ŚRĪ CAITANYA-CARITĀMṚTA

BOOKS by
His Divine Grace A.C. Bhaktivedanta Swami Prabhupāda

Bhagavad-gītā As It Is
Śrīmad-Bhāgavatam, Cantos 1-5 (15 Vols.)
Śrī Caitanya-caritāmṛta (17 Vols.)
Teachings of Lord Caitanya
The Nectar of Devotion
Śrī Īśopaniṣad
Easy Journey to Other Planets
Kṛṣṇa Consciousness: The Topmost Yoga System
Kṛṣṇa, The Supreme Personality of Godhead (3 Vols.)
Transcendental Teachings of Prahlād Mahārāja
Kṛṣṇa, the Reservoir of Pleasure
The Perfection of Yoga
Beyond Birth and Death
On the Way to Kṛṣṇa
Rāja-vidyā: The King of Knowledge
Elevation to Kṛṣṇa Consciousness
Kṛṣṇa Consciousness: The Matchless Gift
Back to Godhead Magazine (Founder)

A complete catalogue is available upon request

International Society for Krishna Consciousness
3764 Watseka Avenue
Los Angeles, California 90034

All Glory to Śrī Guru and Gaurāṅga

ŚRĪ CAITANYA-CARITĀMṚTA

of Kṛṣṇadāsa Kavirāja Gosvāmī

Antya-līlā
Volume One

"The Lord's Pastimes with Śrīla Rūpa Gosvāmī, Junior Haridāsa and Śrīla Haridāsa Ṭhākura"

with the original Bengali text, Roman transliterations, synonyms, translation and elaborate purports

by

HIS DIVINE GRACE

A.C. Bhaktivedanta Swami Prabhupāda

Founder-Ācārya of the International Society for Krishna Consciousness

THE BHAKTIVEDANTA BOOK TRUST
New York · Los Angeles · London · Bombay

Readers interested in the subject matter of this book
are invited by the International Society for Krishna Consciousness
to correspond with its Secretary.

International Society for Krishna Consciousness
3764 Watseka Avenue
Los Angeles, California 90034

Library of Congress Catalogue Card Number: 73-93206
International Standard Book Number: 0-912776-72-2

Printed in the United States of America

Contents

Introduction

Śrī Caitanya-caritāmṛta is the principal work on the life and teachings of Śrī Kṛṣṇa Caitanya. Śrī Caitanya is the pioneer of a great social and religious movement which began in India a little less than five hundred years ago and which has directly and indirectly influenced the subsequent course of religious and philosophical thinking not only in India but in the recent West as well.

Caitanya Mahāprabhu is regarded as a figure of great historical significance. However, our conventional method of historical analysis—that of seeing a man as a product of his times—fails here. Śrī Caitanya is a personality who transcends the limited scope of historical settings.

At a time when, in the West, man was directing his explorative spirit toward studying the structure of the physical universe and circumnavigating the world in search of new oceans and continents, Śrī Kṛṣṇa Caitanya, in the East, was inaugurating and masterminding a revolution directed inward, toward a scientific understanding of the highest knowledge of man's spiritual nature.

The chief historical sources for the life of Śrī Kṛṣṇa Caitanya are the *kaḍacās* (diaries) kept by Murāri Gupta and Svarūpa Dāmodara Gosvāmī. Murāri Gupta, a physician and close associate of Śrī Caitanya's, recorded extensive notes on the first twenty-four years of Śrī Caitanya's life, culminating in his initiation into the renounced order, *sannyāsa*. The events of the rest of Caitanya Mahāprabhu's forty-eight years are recorded in the diary of Svarūpa Dāmodora Gosvāmī, another of Caitanya Mahāprabhu's intimate associates.

Śrī Caitanya-caritāmṛta is divided into three sections called *līlās,* which literally means "pastimes"—*Ādi-līlā* (the early period), *Madhya-līlā* (the middle period) and *Antya-līlā* (the final period). The notes of Murāri Gupta form the basis of the *Ādi-līlā,* and Svarūpa Dāmodara's diary provides the details for the *Madhya-* and *Antya-līlās.*

The first twelve of the seventeen chapters of *Ādi-līlā* constitute the preface for the entire work. By referring to Vedic scriptural evidence, this preface establishes Śrī Caitanya as the *avatāra* (incarnation) of Kṛṣṇa (God) for the age of Kali—the current epoch, beginning five thousand years ago and characterized by materialism, hypocrisy and dissension. In these descriptions, Caitanya Mahāprabhu, who is identical with Lord Kṛṣṇa, descends to liberally grant pure love of God to the fallen souls of this degraded age by propagating *saṅkīrtana*—literally, "congregational glorification of God"—especially by organizing massive public chanting of the *mahā-mantra* (Great Chant for Deliverance). The esoteric purpose of Lord Caitanya's appearance in the world is revealed, his co-*avatāras* and principal devotees are described and his teachings are summarized. The remaining portion of *Ādi-līlā,* chapters thirteen through seventeen, briefly recounts his divine birth and his life until he accepted the renounced order. This includes his childhood miracles, schooling, marriage and early philosophical confrontations, as well as his organization of a widespread *saṅkīrtana* movement and his civil disobedience against the repression of the Mohammedan government.

Śrī Caitanya-caritāmṛta

The subject of *Madhya-līlā,* the longest of the three divisions, is a detailed narration of Lord Caitanya's extensive and eventful travels throughout India as a renounced mendicant, teacher, philosopher, spiritual preceptor and mystic. During this period of six years, Śrī Caitanya transmits his teachings to his principal disciples. He debates and converts many of the most renowned philosophers and theologians of his time, including Śaṅkarites, Buddhists and Muslims, and incorporates their many thousands of followers and disciples into his own burgeoning numbers. A dramatic account of Caitanya Mahāprabhu's miraculous activities at the giant Jagannātha Cart Festival in Orissa is also included in this section.

Antya-līlā concerns the last eighteen years of Śrī Caitanya's manifest presence, spent in semiseclusion near the famous Jagannātha temple at Jagannātha Purī in Orissa. During these final years, Śrī Caitanya drifted deeper and deeper into trances of spiritual ecstasy unparalleled in all of religious and literary history, Eastern or Western. Śrī Caitanya's perpetual and ever-increasing religious beatitude, graphically described in the eyewitness accounts of Svarūpa Dāmodara Gosvāmī, his constant companion during this period, clearly defy the investigative and descriptive abilities of modern psychologists and phenomenologists of religious experience.

The author of this great classic, Kṛṣṇadāsa Kavirāja Gosvāmī, born in the year 1507, was a disciple of Raghunātha dāsa Gosvāmī, a confidential follower of Caitanya Mahāprabhu. Raghunātha dāsa, a renowned ascetic saint, heard and memorized all the activities of Caitanya Mahāprabhu told to him by Svarūpa Dāmodara. After the passing away of Śrī Caitanya and Svarūpa Dāmodara, Raghunātha dāsa, unable to bear the pain of separation from these objects of his complete devotion, traveled to Vṛndāvana, intending to commit suicide by jumping from Govardhana Hill. In Vṛndāvana, however, he encountered Rūpa Gosvāmī and Sanātana Gosvāmī, the most confidential disciples of Caitanya Mahāprabhu. They convinced him to give up his plan of suicide and impelled him to reveal to them the spiritually inspiring events of Lord Caitanya's later life. Kṛṣṇadāsa Kavirāja Gosvāmī was also residing in Vṛndāvana at this time, and Raghunātha dāsa Gosvāmī endowed him with a full comprehension of the transcendental life of Śrī Caitanya.

By this time, several biographical works had already been written on the life of Śrī Caitanya by contemporary and near-contemporary scholars and devotees. These included *Śrī Caitanya-carita* by Murāri Gupta, *Caitanya-maṅgala* by Locana dāsa Ṭhākura and *Caitanya-bhāgavata.* This latter text, a work by Vṛndāvana dāsa Ṭhākura, who was then considered the principal authority on Śrī Caitanya's life, was highly revered. While composing his important work, Vṛndāvana dāsa, fearing that it would become too voluminous, avoided elaborately describing many of the events of Śrī Caitanya's life, particulary the later ones. Anxious to hear of these later pastimes, the devotees of Vṛndāvana requested Kṛṣṇadāsa Kavirāja Gosvāmī, whom they respected as a great saint, to compose a book to narrate these episodes in detail. Upon this request, and with the permission and blessings of the Madana-mohana Deity of Vṛndāvana, he began compiling *Śrī Caitanya-caritāmṛta,* which, due to its biographical excellence and thorough exposition of Lord Caitanya's profound philosophy and teachings, is regarded as the most significant of biographical works on Śrī Caitanya.

He commenced work on the text while in his late nineties and in failing health, as he vividly describes in the text itself: "I have now become too old and disturbed in invalidity. While writing, my hands tremble. I cannot remember anything, nor can I see or hear properly. Still I write, and this is a great wonder." That he nevertheless completed, under such debilitating conditions, the greatest literary gem of medieval India is surely one of the wonders of literary history.

This English translation and commentary is the work of His Divine Grace A. C. Bhaktivedanta Swami Prabhupāda, the world's most distinguished teacher of Indian religious and philosophical thought. His commentary is based upon two Bengali commentaries, one by his teacher Śrīla Bhaktisiddhānta Sarasvatī Gosvāmī, the eminent Vedic scholar who predicted, "The time will come when the people of the world will learn Bengali to read *Śrī Caitanya-caritāmṛta,"* and the other by Śrīla Bhaktisiddhānta's father, Bhaktivinoda Ṭhākura.

His Divine Grace A. C. Bhaktivedanta Swami Prabhupāda is himself a disciplic descendant of Śrī Caitanya Mahāprabhu, and he is the first scholar to execute systematic English translations of the major works of Śrī Caitanya's followers. His consummate Bengali and Sanskrit scholarship and intimate familiarity with the precepts of Śrī Kṛṣṇa Caitanya are a fitting combination that eminently qualifies him to present this important classic to the English-speaking world. The ease and clarity with which he expounds upon difficult philosophical concepts lures even a reader totally unfamiliar with Indian religious tradition into a genuine understanding and appreciation of this profound and monumental work.

The entire text, with commentary, presented in seventeen lavishly illustrated volumes by the Bhaktivedanta Book Trust, represents a contribution of major importance to the intellectual, cultural and spiritual life of contemporary man.

His Divine Grace
A. C. Bhaktivedanta Swami Prabhupāda
Founder-Ācārya of the International Society for Krishna Consciousness

ŚRĪLA BHAKTISIDDHĀNTA SARASVATĪ GOSVĀMĪ MAHĀRĀJA
the spiritual master of
His Divine Grace A.C. Bhaktivedanta Swami Prabhupāda
and foremost scholar and devotee in the recent age.

The historic site where *Śrī Caitanya-caritāmṛta* was completed in the year 1616 by Śrīla Kṛṣṇadāsa Kavirāja Gosvāmī.

The place of worship and chanting beads of Śrīla Rūpa Gosvāmī, the recipient of the special mercy of Lord Caitanya. Being empowered by the Lord, he wrote many transcendental literatures on the science of devotional service.

The Deities and temple of Śrī Śrī Rādhā-Govindajī, established by Śrīla Rūpa Gosvāmī on the order of Caitanya Mahāprabhu.

Distribution of *prasāda* (food offered to Kṛṣṇa) at the Māyāpur-candrodaya-mandira near the birthplace of Śrī Caitanya Mahāprabhu.

The Deities of Lord Caitanya and His associates at the house of Śrīvāsa Ṭhākura, one of the four sites where Caitanya Mahāprabhu would always visit when *kīrtana* was performed.

PLATE ONE

Lord Kṛṣṇa Caitanya surrounded (from left to right by His *avatāra* (Advaita Ācārya), His expansion (Lor Nityānanda), His manifest internal energy (Śr Gadādhara), and His perfect devotee (Śrī Śrīvāsa) These five *tattvas* incarnate with Lord Caitany Mahāprabhu, and thus the Lord executes His *saṅkīrtan* movement with great pleasure.

Śrī Gaurāṅga
Śrī Nityānanda
Śrī Gadādhara
Śrī Advaita
Śrī Śrīvāsa

PLATE TWO

The characteristics of Kṛṣṇa are understood to be a storehouse of transcendental love. Although that storehouse of love certainly came with Kṛṣṇa when He was present, it was sealed. But when Śrī Caitanya Mahāprabhu came with His other associates of the Pañca-tattva, they broke the seal and plundered the storehouse to taste transcendental love for Kṛṣṇa. The more they tasted it, the more their thirst for it grew. Śrī Pañca-tattva themselves danced again and again and thus made it easier to drink nectarean love of Godhead.

PLATE THREE

"When all the devotees came to the place of Ś
Caitanya Mahāprabhu, they saw that the same do
was sitting a little apart from the Lord. Furthermore, Ś
Caitanya Mahāprabhu was throwing remnants of gree
coconut pulp to the dog. Smiling in His own way, H
was saying to the dog, 'Chant the holy names Rāma
Kṛṣṇa and Hari.' Seeing the dog eating the gree
coconut pulp and chanting 'Kṛṣṇa, Kṛṣṇa' again an
again, all the devotees present were very muc
surprised. When he saw the dog sitting in that way an
chanting the name of Kṛṣṇa, Śivānanda, because of hi
natural humility, immediately offered his obeisances t
the dog just to counteract his offenses to it. The ne
day, no one saw that dog, for it had obtained it
spiritual body and departed for Vaikuṇṭha, the spiritu
kingdom." (*pp. 15-17*)

PLATE FOUR

"O most beautiful friend, please accept the Supreme Personality of Godhead, who is standing before you full of transcendental bliss. The borders of His eyes roam from side to side, and His eyebrows move slowly like bumblebees on His lotuslike face. Standing with His right foot placed below the knee of His left leg, the middle of His body curved in three places, and His neck gracefully tilted to the side, He takes His flute to His pursed lips and moves His fingers upon it here and there." (*p. 93*)

PLATE FIVE

"O beautiful-faced one, who is this creative perso standing before us? With the sharp chisels of His lovin glances, He is splitting the hard stones of man women's devotion to their husbands. And with th luster of His body, surpassing the brilliance of countles emeralds, He is simultaneously constructing privat meeting places for His pastimes." (*p. 94*)

PLATE SIX

"Beginning early in the morning, Nṛsiṁhānanda Brahmacārī cooked many varieties of food, including vegetables, cakes, sweet rice and other preparations. After he finished cooking, he brought separate dishes for Jagannātha and Śrī Caitanya Mahāprabhu. He also separately offered dishes to Nṛsiṁhadeva, his worshipable Deity. Thus he divided all the food into three offerings. Then, outside the temple, he began to meditate upon the Lord. In his meditation he saw Śrī Caitanya Mahāprabhu quickly come, sit down and eat all three offerings, leaving behind no remnants." (*pp. 153-154*)

PLATE SEVEN

"Thus at the end of one night, Junior Haridāsa, afte offering Śrī Caitanya Mahāprabhu his respectful obei sances, departed for Prayāga without saying anythin to anyone. Junior Haridāsa had conclusively decided t attain shelter at the lotus feet of Śrī Caitany Mahāprabhu. Thus he entered deep into the water a Triveṇī, the confluence of the Ganges and Yamunā a Prayāga, and in this way gave up his life. Immediatel after committing suicide in this way, he went in hi spiritual body to Śrī Caitanya Mahāprabhu an received the mercy of the Lord. However, he sti remained invisible. In a spiritual body resembling tha of a Gandharva, Junior Haridāsa, although invisible would sing at night for Śrī Caitanya Mahāprabhu t hear. No one but the Lord, however, knew of this." (*pp. 194-195*)

PLATE EIGHT

"After thus instructing the prostitute about the process of chanting the Hare Kṛṣṇa *mantra,* Haridāsa Ṭhākura stood up and left, continuously chanting 'Hari, Hari.' Thereafter, the prostitute distributed to the *brāhmaṇas* whatever household possessions she had, following the order of her spiritual master. The prostitute shaved her head clean in accordance with Vaiṣṇava principles and stayed in that room wearing only one cloth. Following in the footsteps of her spiritual master, she began chanting the Hare Kṛṣṇa *mahā-mantra* 300,000 times a day. She chanted throughout the entire day and night. She worshiped the *tulasī* plant, following in the footsteps of her spiritual master. Instead of eating regularly, she chewed whatever food she received as alms, and if nothing was supplied she would fast. Thus by eating frugally and fasting she conquered her senses, and as soon as her senses were controlled, symptoms of love of Godhead appeared in her person." (*pp. 279-281*)

CHAPTER 1

Śrīla Rūpa Gosvāmī's Second Meeting with the Lord

A summary of the First Chapter is given by Śrīla Bhaktivinoda Ṭhākura in his *Amṛta-pravāha-bhāṣya* as follows. When Śrī Caitanya Mahāprabhu returned to Jagannātha Purī from Vṛndāvana, all His devotees from other parts of India, upon receiving the auspicious news, came to Puruṣottama-kṣetra, or Jagannātha Purī. Śivānanda Sena took a dog with him and even paid fees for it to cross the river. One night, however, the dog could not get any food and therefore went directly to Śrī Caitanya Mahāprabhu at Jagannātha Purī. The next day, when Śivānanda and his party reached Jagannātha Purī, Śivānanda saw the dog eating some coconut pulp offered to it by Śrī Caitanya Mahāprabhu. After this incident, the dog was liberated and went back home, back to Godhead.

Meanwhile, Śrīla Rūpa Gosvāmī reached Bengal, after returning from Vṛndāvana. Although he could not follow the Bengali devotees, after some time he then came to Jagannātha Purī, where he stayed with Haridāsa Ṭhākura. Śrīla Rūpa Gosvāmī composed an important verse, beginning with the words *priyaḥ so 'yam,* and Śrī Caitanya Mahāprabhu relished it very much. One day when Śrī Caitanya Mahāprabhu, Rāmānanda Rāya and Sārvabhauma Bhaṭṭācārya went to see Haridāsa Ṭhākura, the Lord saw the verse Rūpa Gosvāmī had composed as an introduction to his books *Lalita-mādhava* and *Vidagdha-mādhava.* After examining the manuscripts of these two books, Rāmānanda Rāya approved and appreciated them very much. After the period of Cāturmāsya, all the devotees who had come from Bengal returned to their homes. Śrīla Rūpa Gosvāmī, however, remained at Jagannātha Purī for some time.

TEXT 1

পঙ্গুং লঙ্ঘয়তে শৈলং মূকমাবর্তয়েচ্ছ্রুতিম্ ।
যৎকৃপা তমহং বন্দে কৃষ্ণচৈতন্যমীশ্বরম্ ॥ ১ ॥

paṅguṁ laṅghayate śailaṁ
mūkam āvartayec chrutim
yat-kṛpā tam ahaṁ vande
kṛṣṇa-caitanyam īśvaram

SYNONYMS

paṅgum—one who is lame; *laṅghayate*—causes to cross over; *śailam*—a mountain; *mūkam*—one who is dumb; *āvartayet*—can cause to recite; *śrutim*—Vedic literature; *yat-kṛpā*—the mercy of whom; *tam*—unto Him; *aham*—I; *vande*—offer obeisances; *kṛṣṇa-caitanyam*—Śrī Caitanya Mahāprabhu, who is Kṛṣṇa Himself; *īśvaram*—the Lord.

TRANSLATION

I offer my respectful obeisances to Śrī Kṛṣṇa Caitanya Mahāprabhu, by whose mercy even a lame man can cross over a mountain and a dumb man recite Vedic literature.

TEXT 2

দুর্গমে পথি মেঽন্ধস্য স্খলৎপাদগতের্মুহুঃ ।
স্বকৃপা-যষ্টিদানেন সন্তঃ সন্ত্ববলম্বনম্ ॥ ২ ॥

durgame pathi me 'ndhasya
skhalat-pāda-gater muhuḥ
sva-kṛpā-yaṣṭi-dānena
santaḥ santv avalambanam

SYNONYMS

durgame—very difficult; *pathi*—on the path; *me*—of me; *andhasya*—one who is blind; *skhalat*—slipping; *pāda*—on feet; *gateḥ*—whose manner of moving; *muhuḥ*—again and again; *sva-kṛpā*—of their own mercy; *yaṣṭi*—the stick; *dānena*—by giving; *santaḥ*—those saintly persons; *santu*—let that become; *avalambanam*—my support.

TRANSLATION

My path is very difficult. I am blind, and my feet are slipping again and again. Therefore, may the saints help me by granting me the stick of their mercy as my support.

TEXT 3-4

শ্রীরূপ, সনাতন, ভট্ট-রঘুনাথ ।
শ্রীজীব, গোপালভট্ট, দাস-রঘুনাথ ॥ ৩ ॥
এই ছয় গুরুর করোঁ চরণ বন্দন ।
যাহা হৈতে বিঘ্ননাশ, অভীষ্ট-পূরণ ॥ ৪ ॥

śrī-rūpa, sanātana, bhaṭṭa-raghunātha
śrī-jīva, gopāla-bhaṭṭa, dāsa-raghunātha

ei chaya gurura karoṅ caraṇa vandana
yāhā haite vighna-nāśa, abhīṣṭa-pūraṇa

SYNONYMS

śrī-rūpa—of the name Śrī Rūpa; *sanātana*—of the name Sanātana; *bhaṭṭa-raghunātha*—of the name Bhaṭṭa Raghunātha; *śrī-jīva*—of the name Śrī Jīva; *gopāla-bhaṭṭa*—of the name Gopāla Bhaṭṭa; *dāsa-raghunātha*—of the name Dāsa Raghunātha; *ei chaya*—these six; *gurura*—of spiritual masters; *karoṅ*—I offer; *caraṇa vandana*—prayers to the lotus feet; *yāhā haite*—from which; *vighna-nāśa*—destruction of all impediments; *abhīṣṭa-pūraṇa*—fulfillment of desires.

TRANSLATION

I pray to the lotus feet of the six Gosvāmīs—Śrī Rūpa, Sanātana, Bhaṭṭa Raghunātha, Śrī Jīva, Gopāla Bhaṭṭa and Dāsa Raghunātha—so that all impediments to my writing this literature will be annihilated and my real desire will be fulfilled.

PURPORT

If one wants to benefit the entire world, he will certainly find persons like hogs and pigs who will put forward many impediments. That is natural. But if a devotee seeks shelter at the lotus feet of the six Gosvāmīs, the merciful Gosvāmīs will certainly give the Lord's servitor all protection. It is not astonishing that impediments are placed before those who are spreading the Kṛṣṇa consciousness movement all over the world. Nevertheless, if we adhere to the lotus feet of the six Gosvāmīs and pray for their mercy, all impediments will be annihilated, and the transcendental devotional desire to serve the Supreme Lord will be fulfilled.

TEXT 5

জয়তাং সুরতৌ পঙ্গোর্মম মন্দমতের্গতী ।
মৎসর্বস্বপদাম্ভোজৌ রাধা-মদনমোহনৌ ॥ ৫ ॥

jayatāṁ suratau paṅgor
mama manda-mater gatī
mat-sarvasva-padāmbhojau
rādhā-madana-mohanau

SYNONYMS

jayatām—all glory to; *su-ratau*—most merciful, or attached in conjugal love; *paṅgoḥ*—of one who is lame; *mama*—of me; *manda-mateḥ*—foolish; *gatī*—

refuge; *mat*—my; *sarva-sva*—everything; *pada-ambhojau*—whose lotus feet; *rādhā-madana-mohanau*—Rādhārāṇī and Madana-mohana.

TRANSLATION

Glory to the all-merciful Rādhā and Madana-mohana! I am lame and ill-advised, yet They are my directors, and Their lotus feet are everything to me.

TEXT 6

দীব্যদ্বৃন্দারণ্যকল্পদ্রুমাধঃ-
শ্রীমদ্রত্নাগারসিংহাসনস্থৌ।
শ্রীমদ্রাধা-শ্রীলগোবিন্দদেবৌ
প্রেষ্ঠালীভিঃ সেব্যমানৌ স্মরামি ॥ ৬ ॥

dīvyad-vṛndāraṇya-kalpa-drumādhaḥ-
śrīmad-ratnāgāra-siṁhāsana-sthau
śrīmad-rādhā-śrīla-govinda-devau
preṣṭhālībhiḥ sevyamānau smarāmi

SYNONYMS

dīvyat—shining; *vṛndā-araṇya*—in the forest of Vṛndāvana; *kalpa-druma*—desire tree; *adhaḥ*—beneath; *śrīmat*—most beautiful; *ratna-āgāra*—in a temple of jewels; *siṁha-āsana-sthau*—sitting on a throne; *śrīmat*—very beautiful; *rādhā*—Śrīmatī Rādhārāṇī; *śrīla-govinda-devau*—and Śrī Govindadeva; *preṣṭha-ālībhiḥ*—by most confidential associates; *sevyamānau*—being served; *smarāmi*—I remember.

TRANSLATION

In a temple of jewels in Vṛndāvana, underneath a desire tree, Śrī Śrī Rādhā-Govinda, served by Their most confidential associates, sit upon an effulgent throne. I offer my humble obeisances unto Them.

TEXT 7

শ্রীমান্রাসরসারম্ভী বংশীবটতটস্থিতঃ।
কর্ষন্ বেণুস্বনৈর্গোপীর্গোপীনাথঃ শ্রিয়েঽস্তু নঃ ॥ ৭ ॥

śrīmān-rāsa-rasārambhī
vaṁśīvaṭa-taṭa-sthitaḥ
karṣan veṇu-svanair gopīr
gopī-nāthaḥ śriye 'stu naḥ

SYNONYMS

śrīmān—most beautiful; *rāsa*—of the *rāsa* dance; *rasa*—of the mellow; *ārambhī*—the initiator; *vaṁśī-vaṭa*—of the name Vaṁśīvaṭa; *taṭa*—on the shore; *sthitaḥ*—standing; *karṣan*—attracting; *veṇu*—of the flute; *svanaiḥ*—by the sounds; *gopīḥ*—the cowherd girls; *gopī-nāthaḥ*—Śrī Gopīnātha; *śriye*—benediction; *astu*—let there be; *naḥ*—our.

TRANSLATION

Śrī Śrīla Gopīnātha, who originated the transcendental mellow of the rāsa dance, stands on the shore at Vaṁśīvaṭa and attracts the attention of the cowherd damsels with the sound of His celebrated flute. May they all confer upon us their benediction.

TEXT 8

জয় জয় শ্রীচৈতন্য জয় নিত্যানন্দ ।
জয়াদ্বৈতচন্দ্র জয় গৌরভক্তবৃন্দ ॥ ৮ ॥

jaya jaya śrī-caitanya jaya nityānanda
jayādvaita-candra jaya gaura-bhakta-vṛnda

SYNONYMS

jaya jaya śrī caitanya—all glories to Śrī Caitanya Mahāprabhu; *jaya nityānanda*—all glories to Śrī Nityānanda Prabhu; *jaya advaita-candra*—all glories to Advaita Prabhu; *jaya gaura-bhakta-vṛnda*—all glories to the devotees of Śrī Caitanya Mahāprabhu.

TRANSLATION

All glories to Lord Śrī Caitanya Mahāprabhu! All glories to Lord Nityānanda! All glories to Advaita Ācārya! All glories to the devotees of Lord Śrī Caitanya Mahāprabhu!

TEXT 9

মধ্যলীলা সংক্ষেপেতে করিলুঁ বর্ণন ।
অন্ত্যলীলা-বর্ণন কিছু শুন, ভক্তগণ ॥ ৯ ॥

madhya-līlā saṅkṣepete kariluṅ varṇana
antya-līlā-varṇana kichu śuna, bhakta-gaṇa

SYNONYMS

madhya-līlā—pastimes known as *Madhya-līlā*; *saṅkṣepete*—in brief; *kariluṅ varṇana*—I have described; *antya-līlā*—the last pastimes; *varṇana*—description; *kichu*—something; *śuna*—hear; *bhakta-gaṇa*—O devotees.

TRANSLATION

I have briefly described the pastimes of Śrī Caitanya Mahāprabhu in the Madhya-līlā. Now I shall attempt to describe something about His last pastimes, which are known as the Antya-līlā.

TEXT 10

মধ্যলীলা-মধ্যে অন্ত্যলীলা-সূত্রগণ ।
পূর্বগ্রন্থে সংক্ষেপেতে করিয়াছি বর্ণন ॥ ১০ ॥

madhya-līlā-madhye antya-līlā-sūtra-gaṇa
pūrva-granthe saṅkṣepete kariyāchi varṇana

SYNONYMS

madhya-līlā-madhye—within the *Madhya-līlā* chapters; *antya-līlā-sūtra-gaṇa*—the codes of the *Antya-līlā*; *pūrva-granthe*—in the previous chapter; *saṅkṣepete*—in brief; *kariyāchi varṇana*—I have described.

TRANSLATION

I have briefly described the Antya-līlā in codes within the Madhya-līlā.

TEXT 11

আমি জরাগ্রস্ত, নিকটে জানিয়া মরণ ।
অন্ত্য কোনো কোনো লীলা করিয়াছি বর্ণন ॥ ১১ ॥

āmi jarā-grasta, nikaṭe jāniyā maraṇa
antya kono kono līlā kariyāchi varṇana

SYNONYMS

āmi jarā-grasta—I am invalid because of old age; *nikaṭe*—very near; *jāniyā*—knowing; *maraṇa*—death; *antya*—final; *kono kono*—some; *līlā*—pastimes; *kariyāchi varṇana*—I have described.

TRANSLATION

I am now almost an invalid because of old age, and I know that at any moment I may die. Therefore I have already described some portions of the Antya-līlā.

PURPORT

Following in the footsteps of Śrīla Kṛṣṇadāsa Kavirāja Gosvāmī, I am trying to translate the *Bhāgavata* literatures as quickly as possible. However, knowing myself to be an old man and almost an invalid because of rheumatism, I have already translated the essence of all literatures, the Tenth Canto of *Śrīmad-Bhāgavatam,* as a summary study in English. I started the Kṛṣṇa consciousness movement at the age of seventy. Now I am seventy-eight, and so my death is imminent. I am trying to finish the translation of *Śrīmad-Bhāgavatam* as soon as possible, but before finishing it, I have given my readers the book *Kṛṣṇa, the Supreme Personality of Godhead,* so that if I die before finishing the whole task, they may enjoy this book, which is the essence of *Śrīmad-Bhāgavatam.*

TEXT 12

পূর্বলিখিত গ্রন্থসূত্র-অনুসারে ।
যেই নাহি লিখি, তাহা লিখিয়ে বিস্তারে ॥ ১২ ॥

pūrva-likhita grantha-sūtra-anusāre
yei nāhi likhi, tāhā likhiye vistāre

SYNONYMS

pūrva-likhita—previously mentioned; *grantha-sūtra*—the codes of the literature; *anusāre*—according to; *yei*—whatever; *nāhi likhi*—I have not mentioned; *tāhā*—that; *likhiye*—I shall write; *vistāre*—elaborately.

TRANSLATION

In accordance with the codes previously written, I shall describe in detail whatever I have not mentioned.

TEXT 13

বৃন্দাবন হৈতে প্রভু নীলাচলে আইলা ।
স্বরূপ-গোসাঞি গৌড়ে বার্তা পাঠাইলা ॥ ১৩ ॥

vṛndāvana haite prabhu nīlācale āilā
svarūpa-gosāñi gauḍe vārtā pāṭhāilā

SYNONYMS

vṛndāvana haite—from Vṛndāvana; *prabhu*—Śrī Caitanya Mahāprabhu; *nīlācale āilā*—returned to Jagannātha Purī, Nīlācala; *svarūpa-gosāñi*—Svarūpa Dāmodara; *gauḍe*—to Bengal; *vārtā pāṭhāilā*—sent news.

TRANSLATION

When Śrī Caitanya Mahāprabhu returned to Jagannātha Purī from Vṛndāvana, Svarūpa Dāmodara Gosāñi immediately sent news of the Lord's arrival to the devotees in Bengal.

TEXT 14

শুনি' শচী আনন্দিত, সব ভক্তগণ ।
সবে মিলি' নীলাচলে করিলা গমন ॥ ১৪ ॥

śuni' śacī ānandita, saba bhakta-gaṇa
sabe mili' nīlācale karilā gamana

SYNONYMS

śuni'—hearing; *śacī*—mother Śacī; *ānandita*—very pleased; *saba bhakta-gaṇa*—as well as all the other devotees of Navadvīpa; *sabe mili'*—meeting together; *nīlācale*—to Jagannātha Purī, Nīlācala; *karilā gamana*—departed.

TRANSLATION

Upon hearing this news, mother Śacī and all the other devotees of Navadvīpa were very joyful, and they all departed together for Nīlācala [Jagannātha Purī].

TEXT 15

কুলীনগ্রামী ভক্ত আর যত খণ্ডবাসী ।
আচার্য শিবানন্দ সনে মিলিলা সবে আসি' ॥১৫॥

kulīna-grāmī bhakta āra yata khaṇḍa-vāsī
ācārya śivānanda sane mililā sabe āsi'

SYNONYMS

kulīna-grāmī—residents of the village known as Kulīna-grāma; *bhakta*—devotees; *āra*—and; *yata*—all; *khaṇḍa-vāsī*—the residents of Śrī Khaṇḍa; *ācārya*—Advaita Ācārya; *śivānanda*—Śivānanda Sena; *sane*—with; *mililā*—met; *sabe āsi'*—all coming together.

TRANSLATION

Thus all the devotees of Kulīna-grāma and Śrī Khaṇḍa, as well as Advaita Ācārya, came together to meet Śivānanda Sena.

TEXT 16

**শিবানন্দ করে সবার ঘাটি সমাধান ।
সবারে পালন করে, দেয় বাসা-স্থান ॥ ১৬ ॥**

*śivānanda kare sabāra ghāṭi samādhāna
sabāre pālana kare, deya vāsā-sthāna*

SYNONYMS

śivānanda—of the name Śivānanda; *kare*—does; *sabāra*—of everyone; *ghāṭi*—the camp; *samādhāna*—arrangement; *sabāre*—of everyone; *pālana*—maintenance; *kare*—performs; *deya*—gives; *vāsā-sthāna*—residential quarters.

TRANSLATION

Śivānanda Sena arranged for the journey. He maintained everyone and provided residential quarters.

TEXT 17

**এক কুক্কুর চলে শিবানন্দ-সনে ।
ভক্ষ্য দিয়া লঞা চলে করিয়া পালনে ॥ ১৭ ॥**

*eka kukkura cale śivānanda-sane
bhakṣya diyā lañā cale kariyā pālane*

SYNONYMS

eka—one; *kukkura*—dog; *cale*—goes; *śivānanda-sane*—with Śivānanda Sena; *bhakṣya*—food; *diyā*—giving; *lañā*—taking; *cale*—goes; *kariyā pālane*—maintaining the dog.

TRANSLATION

While going to Jagannātha Purī, Śivānanda Sena allowed a dog to go with him. He supplied it food to eat and maintained it.

TEXT 18

**একদিন একস্থানে নদী পার হৈতে ।
উড়িয়া নাবিক কুক্কুর না চড়ায় নৌকাতে ॥ ১৮ ॥**

*eka-dina eka-sthāne nadī pāra haite
uḍiyā nāvika kukkura nā caḍāya naukāte*

SYNONYMS

eka-dina—one day; *eka-sthāne*—in one place; *nadī*—a river; *pāra*—crossing; *haite*—to do; *uḍiyā nāvika*—a boatman who was an Oriyā (Orissan); *kukkura*—the dog; *nā caḍāya*—does not allow to mount; *naukāte*—on the boat.

TRANSLATION

One day, when they needed to cross a river, an Orissan boatman would not allow the dog to get in the boat.

TEXT 19

কুক্কুর রহিলা,—শিবানন্দ দুঃখী হৈলা ।
দশ পণ কড়ি দিয়া কুক্কুরে পার কৈলা ॥ ১৯ ॥

kukkura rahilā,——śivānanda duḥkhī hailā
daśa paṇa kaḍi diyā kukkure pāra kailā

SYNONYMS

kukkura rahilā—the dog remained; *śivānanda duḥkhī hailā*—Śivānanda became very unhappy; *daśa paṇa*—ten *paṇa*; *kaḍi*—small conchshells; *diyā*—paying; *kukkure*—the dog; *pāra kailā*—crossed to the other side of the river.

TRANSLATION

Śivānanda Sena, unhappy that the dog had to stay behind, paid the boatman ten paṇa of conchshells to take the dog across the river.

PURPORT

One *paṇa* is eighty *kaḍis*, or small conchshells. Formerly, even fifty or sixty years ago, there was no paper currency in India. Coins were generally made not of base metal but of gold, silver and copper. In other words, the medium of exchange was really something valuable. Four pieces of *kaḍi* made one *gaṇḍā*, and twenty such *gaṇḍās* equaled one *paṇa*. This *kaḍi* was also used as a medium of exchange; therefore Śivānanda Sena paid for the dog with *daśa paṇa*, or eighty times ten pieces of *kaḍi*. In those days one paisa was also subdivided into small conchshells, but at the present moment the prices for commodities have gone so high that there is nothing one can get in exchange for only one paisa. With one paisa in those days, however, one could purchase sufficient vegetables to provide for a whole family. Even thirty years ago, vegetables were occasionally so inexpensive that one paisa's worth could provide for a whole family for a day.

TEXT 20

একদিন শিবানন্দে ঘাটিয়ালে রাখিলা ।
কুক্কুরকে ভাত দিতে সেবক পাসরিলা ॥ ২০ ॥

eka-dina śivānande ghāṭiyāle rākhilā
kukkurake bhāta dite sevaka pāsarilā

SYNONYMS

eka-dina—one day; *śivānande*—Śivānanda Sena; *ghāṭiyāle*—tollman; *rākhilā*—detained; *kukkurake*—unto the dog; *bhāta dite*—to supply rice; *sevaka*—the servant; *pāsarilā*—forgot.

TRANSLATION

One day while Śivānanda was detained by a tollman, his servant forgot to give the dog its cooked rice.

TEXT 21

রাত্রে আসি' শিবানন্দ ভোজনের কালে ।
'কুক্কুর পাঞাছে ভাত ?'—সেবকে পুছিলে ॥ ২১ ॥

rātre āsi' śivānanda bhojanera kāle
'kukkura pāñāche bhāta?'—sevake puchile

SYNONYMS

rātre āsi'—returning at night; *śivānanda*—Śivānanda Sena; *bhojanera kāle*—at the time of eating; *kukkura*—the dog; *pāñāche*—has gotten; *bhāta*—rice; *sevake*—from the servant; *puchile*—he inquired.

TRANSLATION

At night, when Śivānanda Sena returned and was taking his meal, he inquired from the servant whether the dog had gotten its meals.

TEXT 22

কুক্কুর নাহি পায় ভাত শুনি' দুঃখী হৈলা ।
কুক্কুর চাহিতে দশ-মনুষ্য পাঠাইলা ॥ ২২ ॥

kukkura nāhi pāya bhāta śuni' duḥkhī hailā
kukkura cāhite daśa-manuṣya pāṭhāilā

SYNONYMS

kukkura—the dog; *nāhi*—did not; *pāya*—get; *bhāta*—rice; *śuni'*—hearing; *duḥkhī hailā*—Śivānanda Sena became very unhappy; *kukkura cāhite*—to look for the dog; *daśa-manuṣya*—ten men; *pāṭhāilā*—sent.

TRANSLATION

When he learned that the dog had not been supplied food in his absence, he was very unhappy. He then immediately sent ten men to find the dog.

TEXT 23

চাহিয়া না পাইল কুক্কুর, লোক সব আইলা ।
দুঃখী হঞা শিবানন্দ উপবাস কৈলা ॥ ২৩ ॥

cāhiyā nā pāila kukkura, loka saba āilā
duḥkhī hañā śivānanda upavāsa kailā

SYNONYMS

cāhiyā—looking; *nā*—not; *pāila*—found; *kukkura*—the dog; *loka saba āilā*—all the men returned; *duḥkhī hañā*—being unhappy; *śivānanda*—Śivānanda Sena; *upavāsa*—fast; *kailā*—observed.

TRANSLATION

When the men returned without success, Śivānanda Sena became very unhappy and fasted for the night.

TEXT 24

প্রভাতে কুক্কুর চাহি' কাঁহা না পাইল ।
সকল বৈষ্ণবের মনে চমৎকার হৈল ॥ ২৪ ॥

prabhāte kukkura cāhi' kāṅhā nā pāila
sakala vaiṣṇavera mane camatkāra haila

SYNONYMS

prabhāte—in the morning; *kukkura*—the dog; *cāhi'*—looking for; *kāṅhā*—anywhere; *nā pāila*—not found; *sakala vaiṣṇavera*—of all the Vaiṣṇavas present; *mane*—in the minds; *camatkāra haila*—there was great astonishment.

TRANSLATION

In the morning they looked for the dog, but it could not be found anywhere. All the Vaiṣṇavas were astonished.

PURPORT

Śivānanda Sena's attachment to the dog was a great boon for that animal. The dog appears to have been a street dog. Since it naturally began to follow Śivānanda Sena while he was going to Jagannātha Purī with his party, he accepted it into his party and maintained it the same way he was maintaining the other devotees. It appears that although on one occasion the dog was not allowed aboard a boat, Śivānanda did not leave the dog behind but paid more money just to induce the boatman to take the dog across the river. Then when the servant forgot to feed the dog and the dog disappeared, Śivānanda, being very anxious, sent ten men to find it. When they could not find it, Śivānanda observed a fast. Thus it appears that somehow or other Śivānanda had become attached to the dog.

As will be evident from the following verses, the dog got the mercy of Śrī Caitanya Mahāprabhu and was immediately promoted to Vaikuṇṭha to become an eternal devotee. Śrīla Bhaktivinoda Ṭhākura has therefore sung, *tumi ta' ṭhākura, tomāra kukkura, baliyā jānaha more* (*Śaraṇāgati* 19). He thus offers to become the dog of a Vaiṣṇava. There are many other instances in which the pet animal of a Vaiṣṇava was delivered back home to Vaikuṇṭhaloka, back to Godhead. Such is the benefit of somehow or other becoming the favorite of a Vaiṣṇava. Śrīla Bhaktivinoda Ṭhākura has also sung, *kīṭa-janma ha-u yathā tuyā dāsa* (*Śaraṇāgati* 11). There is no harm in taking birth again and again. Our only desire should be to take birth under the care of a Vaiṣṇava. Fortunately we had the opportunity to be born of a Vaiṣṇava father who took care of us very nicely. He prayed to Śrīmatī Rādhārāṇī that in the future we would become a servant of the eternal consort of Śrī Kṛṣṇa. Thus somehow or other we are now engaged in that service. We may conclude that even as dogs we must take shelter of a Vaiṣṇava. The benefit will be the same as that which accrues to an advanced devotee under a Vaiṣṇava's care.

TEXT 25

উৎকণ্ঠায় চলি' সবে আইলা নীলাচলে ।
পূর্ববৎ মহাপ্রভু মিলিলা সকলে ॥ ২৫ ॥

utkaṇṭhāya cali' sabe āilā nīlācale
pūrvavat mahāprabhu mililā sakale

SYNONYMS

utkaṇṭhāya—in great anxiety; *cali'*—walking; *sabe*—all the devotees; *āilā nīlācale*—came to Jagannātha Purī, Nīlācala; *pūrvavat*—as usual; *mahāprabhu*—Śrī Caitanya Mahāprabhu; *mililā sakale*—met all of them.

TRANSLATION

Thus in great anxiety they all walked to Jagannātha Purī, where Śrī Caitanya Mahāprabhu met them as usual.

TEXT 26

সবা লঞা কৈলা জগন্নাথ দরশন ।
সবা লঞা মহাপ্রভু করেন ভোজন ॥ ২৬ ॥

sabā lañā kailā jagannātha daraśana
sabā lañā mahāprabhu karena bhojana

SYNONYMS

sabā lañā—taking all of them; *kailā*—did; *jagannātha daraśana*—visiting the Jagannātha temple; *sabā lañā*—with all of them; *mahāprabhu*—Śrī Caitanya Mahāprabhu; *karena bhojana*—took *prasāda.*

TRANSLATION

Śrī Caitanya Mahāprabhu went with them to see the Lord in the temple, and on that day He also took lunch in the company of all those devotees.

TEXT 27

পূর্ববৎ সবারে প্রভু পাঠাইলা বাসা-স্থানে ।
প্রভু-ঠাঞি প্রাতঃকালে আইলা আর দিনে ॥ ২৭ ॥

pūrvavat sabāre prabhu pāṭhāilā vāsā-sthāne
prabhu-ṭhāñi prātaḥ-kāle āilā āra dine

SYNONYMS

pūrvavat—as it was previously; *sabāre*—everyone; *prabhu*—Lord Śrī Caitanya Mahāprabhu; *pāṭhāilā*—sent; *vāsā-sthāne*—to their respective residential quarters; *prabhu-ṭhāñi*—to the place of Śrī Caitanya Mahāprabhu; *prātaḥ-kāle*—in the morning; *āilā*—they came; *āra dine*—on the next day.

TRANSLATION

As previously, the Lord provided them all with residential quarters. And the next morning all the devotees came to see the Lord.

TEXT 28

আসিয়া দেখিল সবে সেই ত কুক্কুরে ।
প্রভু-পাশে বসিয়াছে কিছু অল্পদূরে ॥ ২৮ ॥

āsiyā dekhila sabe sei ta kukkure
prabhu-pāśe vasiyāche kichu alpa-dūre

SYNONYMS

āsiyā—coming; *dekhila*—they saw; *sabe*—everyone; *sei ta kukkure*—that very same dog; *prabhu-pāśe*—near Lord Śrī Caitanya Mahāprabhu; *vasiyāche*—sat; *kichu alpa-dūre*—a little bit away from the Lord.

TRANSLATION

When all the devotees came to the place of Śrī Caitanya Mahāprabhu, they saw that the same dog was sitting a little apart from the Lord.

TEXT 29

প্রসাদ নারিকেল-শস্য দেন ফেলাঞা ।
'রাম' 'কৃষ্ণ' 'হরি' কহ'—বলেন হাসিয়া ॥ ২৯ ॥

prasāda nārikela-śasya dena phelāñā
'rāma' 'kṛṣṇa' 'hari' kaha'——balena hāsiyā

SYNONYMS

prasāda—food; *nārikela-śasya*—the pulp of green coconut; *dena*—gives; *phelāñā*—throwing; *rāma*—Lord Rāmacandra; *kṛṣṇa*—Śrī Kṛṣṇa; *hari*—the holy name of Hari; *kaha*—say; *balena*—Śrī Caitanya Mahāprabhu says; *hāsiyā*—smiling.

TRANSLATION

Furthermore, Śrī Caitanya Mahāprabhu was throwing remnants of green coconut pulp to the dog. Smiling in His own way, He was saying to the dog, "Chant the holy names Rāma, Kṛṣṇa, and Hari."

TEXT 30

শস্য খায় কুক্কুর, 'কৃষ্ণ' কহে বার বার ।
দেখিয়া লোকের মনে হৈল চমৎকার ॥ ৩০ ॥

śasya khāya kukkura, 'kṛṣṇa' kahe bāra bāra
dekhiyā lokera mane haila camatkāra

SYNONYMS

śasya khāya—eats the pulp of green coconut; *kukkura*—the dog; *kṛṣṇa*—the holy name of Kṛṣṇa; *kahe*—chants; *bāra bāra*—again and again; *dekhiyā*—seeing this; *lokera*—of all the people; *mane*—in the minds; *haila*—there was; *camatkāra*—astonishment.

TRANSLATION

Seeing the dog eating the green coconut pulp and chanting "Kṛṣṇa, Kṛṣṇa" again and again, all the devotees present were very much surprised.

TEXT 31

শিবানন্দ কুক্কুর দেখি' দণ্ডবৎ কৈলা ।
দৈন্য করি' নিজ অপরাধ ক্ষমাইলা ॥ ৩১ ॥

śivānanda kukkura dekhi' daṇḍavat kailā
dainya kari' nija aparādha kṣamāilā

SYNONYMS

śivānanda—Śivānanda Sena; *kukkura*—the dog; *dekhi'*—seeing there; *daṇḍavat kailā*—offered obeisances; *dainya kari'*—exhibiting humbleness; *nija*—personal; *aparādha*—offenses; *kṣamāilā*—was forgiven.

TRANSLATION

When he saw the dog sitting in that way and chanting the name of Kṛṣṇa, Śivānanda, because of his natural humility, immediately offered his obeisances to the dog just to counteract his offenses to it.

TEXT 32

আর দিন কেহ তার দেখা না পাইলা ।
সিদ্ধ-দেহ পাঞা কুক্কুর বৈকুণ্ঠেতে গেলা ॥ ৩২ ॥

āra dina keha tāra dekhā nā pāilā
siddha-deha pāñā kukkura vaikuṇṭhete gelā

SYNONYMS

āra dina—the next day; *keha*—all of them; *tāra*—of the dog; *dekhā nā pāilā*—did not get sight; *siddha-deha pāñā*—obtaining a spiritual body; *kukkura*—the dog; *vaikuṇṭhete gelā*—went to the spiritual kingdom, Vaikuṇṭha.

TRANSLATION

The next day, no one saw that dog, for it had obtained its spiritual body and departed for Vaikuṇṭha, the spiritual kingdom.

PURPORT

This is the result of *sādhu-saṅga,* consequent association with Śrī Caitanya Mahāprabhu and promotion back home, back to Godhead. This result is possible even for a dog, by the mercy of the Vaiṣṇava. Therefore, everyone in the human form of life should be induced to associate with devotees. By rendering a little service, even by eating *prasāda,* not to speak of chanting and dancing, everyone could be promoted to Vaikuṇṭhaloka. It is therefore requested that all our devotees in the ISKCON community become pure Vaiṣṇavas, so that by their mercy all the people of the world will be transferred to Vaikuṇṭhaloka, even without their knowledge. Everyone should be given a chance to take *prasāda* and thus be induced to chant the holy names Hare Kṛṣṇa and also dance in ecstasy. By these three processes, although performed without knowledge or education, even an animal went back to Godhead.

TEXT 33

ঐছে দিব্যলীলা করে শচীর নন্দন ।
কুক্কুরকে কৃষ্ণ কহাঞা করিলা মোচন ॥ ৩৩ ॥

aiche divya-līlā kare śacīra nandana
kukkurake kṛṣṇa kahāñā karilā mocana

SYNONYMS

aiche—in that way; *divya-līlā*—transcendental activities; *kare*—performs; *śacīra nandana*—the son of mother Śacī; *kukkurake*—even a dog; *kṛṣṇa kahāñā*—inducing to chant the holy name "Kṛṣṇa"; *karilā mocana*—delivered.

TRANSLATION

Such are the transcendental pastimes of Śrī Caitanya Mahāprabhu, the son of mother Śacī. He even delivered a dog simply by inducing it to chant the mahā-mantra, Hare Kṛṣṇa.

TEXT 34

এথা প্রভু-আজ্ঞায় রূপ আইলা বৃন্দাবন।
কৃষ্ণলীলা-নাটক করিতে হৈল মন ॥ ৩৪ ॥

ethā prabhu-ājñāya rūpa āilā vṛndāvana
kṛṣṇa-līlā-nāṭaka karite haila mana

SYNONYMS

ethā—on the other side; *prabhu-ājñāya*—upon the order of Śrī Caitanya Mahāprabhu; *rūpa*—Rūpa Gosvāmī; *āilā*—went; *vṛndāvana*—to Vṛndāvana; *kṛṣṇa-līlā-nāṭaka*—a drama on Lord Kṛṣṇa's pastimes; *karite*—to compose; *haila*—it was; *mana*—the mind.

TRANSLATION

Meanwhile, following the order of Śrī Caitanya Mahāprabhu, Śrīla Rūpa Gosvāmī returned to Vṛndāvana. He desired to write dramas concerning the pastimes of Lord Kṛṣṇa.

TEXT 35

বৃন্দাবনে নাটকের আরম্ভ করিলা।
মঙ্গলাচরণ 'নান্দী-শ্লোক' তথাই লিখিলা ॥ ৩৫ ॥

vṛndāvane nāṭakera ārambha karilā
maṅgalācaraṇa 'nāndī-śloka' tathāi likhilā

SYNONYMS

vṛndāvane—at Vṛndāvana; *nāṭakera*—of the drama; *ārambha*—the beginning; *karilā*—wrote; *maṅgalācaraṇa*—invoking auspiciousness; *nāndī-śloka*—introductory verse; *tathāi*—there; *likhilā*—he wrote.

TRANSLATION

In Vṛndāvana, Rūpa Gosvāmī began to write a drama. In particular, he composed the introductory verses to invoke good fortune.

PURPORT

Śrīla Bhaktisiddhānta Sarasvatī Ṭhākura quotes his notes from the *Nāṭaka-candrikā,* wherein he has written:

prastāvanāyās tu mukhe
nāndī kāryāśubhāvahā
āśīr-namaskriyā-vastu-
nirdeśānyatamānvitā

aṣṭābhir daśabhir yuktā
kiṁvā dvādaśabhiḥ padaiḥ
candranāmāṅkitā prāyo
maṅgalārtha-padojjvalā
maṅgalaṁ cakra-kamala-
cakora-kumudādikam

Similarly, in the Sixth Chapter of the *Sāhitya-darpaṇa,* text 282, he has said:

āśīr-vacana-saṁyuktā
stutir yasmāt prayujyate
deva-dvija-nṛ-pādīnāṁ
tasmān nāndīti saṁjñitā

The introductory portion of a drama, which is written to invoke good fortune, is called *nāndī-śloka.*

TEXT 36

পথে চলি' আইসে নাটকের ঘটনা ভাবিতে ।
কড়চা করিয়া কিছু লাগিলা লিখিতে ॥ ৩৬ ॥

pathe cali' āise nāṭakera ghaṭanā bhāvite
kaḍacā kariyā kichu lāgilā likhite

SYNONYMS

pathe cali'—walking on the road; *āise*—goes; *nāṭakera*—of the drama; *ghaṭanā*—events; *bhāvite*—thinking of; *kaḍacā kariyā*—making notes; *kichu*—something; *lāgilā likhite*—he began to write.

TRANSLATION

On his way to Gauḍa-deśa, Rūpa Gosvāmī had been thinking of how to write the action of the drama. Thus he had made some notes and begun to write.

TEXT 37

এইমতে দুই ভাই গৌড়দেশে আইলা ।
গৌড়ে আসি' অনুপমের গঙ্গা-প্রাপ্তি হৈলা ॥ ৩৭ ॥

ei-mate dui bhāi gauḍa-deśe āilā
gauḍe āsi' anupamera gaṅgā-prāpti hailā

SYNONYMS

ei-mate—in this way; *dui bhāi*—Rūpa Gosvāmī and his younger brother, Anupama; *gauḍa-deśe āilā*—reached Bengal, which is known as Gauḍa-deśa; *gauḍe āsi'*—coming to Gauḍa; *anupamera*—of Anupama; *gaṅgā-prāpti hailā*—there was obtainment of the shelter of mother Ganges (passing away).

TRANSLATION

In this way the two brothers Rūpa and Anupama reached Bengal, but when they arrived there Anupama died.

PURPORT

Formerly when a person died it was commonly said that he had attained the shelter of mother Ganges, even if he did not die on the bank of the Ganges. It is customary among Hindus to carry a dying person to a nearby bank of the Ganges, for if one dies on the bank of the Ganges, his soul is considered to reach the lotus feet of Lord Viṣṇu, wherefrom the Ganges flows.

TEXT 38

রূপ-গোসাঞি প্রভুপাশে করিলা গমন ।
প্রভুরে দেখিতে তাঁর উৎকণ্ঠিত মন ॥ ৩৮ ॥

rūpa-gosāñi prabhu-pāśe karilā gamana
prabhure dekhite tāṅra utkaṇṭhita mana

SYNONYMS

rūpa-gosāñi—of the name Rūpa Gosvāmī; *prabhu-pāśe*—the place of Śrī Caitanya Mahāprabhu; *karilā gamana*—departed for; *prabhure dekhite*—to see Lord Śrī Caitanya Mahāprabhu; *tāṅra*—his; *utkaṇṭhita*—full of anxiety; *mana*—mind.

TRANSLATION

Rūpa Gosvāmī then departed to see Śrī Caitanya Mahāprabhu, for he was very eager to see Him.

TEXT 39

অনুপমের লাগি' তাঁর কিছু বিলম্ব হইল ।
ভক্তগণ-পাশ আইলা, লাগ্ না পাইল ॥ ৩৯ ॥

anupamera lāgi' tāṅra kichu vilamba ha-ila
bhakta-gaṇa-pāśa āilā, lāg nā pāila

SYNONYMS

anupamera lāgi'—on account of the passing away of Anupama; *tāṅra*—of Rūpa Gosvāmī; *kichu*—some; *vilamba*—delay; *ha-ila*—there was; *bhakta-gaṇa-pāśa*—to the devotees in Bengal; *āilā*—came; *lāg nā pāila*—he could not contact them.

TRANSLATION

There was some delay because of the death of Anupama, and therefore when Rūpa Gosvāmī went to Bengal to see the devotees there, he could not get in touch with them because they had already left.

TEXT 40

উড়িয়া-দেশে 'সত্যভামাপুর'-নামে গ্রাম ।
এক রাত্রি সেই গ্রামে করিলা বিশ্রাম ॥ ৪০ ॥

uḍiyā-deśe 'satyabhāmā-pura'-nāme grāma
eka rātri sei grāme karilā viśrāma

SYNONYMS

uḍiyā-deśe—in the state of Orissa; *satyabhāmā-pura*—Satyabhāmā-pura; *nāme*—named; *grāma*—a village; *eka rātri*—one night; *sei grāme*—in that village; *karilā viśrāma*—he rested.

TRANSLATION

In the province of Orissa there is a place known as Satyabhāmā-pura. Śrīla Rūpa Gosvāmī rested for a night in that village on his way to Jagannātha Purī.

PURPORT

There is a place known as Satyabhāmā-pura in the district of Kaṭaka (Cuttak) in Orissa. It is near the village known as Jānkādei-pura.

TEXT 41

রাত্রে স্বপ্নে দেখে,—এক দিব্যরূপা নারী ।
সম্মুখে আসিয়া আজ্ঞা দিলা বহু কৃপা করি' ॥ ৪১ ॥

rātre svapne dekhe,——eka divya-rūpā nārī
sammukhe āsiyā ājñā dilā bahu kṛpā kari'

SYNONYMS

rātre—at night; *svapne dekhe*—he dreamed; *eka*—one; *divya-rūpā nārī*—celestially beautiful woman; *sammukhe āsiyā*—coming before him; *ājñā dilā*—ordered; *bahu kṛpā kari'*—showing him much mercy.

TRANSLATION

While resting in Satyabhāmā-pura, he dreamed that a celestially beautiful woman had come before him and very mercifully gave him the following order.

TEXT 42

"আমার নাটক পৃথক্ করহ রচন।
আমার কৃপাতে নাটক হৈবে বিলক্ষণ॥"৪২॥

"āmāra nāṭaka pṛthak karaha racana
āmāra kṛpāte nāṭaka haibe vilakṣaṇa"

SYNONYMS

āmāra nāṭaka—my drama; *pṛthak karaha racana*—write separately; *āmāra kṛpāte*—by my mercy; *nāṭaka*—the drama; *haibe*—will be; *vilakṣaṇa*—extraordinarily beautiful.

TRANSLATION

"Write a separate drama about me," she said. "By my mercy, it will be extraordinarily beautiful."

TEXT 43

স্বপ্ন দেখি' রূপ-গোসাঞি করিলা বিচার।
সত্যভামার আজ্ঞা—পৃথক্ নাটক করিবার॥ ৪৩॥

svapna dekhi' rūpa-gosāñi karilā vicāra
satya-bhāmāra ājñā—pṛthak nāṭaka karibāra

SYNONYMS

svapna dekhi'—after dreaming; *rūpa-gosāñi*—Rūpa Gosvāmī; *karilā vicāra*—considered; *satya-bhāmāra ājñā*—the order of Śrīmatī Satyabhāmā; *pṛthak nāṭaka karibāra*—to write a separate drama.

TRANSLATION

After having that dream, Śrīla Rūpa Gosvāmī considered, "It is the order of Satyabhāmā that I write a separate drama for her.

TEXT 44

ব্রজ-পুর-লীলা একত্র করিয়াছি ঘটনা ।
দুই ভাগ করি' এবে করিমু রচনা ॥ ৪৪ ॥

vraja-pura-līlā ekatra kariyāchi ghaṭanā
dui bhāga kari' ebe karimu racanā

SYNONYMS

vraja-pura-līlā—Lord Kṛṣṇa's pastimes in Vraja and Dvārakā; *ekatra*—in one place; *kariyāchi*—I have collected; *ghaṭanā*—all the events; *dui bhāga kari'*—dividing into two different parts; *ebe*—now; *karimu racanā*—I shall write.

TRANSLATION

"I have brought together in one work all the pastimes performed by Lord Kṛṣṇa in Vṛndāvana and in Dvārakā. Now I shall have to divide them into two dramas."

TEXT 45

ভাবিতে ভাবিতে শীঘ্র আইলা নীলাচলে ।
আসি' উত্তরিলা হরিদাস-বাসাস্থলে ॥ ৪৫ ॥

bhāvite bhāvite śīghra āilā nīlācale
āsi' uttarilā haridāsa-vāsā-sthale

SYNONYMS

bhāvite bhāvite—thinking and thinking; *śīghra*—very soon; *āilā nīlācale*—reached Nīlācala (Jagannātha Purī); *āsi'*—coming; *uttarilā*—approached; *haridāsa-vāsā-sthale*—the place where Haridāsa Ṭhākura was residing.

TRANSLATION

Thus absorbed in thought, he quickly reached Jagannātha Purī. When he arrived, he approached the hut of Haridāsa Ṭhākura.

TEXT 46

হরিদাস-ঠাকুর তাঁরে বহুকৃপা কৈলা ।
'তুমি আসিবে,—মোরে প্রভু যে কহিলা' ॥ ৪৬ ॥

haridāsa-ṭhākura tāṅre bahu-kṛpā kailā
'tumi āsibe,——more prabhu ye kahilā'

SYNONYMS

hari-dāsa-ṭhākura—of the name Haridāsa Ṭhākura; *tāṅre*—unto him; *bahu-kṛpā kailā*—showed much affection because of love and mercy; *tumi āsibe*—you will come; *more*—me; *prabhu*—Śrī Caitanya Mahāprabhu; *ye*—that; *kahilā*—informed.

TRANSLATION

Out of affectionate love and mercy, Haridāsa Ṭhākura told Śrīla Rūpa Gosvāmī, "Śrī Caitanya Mahāprabhu has already informed me that you would come here."

TEXT 47

'উপল-ভোগ' দেখি' হরিদাসেরে দেখিতে ।
প্রতিদিন আইসেন, প্রভু আইলা আচম্বিতে ॥ ৪৭ ॥

'upala-bhoga' dekhi' haridāsere dekhite
pratidina āisena, prabhu āilā ācambite

SYNONYMS

upala-bhoga—the offering of food to Lord Jagannātha at noon; *dekhi'*—seeing; *hari-dāsere dekhite*—to see Haridāsa Ṭhākura; *pratidina*—daily; *āisena*—comes; *prabhu*—Śrī Caitanya Mahāprabhu; *āilā*—He reached there; *ācambite*—all of a sudden.

TRANSLATION

After seeing the upala-bhoga ceremony at the Jagannātha temple, Lord Śrī Caitanya Mahāprabhu would regularly come to see Haridāsa every day. Thus He suddenly arrived there.

TEXT 48

'রূপ দণ্ডবৎ করে',—হরিদাস কহিলা ।
হরিদাসে মিলি' প্রভু রূপে আলিঙ্গিলা ॥ ৪৮ ॥

'rūpa daṇḍavat kare',——haridāsa kahilā
haridāse mili' prabhu rūpe āliṅgilā

SYNONYMS

rūpa—Rūpa Gosvāmī; *daṇḍavat kare*—offers You obeisances; *hari-dāsa kahilā*—Haridāsa informed Śrī Caitanya Mahāprabhu; *hari-dāse mili'*—after meeting Haridāsa; *prabhu*—Śrī Caitanya Mahāprabhu; *rūpe āliṅgilā*—embraced Rūpa Gosvāmī.

TRANSLATION

When the Lord arrived, Rūpa Gosvāmī immediately offered his obeisances. Haridāsa informed the Lord, "This is Rūpa Gosvāmī offering You obeisances," and the Lord embraced him.

TEXT 49

হরিদাস-রূপে লঞা প্রভু বসিলা একস্থানে ।
কুশল-প্রশ্ন, ইষ্টগোষ্ঠী কৈলা কতক্ষণে ॥ ৪৯ ॥

haridāsa-rūpe lañā prabhu vasilā eka-sthāne
kuśala-praśna, iṣṭa-goṣṭhī kailā kata-kṣaṇe

SYNONYMS

hari-dāsa-rūpe—both Haridāsa Ṭhākura and Rūpa Gosvāmī; *lañā*—with; *prabhu*—Śrī Caitanya Mahāprabhu; *vasilā*—sat down; *eka-sthāne*—in one place; *kuśala-praśna*—questions about auspicious news; *iṣṭa-goṣṭhī*—talking together; *kailā kata-kṣaṇe*—continued for some time.

TRANSLATION

Śrī Caitanya Mahāprabhu then sat down with Haridāsa and Rūpa Gosvāmī. They inquired from one another about auspicious news, and then continued to talk together for some time.

TEXT 50

সনাতনের বার্তা যবে গোসাঞি পুছিল ।
রূপ কহে,—'তার সঙ্গে দেখা না হইল ॥ ৫০ ॥

sanātanera vārtā yabe gosāñi puchila
rūpa kahe,——'tāra saṅge dekhā nā ha-ila

SYNONYMS

sanātanera vārtā—news of Sanātana Gosvāmī; *yabe*—when; *gosāñi*—Śrī Caitanya Mahāprabhu; *puchila*—inquired; *rūpa kahe*—Rūpa Gosvāmī says; *tāra saṅge*—with him; *dekhā nā ha-ila*—there was not meeting.

TRANSLATION

When Śrī Caitanya Mahāprabhu inquired about Sanātana Gosvāmī, Rūpa Gosvāmī replied, "I did not meet him.

TEXT 51

আমি গঙ্গাপথে আইলাঙ, তিঁহো রাজপথে ।
অতএব আমার দেখা নহিল তাঁর সাথে ॥ ৫১ ॥

āmi gaṅgā-pathe āilāṅa, tiṅho rāja-pathe
ataeva āmāra dekhā nahila tāṅra sāthe

SYNONYMS

āmi—I; *gaṅgā-pathe*—on the path on the bank of the Ganges; *āilāṅa*—I came; *tiṅho*—he; *rāja-pathe*—on the public road; *ataeva*—therefore; *āmāra*—my; *dekhā*—meeting; *nahila*—was not possible; *tāṅra sāthe*—with him.

TRANSLATION

"I came by the path on the bank of the Ganges, whereas Sanātana Gosvāmī came by the public road. Therefore we did not meet.

TEXT 52

প্রয়াগে শুনিলুঁ,– তেঁহো গেলা বৃন্দাবনে ।
অনুপমের গঙ্গা-প্রাপ্তি' কৈল নিবেদনে ॥" ৫২ ॥

prayāge śuniluṅ,——teṅho gelā vṛndāvane
anupamera gaṅgā-prāpti kaila nivedane"

SYNONYMS

prayāge—in Prayāga; *śuniluṅ*—I heard; *teṅho*—he; *gelā vṛndāvane*—has gone to Vṛndāvana; *anupamera*—of Anupama; *gaṅgā-prāpti*—getting the mercy of the Ganges (death); *kaila nivedane*—he informed.

TRANSLATION

"In Prayāga I heard that he had already gone to Vṛndāvana." Rūpa Gosvāmī next informed the Lord about the death of Anupama.

TEXT 53

রূপে তাহাঁ বাসা দিয়া গোসাঞি চলিলা ।
গোসাঞির সঙ্গী ভক্ত রূপেরে মিলিলা ॥ ৫৩ ॥

rūpe tāhāṅ vāsā diyā gosāñi calilā
gosāñira saṅgī bhakta rūpere mililā

SYNONYMS

rūpe—to Rūpa; *tāhāṅ*—there; *vāsā diyā*—offered a residence; *gosāñi calilā*—Śrī Caitanya Mahāprabhu left the place; *gosāñira saṅgī*—the associates of Śrī Caitanya Mahāprabhu; *bhakta*—all the devotees; *rūpere mililā*—met Rūpa Gosvāmī.

TRANSLATION

After allotting residential quarters there to Rūpa Gosvāmī, Śrī Caitanya Mahāprabhu left. Then all of the Lord's personal associates met Śrīla Rūpa Gosvāmī.

TEXT 54

আর দিন মহাপ্রভু সব ভক্ত লঞা ।
রূপে মিলাইলা সবায় কৃপা ত' করিয়া ॥ ৫৪ ॥

āra dina mahāprabhu saba bhakta lañā
rūpe milāilā sabāya kṛpā ta' kariyā

SYNONYMS

āra dina—the next day; *mahāprabhu*—Śrī Caitanya Mahāprabhu; *saba*—all; *bhakta lañā*—taking the devotees; *rūpe milāilā*—introduced Rūpa Gosvāmī; *sabāya*—to all of them; *kṛpā ta' kariyā*—showing His mercy.

TRANSLATION

On the next day, Caitanya Mahāprabhu again met Rūpa Gosvāmī, and with great mercy the Lord introduced him to all the devotees.

TEXT 55

সবার চরণ রূপ করিলা বন্দন ।
কৃপা করি' রূপে সবে কৈলা আলিঙ্গন ॥ ৫৫ ॥

sabāra caraṇa rūpa karilā vandana
kṛpā kari' rūpe sabe kailā āliṅgana

SYNONYMS

sabāra—of all the devotees; *caraṇa*—to the lotus feet; *rūpa*—Śrīla Rūpa Gosvāmī; *karilā vandana*—offered prayers; *kṛpā kari'*—showing great mercy; *rūpe*—Rūpa Gosvāmī; *sabe*—all the devotees; *kailā*—did; *āliṅgana*—embracing.

TRANSLATION

Śrīla Rūpa Gosvāmī offered his respectful obeisances unto the lotus feet of them all, and all the devotees, by their mercy, embraced him.

TEXT 56

'অদ্বৈত নিত্যানন্দ, তোমরা দুইজনে ।
প্রভু কহে—রূপে কৃপা কর কায়মনে ॥ ৫৬ ॥

'advaita nityānanda, tomarā dui-jane
prabhu kahe——rūpe kṛpā kara kāya-mane

SYNONYMS

advaita—Advaita Ācārya; *nityānanda*—Nityānanda Prabhu; *tomarā dui-jane*—both of You; *prabhu kahe*—Lord Caitanya Mahāprabhu says; *rūpe*—to Rūpa Gosvāmī; *kṛpā*—mercy; *kara*—show; *kāya-mane*—wholeheartedly.

TRANSLATION

Śrī Caitanya Mahāprabhu told Advaita Ācārya and Nityānanda Prabhu, "You should both show Your mercy wholeheartedly to Rūpa Gosvāmī.

TEXT 57

তোমা-দুঁহার কৃপাতে ইহাঁর হউ তৈছে শক্তি ।
যাতে বিবরিতে পারেন কৃষ্ণরসভক্তি ॥ ৫৭ ॥

tomā-duṅhāra kṛpāte iṅhāra ha-u taiche śakti
yāte vivarite pārena kṛṣṇa-rasa-bhakti

SYNONYMS

tomā-duṅhāra kṛpāte—by the mercy of both of You; *iṅhāra*—of Rūpa Gosvāmī; *ha-u*—let there be; *taiche*—such; *śakti*—power; *yāte*—by which; *vivarite*—to describe; *pārena*—is able; *kṛṣṇa-rasa-bhakti*—the transcendental mellows of devotional service.

TRANSLATION

"May Rūpa Gosvāmī, by Your mercy, become so powerful that he will be able to describe the transcendental mellows of devotional service."

TEXT 58

গৌড়িয়া, উড়িয়া, যত প্রভুর ভক্তগণ ।
সবার হইল রূপ স্নেহের ভাজন ॥ ৫৮ ॥

gauḍiyā, uḍiyā, yata prabhura bhakta-gaṇa
sabāra ha-ila rūpa snehera bhājana

SYNONYMS

gauḍiyā—devotees from Bengal; *uḍiyā*—devotees belonging to Orissa; *yata*—all; *prabhura bhakta-gaṇa*—devotees of Lord Śrī Caitanya Mahāprabhu; *sabāra*—of all of them; *ha-ila*—was; *rūpa*—Rūpa Gosvāmī; *snehera bhājana*—an object of love and affection.

TRANSLATION

Thus Rūpa Gosvāmī became the object of love and affection for all the devotees of the Lord, including those who came from Bengal and those who resided in Orissa.

TEXT 59

প্রতিদিন আসি' রূপে করেন মিলনে ।
মন্দিরে যে প্রসাদ পান, দেন দুই জনে ॥ ৫৯ ॥

pratidina āsi' rūpe karena milane
mandire ye prasāda pāna, dena dui jane

SYNONYMS

pratidina—every day; *āsi'*—going; *rūpe*—Rūpa Gosvāmī; *karena milane*—Caitanya Mahāprabhu meets; *mandire*—at the Jagannātha temple; *ye*—whatever; *prasāda pāna*—*prasāda* He gets; *dena*—gives; *dui jane*—to two persons, Śrīla Rūpa Gosvāmī and Haridāsa Ṭhākura.

TRANSLATION

Every day Śrī Caitanya Mahāprabhu would go to see Rūpa Gosvāmī, and whatever prasāda He received from the temple He would deliver to Rūpa Gosvāmī and Haridāsa Ṭhākura.

TEXT 60

ইষ্টগোষ্ঠী দুঁহা সনে করি' কতক্ষণ ।
মধ্যাহ্ন করিতে প্রভু করিলা গমন ॥ ৬০ ॥

iṣṭa-goṣṭhī duṅhā sane kari' kata-kṣaṇa
madhyāhna karite prabhu karilā gamana

SYNONYMS

iṣṭa-goṣṭhī—conversation; *duṅhā sane*—with both Rūpa Gosvāmī and Haridāsa; *kari'*—doing; *kata-kṣaṇa*—for some time; *madhya-ahna karite*—to execute daily noontime duties; *prabhu*—Śrī Caitanya Mahāprabhu; *karilā gamana*—left that place.

TRANSLATION

He would talk for some time with them both and then leave to perform His noontime duties.

TEXT 61

এইমত প্রতিদিন প্রভুর ব্যবহার ।
প্রভুকৃপা পাঞা রূপের আনন্দ অপার ॥ ৬১ ॥

ei-mata pratidina prabhura vyavahāra
prabhu-kṛpā pāñā rūpera ānanda apāra

SYNONYMS

ei-mata—in this way; *pratidina*—daily; *prabhura vyavahāra*—the dealings of Śrī Caitanya Mahāprabhu; *prabhu-kṛpā*—the mercy of Lord Caitanya; *pāñā*—getting; *rūpera*—of Śrīla Rūpa Gosvāmī; *ānanda apāra*—unlimited happiness.

TRANSLATION

In this way Lord Caitanya Mahāprabhu's dealings with them continued every day. Thus receiving the transcendental favor of the Lord, Śrīla Rūpa Gosvāmī felt unlimited pleasure.

TEXT 62

ভক্তগণ লঞা কৈলা গুণ্ডিচা মার্জন ।
আইটোটা আসি' কৈলা বন্য-ভোজন ॥ ৬২ ॥

bhakta-gaṇa lañā kailā guṇḍicā mārjana
āiṭoṭā āsi' kailā vanya-bhojana

SYNONYMS

bhakta-gaṇa—all the devotees; *lañā*—taking; *kailā*—performed; *guṇḍicā mārjana*—cleansing and washing of the Guṇḍicā temple; *āiṭoṭā āsi'*—coming to the nearby garden named Āiṭoṭā; *kailā*—had; *vanya-bhojana*—a picnic within the garden.

TRANSLATION

After Śrī Caitanya Mahāprabhu, taking all His devotees with Him, performed the Guṇḍicā-mārjana [washing and cleansing the temple Guṇḍicā], He went to the garden known as Āiṭoṭā and accepted prasāda at a picnic within the garden.

TEXT 63

প্রসাদ খায়, 'হরি' বলে সর্বভক্তজন ।
দেখি' হরিদাস-রূপের হরষিত মন ॥ ৬৩ ॥

prasāda khāya, 'hari' bale sarva-bhakta-jana
dekhi' haridāsa-rūpera harașita mana

SYNONYMS

prasāda khāya—eat the *prasāda*; *hari bale*—chant the holy name of Hari; *sarva-bhakta-jana*—all the devotees; *dekhi'*—seeing this; *hari-dāsa*—of Haridāsa Ṭhākura; *rūpera*—and of Rūpa Gosvāmī; *harașita*—jubilant; *mana*—the minds.

TRANSLATION

When Haridāsa Ṭhākura and Rūpa Gosvāmī saw that all the devotees were accepting prasāda and chanting the holy name of Hari, they both were greatly pleased.

TEXT 64

গোবিন্দদ্বারা প্রভুর শেষ-প্রসাদ পাইলা ।
প্রেমে মত্ত দুইজন নাচিতে লাগিলা ॥ ৬৪ ॥

govinda-dvārā prabhura śeṣa-prasāda pāilā
preme matta dui-jana nācite lāgilā

SYNONYMS

govinda-dvārā—through Govinda; *prabhura*—of Śrī Caitanya Mahāprabhu; *śeṣa-prasāda*—remnants of food; *pāilā*—they got; *preme matta*—overwhelmed by ecstasy; *dui-jana*—both of them; *nācite lāgilā*—began to dance.

TRANSLATION

When they received the remnants of Śrī Caitanya Mahāprabhu's prasāda through Govinda, they respected it, and then they both began to dance in ecstasy.

TEXT 65

আর দিন প্রভু রূপে মিলিয়া বসিলা ।
সর্বজ্ঞ-শিরোমণি প্রভু কহিতে লাগিলা ॥ ৬৫ ॥

āra dina prabhu rūpe miliyā vasilā
sarvajña-śiromaṇi prabhu kahite lāgilā

SYNONYMS

āra dina—the next day; *prabhu*—Śrī Caitanya Mahāprabhu; *rūpe*—with Śrīla Rūpa Gosvāmī; *miliyā*—meeting; *vasilā*—sat down; *sarva-jña-śiromaṇi*—Śrī Caitanya Mahāprabhu, the best of the omniscient; *prabhu*—Śrī Caitanya Mahāprabhu; *kahite lāgilā*—began to speak.

TRANSLATION

On the next day, when Śrī Caitanya Mahāprabhu went to see Śrīla Rūpa Gosvāmī, the omniscient Lord spoke as follows.

TEXT 66

“কৃষ্ণেরে বাহির নাহি করিহ ব্রজ হৈতে ।
ব্রজ ছাড়ি’ কৃষ্ণ কভু না যান কাহাঁতে ॥ ৬৬ ॥

"kṛṣṇere bāhira nāhi kariha vraja haite
vraja chāḍi' kṛṣṇa kabhu nā yāna kāhāṅte

SYNONYMS

kṛṣṇere—Kṛṣṇa; *bāhira*—outside; *nāhi*—do not; *kariha*—take; *vraja haite*—from Vṛndāvana; *vraja chāḍi'*—leaving Vṛndāvana; *kṛṣṇa*—Lord Kṛṣṇa; *kabhu*—at any time; *nā*—not; *yāna*—goes; *kāhāṅte*—anywhere.

TRANSLATION

"Do not try to take Kṛṣṇa out of Vṛndāvana, for He does not go anywhere else at any time.

TEXT 67

কৃষ্ণোঽন্যো যদুসম্ভূতো যঃ পূর্ণঃ সোঽস্ত্যতঃ পরঃ ।
বৃন্দাবনং পরিত্যজ্য স ক্বচিন্নৈব গচ্ছতি ॥ ৬৭ ॥

kṛṣṇo 'nyo yadu-sambhūto
yaḥ pūrṇaḥ so 'sty ataḥ paraḥ
vṛndāvanaṁ parityajya
sa kvacin naiva gacchati

SYNONYMS

kṛṣṇaḥ—Lord Kṛṣṇa; *anyaḥ*—another Lord Vāsudeva; *yadu-sambhūtaḥ*—born in the Yadu dynasty; *yaḥ*—who; *pūrṇaḥ*—the full Supreme Personality of Godhead, Kṛṣṇa; *saḥ*—He; *asti*—is; *ataḥ*—than Him (Vāsudeva); *paraḥ*—different; *vṛndāvanam*—the place Vṛndāvana; *parityajya*—giving up; *saḥ*—He; *kvacit*—at any time; *na eva gacchati*—does not go.

TRANSLATION

" 'The Kṛṣṇa known as Yadukumāra is Vāsudeva Kṛṣṇa. He is different from the Kṛṣṇa who is the son of Nanda Mahārāja. Yadukumāra Kṛṣṇa manifests His pastimes in the cities of Mathurā and Dvārakā, but Kṛṣṇa the son of Nanda Mahārāja never at any time leaves Vṛndāvana.' "

PURPORT

This verse is included in the *Laghu-bhāgavatāmṛta* (1.5.461), by Śrīla Rūpa Gosvāmī.

TEXT 68

এত কহি' মহাপ্রভু মধ্যাহ্নে চলিলা ।
রূপ-গোসাঞি মনে কিছু বিস্ময় হইলা ॥ ৬৮ ॥

eta kahi' mahāprabhu madhyāhne calilā
rūpa-gosāñi mane kichu vismaya ha-ilā

SYNONYMS

eta kahi'—saying this; *mahāprabhu*—Śrī Caitanya Mahāprabhu; *madhya-ahne calilā*—left to execute noon duties; *rūpa-gosāñi*—Śrīla Rūpa Gosvāmī; *mane*—in mind; *kichu*—some; *vismaya ha-ilā*—there was surprise.

TRANSLATION

After saying this, Caitanya Mahāprabhu went to perform His noontime duties, leaving Śrīla Rūpa Gosvāmī somewhat surprised.

TEXT 69

"পৃথক্ নাটক করিতে সত্যভামা আজ্ঞা দিল ।
জানিলু, পৃথক্ নাটক করিতে প্রভু-আজ্ঞা হৈল ॥৬৯॥

"pṛthak nāṭaka karite satyabhāmā ājñā dila
jānilu, pṛthak nāṭaka karite prabhu-ājñā haila

SYNONYMS

pṛthak nāṭaka—different dramas; *karite*—to write; *satyabhāmā*—of the name Satyabhāmā; *ājñā dila*—ordered; *jānilu*—now I understand; *pṛthak nāṭaka*—different dramas; *karite*—to write; *prabhu-ājñā*—the order of the Lord; *haila*—there was.

TRANSLATION

"Satyabhāmā ordered me to write two different dramas," Śrīla Rūpa Gosvāmī thought. "Now I understand that this order has been confirmed by Śrī Caitanya Mahāprabhu.

TEXT 70

পূর্বে দুই নাটক ছিল একত্র রচনা ।
দুইভাগ করি এবে করিমু ঘটনা ॥ ৭০ ॥

pūrve dui nāṭaka chila ekatra racanā
dui-bhāga kari ebe karimu ghaṭanā

SYNONYMS

pūrve—previously; *dui nāṭaka*—two dramas; *chila*—there was; *ekatra*—together; *racanā*—composition; *dui-bhāga kari*—dividing into two; *ebe*—now; *karimu ghaṭanā*—I shall write the incidents.

TRANSLATION

"Formerly I wrote the two dramas as one composition. Now I shall divide it and describe the incidents in two separate works.

TEXT 71

দুই 'নান্দী' 'প্রস্তাবনা', দুই 'সংঘটনা'।
পৃথক্ করিয়া লিখি করিয়া ভাবনা ॥ ৭১ ॥

dui 'nāndī' 'prastāvanā', dui 'saṁghaṭanā'
pṛthak kariyā likhi kariyā bhāvanā

SYNONYMS

dui nāndī—two invocations of good fortune; *prastāvanā*—introductions; *dui*—two; *saṁghaṭanā*—chains of events; *pṛthak kariyā*—making separate; *likhi*—I shall write; *kariyā bhāvanā*—thinking about them.

TRANSLATION

"I shall write two separate invocations of good fortune and two different introductions. Let me think deeply about the matter and then describe two different sets of incidents."

PURPORT

The two works are *Vidagdha-mādhava* and *Lalita-mādhava. Vidagdha-mādhava* describes pastimes in Vṛndāvana, and *Lalita-mādhava* describes pastimes in Dvārakā and Mathurā.

TEXT 72

রথযাত্রায় জগন্নাথ দর্শন করিলা।
রথ-অগ্রে প্রভুর নৃত্য-কীর্তন দেখিলা ॥ ৭২ ॥

ratha-yātrāya jagannātha darśana karilā
ratha-agre prabhura nṛtya-kīrtana dekhilā

SYNONYMS

ratha-yātrāya—during the function of Ratha-yātrā; *jagannātha*—Lord Jagannātha; *darśana karilā*—he saw; *ratha-agre*—the front of the *ratha,* or chariot; *prabhura*—of Śrī Caitanya Mahāprabhu; *nṛtya*—dancing; *kīrtana*—chanting; *dekhilā*—he saw.

TRANSLATION

During the Ratha-yātrā ceremony Rūpa Gosvāmī saw Lord Jagannātha. He also saw Lord Caitanya Mahāprabhu dancing and chanting in front of the ratha.

TEXT 73

প্রভুর নৃত্য-শ্লোক শুনি' শ্রীরূপ-গোসাঞি।
সেই শ্লোকার্থ লঞা শ্লোক করিলা তথাই ॥ ৭৩ ॥

prabhura nṛtya-śloka śuni' śrī-rūpa-gosāñi
sei ślokārtha lañā śloka karilā tathāi

SYNONYMS

prabhura—of Śrī Caitanya Mahāprabhu; *nṛtya-śloka*—verse uttered during His dancing; *śuni'*—hearing; *śrī-rūpa-gosāñi*—Śrīla Rūpa Gosvāmī; *sei śloka-artha*—the meaning of that verse; *lañā*—taking; *śloka karilā*—composed another verse; *tathāi*—on the spot.

TRANSLATION

When Rūpa Gosvāmī heard a verse uttered by Śrī Caitanya Mahāprabhu during the ceremony, he immediately composed another verse dealing with the same subject.

TEXT 74

পূর্বে সেই সব কথা করিয়াছি বর্ণন।
তথাপি কহিয়ে কিছু সংক্ষেপে কথন ॥ ৭৪ ॥

pūrve sei saba kathā kariyāchi varṇana
tathāpi kahiye kichu saṅkṣepe kathana

SYNONYMS

pūrve—previously; *sei*—these; *saba*—all; *kathā*—words; *kariyāchi varṇana*—I have described; *tathāpi*—still; *kahiye*—let me say; *kichu*—something; *saṅkṣepe*—in brief; *kathana*—telling.

TRANSLATION

I have already described all these incidents, but I still wish to add briefly something more.

TEXT 75

সামান্য এক শ্লোক প্রভু পড়েন কীর্তনে।
কেনে শ্লোক পড়ে—ইহা কেহ নাহি জানে ॥ ৭৫ ॥

sāmānya eka śloka prabhu paḍena kīrtane
kene śloka paḍe——ihā keha nāhi jāne

SYNONYMS

sāmānya—generally; *eka*—one; *śloka*—verse; *prabhu*—Śrī Caitanya Mahāprabhu; *paḍena*—recites; *kīrtane*—while chanting; *kene*—why; *śloka*—that verse; *paḍe*—He recites; *ihā*—this; *keha nāhi jāne*—no one knows.

TRANSLATION

Generally Śrī Caitanya Mahāprabhu recited a verse while dancing and chanting before the ratha, but no one knew why He was reciting that particular verse.

TEXT 76

সবে একা স্বরূপ গোসাঞি শ্লোকের অর্থ জানে।
শ্লোকানুরূপ পদ প্রভুকে করান আস্বাদনে ॥ ৭৬ ॥

sabe ekā svarūpa gosāñi ślokera artha jāne
ślokānurūpa pada prabhuke karāna āsvādane

SYNONYMS

sabe—only; *ekā*—one; *svarūpa gosāñi*—Svarūpa Dāmodara Gosvāmī; *ślokera artha*—the meaning of that verse; *jāne*—knows; *śloka-anurūpa pada*—other verses following that particular verse; *prabhuke*—Śrī Caitanya Mahāprabhu; *karāna*—causes; *āsvādane*—tasting.

TRANSLATION

Only Svarūpa Dāmodara Gosvāmī knew the purpose for which the Lord recited that verse. According to the Lord's attitude, he used to quote other verses to enable the Lord to relish mellows.

TEXT 77

রূপ-গোসাঞি প্রভুর জানিয়া অভিপ্রায়।
সেই অর্থে শ্লোক কৈলা প্রভুরে যে ভায় ॥ ৭৭ ॥

rūpa-gosāñi prabhura jāniyā abhiprāya
sei arthe śloka kailā prabhure ye bhāya

SYNONYMS

rūpa-gosāñi—Śrīla Rūpa Gosvāmī; *prabhura*—of Śrī Caitanya Mahāprabhu; *jāniyā*—knowing; *abhiprāya*—the intention; *sei arthe*—in that meaning; *śloka*—a verse; *kailā*—composed; *prabhure*—to Śrī Caitanya Mahāprabhu; *ye*—which; *bhāya*—appealed.

TRANSLATION

Rūpa Gosvāmī, however, could understand the intention of the Lord, and thus he composed another verse that appealed to Śrī Caitanya Mahāprabhu.

TEXT 78

যঃ কৌমারহরঃ স এব হি বরস্তা এব চৈত্রক্ষপা-
স্তে চোন্মীলিতমালতীসুরভয়ঃ প্রৌঢ়াঃ কদম্বানিলাঃ ।
সা চৈবাস্মি তথাপি তত্র সুরতব্যাপারলীলাবিধৌ
রেবারোধসি বেতসীতরুতলে চেতঃ সমুৎকণ্ঠতে ॥ ৭৮ ॥

yaḥ kaumāra-haraḥ sa eva hi varas tā eva caitra-kṣapās
te conmīlita-mālatī-surabhayaḥ prauḍhāḥ kadambānilāḥ
sā caivāsmi tathāpi tatra surata-vyāpāra-līlā-vidhau
revā-rodhasi vetasī-taru-tale cetaḥ samutkaṇṭhate

SYNONYMS

yaḥ—that same person who; *kaumāra-haraḥ*—the thief of my heart during youth; *saḥ*—he; *eva hi*—certainly; *varaḥ*—lover; *tāḥ*—these; *eva*—certainly; *caitra-kṣapāḥ*—moonlit nights of the month of Caitra; *te*—those; *ca*—and; *unmīlita*—fructified; *mālatī*—of *mālatī* flowers; *surabhayaḥ*—fragrances; *prauḍhāḥ*—full; *kadamba*—with the fragrance of the *kadamba* flower; *anilāḥ*—the breezes; *sā*—that one; *ca*—also; *eva*—certainly; *asmi*—I am; *tathāpi*—still; *tatra*—there; *surata-vyāpāra*—in intimate transactions; *līlā*—of pastimes; *vidhau*—in the manner; *revā*—of the river named Revā; *rodhasi*—on the bank; *vetasī*—of the name Vetasī; *taru-tale*—underneath the tree; *cetaḥ*—my mind; *samutkaṇṭhate*—is very eager to go.

TRANSLATION

"That very personality who stole my heart during my youth is now again my master. These are the same moonlit nights of the month of Caitra. The same fragrance of mālatī flowers is there, and the same sweet breezes are blowing from the kadamba forest. In our intimate relationship, I am also the same lover, yet still my mind is not happy here. I am eager to go back to that place on the bank of the Revā under the Vetasī tree. That is my desire."

PURPORT

This is the verse recited by Śrī Caitanya Mahāprabhu.

TEXT 79

প্রিয়ঃ সোঽয়ং কৃষ্ণঃ সহচরি কুরুক্ষেত্রমিলিত-
স্তথাহং সা রাধা তদিদমুভয়োঃ সঙ্গমসুখম্ ।
তথাপ্যন্তঃখেলন্মধুরমুরলীপঞ্চমজুষে
মনো মে কালিন্দীপুলিনবিপিনায় স্পৃহয়তি ॥ ৭৯ ॥

priyaḥ so 'yaṁ kṛṣṇaḥ sahacari kuru-kṣetra-militas
tathāhaṁ sā rādhā tad idam ubhayoḥ saṅgama-sukham
tathāpy antaḥ-khelan-madhura-muralī-pañcama-juṣe
mano me kālindī-pulina-vipināya spṛhayati

SYNONYMS

priyaḥ—very dear; *saḥ*—He; *ayam*—this; *kṛṣṇaḥ*—Lord Kṛṣṇa; *saha-cari*—O My dear friend; *kuru-kṣetra-militaḥ*—who is met on the field of Kurukṣetra; *tathā*—also; *aham*—I; *sā*—that; *rādhā*—Rādhārāṇī; *tat*—that; *idam*—this; *ubhayoḥ*—of both of Us; *saṅgama-sukham*—the happiness of meeting; *tathāpi*—still; *antaḥ*—within; *khelan*—playing; *madhura*—sweet; *muralī*—of the flute; *pañcama*—the fifth note; *juṣe*—which delights in; *manaḥ*—the mind; *me*—My; *kālindī*—of the River Yamunā; *pulina*—on the bank; *vipināya*—the trees; *spṛhayati*—desires.

TRANSLATION

"My dear friend, now I have met My very old and dear friend Kṛṣṇa on this field of Kurukṣetra. I am the same Rādhārāṇī, and now We are meeting together. It is very pleasant, but I would still like to go to the bank of the Yamunā beneath the trees of the forest there. I wish to hear the vibration of His sweet flute playing the fifth note within that forest of Vṛndāvana."

PURPORT

This is the verse composed by Śrīla Rūpa Gosvāmī. It is included in his book *Padyāvalī* (383).

TEXT 80

তালপত্রে শ্লোক লিখি' চালেতে রাখিলা ।
সমুদ্রস্নান করিবারে রূপ-গোসাঞি গেলা ॥ ৮০ ॥

tāla-patre śloka likhi' cālete rākhilā
samudra-snāna karibāre rūpa-gosāñi gelā

SYNONYMS

tāla-patre—on a palm leaf; *śloka*—the verse; *likhi'*—writing; *cālete*—in the thatched roof; *rākhilā*—kept it; *samudra-snāna*—bath in the sea; *karibāre*—for taking; *rūpa-gosāñi*—of the name Rūpa Gosvāmī; *gelā*—departed.

TRANSLATION

After writing this verse on a palm leaf, Rūpa Gosvāmī put it somewhere in his thatched roof and went to bathe in the sea.

TEXT 81

হেনকালে প্রভু আইলা তাঁহারে মিলিতে।
চালে শ্লোক দেখি প্রভু লাগিলা পড়িতে॥ ৮১॥

hena-kāle prabhu āilā tāṅhāre milite
cāle śloka dekhi prabhu lāgilā paḍite

SYNONYMS

hena-kāle—at that time; *prabhu*—Śrī Caitanya Mahāprabhu; *āilā*—came there; *tāṅhāre milite*—to meet him; *cāle*—in the thatched roof; *śloka*—verse; *dekhi*—seeing; *prabhu*—Śrī Caitanya Mahāprabhu; *lāgilā*—began; *paḍite*—to read.

TRANSLATION

At that time, Śrī Caitanya Mahāprabhu went there to meet him, and when He saw the leaf pushed into the roof and saw the verse, He began to read it.

TEXT 82

শ্লোক পড়ি' প্রভু সুখে প্রেমাবিষ্ট হৈলা।
হেনকালে রূপ-গোসাঞি স্নান করি' আইলা॥ ৮২॥

śloka paḍi' prabhu sukhe premāviṣṭa hailā
hena-kāle rūpa-gosāñi snāna kari' āilā

SYNONYMS

śloka paḍi'—reading this verse; *prabhu*—Śrī Caitanya Mahāprabhu; *sukhe*—in great happiness; *prema-āviṣṭa hailā*—became overwhelmed by ecstatic love;

hena-kāle—at that time; *rūpa-gosāñi*—Śrīla Rūpa Gosvāmī; *snāna kari'*—after taking his bath; *āilā*—came back.

TRANSLATION

After reading the verse, Śrī Caitanya Mahāprabhu was overwhelmed by ecstatic love. At that very time, Rūpa Gosvāmī returned, having finished bathing in the sea.

TEXT 83

প্রভু দেখি' দণ্ডবৎ প্রাঙ্গণে পড়িলা ।
প্রভু তাঁরে চাপড় মারি' কহিতে লাগিলা ॥ ৮৩ ॥

prabhu dekhi' daṇḍavat prāṅgaṇe paḍilā
prabhu tāṅre cāpaḍa māri' kahite lāgilā

SYNONYMS

prabhu dekhi'—after seeing the Lord there; *daṇḍavat*—obeisances; *prāṅgaṇe*—in the courtyard; *paḍilā*—fell down; *prabhu*—Śrī Caitanya Mahāprabhu; *tāṅre*—to Rūpa Gosvāmī; *cāpaḍa māri'*—giving a mild slap; *kahite lāgilā*—began to speak.

TRANSLATION

Seeing the Lord, Śrī Rūpa Gosvāmī fell flat in the courtyard to offer obeisances. The Lord slapped him mildly in love and spoke as follows.

TEXT 84

'গূঢ় মোর হৃদয় তুঞি জানিলা কেমনে ?'
এত কহি' রূপে কৈলা দৃঢ় আলিঙ্গনে ॥ ৮৪ ॥

'gūḍha mora hṛdaya tuñi jānilā kemane?'
eta kahi' rūpe kailā dṛḍha āliṅgane

SYNONYMS

gūḍha—very confidential; *mora*—My; *hṛdaya*—heart; *tuñi*—you; *jānilā*—knew; *kemane*—how; *eta kahi'*—saying this; *rūpe*—to Rūpa Gosvāmī; *kailā*—did; *dṛḍha āliṅgane*—firm embracing.

TRANSLATION

"My heart is very confidential. How did you know My mind in this way?" After saying this, He firmly embraced Rūpa Gosvāmī.

TEXT 85

সেই শ্লোক লঞা প্রভু স্বরূপে দেখাইলা।
স্বরূপের পরীক্ষা লাগি' তাঁহারে পুছিলা ॥ ৮৫ ॥

sei śloka lañā prabhu svarūpe dekhāilā
svarūpera parīkṣā lāgi' tāṅhāre puchilā

SYNONYMS

sei śloka—that verse; *lañā*—taking; *prabhu*—Śrī Caitanya Mahāprabhu; *svarūpe dekhāilā*—showed to Svarūpa Dāmodara; *svarūpera*—of Svarūpa Dāmodara Gosāñi; *parīkṣā lāgi'*—for the examination; *tāṅhāre puchilā*—He inquired from him.

TRANSLATION

Śrī Caitanya Mahāprabhu took that verse and showed it to Svarūpa Dāmodara for him to examine. Then the Lord questioned him.

TEXT 86

'মোর অন্তর-বার্তা রূপ জানিল কেমনে?'
স্বরূপ কহে—"জানি, কৃপা করিয়াছ আপনে ॥ ৮৬ ॥

'mora antara-vārtā rūpa jānila kemane?'
svarūpa kahe——"jāni, kṛpā kariyācha āpane

SYNONYMS

mora antara-vārtā—My internal intentions; *rūpa*—Rūpa Gosvāmī; *jānila*—knew; *kemane*—how; *svarūpa kahe*—Svarūpa replied; *jāni*—I can understand; *kṛpā kariyācha*—You have bestowed Your mercy; *āpane*—personally.

TRANSLATION

"How could Rūpa Gosvāmī have understood My heart?" the Lord asked. Svarūpa Dāmodara replied, "I can understand that You have already bestowed Your causeless mercy upon him.

TEXT 87

অন্যথা এ অর্থ কার নাহি হয় জ্ঞান।
তুমি পূর্বে কৃপা কৈলা, করি অনুমান ॥" ৮৭ ॥

anyathā e artha kāra nāhi haya jñāna
tumi pūrve kṛpā kailā, kari anumāna"

SYNONYMS

anyathā—otherwise; *e artha*—this confidential meaning; *kāra*—of anyone; *nāhi*—not; *haya*—is; *jñāna*—the knowledge; *tumi*—You; *pūrve*—before this; *kṛpā kailā*—bestowed mercy; *kari anumāna*—I can conjecture.

TRANSLATION

"No one could otherwise understand this meaning. I can therefore guess that previously You bestowed upon him Your causeless mercy."

TEXT 88

প্রভু কহে,—"ইঁহো আমায় প্রয়াগে মিলিল।
যোগ্যপাত্র জানি ইঁহায় মোর কৃপা ত' হইল ॥৮৮॥

prabhu kahe,—"iṅho āmāya prayāge milila
yogya-pātra jāni iṅhāya mora kṛpā ta' ha-ila

SYNONYMS

prabhu kahe—Śrī Caitanya Mahāprabhu replies; *iṅho*—Rūpa Gosvāmī; *āmāya*—with Me; *prayāge*—at Prayāga; *milila*—met; *yogya-pātra jāni* —knowing him to be a suitable person; *iṅhāya*—unto him; *mora*—My; *kṛpā ta' ha-ila*—there was mercy.

TRANSLATION

Śrī Caitanya Mahāprabhu replied, "Rūpa Gosvāmī met Me at Prayāga. Knowing him to be a suitable person, I naturally bestowed My mercy upon him.

TEXT 89

তবে শক্তি সঞ্চারি' আমি কৈলুঁ উপদেশ।
তুমিহ কহিও ইহাঁয় রসের বিশেষ ॥" ৮৯ ॥

tabe śakti sañcāri' āmi kailuṅ upadeśa
tumiha kahio ihāṅya rasera viśeṣa"

SYNONYMS

tabe—thereupon; *śakti sañcāri'*—empowering him with My transcendental potency; *āmi*—I; *kailuṅ upadeśa*—gave instruction; *tumiha*—you also; *kahio*—

inform; *inhāṅya*—unto him; *rasera viśeṣa*—particular information about transcendental mellows.

TRANSLATION

"I thereupon also bestowed upon him My transcendental potency. Now you also should give him instructions. In particular, instruct him in transcendental mellows."

TEXT 90

স্বরূপ কহে—"যাতে এই শ্লোক দেখিলুঁ ।
তুমি করিয়াছ কৃপা, তবঁহি জানিলু ॥ ৯০ ॥

svarūpa kahe——"yāte ei śloka dekhiluṅ
tumi kariyācha kṛpā, tavaṅhi jānilu

SYNONYMS

svarūpa kahe—Svarūpa Dāmodara says; *yāte*—since; *ei śloka*—this verse; *dekhiluṅ*—I have seen; *tumi*—You; *kariyācha kṛpā*—have bestowed Your mercy; *tavaṅhi*—immediately; *jānilu*—I could understand.

TRANSLATION

Svarūpa Dāmodara said, "As soon as I saw the unique composition of this verse, I could immediately understand that You had bestowed upon him Your special mercy.

TEXT 91

"ফলেন ফলকারণমনুমীয়তে ॥" ৯১ ॥

phalena phala-kāraṇam anumīyate

SYNONYMS

phalena—by the result; *phala-kāraṇam*—the origin of the result; *anumīyate*—one can guess.

TRANSLATION

" 'By seeing a result, one can understand the cause of that result.'

PURPORT

This verse is from the doctrines of *nyāya,* or logic.

TEXT 92

"স্বর্গাপগা-হেমমৃণালিনীনাং
নানা-মৃণালাগ্রভুজো ভজামঃ ।
অন্নানুরূপাং তনুরূপঋদ্ধিং
কার্যং নিদানাদ্ধি গুণানধীতে ॥" ৯২ ॥

svargāpagā-hema-mṛṇālinīnāṁ
nānā-mṛṇālāgra-bhujo bhajāmaḥ
annānurūpāṁ tanu-rūpa-ṛddhiṁ
kāryaṁ nidānād dhi guṇān adhīte

SYNONYMS

svarga-āpagā—of the Ganges water flowing in the heavenly planets; *hema*—golden; *mṛṇālinīnām*—of the lotus flowers; *nānā*—various; *mṛṇāla-agra-bhujaḥ*—those who eat the tops of the stems; *bhajāmaḥ*—we get; *anna-anurūpām*—according to the food; *tanu-rūpa-ṛddhim*—an abundance of bodily beauty; *kāryam*—the effect; *nidānāt*—from the cause; *hi*—certainly; *guṇān*—qualities; *adhīte*—one obtains.

TRANSLATION

" 'The River Ganges flowing from the heavenly planets is full of golden lotus flowers, and we, the residents of those planets, eat the stems of the flowers. Thus we are very beautiful, more so than the inhabitants of any other planet. This is due to the law of cause and effect, for if one eats food in the mode of goodness, the mode of goodness increases the beauty of his body.' "

PURPORT

One's bodily luster and beauty, one's constitution, one's activities and one's qualities all depend on the law of cause and effect. There are three qualities in material nature, and as stated in *Bhagavad-gītā* (13.22), *kāraṇaṁ guṇa-saṅgo 'sya sad-asad-yoni-janmasu:* one takes birth in a good or bad family according to his previous association with the qualities of material nature. Therefore one seriously eager to achieve transcendental perfection, Kṛṣṇa consciousness, must eat Kṛṣṇa *prasāda.* Such food is *sāttvika,* or in the material quality of goodness, but when offered to Kṛṣṇa it becomes transcendental. Our Kṛṣṇa consciousness movement distributes Kṛṣṇa *prasāda,* and those who eat such transcendental food are sure to become devotees of the Lord. This is a very scientific method, as stated in this verse from *Nala-naiṣadha* (3.17): *kāryaṁ nidānād dhi guṇān adhīte.* If in all one's activities he strictly adheres to the mode of goodness, he will certainly develop his dormant Kṛṣṇa consciousness and ultimately become a pure devotee of Lord Kṛṣṇa.

Unfortunately at the present moment the bodily constitutions of the leaders of society, especially the governmental leaders, are polluted. As described in *Śrīmad-Bhāgavatam* (12.1.42):

asaṁskṛtāḥ kriyā-hīnā
rajasā tamasāvṛtāḥ
prajās te bhakṣayiṣyanti
mlecchā rājany arūpiṇaḥ

Such leaders have no chance to purify their eating. Politicians meet together and exchange good wishes by drinking liquor, which is so polluted and sinful that naturally drunkards and meateaters develop a degraded mentality in the mode of ignorance. The processes of eating in different modes are explained in *Bhagavad-gītā,* wherein it is stated that those who eat rice, wheat, vegetables, milk products, fruit and sugar are situated in the elevated quality of goodness. Therefore if we want a happy and tranquil political situation, we must select leaders who eat Kṛṣṇa *prasāda.* Otherwise the leaders will eat meat and drink wine, and thus they will be *asaṁskṛtāḥ,* unreformed, and *kriyā-hīnāḥ,* devoid of spiritual behavior. In other words, they will be *mlecchas* and *yavanas,* or men who are unclean in their habits. Through taxation, such men exploit the citizens as much as possible, and in this way they devour the citizens of the state instead of benefiting them. We therefore cannot expect a government to be efficient if it is headed by such unclean *mlecchas* and *yavanas.*

TEXT 93

চাতুর্মাস্য রহি' গৌড়ে বৈষ্ণব চলিলা ।
রূপ-গোসাঞি মহাপ্রভুর চরণে রহিলা ॥ ৯৩ ॥

cāturmāsya rahi' gauḍe vaiṣṇava calilā
rūpa-gosāñi mahāprabhura caraṇe rahilā

SYNONYMS

cāturmāsya rahi'—remaining four months for Cāturmāsya; *gauḍe*—to Bengal; *vaiṣṇava*—all the devotees; *calilā*—returned; *rūpa-gosāñi*—Śrīla Rūpa Gosvāmī; *mahāprabhura*—of Śrī Caitanya Mahāprabhu; *caraṇe*—at the shelter of His lotus feet; *rahilā*—remained.

TRANSLATION

After the four months of Cāturmāsya [Śrāvaṇa, Bhādra, Āśvina and Kārttika], all the Vaiṣṇavas of Bengal returned to their homes, but Śrīla Rūpa Gosvāmī

remained in Jagannātha Purī under the shelter of the lotus feet of Śrī Caitanya Mahāprabhu.

TEXT 94

একদিন রূপ করেন নাটক লিখন ।
আচম্বিতে মহাপ্রভুর হৈল আগমন ॥ ৯৪ ॥

eka-dina rūpa karena nāṭaka likhana
ācambite mahāprabhura haila āgamana

SYNONYMS

eka-dina—one day; *rūpa*—Rūpa Gosvāmī; *karena*—does; *nāṭaka*—drama; *likhana*—writing; *ācambite*—all of a sudden; *mahāprabhura*—of Śrī Caitanya Mahāprabhu; *haila*—there was; *āgamana*—the coming.

TRANSLATION

One day while Rūpa Gosvāmī was writing his book, Śrī Caitanya Mahāprabhu suddenly appeared.

TEXT 95

সম্ভ্রমে দুঁহে উঠি' দণ্ডবৎ হৈলা ।
দুঁহে আলিঙ্গিয়া প্রভু আসনে বসিলা ॥ ৯৫ ॥

sambhrame duṅhe uṭhi' daṇḍavat hailā
duṅhe āliṅgiyā prabhu āsane vasilā

SYNONYMS

sambhrame—with great respect; *duṅhe*—Haridāsa Ṭhākura and Rūpa Gosvāmī; *uṭhi'*—standing up; *daṇḍavat hailā*—fell down to offer obeisances; *duṅhe*—the two of them; *āliṅgiyā*—embracing; *prabhu*—Śrī Caitanya Mahāprabhu; *āsane vasilā*—sat down on a seat.

TRANSLATION

As soon as Haridāsa Ṭhākura and Rūpa Gosvāmī saw the Lord coming, they both stood up and then fell down to offer Him their respectful obeisances. Śrī Caitanya Mahāprabhu embraced them both and then sat down.

TEXT 96

'ক্যা পুঁথি লিখ ?' বলি' একপত্র নিলা ।
অক্ষর দেখিয়া প্রভু মনে সুখী হৈলা ॥ ৯৬ ॥

'kyā puṅthi likha?' bali' eka-patra nilā
akṣara dekhiyā prabhu mane sukhī hailā

SYNONYMS

kyā—what; *puṅthi*—book; *likha*—you are writing; *bali'*—saying this; *eka-patra nilā*—took one page written on a palm leaf; *akṣara*—the good handwriting; *dekhiyā*—seeing; *prabhu*—Śrī Caitanya Mahāprabhu; *mane*—in the mind; *sukhī hailā*—became very happy.

TRANSLATION

The Lord inquired, "What kind of book are you writing?" He held up a palm leaf that was a page of the manuscript, and when He saw the fine handwriting, His mind was very pleased.

TEXT 97

শ্রীরূপের অক্ষর—যেন মুকুতার পাঁতি ।
প্রীত হঞা করেন প্রভু অক্ষরের স্তুতি ॥ ৯৭ ॥

śrī-rūpera akṣara——yena mukutāra pāṅti
prīta hañā karena prabhu akṣarera stuti

SYNONYMS

śrī-rūpera akṣara—the handwriting of Rūpa Gosvāmī; *yena*—like; *mukutāra pāṅti*—a row of pearls; *prīta hañā*—being pleased; *karena*—does; *prabhu*—Śrī Caitanya Mahāprabhu; *akṣarera stuti*—praise of the handwriting of Śrīla Rūpa Gosvāmī.

TRANSLATION

Thus being pleased, the Lord praised the writing by saying, "The handwriting of Rūpa Gosvāmī is just like rows of pearls."

TEXT 98

সেই পত্রে প্রভু এক শ্লোক যে দেখিলা ।
পড়িতেই শ্লোক, প্রেমে আবিষ্ট হইলা ॥ ৯৮ ॥

sei patre prabhu eka śloka ye dekhilā
paḍitei śloka, preme āviṣṭa ha-ilā

SYNONYMS

sei patre—on that palm leaf; *prabhu*—Śrī Caitanya Mahāprabhu; *eka śloka*—one verse; *ye*—which; *dekhilā*—He saw; *paḍitei*—by reading; *śloka*—the verse; *preme*—ecstatic love; *āviṣṭa ha-ilā*—was overwhelmed.

TRANSLATION

While reading the manuscript, Śrī Caitanya Mahāprabhu saw a verse on that page, and as soon as He read it He was overwhelmed by ecstatic love.

TEXT 99

তুণ্ডে তাণ্ডবিনী রতিং বিতনুতে তুণ্ডাবলীলব্ধয়ে
কর্ণক্রোড়কড়ম্বিনী ঘটয়তে কর্ণার্বুদেভ্যঃ স্পৃহাম্ ।
চেতঃপ্রাঙ্গণসঙ্গিনী বিজয়তে সর্বেন্দ্রিয়াণাং কৃতিং
নো জানে জনিতা কিয়দ্ভিরমৃতৈঃ কৃষ্ণেতি বর্ণদ্বয়ী ॥ ৯৯ ॥

tuṇḍe tāṇḍavinī ratiṁ vitanute tuṇḍāvalī-labdhaye
karṇa-kroḍa-kaḍambinī ghaṭayate karṇārbudebhyaḥ spṛhām
cetaḥ-prāṅgaṇa-saṅginī vijayate sarvendriyāṇāṁ kṛtiṁ
no jāne janitā kiyadbhir amṛtaiḥ kṛṣṇeti varṇa-dvayī

SYNONYMS

tuṇḍe—in the mouth; *tāṇḍavinī*—dancing; *ratim*—the inspiration; *vitanute*—expands; *tuṇḍa-āvalī-labdhaye*—to achieve many mouths; *karṇa*—of the ear; *kroḍa*—in the hole; *kaḍambinī*—sprouting; *ghaṭayate*—causes to appear; *karṇa-arbudebhyaḥ spṛhām*—the desire for millions of ears; *cetaḥ-prāṅgaṇa*—in the courtyard of the heart; *saṅginī*—being a companion; *vijayate*—conquers; *sarva-indriyāṇām*—of all the senses; *kṛtim*—the activity; *no*—not; *jāne*—I know; *janitā*—produced; *kiyadbhiḥ*—of what measure; *amṛtaiḥ*—by nectar; *kṛṣṇa*—the name of Kṛṣṇa; *iti*—thus; *varṇa-dvayī*—the two syllables.

TRANSLATION

"I do not know how much nectar the two syllables 'Kṛṣ-ṇa' have produced. When the holy name of Kṛṣṇa is chanted, it appears to dance within the mouth. We then desire many, many mouths. When that name enters the holes of the ears, we desire many millions of ears. And when the holy name dances in the courtyard of the heart, it conquers the activities of the mind, and therefore all the senses become inert."

PURPORT

This verse is included in the *Vidagdha-mādhava* (1.15), a seven-act play written by Śrīla Rūpa Gosvāmī describing the pastimes of Śrī Kṛṣṇa in Vṛndāvana.

TEXT 100

শ্লোক শুনি' হরিদাস হইলা উল্লাসী ।
নাচিতে লাগিলা শ্লোকের অর্থ প্রশংসি' ॥ ১০০ ॥

śloka śuni' haridāsa ha-ilā ullāsī
nācite lāgilā ślokera artha praśaṁsi'

SYNONYMS

śloka śuni'—hearing this verse; *hari-dāsa*—Haridāsa Ṭhākura; *ha-ilā ullāsī*—became very jubilant; *nācite lāgilā*—he began to dance; *ślokera*—of the verse; *artha praśaṁsi'*—praising the meaning.

TRANSLATION

When Śrī Caitanya Mahāprabhu chanted this verse, Haridāsa Ṭhākura, upon hearing the vibration, became jubilant and began dancing and praising its meaning.

TEXT 101

কৃষ্ণনামের মহিমা শাস্ত্র-সাধু-মুখে জানি ।
নামের মাধুরী ঐছে কাহাঁ নাহি শুনি ॥ ১০১ ॥

kṛṣṇa-nāmera mahimā śāstra-sādhu-mukhe jāni
nāmera mādhurī aiche kāhāṅ nāhi śuni

SYNONYMS

kṛṣṇa-nāmera mahimā—the glories of the holy name of Lord Kṛṣṇa; *śāstra*—of the revealed scriptures; *sādhu*—of the devotees; *mukhe*—in the mouth; *jāni*—we can understand; *nāmera mādhurī*—the sweetness of the holy name; *aiche*—in that way; *kāhāṅ*—anywhere else; *nāhi śuni*—we do not hear.

TRANSLATION

One has to learn about the beauty and transcendental position of the holy name of the Lord by hearing the revealed scriptures from the mouths of devotees. Nowhere else can we hear of the sweetness of the Lord's holy name.

PURPORT

It is said in the *Padma Purāṇa, ataḥ śrī-kṛṣṇa-nāmādi na bhaved grāhyam indriyaiḥ*. Chanting and hearing of the transcendental holy name of the Lord cannot be performed by the ordinary senses. The transcendental vibration of the Lord's holy name is completely spiritual. Thus it must be received from spiritual sources and must be chanted after having been heard from a spiritual master. One who hears the chanting of the Hare Kṛṣṇa *mantra* must receive it from the spiritual master by aural reception. Śrīla Sanātana Gosvāmī has forbidden us to hear the holy name of Kṛṣṇa chanted by non-Vaiṣṇavas, such as professional actors and singers, for it will have no effect. It is like milk touched by the lips of a serpent, as stated in the *Padma Purāṇa:*

avaiṣṇava-mukhodgīrṇaṁ
pūtaṁ hari-kathāmṛtam
śravaṇaṁ naiva kartavyaṁ
sarpocchiṣṭaṁ yathā payaḥ

As far as possible, therefore, the devotees in the Kṛṣṇa consciousness movement gather to chant the holy name of Kṛṣṇa in public so that both the chanters and the listeners may benefit.

TEXT 102

তবে মহাপ্রভু দুঁহে করি' আলিঙ্গন।
মধ্যাহ্ন করিতে সমুদ্রে করিলা গমন ॥ ১০২ ॥

tabe mahāprabhu duṅhe kari' āliṅgana
madhyāhna karite samudre karilā gamana

SYNONYMS

tabe—then; *mahāprabhu*—Śrī Caitanya Mahāprabhu; *duṅhe*—unto both Rūpa Gosvāmī and Haridāsa Ṭhākura; *kari'*—doing; *āliṅgana*—embracing; *madhya-ahna karite*—to perform His noontime duties; *samudre*—to the seaside; *karilā gamana*—went.

TRANSLATION

Thus Śrī Caitanya Mahāprabhu embraced both Haridāsa and Rūpa Gosvāmī and left for the seaside to perform His noontime duties.

TEXTS 103-104

আর দিন মহাপ্রভু দেখি' জগন্নাথ।
সার্বভৌম-রামানন্দ-স্বরূপাদি-সাথ ॥ ১০৩ ॥

সবে মিলি' চলি আইলা শ্রীরূপে মিলিতে।
পথে তাঁর গুণ সবারে লাগিলা কহিতে ॥ ১০৪ ॥

āra dina mahāprabhu dekhi' jagannātha
sārvabhauma-rāmānanda-svarūpādi-sātha

sabe mili' cali āilā śrī-rūpe milite
pathe tāṅra guṇa sabāre lāgilā kahite

SYNONYMS

āra dina—the next day; *mahāprabhu*—Śrī Caitanya Mahāprabhu; *dekhi'*—seeing; *jagannātha*—Lord Jagannātha in the temple; *sārvabhauma*—Sārvabhauma Bhaṭṭācārya; *rāmānanda*—Rāmānanda Rāya; *svarūpa-ādi*—Svarūpa Dāmodara Gosvāmī; *sātha*—along with; *sabe mili'*—meeting all together; *cali āilā*—came there; *śrī-rūpe milite*—to meet Śrīla Rūpa Gosvāmī; *pathe*—on the way; *tāṅra*—of Rūpa Gosvāmī; *guṇa*—all the good qualities; *sabāre*—unto all the personal associates; *lāgilā kahite*—began to speak.

TRANSLATION

On the next day, after visiting the temple of Jagannātha as usual, Śrī Caitanya Mahāprabhu met Sārvabhauma Bhaṭṭācārya, Rāmānanda Rāya and Svarūpa Dāmodara. They all went together to Śrīla Rūpa Gosvāmī, and on the way the Lord greatly praised his qualities.

TEXT 105

দুই শ্লোক কহি' প্রভুর হৈল মহাসুখ।
নিজ-ভক্তের গুণ কহে হঞা পঞ্চমুখ ॥ ১০৫ ॥

dui śloka kahi' prabhura haila mahā-sukha
nija-bhaktera guṇa kahe hañā pañca-mukha

SYNONYMS

dui śloka kahi'—reciting two verses; *prabhura*—of Śrī Caitanya Mahāprabhu; *haila*—there was; *mahā-sukha*—great pleasure; *nija-bhaktera*—of His own devotee; *guṇa*—the qualities; *kahe*—describes; *hañā*—as if becoming; *pañca-mukha*—five-mouthed.

TRANSLATION

When Śrī Caitanya Mahāprabhu recited the two important verses, He felt great pleasure; thus, as if He had five mouths, He began to praise His devotee.

PURPORT

The two verses referred to are those beginning with *priyaḥ so 'yam* (79) and *tuṇḍe tāṇḍavinī* (99).

TEXT 106

সার্বভৌম-রামানন্দে পরীক্ষা করিতে ।
শ্রীরূপের গুণ দুঁহারে লাগিলা কহিতে ॥ ১০৬ ॥

sārvabhauma-rāmānande parīkṣā karite
śrī-rūpera guṇa duṅhāre lāgilā kahite

SYNONYMS

sārvabhauma-rāmānande—Sārvabhauma Bhaṭṭācārya and Rāmānanda Rāya; *parīkṣā karite*—to examine; *śrī-rūpera guṇa*—the transcendental qualities of Śrīla Rūpa Gosvāmī; *duṅhāre*—unto both of them; *lāgilā kahite*—He began to praise.

TRANSLATION

Just to examine Sārvabhauma Bhaṭṭācārya and Rāmānanda Rāya, the Lord began to praise the transcendental qualities of Śrī Rūpa Gosvāmī before them.

TEXT 107

'ঈশ্বর-স্বভাব'—ভক্তের না লয় অপরাধ ।
অল্পসেবা বহু মানে আত্মপর্যন্ত প্রসাদ ॥ ১০৭ ॥

'īśvara-svabhāva'——bhaktera nā laya aparādha
alpa-sevā bahu māne ātma-paryanta prasāda

SYNONYMS

īśvara-svabhāva—the characteristic of the Supreme Personality of Godhead; *bhaktera*—of the pure devotee; *nā laya*—does not take; *aparādha*—any offense; *alpa-sevā*—very small service; *bahu māne*—the Lord accepts as very great; *ātma-paryanta*—giving Himself; *prasāda*—mercy.

TRANSLATION

Characteristically, the Supreme Personality of Godhead does not take seriously an offense committed by a pure devotee. The Lord accepts whatever small service a devotee renders as being such a great service that He is prepared to give even Himself, not to speak of other benedictions.

TEXT 108

ভৃত্যস্য পশ্যতি গুরূনপি নাপরাধান্
সেবাং মনাগপি কৃতাং বহুধাভ্যুপৈতি ।
আবিষ্করোতি পিশুনেষ্বপি নাভ্যসূয়াং
শীলেন নির্মলমতিঃ পুরুষোত্তমোঽয়ম্ ॥ ১০৮ ॥

bhṛtyasya paśyati gurūn api nāparādhān
sevāṁ manāg api kṛtāṁ bahudhābhyupaiti
āviṣkaroti piśuneṣv api nābhyasūyāṁ
śīlena nirmala-matiḥ puruṣottamo 'yam

SYNONYMS

bhṛtyasya—of the servant; *paśyati*—He sees; *gurūn*—very great; *api*—although; *na*—not; *aparādhān*—the offenses; *sevām*—service; *manāk api*—however small; *kṛtām*—performed; *bahu-dhā*—as great; *abhyupaiti*—accepts; *āviṣkaroti*—manifests; *piśuneṣu*—on the enemies; *api*—also; *na*—not; *abhyasūyām*—envy; *śīlena*—by gentle behavior; *nirmala-matiḥ*—naturally clean-minded; *puruṣottamaḥ*—the Supreme Personality of Godhead, the best of all personalities; *ayam*—this.

TRANSLATION

"The Supreme Personality of Godhead, who is known as Puruṣottama, the greatest of all persons, has a pure mind. He is so gentle that even if His servant is implicated in a great offense, He does not take it very seriously. Indeed, if His servant renders some small service, the Lord accepts it as being very great. Even if an envious person blasphemes the Lord, the Lord never manifests anger against him. Such are His great qualities."

PURPORT

This verse is from the *Bhakti-rasāmṛta-sindhu* (2.1.138) by Śrīla Rūpa Gosvāmī.

TEXT 109

ভক্তসঙ্গে প্রভু আইলা, দেখি' দুই জন ।
দণ্ডবৎ হঞা কৈলা চরণ বন্দন ॥ ১০৯ ॥

bhakta-saṅge prabhu āilā, dekhi' dui jana
daṇḍavat hañā kailā caraṇa vandana

SYNONYMS

bhakta-saṅge—accompanied by other devotee associates; *prabhu*—Śrī Caitanya Mahāprabhu; *āilā*—came; *dekhi'*—seeing this; *dui jana*—Rūpa Gosvāmī and Haridāsa Ṭhākura; *daṇḍavat hañā*—falling flat like logs; *kailā*—did; *caraṇa vandana*—prayers to their lotus feet.

TRANSLATION

When Haridāsa Ṭhākura and Rūpa Gosvāmī saw that Śrī Caitanya Mahāprabhu had come with His intimate devotees, they both immediately fell down like logs and offered prayers to their lotus feet.

TEXT 110

ভক্তসঙ্গে কৈলা প্রভু দুঁহারে মিলন ।
পিণ্ডাতে বসিলা প্রভু লঞা ভক্তগণ ॥ ১১০ ॥

bhakta-saṅge kailā prabhu duṅhāre milana
piṇḍāte vasilā prabhu lañā bhakta-gaṇa

SYNONYMS

bhakta-saṅge—with His intimate associates; *kailā*—did; *prabhu*—Śrī Caitanya Mahāprabhu; *duṅhāre*—the two (Rūpa Gosvāmī and Haridāsa Ṭhākura); *milana*—meeting; *piṇḍāte*—on a raised place; *vasilā*—sat down; *prabhu*—Śrī Caitanya Mahāprabhu; *lañā bhakta-gaṇa*—with His personal devotees.

TRANSLATION

Thus Śrī Caitanya Mahāprabhu and His personal devotees met Rūpa Gosvāmī and Haridāsa Ṭhākura. The Lord then sat down in an elevated place with His devotees.

TEXT 111

রূপ হরিদাস দুঁহে বসিলা পিণ্ডাতলে ।
সবার আগ্রহে না উঠিলা পিঁড়ার উপরে ॥ ১১১ ॥

rūpa haridāsa duṅhe vasilā piṇḍā-tale
sabāra āgrahe nā uṭhilā piṅḍāra upare

SYNONYMS

rūpa hari-dāsa—Rūpa Gosvāmī and Haridāsa Ṭhākura; *duṅhe*—both of them; *vasilā*—sat down; *piṇḍā-tale*—at the foot of the raised place where Śrī Caitanya

Mahāprabhu was sitting; *sabāra*—of all of the devotees; *āgrahe*—the insistence; *nā uṭhilā*—did not rise; *piṅḍāra upare*—the top of the raised place where Śrī Caitanya Mahāprabhu was sitting with His devotees.

TRANSLATION

Rūpa Gosvāmī and Haridāsa Ṭhākura sat at the foot of the elevated place where Śrī Caitanya Mahāprabhu was sitting. Although everyone asked them to sit on the same level as the Lord and His associates, they did not do so.

TEXT 112

'পূর্বশ্লোক পড়, রূপ, প্রভু আজ্ঞা কৈলা ।
লজ্জাতে না পড়ে রূপ মৌন ধরিলা ॥ ১১২ ॥

'pūrva-śloka paḍa, rūpa' prabhu ājñā kailā
lajjāte nā paḍe rūpa mauna dharilā

SYNONYMS

pūrva-śloka—the previous verse; *paḍa*—just read; *rūpa*—My dear Rūpa; *prabhu*—Śrī Caitanya Mahāprabhu; *ājñā kailā*—ordered; *lajjāte*—in great shyness; *nā paḍe*—did not read; *rūpa*—Rūpa Gosvāmī; *mauna dharilā*—remained silent.

TRANSLATION

When Śrī Caitanya Mahāprabhu ordered Rūpa Gosvāmī to read the verse they had previously heard, Rūpa Gosvāmī, because of great shyness, did not read it but instead remained silent.

TEXT 113

স্বরূপ-গোসাঞি তবে সেই শ্লোক পড়িল ।
শুনি' সবাকার চিত্তে চমৎকার হৈল ॥ ১১৩ ॥

svarūpa-gosāñi tabe sei śloka paḍila
śuni' sabākāra citte camatkāra haila

SYNONYMS

svarūpa-gosāñi—Svarūpa Dāmodara Gosāñi; *tabe*—then; *sei*—that; *śloka paḍila*—recited the verse; *śuni'*—hearing this; *sabākāra*—of all of them; *citte*—in the minds; *camatkāra haila*—there was great wonder.

TRANSLATION

Then Svarūpa Dāmodara Gosvāmī recited the verse, and when all the devotees heard it, their minds were struck with wonder.

TEXT 114

প্রিয়ঃ সোঽয়ং কৃষ্ণঃ সহচরি কুরুক্ষেত্রমিলিত-
স্তথাহং সা রাধা তদিদমুভয়োঃ সঙ্গমসুখম্ ।
তথাপ্যন্তঃখেলন্মধুরমুরলীপঞ্চমজুষে
মনো মে কালিন্দীপুলিনবিপিনায় স্পৃহয়তি ॥ ১১৪ ॥

priyaḥ so 'yaṁ kṛṣṇaḥ sahacari kuru-kṣetra-militas
tathāhaṁ sā rādhā tad idam ubhayoḥ saṅgama-sukham
tathāpy antaḥ-khelan-madhura-muralī-pañcama-juṣe
mano me kālindī-pulina-vipināya spṛhayati

SYNONYMS

priyaḥ—very dear; *saḥ*—He; *ayam*—this; *kṛṣṇaḥ*—Lord Kṛṣṇa; *saha-cari*—O My dear friend; *kuru-kṣetra-militaḥ*—who is met on the field of Kurukṣetra; *tathā*—also; *aham*—I; *sā*—that; *rādhā*—Rādhārāṇī; *tat*—that; *idam*—this; *ubhayoḥ*—of both of Us; *saṅgama-sukham*—the happiness of meeting; *tathāpi*—still; *antaḥ*—within; *khelan*—playing; *madhura*—sweet; *muralī*—of the flute; *pañcama*—the fifth note; *juṣe*—which delights in; *manaḥ*—the mind; *me*—My; *kālindī*—of the River Yamunā; *pulina*—on the bank; *vipināya*—the trees; *spṛhayati*—desires.

TRANSLATION

"My dear friend, now I have met My very old and dear friend Kṛṣṇa on this field of Kurukṣetra. I am the same Rādhārāṇī, and now We are meeting together. It is very pleasant, but I would still like to go to the bank of the Yamunā beneath the trees of the forest there. I wish to hear the vibration of His sweet flute playing the fifth note within that forest of Vṛndāvana."

TEXT 115

রায়, ভট্টাচার্য বলে,—"তোমার প্রসাদ বিনে ।
তোমার হৃদয় এই জানিল কেমনে ॥ ১১৫ ॥

rāya, bhaṭṭācārya bale,—"tomāra prasāda vine
tomāra hṛdaya ei jānila kemane

SYNONYMS

rāya—Rāmānanda Rāya; *bhaṭṭācārya*—Sārvabhauma Bhaṭṭācārya; *bale*—say; *tomāra prasāda vine*—without Your special mercy; *tomāra hṛdaya*—Your mind; *ei*—this Rūpa Gosvāmī; *jānila*—understood; *kemane*—how.

TRANSLATION

After hearing this verse, both Rāmānanda Rāya and Sārvabhauma Bhaṭṭācārya said to Caitanya Mahāprabhu, "Without Your special mercy, how could this Rūpa Gosvāmī have understood Your mind?"

TEXT 116

আমাতে সঞ্চারি' পূর্বে কহিলা সিদ্ধান্ত ।
যে সব সিদ্ধান্তে ব্রহ্মা নাহি পায় অন্ত ॥ ১১৬ ॥

āmāte sañcāri' pūrve kahilā siddhānta
ye saba siddhānte brahmā nāhi pāya anta

SYNONYMS

āmāte—within me; *sañcāri'*—creating all logical truths; *pūrve*—previously; *kahilā*—You express; *siddhānta*—conclusive statements; *ye*—which; *saba*—all of; *siddhānte*—conclusive statements; *brahmā*—even Lord Brahmā; *nāhi pāya anta*—cannot understand the limit.

TRANSLATION

Śrīla Rāmānanda Rāya admitted that previously Śrī Caitanya Mahāprabhu had empowered his heart so that he could express elevated and conclusive statements to which even Lord Brahmā has no access.

TEXT 117

তাতে জানি—পূর্বে তোমার পাঞাছে প্রসাদ ।
তাহা বিনা নহে তোমার হৃদয়ানুবাদ ॥" ১১৭ ॥

tāte jāni——pūrve tomāra pāñāche prasāda
tāhā vinā nahe tomāra hṛdayānuvāda"

SYNONYMS

tāte—in such instances; *jāni*—I can understand; *pūrve*—previously; *tomāra*—Your; *pāñāche prasāda*—he has obtained special mercy; *tāhā vinā*—without that; *nahe*—there is not; *tomāra*—Your; *hṛdaya-anuvāda*—expression of feelings.

TRANSLATION

"Had you not previously bestowed Your mercy on him," they said, "it would not have been possible for him to express Your internal feelings."

PURPORT

Devotees acknowledge Śrī Caitanya Mahāprabhu's special mercy upon Śrīla Rūpa Gosvāmī in the following words:

śrī-caitanya-mano 'bhīṣṭaṁ
sthāpitaṁ yena bhū-tale
svayaṁ rūpaḥ kadā mahyaṁ
dadāti sva-padāntikam

"When will Śrīla Rūpa Gosvāmī Prabhupāda, who has established within this material world the mission to fulfill the desire of Lord Caitanya, give me shelter under his lotus feet?"

The special function of Śrīla Rūpa Gosvāmī is to establish the feelings of Śrī Caitanya Mahāprabhu. These feelings are His desires that His special mercy be spread throughout the world in this Kali-yuga.

pṛthivīte āche yata nagarādi-grāma
sarvatra pracāra haibe mora nāma

His desire is that all over the world everyone, in every village and every town, know of Śrī Caitanya Mahāprabhu and His *saṅkīrtana* movement. These are the inner feelings of Śrī Caitanya Mahāprabhu. Śrī Rūpa Gosvāmī committed to writing all these feelings of the Lord. Now again, by the mercy of Śrī Caitanya Mahāprabhu, the same feelings are being spread all over the world by the servants of the Gosvāmīs, and devotees who are pure and simple will appreciate this attempt. As concluded by Śrīla Kṛṣṇadāsa Kavirāja Gosvāmī, however, those who are on the level of hogs and dogs will never appreciate such a great attempt. Yet this does not matter to the preachers of Śrī Caitanya Mahāprabhu's cult, for all over the world they will continue to perform this responsible work, even though persons who are like cats and dogs do not appreciate them.

TEXT 118

প্রভু কহে,—কহ "রূপ, নাটকের শ্লোক ।
যে শ্লোক শুনিলে লোকের যায় দুঃখ-শোক ॥ ১১৮॥

prabhu kahe,—"kaha rūpa, nāṭakera śloka
ye śloka śunile lokera yāya duḥkha-śoka

SYNONYMS

prabhu kahe—Śrī Caitanya Mahāprabhu said; *kaha*—please recite; *rūpa*—My dear Rūpa; *nāṭakera śloka*—the verse of your drama; *ye*—which; *śloka*—verse; *śunile*—hearing; *lokera*—of all people; *yāya*—go away; *duḥkha-śoka*—the unhappiness and lamentation.

TRANSLATION

Thus Śrī Caitanya Mahāprabhu said, "My dear Rūpa, please recite that verse from your drama which, upon being heard, makes all people's unhappiness and lamentation go away."

TEXT 119

বার বার প্রভু যদি তারে আজ্ঞা দিল।
তবে সেই শ্লোক রূপগোসাঞি কহিল॥ ১১৯ ॥

bāra bāra prabhu yadi tāre ājñā dila
tabe sei śloka rūpa-gosāñi kahila

SYNONYMS

bāra bāra—again and again; *prabhu*—Śrī Caitanya Mahāprabhu; *yadi*—when; *tāre*—him; *ājñā dila*—ordered; *tabe*—at that time; *sei śloka*—that particular verse; *rūpa-gosāñi*—of the name Rūpa Gosvāmī; *kahila*—recited.

TRANSLATION

When the Lord persisted in asking this again and again, Rūpa Gosvāmī recited that verse [as follows].

TEXT 120

তুণ্ডে তাণ্ডবিনী রতিং বিতনুতে তুণ্ডাবলীলব্ধয়ে
কর্ণক্রোড়কড়ম্বিনী ঘটয়তে কর্ণার্বুদেভ্যঃ স্পৃহাম্।
চেতঃপ্রাঙ্গণসঙ্গিনী বিজয়তে সর্বেন্দ্রিয়াণাং কৃতিং
নো জানে জনিতা কিয়দ্ভিরমৃতৈঃ কৃষ্ণেতি বর্ণদ্বয়ী॥ ১২০ ॥

tuṇḍe tāṇḍavinī ratiṁ vitanute tuṇḍāvalī-labdhaye
karṇa-kroḍa-kaḍambinī ghaṭayate karṇārbudebhyaḥ spṛhām
cetaḥ-prāṅgaṇa-saṅginī vijayate sarvendriyāṇāṁ kṛtiṁ
no jāne janitā kiyadbhir amṛtaiḥ kṛṣṇeti varṇa-dvayī

SYNONYMS

tuṇḍe—in the mouth; *tāṇḍavinī*—dancing; *ratim*—the inspiration; *vitanute*—expands; *tuṇḍa-āvalī-labdhaye*—to achieve many mouths; *karṇa*—of the ear; *kroḍa*—in the hole; *kaḍambinī*—sprouting; *ghaṭayate*—causes to appear; *karṇa-arbudebhyaḥ spṛhām*—the desire for millions of ears; *cetaḥ-prāṅgaṇa*—in the courtyard of the heart; *saṅginī*—being a companion; *vijayate*—conquers; *sarva-indriyāṇām*—of all the senses; *kṛtim*—the activity; *no*—not; *jāne*—I know; *janitā*—produced; *kiyadbhiḥ*—of what measures by; *amṛtaiḥ*—by nectar; *kṛṣṇa*—the name of Kṛṣṇa; *iti*—thus; *varṇa-dvayī*—the two syllables.

TRANSLATION

"I do not know how much nectar the two syllables 'Kṛṣ-ṇa' have produced. When the holy name of Kṛṣṇa is chanted, it appears to dance within the mouth. We then desire many, many mouths. When that name enters the holes of the ears, we desire many millions of ears. And when the holy name dances in the courtyard of the heart, it conquers the activities of the mind, and therefore all the senses become inert."

TEXT 121

যত ভক্তবৃন্দ আর রামানন্দ রায় ।
শ্লোক শুনি' সবার হইল আনন্দ-বিস্ময় ॥ ১২১ ॥

yata bhakta-vṛnda āra rāmānanda rāya
śloka śuni' sabāra ha-ila ānanda-vismaya

SYNONYMS

yata bhakta-vṛnda—all the personal devotees of Śrī Caitanya Mahāprabhu; *āra*—and; *rāmānanda rāya*—of the name Rāmānanda Rāya; *śloka śuni'*—hearing this verse; *sabāra*—of everyone; *ha-ila*—there was; *ānanda-vismaya*—transcendental bliss and astonishment.

TRANSLATION

When all the devotees of Śrī Caitanya Mahāprabhu, especially Śrī Rāmānanda Rāya, heard this verse, they were all filled with transcendental bliss and were struck with wonder.

TEXT 122

সবে বলে,—'নাম-মহিমা শুনিয়াছি অপার ।
এমন মাধুর্য কেহ নাহি বর্ণে আর ॥ ১২২ ॥

sabe bale,—'nāma-mahimā śuniyāchi apāra
emana mādhurya keha nāhi varṇe āra'

SYNONYMS

sabe bale—every one of them said; *nāma-mahimā*—the glories of chanting the holy name; *śuniyāchi*—we have heard; *apāra*—many times; *emana*—this kind of; *mādhurya*—sweetness; *keha*—someone; *nāhi*—not; *varṇe*—describes; *āra*—else.

TRANSLATION

Everyone admitted that although they had heard many statements glorifying the holy name of the Lord, they had never heard such sweet descriptions as those of Rūpa Gosvāmī.

TEXT 123

রায় কহে,—কোন্ গ্রন্থ কর হেন জানি ?
যাহার ভিতরে এই সিদ্ধান্তের খনি ?" ১২৩ ॥

rāya kahe,—"kon grantha kara hena jāni?
yāhāra bhitare ei siddhāntera khani?"

SYNONYMS

rāya kahe—Rāmānanda Rāya inquired; *kon*—what; *grantha*—dramatic literature; *kara*—you are writing; *hena*—such; *jāni*—I can understand; *yāhāra bhitare*—within which; *ei*—these; *siddhāntera khani*—a mine of conclusive statements.

TRANSLATION

Rāmānanda Rāya inquired, "What kind of drama are you writing? We can understand that it is a mine of conclusive statements."

TEXT 124

স্বরূপ কহে,—কৃষ্ণলীলার নাটক করিতে ।
ব্রজলীলা-পুরলীলা একত্র বর্ণিতে ॥ ১২৪ ॥

svarūpa kahe,—"kṛṣṇa-līlāra nāṭaka karite
vraja-līlā-pura-līlā ekatra varṇite

SYNONYMS

svarūpa kahe—Svarūpa Dāmodara replied on behalf of Rūpa Gosvāmī; *kṛṣṇa-līlāra*—of the pastimes of Lord Kṛṣṇa; *nāṭaka karite*—composing a drama; *vraja-*

līlā-pura-līlā—His pastimes in Vṛndāvana and His pastimes in Mathurā and Dvārakā; *ekatra*—in one book; *varṇite*—to describe.

TRANSLATION

Svarūpa Dāmodara replied for Śrīla Rūpa Gosvāmī: "He wanted to compose a drama about the pastimes of Lord Kṛṣṇa. He planned to describe in one book both the pastimes of Vṛndāvana and those of Dvārakā and Mathurā.

TEXT 125

আরম্ভিয়াছিলা, এবে প্রভু-আজ্ঞা পাঞা ।
দুই নাটক করিতেছে বিভাগ করিয়া ॥ ১২৫ ॥

ārambhiyāchilā, ebe prabhu-ājñā pāñā
dui nāṭaka kariteche vibhāga kariyā

SYNONYMS

ārambhiyāchilā—Śrīla Rūpa Gosvāmī began; *ebe*—now; *prabhu-ājñā pāñā*—getting the order of Śrī Caitanya Mahāprabhu; *dui nāṭaka*—two different dramas; *kariteche*—he is compiling; *vibhāga kariyā*—dividing the original idea.

TRANSLATION

"He began it in that way, but now, following the order of Śrī Caitanya Mahāprabhu, he has divided it in two and is writing two plays, one concerning the pastimes of Mathurā and Dvārakā and the other concerning the pastimes of Vṛndāvana.

TEXT 126

বিদগ্ধমাধব আর ললিতমাধব ।
দুই নাটকে প্রেমরস অদভুত সব ॥" ১২৬ ॥

vidagdha-mādhava āra lalita-mādhava
dui nāṭake prema-rasa adabhuta saba"

SYNONYMS

vidagdha-mādhava—one is named *Vidagdha-mādhava*; *āra*—and; *lalita-mādhava*—named *Lalita-mādhava*; *dui nāṭake*—in two plays; *prema-rasa*—ecstatic mellows of emotional love for Kṛṣṇa; *adabhuta*—wonderful; *saba*—all.

TRANSLATION

"The two plays are called Vidagdha-mādhava and Lalita-mādhava. Both of them wonderfully describe ecstatic emotional love of God."

PURPORT

Śrīla Bhaktisiddhānta Sarasvatī Ṭhākura informs us in this connection that Śrīla Rūpa Gosvāmī composed the drama known as *Vidagdha-mādhava* in the year Śakābda 1454, and he finished *Lalita-mādhava* in Śakābda 1459. The discussion between Rāmānanda Rāya and Śrīla Rūpa Gosvāmī at Jagannātha Purī took place in Śakābda 1437.

TEXT 127

রায় কহে,—"নান্দী-শ্লোক পড় দেখি, শুনি ?"
শ্রীরূপ শ্লোক পড়ে প্রভু-আজ্ঞা মানি' ॥ ১২৭ ॥

rāya kahe,——"nāndī-śloka paḍa dekhi, śuni?"
śrī-rūpa śloka paḍe prabhu-ājñā māni'

SYNONYMS

rāya kahe—Śrī Rāmānanda Rāya says; *nāndī-śloka paḍa*—please recite the introductory verse; *dekhi*—so that I can see; *śuni*—so that I can hear; *śrī-rūpa śloka paḍe*—Rūpa Gosvāmī recites the verse; *prabhu-ājñā māni'*—accepting the order of Śrī Caitanya Mahāprabhu.

TRANSLATION

Rāmānanda Rāya said, "Please recite the introductory verse of Vidagdha-mādhava so that I can hear and examine it." Thus Śrī Rūpa Gosvāmī, being ordered by Śrī Caitanya Mahāprabhu, recited the verse (1.1).

TEXT 128

সুধানাং চান্দ্রীণামপি মধুরিমোন্মাদ-দমনী
দধানা রাধাদিপ্রণয়ঘনসারৈঃ সুরভিতাম্ ।
সমন্তাৎ সন্তাপোদ্গম-বিষমসংসার-সরণী-
প্রণীতাং তে তৃষ্ণাং হরতু হরিলীলা-শিখরিণী ॥ ১২৮ ॥

sudhānāṁ cāndrīṇām api madhurimonmāda-damanī
dadhānā rādhādi-praṇaya-ghana-sāraiḥ surabhitām
samantāt santāpodgama-viṣama-saṁsāra-saraṇī-
praṇītāṁ te tṛṣṇāṁ haratu hari-līlā-śikhariṇī

SYNONYMS

sudhānām—of the nectar; *cāndrīṇām*—produced on the moon; *api*—even; *madhurimā*—the sweetness; *unmāda-damanī*—overpowering the pride; *dadhānā*—distributing; *rādhā-ādi*—of Śrīmatī Rādhārāṇī and Her companions; *praṇaya-ghana*—of the concentrated loving affairs; *sāraiḥ*—by the essence; *surabhitām*—a good fragrance; *samantāt*—everywhere; *santāpa*—miserable conditions; *udgama*—generating; *viṣama*—very dangerous; *saṁsāra-saraṇī*—on the path of material existence; *praṇītām*—created; *te*—your; *tṛṣṇām*—desires; *haratu*—let it take away; *hari-līlā*—the pastimes of Śrī Kṛṣṇa; *śikhariṇī*—exactly like a combination of yogurt and sugar candy.

TRANSLATION

"May the pastimes of Śrī Kṛṣṇa reduce the miseries existing in the material world and nullify all unwanted desires. The pastimes of the Supreme Personality of Godhead are like śikhariṇī, a blend of yogurt and sugar candy. They overpower the pride of even the nectar produced on the moon, for they distribute the sweet fragrance of the concentrated loving affairs of Śrīmatī Rādhārāṇī and the gopīs."

TEXT 129

রায় কহে,—'কহ ইষ্টদেবের বর্ণন' ।
প্রভুর সঙ্কোচে রূপ না করে পঠন ॥ ১২৯ ॥

rāya kahe,——'kaha iṣṭa-devera varṇana'
prabhura saṅkoce rūpa nā kare paṭhana

SYNONYMS

rāya kahe—Rāmānanda Rāya says; *kaha*—now speak; *iṣṭa-devera varṇana*—description of your worshipable Deity; *prabhura saṅkoce*—embarrassment in the presence of Śrī Caitanya Mahāprabhu; *rūpa*—Rūpa Gosvāmī; *nā kare*—does not do; *paṭhana*—recitation.

TRANSLATION

Rāmānanda Rāya said, "Now please recite the description of the glories of your worshipable Deity." Rūpa Gosvāmī, however, hesitated due to embarrassment because Śrī Caitanya Mahāprabhu was present.

TEXT 130

প্রভু কহে,—"কহ, কেনে কর সঙ্কোচ-লাজে ?
গ্রন্থের ফল শুনাইবা বৈষ্ণব-সমাজে ?" ১৩০ ॥

prabhu kahe,——"kaha, kene kara saṅkoca-lāje?
granthera phala śunāibā vaiṣṇava samāje?"

SYNONYMS

prabhu kahe—Śrī Caitanya Mahāprabhu says; *kaha*—speak up; *kene*—why; *kara*—you do; *saṅkoca-lāje*—in shame and embarrassment; *granthera*—of the book; *phala*—the fruit; *śunāibā*—you should make heard; *vaiṣṇava-samāje*—in the society of pure devotees.

TRANSLATION

The Lord, however, encouraged Rūpa Gosvāmī, saying, "Why are you embarrassed? You should recite it so the devotees can hear the good fruit of your writing."

TEXT 131

তবে রূপ-গোসাঞি যদি শ্লোক পড়িল ।
শুনি' প্রভু কহে,—'এই অতি স্তুতি হৈল' ॥ ১৩১ ॥

tabe rūpa-gosāñi yadi śloka paḍila
śuni' prabhu kahe,——'ei ati stuti haila'

SYNONYMS

tabe—at that time; *rūpa-gosāñi*—of the name Rūpa Gosvāmī; *yadi*—when; *śloka paḍila*—recited the verse; *śuni'*—hearing this; *prabhu kahe*—Śrī Caitanya Mahāprabhu says; *ei*—this; *ati stuti*—exaggerated offering of prayers; *haila*—was.

TRANSLATION

When Rūpa Gosvāmī thus recited his verse, Caitanya Mahāprabhu disapproved of it because it described His personal glories. He expressed the opinion that it was an exaggerated explanation.

TEXT 132

অনর্পিতচরীং চিরাৎ করুণয়াবতীর্ণঃ কলৌ
সমর্পয়িতুমুন্নতোজ্জ্বলরসাং স্বভক্তিশ্রিয়ম্ ।
হরিঃ পুরটসুন্দরদ্যুতিকদম্বসন্দীপিতঃ
সদা হৃদয়কন্দরে স্ফুরতু বঃ শচীনন্দনঃ ॥ ১৩২ ॥

anarpita-carīṁ cirāt karuṇayāvatīrṇaḥ kalau
samarpayitum unnatojjvala-rasāṁ sva-bhakti-śriyam
hariḥ puraṭa-sundara-dyuti-kadamba-sandīpitaḥ
sadā hṛdaya-kandare sphuratu vaḥ śacī-nandanaḥ

SYNONYMS

anarpita—not bestowed; *carīm*—having been formerly; *cirāt*—for a long time; *karuṇayā*—by causeless mercy; *avatīrṇaḥ*—descended; *kalau*—in the age of Kali; *samarpayitum*—to bestow; *unnata*—elevated; *ujjvala-rasām*—the conjugal mellow; *sva-bhakti*—of His own service; *śriyam*—the treasure; *hariḥ*—the Supreme Lord; *puraṭa*—than gold; *sundara*—more beautiful; *dyuti*—of splendor; *kadamba*—with a multitude; *sandīpitaḥ*—illuminated; *sadā*—always; *hṛdaya-kandare*—in the cavity of the heart; *sphuratu*—let Him be manifest; *vaḥ*—your; *śacī-nandanaḥ*—the son of mother Śacī.

TRANSLATION

"May the Supreme Lord, who is known as the son of Śrīmatī Śacīdevī, be transcendentally situated in the innermost core of your heart. Resplendent with the radiance of molten gold, He has descended in the age of Kali by His causeless mercy to bestow what no incarnation has ever offered before: the most elevated mellow of devotional service, the mellow of conjugal love."

PURPORT

This verse (*Vidagdha-mādhava* 1.2) also appears in *Ādi-līlā* (1.4 and 3.4). In his commentary on *Vidagdha-mādhava,* Śrīla Viśvanātha Cakravartī Ṭhākura remarks: *mahā-prabhoḥ sphūrtiṁ vinā hari-līlā-rasāsvādanānupapatter iti bhāvaḥ.* Without the mercy of Śrī Caitanya Mahāprabhu, one cannot describe the pastimes of the Supreme Personality of Godhead. Therefore Śrīla Rūpa Gosvāmī said, *vaḥ yuṣmākaṁ hṛdaya-rūpa-guhāyāṁ śacī-nandano hariḥ, pakṣe, siṁhaḥ sphuratu*: "May Śrī Caitanya Mahāprabhu, who is exactly like a lion that kills all the elephants of desire, be awakened within everyone's heart, for by His merciful blessings one can understand the transcendental pastimes of Kṛṣṇa."

TEXT 133

সব ভক্তগণ কহে শ্লোক শুনিয়া ।
কৃতার্থ করিলা সবায় শ্লোক শুনাঞা ॥১৩৩ ॥

saba bhakta-gaṇa kahe śloka śuniyā
kṛtārtha karilā sabāya śloka śunāñā

SYNONYMS

saba bhakta-gaṇa—all the devotees present there; *kahe*—say; *śloka śuniyā*—hearing this verse; *kṛta-artha karilā*—you have obliged; *sabāya*—everyone; *śloka śunāñā*—by reciting this verse.

TRANSLATION

All the devotees present so greatly appreciated this verse that they expressed their gratitude to Śrī Rūpa Gosvāmī for his transcendental recitation.

TEXT 134

রায় কহে,—"কোন্ আমুখে পাত্র-সন্নিধান ?"
রূপ কহে,—"কালসাম্যে 'প্রবর্তক' নাম" ॥ ১৩৪ ॥

rāya kahe,——"kon āmukhe pātra-sannidhāna?"
rūpa kahe,——"kāla-sāmye 'pravartaka' nāma"

SYNONYMS

rāya kahe—Rāmānanda Rāya says; *kon*—what; *āmukhe*—by introduction; *pātra-sannidhāna*—presence of the players; *rūpa kahe*—Śrīla Rūpa Gosvāmī replies; *kāla-sāmye*—in agreement of time; *pravartaka nāma*—the introduction called *pravartaka.*

TRANSLATION

Rāmānanda Rāya inquired, "How have you introduced the assembly of the players?" Rūpa Gosvāmī replied, "The players assemble at a suitable time under the heading of pravartaka.

PURPORT

In a drama all the actors are called *pātra,* or players. This is stated by Viśvanātha Kavirāja in the *Sāhitya-darpaṇa* (6.283):

divya-martye sa tad-rūpo
miśram anyataras tayoḥ
sūcayed vastu-bījaṁ vā-
mukhaṁ pātram athāpi vā

The meaning of *āmukha* is stated by Śrīla Rūpa Gosvāmī in the *Nāṭaka-candrikā:*

sūtra-dhāro naṭī brūte
sva-kāryaṁ pratiyuktitaḥ

prastutākṣepicitroktyā
yat tad āmukham īritam

When Śrīla Rāmānanda Rāya inquired about the arrangement for introducing the assembly of players in the drama, Rūpa Gosvāmī replied that when the players first enter the stage in response to the time, the introduction is technically called *pravartaka.* For an example one may consult the *Antya-līlā,* First Chapter, verse 17. Śrīla Bhaktisiddhānta Sarasvatī Ṭhākura says that the introduction, which is technically called *āmukha,* may be of five different kinds, according to the *Sāhitya-darpaṇa* (6.288):

udghātyakaḥ kathodghātaḥ
prayogātiśayas tathā
pravartakāvalagite
pañca prastāvanā-bhidāḥ

Introductions may be classified as follows: (1) *udghātyaka,* (2) *kathodghāta,* (3) *prayogātiśaya,* (4) *pravartaka* and (5) *avalagita.* These five kinds of introduction are called *āmukha.* Thus Śrīla Rāmānanda Rāya asked which of the five introductions had been employed, and Śrīla Rūpa Gosvāmī replied that he had used the introduction called the *pravartaka.*

TEXT 135

আক্ষিপ্তঃ কালসাম্যেন প্রবেশঃ স্যাৎ প্রবর্তকঃ ॥ ১৩৫ ॥

ākṣiptaḥ kāla-sāmyena
praveśaḥ syāt pravartakaḥ

SYNONYMS

ākṣiptaḥ—set in motion; *kāla-sāmyena*—by a suitable time; *praveśaḥ*—the entrance; *syāt*—should be; *pravartakaḥ*—named *pravartaka.*

TRANSLATION

" 'When the entrance of the actors is set in motion by the arrival of a suitable time, the entrance is called pravartaka.'

PURPORT

This verse is from *Nāṭaka-candrikā* (12) by Śrīla Rūpa Gosvāmī.

TEXT 136

সোঽয়ং বসন্তসময়ঃ সমিয়ায় যস্মিন্
পূর্ণং তমীশ্বরমুপোঢ়-নবানুরাগম্ ।

গূঢ়গ্রহা রুচিরয়া সহ রাধয়াসৌ
রঙ্গায় সঙ্গময়িতা নিশি পৌর্ণমাসী ॥ ১৩৬ ॥

so 'yaṁ vasanta-samayaḥ samiyāya yasmin
pūrṇaṁ tam īśvaram upoḍha-navānurāgam
gūḍha-grahā ruciraya saha rādhayāsau
raṅgāya saṅgamayitā niśi paurṇamāsī

SYNONYMS

saḥ—that; *ayam*—this; *vasanta-samayaḥ*—springtime; *samiyāya*—had arrived; *yasmin*—in which; *pūrṇam*—the complete; *tam*—Him; *īśvaram*—the Supreme Personality of Godhead; *upoḍha*—obtained; *nava-anurāgam*—new attachment; *gūḍha-grahā*—which covered the stars; *rucirayā*—very beautiful; *saha*—with; *rādhayā*—Śrīmatī Rādhārāṇī; *asau*—that full-moon night; *raṅgāya*—for increasing the beauty; *saṅgamayitā*—caused to meet; *niśi*—at night; *paurṇamāsī*—the full-moon night.

TRANSLATION

" 'Springtime had arrived, and the full moon of that season inspired the Supreme Personality of Godhead, who is complete in everything, with new attraction to meet the beautiful Śrīmatī Rādhārāṇī at night to increase the beauty of Their pastimes.' "

PURPORT

Śrīla Bhaktivinoda Ṭhākura interprets this verse (*Vidagdha-mādhava* 1.10) in two ways, for Lord Kṛṣṇa and for Śrīmatī Rādhārāṇī. When interpreted for Kṛṣṇa, the night is understood to have been a dark moon night, and when interpreted for Śrīmatī Rādhārāṇī, it is considered to have been a full moon night.

TEXT 137

রায় কহে,—"প্ররোচনাদি কহ দেখি, শুনি ?"
রূপ কহে,—মহাপ্রভুর শ্রবণেচ্ছা জানি ॥ ১৩৭ ॥

rāya kahe,—"prarocanādi kaha dekhi, śuni?"
rūpa kahe,—"mahāprabhura śravaṇecchā jāni"

SYNONYMS

rāya kahe—Śrīla Rāmānanda Rāya says; *prarocanādi kaha*—please recite the *prarocanā*; *dekhi*—I shall see; *śuni*—and hear; *rūpa kahe*—Śrīla Rūpa Gosāñi replies; *mahāprabhura*—of Śrī Caitanya Mahāprabhu; *śravaṇa-icchā*—desired to hear; *jāni*—I think.

TRANSLATION

Rāmānanda Rāya said, "Please recite the prarocanā portion so that I may hear and examine it." Śrī Rūpa replied, "I think that the desire to hear of Śrī Caitanya Mahāprabhu is prarocanā.

PURPORT

The method of inducing the audience to become more and more eager to hear by praising the time and place, the hero and the audience is called *prarocanā*. This is the statement regarding *prarocanā* in the *Nāṭaka-candrikā*:

deśa-kāla-kathā-vastu-
sabhyādīnāṁ praśaṁsayā
śrotṝṇām unmukhī-kāraḥ
kathiteyaṁ prarocanā

Similarly the *Sāhitya-darpaṇa* (6.286) says:

tasyāḥ prarocanā vīthī
tathā prahasanā-mukhe
aṅgānyatronmukhī-kāraḥ
praśaṁsātaḥ prarocanā

Any literature presented in Sanskrit must follow the rules and regulations mentioned in the authoritative reference books. The technical inquiries by Śrīla Rāmānanda Rāya and the replies of Śrīla Rūpa Gosvāmī indicate that both of them were expert and fully conversant with the techniques of writing drama.

TEXT 138

ভক্তানামুদগাদনর্গলধিয়াং বর্গো নিসর্গোজ্জ্বলঃ
শীলৈঃ পল্লবিতঃ স বল্লববধূবন্ধোঃ প্রবন্ধোঽপ্যসৌ।
লেভে চত্বরতাঞ্চ তাণ্ডববিধের্বৃন্দাটবীগর্ভভূ-
র্মন্যে মদ্বিধপুণ্যমণ্ডলপরীপাকোঽয়মুন্মীলতি ॥ ১৩৮ ॥

bhaktānām udagād anargala-dhiyāṁ vargo nisargojjvalaḥ
śīlaiḥ pallavitaḥ sa ballava-vadhū-bandho prabandho 'py asau
lebhe catvaratāṁ ca tāṇḍava-vidher vṛndāṭavī-garbha-bhūr
manye mad-vidha-puṇya-maṇḍala-parīpāko 'yam unmīlati

SYNONYMS

bhaktānām—of devotees; *udagāt*—has appeared; *anargala-dhiyām*—constantly thinking of Rādhā-Kṛṣṇa; *vargaḥ*—the assembly; *nisarga-ujjvalaḥ*—naturally very advanced; *śīlaiḥ*—with natural poetic decorations; *pallavitaḥ*—spread like the leaves of a tree; *saḥ*—that; *ballava-vadhū-bandhaḥ*—of the friend of the *gopīs,* Śrī Kṛṣṇa; *prabandhaḥ*—a literary composition; *api*—even; *asau*—that; *lebhe*—has achieved; *catvaratām*—the quality of a quadrangular place with level ground; *ca*—and; *tāṇḍava-vidheḥ*—for dancing; *vṛndā-aṭavī*—of the forest of Vṛndāvana; *garbha-bhūḥ*—the inner grounds; *manye*—I consider; *mat-vidha*—of persons like me; *puṇya-maṇḍala*—of groups of pious activities; *parīpākaḥ*—the full development; *ayam*—this; *unmīlati*—appears.

TRANSLATION

" 'The devotees now present are constantly thinking of the Supreme Lord and are therefore highly advanced. This work named Vidagdha-mādhava depicts the characteristic pastimes of Lord Kṛṣṇa with decorations of poetic ornaments. And the inner grounds of the forest of Vṛndāvana provide a suitable platform for the dancing of Kṛṣṇa with the gopīs. Therefore I think that the pious activities of persons like us, who have tried to advance in devotional service, have now attained maturity.'

PURPORT

This is verse eight of the First Act of *Vidagdha-mādhava.*

TEXT 139

অভিব্যক্তা মত্তঃ প্রকৃতিলঘুরূপাদপি বুধা
বিধাত্রী সিদ্ধার্থান্ হরিগুণময়ী বঃ কৃতিরিয়ম্ ।
পুলিন্দেনাপ্যগ্নিঃ কিমু সমিধমুন্মথ্য জনিতো
হিরণ্যশ্রেণীনামপহরতি নান্তঃকলুষতাম্ ॥ ১৩৯॥

abhivyaktā mattaḥ prakṛti-laghu-rūpād api budhā
vidhātrī siddhārthān hari-guṇa-mayī vaḥ kṛtir iyam
pulindenāpy agniḥ kimu samidham-unmathya janito
hiraṇya-śreṇīnām apaharati nāntaḥ-kaluṣatām

SYNONYMS

abhivyaktā—manifested; *mattaḥ*—from me; *prakṛti*—by nature; *laghu-rūpāt*—situated in a lower position; *api*—although; *budhāḥ*—O learned devotees;

vidhātrī—which may bring about; *siddha-arthān*—all the objects of perfection; *hari-guṇa-mayī*—whose subject matter is the attributes of Kṛṣṇa; *vaḥ*—of you; *kṛtiḥ*—the poetic play known as *Vidagdha-mādhava*; *iyam*—this; *pulindena*—by the lowest class of men; *api*—although; *agniḥ*—a fire; *kimu*—whether; *samidham*—the wood; *unmathya*—rubbing; *janitaḥ*—produced; *hiraṇya*—of gold; *śreṇīnām*—of quantities; *apaharati*—vanquishes; *na*—not; *antaḥ*—inner; *kaluṣatām*—dirty things.

TRANSLATION

" 'O learned devotees, I am by nature ignorant and low, yet even though it is from me that Vidagdha-mādhava has come, it is filled with descriptions of the transcendental attributes of the Supreme Personality of Godhead. Therefore, will not such literature bring about the attainment of the highest goal of life? Although its wood may be ignited by a low-class man, fire can nevertheless purify gold. Although I am very low by nature, this book may help cleanse the dirt from within the hearts of the golden devotees.' "

PURPORT

This verse is also from *Vidagdha-mādhava* (1.6).

TEXT 140

রায় কহে,—"কহ দেখি প্রেমোৎপত্তি-কারণ?
পূর্ব্বরাগ, বিকার, চেষ্টা, কামলিখন?" ॥ ১৪০ ॥

rāya kahe,—"kaha dekhi premotpatti-kāraṇa?
pūrva-rāga, vikāra, ceṣṭā, kāma-likhana?"

SYNONYMS

rāya kahe—Śrīla Rāmānanda Rāya further inquires; *kaha*—please recite; *dekhi*—so that I may know; *prema-utpatti-kāraṇa*—the causes of awakening the loving propensity; *pūrva-rāga*—previous attachment; *vikāra*—transformation; *ceṣṭā*—endeavor; *kāma-likhana*—writing of letters disclosing the *gopīs'* attachment for Kṛṣṇa.

TRANSLATION

Then Rāmānanda Rāya inquired from Rūpa Gosvāmī about the causes of the loving affairs between Kṛṣṇa and the gopīs, such as previous attachment, transformations of love, endeavors for love, and exchanges of letters disclosing the gopīs' awakening love for Kṛṣṇa.

TEXT 141

ক্রমে শ্রীরূপ-গোসাঞি সকলি কহিল ।
শুনি' প্রভুর ভক্তগণের চমৎকার হৈল ॥ ১৪১ ॥

krame śrī-rūpa-gosāñi sakali kahila
śuni' prabhura bhakta-gaṇera camatkāra haila

SYNONYMS

krame—gradually; *śrī-rūpa-gosāñi*—Śrīla Rūpa Gosvāmī; *sakali kahila*—explained everything; *śuni'*—hearing; *prabhura*—of Śrī Caitanya Mahāprabhu; *bhakta-gaṇera*—of the devotees; *camatkāra*—astonishment; *haila*—there was.

TRANSLATION

Śrīla Rūpa Gosvāmī gradually informed Rāmānanda Rāya about everything he asked. Hearing his explanations, all the devotees of Śrī Caitanya Mahāprabhu were struck with wonder.

PURPORT

Śrīla Rūpa Gosvāmī has explained *kāma-likhana* in his book *Ujjvala-nīlamaṇi* (*Vipralambha-prakaraṇa* 26):

sa lekhaḥ kāma-lekhaḥ syāt
yaḥ sva-prema-prakāśakaḥ
yuvatyā yūni yūnā ca
yuvatyāṁ saṁprahīyate

"Exchanges of letters between a young boy and young girl concerning their awakening of attachment for one another are called *kāma-lekha.*"

TEXT 142

একস্য শ্রুতমেব লুম্পতি মতিং কৃষ্ণেতি নামাক্ষরং
সান্দ্রোন্মাদ-পরম্পরামুপনয়ত্যন্যস্য বংশীকলঃ ।
এষ স্নিগ্ধঘনদ্যুতির্মনসি মে লগ্নঃ পটে বীক্ষণাৎ
কষ্টং ধিক্ পুরুষত্রয়ে রতিরভূন্মন্যে মৃতিঃ শ্রেয়সী ॥ ১৪২ ॥

ekasya śrutam eva lumpati matiṁ kṛṣṇeti nāmākṣaraṁ
sāndronmāda-paramparām upanayaty anyasya vaṁśī-kalaḥ

eṣa snigdha-ghana-dyutir manasi me lagnaḥ paṭe vīkṣaṇāt
kaṣṭaṁ dhik puruṣa-traye ratir abhūn manye mṛtiḥ śreyasī

SYNONYMS

ekasya—of one person; *śrutam*—heard; *eva*—certainly; *lumpati*—take away; *matim*—the mind; *kṛṣṇa iti*—Kṛṣṇa; *nāma-akṣaram*—the letters of the name; *sāndra-unmāda*—of intense madness; *paramparām*—a shower; *upanayati*—brings; *anyasya*—of another; *vaṁśī-kalaḥ*—the sound vibration of the flute; *eṣaḥ*—this third one; *snigdha*—giving love; *ghana-dyutiḥ*—lightninglike effulgence; *manasi*—in the mind; *me*—My; *lagnaḥ*—attachment; *paṭe*—in the picture; *vīkṣaṇāt*—by seeing; *kaṣṭam dhik*—oh, shame upon Me; *puruṣa-traye*—to three persons; *ratiḥ*—attachment; *abhūt*—has appeared; *manye*—I think; *mṛtiḥ*—death; *śreyasī*—better.

TRANSLATION

Experiencing previous attachment to Kṛṣṇa [pūrva-rāga], Śrīmatī Rādhārāṇī thought: "Since I have heard the name of a person called Kṛṣṇa, I have practically lost My good sense. Then, there is another person who plays His flute in such a way that after I hear the vibration, intense madness arises in My heart. And again there is still another person to whom My mind becomes attached when I see His beautiful lightning effulgence in His picture. Therefore I think that I am greatly condemned, for I have become simultaneously attached to three persons. It would be better for Me to die because of this."

PURPORT

This verse is from *Vidagdha-mādhava* (2.9).

TEXT 143

ইয়ং সখি সুদুঃসাধ্যা রাধা-হৃদয়বেদনা ।
কৃতা যত্র চিকিৎসাপি কুৎসায়াং পর্যবস্যতি ॥ ১৪৩ ॥

iyaṁ sakhi suduḥsādhyā
rādhā hṛdaya-vedanā
kṛtā yatra cikitsāpi
kutsāyāṁ paryavasyati

SYNONYMS

iyam—this; *sakhi*—my dear friend; *suduḥsādhyā*—incurable; *rādhā*—of Śrīmatī Rādhārāṇī; *hṛdaya-vedanā*—palpitation of the heart; *kṛtā*—done; *yatra*—

in which; *cikitsā*—treatment; *api*—although; *kutsāyām*—in defamation; *paryavasyati*—ends in.

TRANSLATION

"My dear friend, these palpitations of Śrīmatī Rādhārāṇī's heart are extremely difficult to cure. Even if one applied some medical treatment, it would only end in defamation."

PURPORT

This verse (*Vidagdha-mādhava* 2.8) is spoken by Śrīmatī Rādhārāṇī Herself.

TEXT 144

ধরিঅ পড়িচ্ছন্দগুণং
স্থন্দর মহ মন্দিরে তুমং বসসি।
তহ তহ রুন্ধসি বলিঅং
জহ জহ চইদা পলাএম্‌হি ? ১৪৪ ॥

dhari-a paḍicchanda-guṇaṁ
sundara maha mandire tumaṁ vasasi
taha taha rundhasi bali-aṁ
jaha jaha ca-idā palāemhi

SYNONYMS

dhari-a—capturing; *paḍicchanda-guṇam*—the quality of an artistic picture; *sundara*—O most beautiful one; *maha*—my; *mandire*—within the heart; *tumam*—You; *vasasi*—reside; *taha taha*—that much; *rundhasi*—You block; *bali-am*—by force; *jaha jaha*—as much as; *ca-idā*—being disturbed; *palāemhi*—I try to escape.

TRANSLATION

"O dearly beautiful, the artistic loveliness of Your picture is now impressed within My mind. Since You are now living within My mind, wherever I wish to run because I am agitated by impressions of You, I find that You, O My friend, are blocking My way."

PURPORT

This verse (*Vidagdha-mādhava* 2.33) is written in the Prākṛta language, not in Sanskrit. When transformed into Sanskrit, it reads as follows:

dhṛtvā praticchanda-guṇaṁ sundara mama mandire tvaṁ vasasi
tathā tathā ruṇatsi balitaṁ yathā yathā cakitā palāye

The meaning is the same, but the native language is different. It was spoken by Madhumaṅgala to Śrī Kṛṣṇa.

TEXT 145

অগ্রে বীক্ষ্য শিখণ্ডখণ্ডমচিরাদুৎকম্পমালম্বতে
গুঞ্জানাঞ্চ বিলোকনান্মুহুরসৌ সাস্রং পরিক্রোশতি ।
নো জানে জনয়ন্নপূর্বনটনক্রীড়া-চমৎকারিতাং
বালায়াঃ কিল চিত্তভূমিমবিশৎ কোঽয়ং নবীনগ্রহঃ ॥১৪৫॥

agre vīkṣya śikhaṇḍa-khaṇḍam acirād utkampam ālambate
guñjānāṁ ca vilokanān muhur asau sāsraṁ parikrośati
no jāne janayann apūrva-naṭana-krīḍā-camatkāritāṁ
bālāyāḥ kila citta-bhūmim aviśat ko 'yaṁ navīna-grahaḥ

SYNONYMS

agre—in front; *vīkṣya*—seeing; *śikhaṇḍa-khaṇḍam*—some peacock feathers; *acirāt*—all of a sudden; *utkampam*—trembling of the heart and body; *ālambate*—takes to; *guñjānām*—of a garland of *guñjā* (small conchshells); *ca*—also; *vilokanāt*—by seeing; *muhuḥ*—constantly; *asau*—She; *sa-asram*—with tears; *parikrośati*—goes around crying; *no*—not; *jāne*—I know; *janayan*—awakening; *apūrva-naṭana*—like unheard-of dramatic dancing; *krīḍā*—of activities; *camatkāritām*—the madness; *bālāyāḥ*—of this poor girl; *kila*—certainly; *citta-bhūmim*—within the heart; *aviśat*—has entered; *kaḥ*—what; *ayam*—this; *navīna-grahaḥ*—new ecstatic influence.

TRANSLATION

"Upon seeing peacock feathers in front of Her, this girl suddenly begins trembling. When She sometimes sees a necklace of guñjā [small conchshells], She sheds tears and cries loudly. I do not know what kind of new ecstatic influence has entered the heart of this poor girl. It has imbued Her with the dancing attitude of a player creating wonderful, unprecedented dances on a stage."

PURPORT

This verse (*Vidagdha-mādhava* 2.15) is spoken by Mukharā, Lord Kṛṣṇa's grandmother, in a conversation with the grandmother of Rādhārāṇī, Paurṇamāsī.

TEXT 146

অকারুণ্যঃ কৃষ্ণো যদি ময়ি তবাগঃ কথমিদং
মুধা মা রোদীর্মে কুরু পরমিমামুত্তরকৃতিম্।
তমালস্য স্কন্ধে বিনিহিত-ভুজবল্লরিরিয়ং
যথা বৃন্দারণ্যে চিরমবিচলা তিষ্ঠতি তনুঃ ॥ ১৪৬ ॥

akāruṇyaḥ kṛṣṇo yadi mayi tavāgaḥ katham idaṁ
mudhā mā rodīr me kuru param imām uttara-kṛtim
tamālasya skandhe vinihita-bhuja-vallarir iyaṁ
yathā vṛndāraṇye ciram avicalā tiṣṭhati tanuḥ

SYNONYMS

akāruṇyaḥ—very cruel; *kṛṣṇaḥ*—Lord Kṛṣṇa; *yadi*—if; *mayi*—unto Me; *tava*—your; *āgaḥ*—offense; *katham*—how; *idam*—this; *mudhā*—uselessly; *mā rodīḥ*—do not cry; *me*—for Me; *kuru*—do; *param*—but afterwards; *imām*—this; *uttara-kṛtim*—final act; *tamālasya*—of a *tamāla* tree; *skandhe*—the trunk; *vinihita*—fixed upon; *bhuja-vallariḥ*—arms like creepers; *iyam*—this; *yathā*—as far as possible; *vṛndā-araṇye*—in the forest of Vṛndāvana; *ciram*—forever; *avicalā*—without being disturbed; *tiṣṭhati*—remains; *tanuḥ*—the body.

TRANSLATION

Śrīmatī Rādhārāṇī said to Her constant companion Viśākhā: "My dear friend, if Kṛṣṇa is unkind to Me, there will be no need for you to cry, for it will not be due to any fault of yours. I shall then have to die, but afterwards please do one thing for Me: to observe My funeral ceremony, place My body with its arms embracing a tamāla tree like creepers so that I may remain forever in Vṛndāvana undisturbed. That is My last request." (Vidagdha-mādhava 2.47)

TEXT 147

রায় কহে,—"কহ দেখি ভাবের স্বভাব ?"
রূপ কহে,—"ঐছে হয় কৃষ্ণবিষয়ক 'ভাব' ॥" ১৪৭ ॥

rāya kahe,—"kaha dekhi bhāvera svabhāva?"
rūpa kahe,—"aiche haya kṛṣṇa-viṣayaka 'bhāva' "

SYNONYMS

rāya kahe—Rāmānanda Rāya says; *kaha*—kindly recite; *dekhi*—so that I may see; *bhāvera svabhāva*—the characteristic of emotional love; *rūpa kahe*—Rūpa

Gosvāmī replies; *aiche*—such; *haya*—is; *kṛṣṇa-viṣayaka*—concerning Kṛṣṇa; *bhāva*—emotional love.

TRANSLATION

Rāmānanda Rāya inquired, "What are the characteristics of emotional love?" Rūpa Gosvāmī replied, "This is the nature of emotional love for Kṛṣṇa.

TEXT 148

পীড়াভির্নবকালকূটকটুতা-গর্বস্য নির্বাসনো
নিঃস্যন্দেন মুদাং সুধা-মধুরিমাহঙ্কার-সঙ্কোচনঃ ।
প্রেমা সুন্দরি নন্দনন্দনপরো জাগর্তি যস্যান্তরে
জ্ঞায়ন্তে স্ফুটমস্য বক্রমধুরাস্তেনৈব বিক্রান্তয়ঃ ॥ ১৪৮ ॥

pīḍābhir nava-kāla-kūṭa-kaṭutā-garvasya nirvāsano
nisyandena mudāṁ sudhā-madhurimāhaṅkāra-saṅkocanaḥ
premā sundari nanda-nandana-paro jāgarti yasyāntare
jñāyante sphuṭam asya vakra-madhurās tenaiva vikrāntayaḥ

SYNONYMS

pīḍābhiḥ—by the sufferings; *nava*—fresh; *kāla-kūṭa*—of poison; *kaṭutā*—of the severity; *garvasya*—of pride; *nirvāsanaḥ*—banishment; *nisyandena*—by pouring down; *mudām*—happiness; *sudhā*—of nectar; *madhurimā*—of the sweetness; *ahaṅkāra*—the pride; *saṅkocanaḥ*—minimizing; *premā*—love; *sundari*—beautiful friend; *nanda-nandana-paraḥ*—fixed upon the son of Mahārāja Nanda; *jāgarti*—develops; *yasya*—of whom; *antare*—in the heart; *jñāyante*—are perceived; *sphuṭam*—explicitly; *asya*—of that; *vakra*—crooked; *madhurāḥ*—and sweet; *tena*—by him; *eva*—alone; *vikrāntayaḥ*—the influences.

TRANSLATION

" 'My dear beautiful friend, if one develops love of Godhead, love of Kṛṣṇa, the son of Nanda Mahārāja, all the bitter and sweet influences of this love will manifest in one's heart. Such love of Godhead acts in two ways. The poisonous effects of love of Godhead defeat the severe and fresh poison of the serpent. Yet there is simultaneously transcendental bliss, which pours down and defeats the poisonous effects of a snake, as well as the happiness derived from pouring nectar on one's head. It is perceived as doubly effective, simultaneously poisonous and nectarean.' "

PURPORT

This verse is from the *Vidagdha-mādhava* (2.18). It also appears in *Madhya-līlā,* Chapter Two, verse 52. It is spoken by Paurṇamāsī.

TEXT 149

রায় কহে'—"কহ সহজ-প্রেমের লক্ষণ"।
রূপ-গোসাঞি কহে, "সাহজিক প্রেমধর্ম" ॥১৪৯॥

rāya kahe,——"kaha sahaja-premera lakṣaṇa"
rūpa-gosāñi kahe,——"sāhajika prema-dharma"

SYNONYMS

rāya kahe—Śrīla Rāmānanda Rāya inquires; *kaha*—please tell me; *sahaja-premera*—of natural love; *lakṣaṇa*—the characteristics; *rūpa-gosāñi kahe*—Rūpa Gosvāmī replies; *sāhajika*—spontaneous; *prema-dharma*—character of love of Godhead.

TRANSLATION

Rāmānanda Rāya further inquired, "What are the natural characteristics of awakening love of Godhead?" Rūpa Gosvāmī replied, "These are the natural characteristics of love of God.

TEXT 150

স্তোত্রং যত্র তটস্থতাং প্রকটয়চ্চিত্তস্য ধত্তে ব্যথাং
নিন্দাপি প্রমদং প্রযচ্ছতি পরীহাসশ্রিয়ং বিভ্রতী।
দোষেণ ক্ষয়িতাং গুণেন গুরুতাং কেনাপ্যনাতন্বতী
প্রেম্ণঃ স্বারসিকস্য কস্যচিদিয়ং বিক্রীড়তি প্রক্রিয়া॥১৫০॥

stotraṁ yatra taṭa-sthatāṁ prakaṭayac cittasya ḍhatte vyathāṁ
nindāpi pramadaṁ prayacchati parīhāsa-śriyaṁ bibhratī
doṣeṇa kṣayitāṁ guṇena gurutāṁ kenāpy anātanvatī
premṇaḥ svārasikasya kasyacid iyaṁ vikrīḍati prakriyā

SYNONYMS

stotram—praising; *yatra*—in which; *taṭa-sthatām*—neutrality; *prakaṭayat*—manifesting; *cittasya*—to the heart; *dhatte*—gives; *vyathām*—painful reaction; *nindā*—blaspheming; *api*—also; *pramadam*—pleasure; *prayacchati*—delivers; *parīhāsa*—of joking; *śriyam*—the beauty; *bibhratī*—bringing forth; *doṣeṇa*—by accusation; *kṣayitām*—the quality of diminishing; *guṇena*—by good qualities; *gurutām*—the importance; *kena api*—by any; *anātanvatī*—not increasing; *premṇaḥ*—of love of Godhead; *svārasikasya*—spontaneous; *kasyacit*—of any; *iyam*—this; *vikrīḍati*—acts within the heart; *prakriyā*—the manner of action.

TRANSLATION

" 'When one hears praise from his beloved, he outwardly remains neutral but feels pain within his heart. When he hears his beloved making accusations about him, he takes them to be jokes and enjoys pleasure. When he finds faults in his beloved, they do not diminish his love, nor do the beloved's good qualities increase his spontaneous affection. Thus spontaneous love continues under all circumstances. That is how spontaneous love of Godhead acts within the heart.'

PURPORT

This verse from *Vidagdha-mādhava* (5.4) is spoken by Paurṇamāsī, the grandmother of Rādhārāṇī and mother of Sāndīpani Muni.

TEXT 151

শ্রুত্বা নিষ্ঠুরতাং মমেন্দুবদনা প্রেমাঙ্কুরং ভিন্দতী
স্বান্তে শান্তিধুরাং বিধায় বিধুরে প্রায়ঃ পরাঞ্চিষ্যতি।
কিংবা পামর-কাম-কার্মুকপরিত্রস্তা বিমোক্ষ্যত্যসূন্
হা মৌগ্ধ্যাৎ ফলিনী মনোরথলতা মৃদ্বী ময়োন্মূলিতা ॥১৫১

śrutvā niṣṭhuratāṁ mamendu-vadanā premāṅkuraṁ bhindatī
svānte śānti-dhurāṁ vidhāya vidhure prāyaḥ parāñciṣyati
kiṁvā pāmara-kāma-kārmuka-paritrastā vimokṣyaty asūn
hā maugdhyāt phalinī manoratha-latā mṛdvī mayonmūlitā

SYNONYMS

śrutvā—by hearing; *niṣṭhuratām*—cruelty; *mama*—My; *indu-vadanā*—moon-faced; *prema-aṅkuram*—the seed of love; *bhindatī*—splitting; *sva-ante*—within Her heart; *śānti-dhurām*—great toleration; *vidhāya*—taking; *vidhure*—aggrieved; *prāyaḥ*—almost; *parāñciṣyati*—may turn against; *kiṁvā*—or; *pāmara*—most formidable; *kāma*—of lusty desires or Cupid; *kārmuka*—of the bow; *paritrastā*—frightened; *vimokṣyati*—will give up; *asūn*—life; *hā*—alas; *maugdhyāt*—on account of bewilderment; *phalinī*—almost fruitful; *manaḥ-ratha-latā*—the creeper of growing love; *mṛdvī*—very soft; *mayā*—by Me; *unmūlitā*—uprooted.

TRANSLATION

" 'Upon hearing of My cruelty, moon-faced Rādhārāṇī may establish some kind of tolerance in Her aggrieved heart. But then She might turn against Me. Or, indeed, being fearful of the lusty desires invoked by the bow of formidable Cupid, She might even give up Her life. Alas! I have foolishly uprooted the soft creeper of Her desire just when it was ready to bear fruit.'

PURPORT

Having been very cruel to Śrīmatī Rādhārāṇī, Kṛṣṇa is repenting in this way (*Vidagdha-mādhava* 2.40).

TEXT 152

যস্যোৎসঙ্গসুখাশয়া শিথিলিতা গুর্বী গুরুভ্যস্ত্রপা
প্রাণেভ্যোঽপি সুহৃত্তমাঃ সখি তথা যূয়ং পরিক্লেশিতাঃ।
ধর্মঃ সোঽপি মহান্ময়া ন গণিতঃ সাধ্বীভিরধ্যাসিতো
ধিগ্ ধৈর্যং তদুপেক্ষিতাপি যদহং জীবামি পাপীয়সী ॥১৫২॥

yasyotsaṅga-sukhāśayā śithilitā gurvī gurubhyas trapā
prāṇebhyo 'pi suhṛt-tamāḥ sakhi tathā yūyaṁ parikleśitāḥ
dharmaḥ so 'pi mahān mayā na gaṇitaḥ sādhvībhir adhyāsito
dhig dhairyaṁ tad-upekṣitāpi yad ahaṁ jīvāmi pāpīyasī

SYNONYMS

yasya—of whom; *utsaṅga-sukha-āśayā*—by the desire for the happiness of the association; *śithilitā*—slackened; *gurvī*—very great; *gurubhyaḥ*—unto the superiors; *trapā*—bashfulness; *prāṇebhyaḥ*—than My life; *api*—although; *suhṛt-tamāḥ*—more dear; *sakhi*—O My dear friend; *tathā*—similarly; *yūyam*—you; *parikleśitāḥ*—so much troubled; *dharmaḥ*—duties to My husband; *saḥ*—that; *api*—also; *mahān*—very great; *mayā*—by Me; *na*—not; *gaṇitaḥ*—cared for; *sādhvībhiḥ*—by the most chaste women; *adhyāsitaḥ*—practiced; *dhik dhairyam*—to hell with patience; *tat*—by Him; *upekṣitā*—neglected; *api*—although; *yat*—which; *aham*—I; *jīvāmi*—am living; *pāpīyasī*—the most sinful.

TRANSLATION

" 'Desiring the happiness of His association and embraces, My dear friend, I disregarded even My superiors and relaxed My shyness and gravity before them. Furthermore, although you are My best friend, more dear to Me than My own life, I have given you so much trouble. Indeed, I even put aside the vow of dedication to My husband, a vow kept by the most elevated women. Oh, alas! Although He is now neglecting Me, I am so sinful that I am still living. Therefore I must condemn My so-called patience.'

PURPORT

Śrīmatī Rādhārāṇī is speaking this verse (*Vidagdha-mādhava* 2.41) to Her intimate friend Viśākhādevī.

TEXT 153

গৃহান্তঃখেলন্ত্যো নিজসহজবাল্যস্য বলনা-
দভদ্রং ভদ্রং বা কিমপি হি ন জানীমহি মনাক্ ।
বয়ং নেতুং যুক্তাঃ কথমশরণাং কামপি দশাং
কথং বা ন্যায্যা তে প্রথয়িতুমুদাসীনপদবী ॥ ১৫৩ ॥

gṛhāntaḥ-khelantyo nija-sahaja-bālyasya balanād
abhadraṁ bhadraṁ vā kim api hi na jānīmahi manāk
vayaṁ netuṁ yuktāḥ katham aśaraṇāṁ kām api daśāṁ
kathaṁ vā nyāyyā te prathayitum udāsīna-padavī

SYNONYMS

gṛha-antaḥ-khelantyaḥ—who were engaged in childish play within the house; *nija*—one's own; *sahaja*—simple; *bālyasya*—of childhood; *balanāt*—on account of influence; *abhadram*—bad; *bhadram*—good; *vā*—or; *kim api*—what; *hi*—certainly; *na*—not; *jānīmahi*—we did know; *manāk*—even slightly; *vayam*—we; *netum*—to lead; *yuktāḥ*—suitable; *katham*—how; *aśaraṇām*—without surrender; *kām api*—such as this; *daśām*—to the condition; *katham*—how; *vā*—or; *nyāyyā*—correct; *te*—of You; *prathayitum*—to manifest; *udāsīna*—of carelessness; *padavī*—the position.

TRANSLATION

" 'I was engaged in My own playful activities in My home, and because of My childish innocence I did not know right from wrong. Therefore, is it good for You to have forced us into being so much attracted to You and then to have neglected us? Now You are indifferent to us. Do You think that is right?'

PURPORT

This verse (*Vidagdha-mādhava* 2.46) is spoken to Kṛṣṇa by Śrīmatī Rādhārāṇī.

TEXT 154

অন্তঃক্লেশকলঙ্কিতাঃ কিল বয়ং যামোঽদ্য যাম্যাং পুরীং
নায়ং বঞ্চনসঞ্চয়প্রণয়িনং হাসং তথাপ্যুজ্ঝতি ।
অস্মিন্ সম্পুটিতে গভীরকপটৈরাভীরপল্লীবিটে
হা মেধাবিনি রাধিকে তব কথং প্রেমা গরীয়ানভূৎ ॥ ১৫৪॥

antaḥ-kleśa-kalaṅkitāḥ kila vayaṁ yāmo 'dya yāmyāṁ purīṁ
nāyaṁ vañcana-sañcaya-praṇayinaṁ hāsaṁ tathāpy ujjhati

asmin samputite gabhīra-kapaṭair ābhīra-pallī-viṭe
hā medhāvini rādhike tava kathaṁ premā garīyān abhūt

SYNONYMS

antaḥ-kleśa-kalaṅkitāḥ—polluted by inner miserable conditions that continue even after death; *kila*—certainly; *vayam*—all of us; *yāmaḥ*—are going; *adya*—now; *yāmyām*—of Yamarāja; *purīm*—to the abode; *na*—not; *ayam*—this; *vañcana-sañcaya*—cheating activities; *praṇayinam*—aiming at; *hāsam*—smiling; *tathāpi*—still; *ujjhati*—gives up; *asmin*—in this; *samputite*—filled; *gabhīra*—deep; *kapaṭaiḥ*—with deceit; *ābhīra-pallī*—from the village of the cowherd men; *viṭe*—in a debauchee; *hā*—alas; *medhāvini*—O intelligent one; *rādhike*—Śrīmatī Rādhārāṇī; *tava*—Your; *katham*—how; *premā*—love; *garīyān*—so great; *abhūt*—became.

TRANSLATION

" 'Our hearts are so polluted by miserable conditions that we are certainly going to Pluto's kingdom. Nevertheless, Kṛṣṇa does not give up His beautiful loving smiling, which is full of cheating tricks. O Śrīmatī Rādhārāṇī, You are very intelligent. How could You have developed such great loving affection for this deceitful debauchee from the neighborhood of the cowherds?'

PURPORT

This verse (*Vidagdha-mādhava* 2.37) is spoken to Rādhārāṇī by Lalitā-sakhī, another confidential friend.

TEXT 155

হিত্বা দূরে পথি ধবতরোরন্তিকং ধর্ম্মসেতো-
র্ভঙ্গোদগ্রা গুরুশিখরিণং রংহসা লঙ্ঘয়ন্তী।
লেভে কৃষ্ণার্ণব নবরসা রাধিক-বাহিনী ত্বাং
বাগ্বীচিভিঃ কিমিব বিমুখীভাবমস্যাস্তনোষি ॥ ১৫৫ ॥

hitvā dūre pathi dhava-taror antikaṁ dharma-setor
bhaṅgodagrā guru-śikhariṇaṁ raṁhasā laṅghayantī
lebhe kṛṣṇārṇava nava-rasā rādhikā-vāhinī tvāṁ
vāg-vīcibhiḥ kim iva vimukhī-bhāvam asyās tanoṣi

SYNONYMS

hitvā—giving up; *dūre*—far away; *pathi*—on the road; *dhava-taroḥ*—of the tree of the husband; *antikam*—the vicinity; *dharma-setoḥ*—the bridge of religion; *bhaṅga-udagrā*—being strong enough for breaking; *guru-śikhariṇam*—the hill of the superior relatives; *raṁhasā*—with great force; *laṅghayantī*—crossing over; *lebhe*—has obtained; *kṛṣṇa-arṇava*—O ocean of Kṛṣṇa; *nava-rasā*—being influenced by new ecstatic love; *rādhikā*—Śrīmatī Rādhārāṇī; *vāhinī*—like a river; *tvām*—You; *vāk-vīcibhiḥ*—only by the waves of words; *kim*—how; *iva*—like this; *vimukhī-bhāvam*—indifference; *asyāḥ*—toward Her; *tanoṣi*—You are spreading.

TRANSLATION

" 'O Lord Kṛṣṇa, You are just like an ocean. The river of Śrīmatī Rādhārāṇī has reached You from a long distance—leaving far behind the tree of Her husband, breaking through the bridge of social convention, and forcibly crossing the hills of elder relatives. Coming here because of fresh feelings of love for You, that river has now received Your shelter, but now You are trying to turn Her back by the waves of unfavorable words. How is it that You are spreading this attitude?' "

PURPORT

This verse from *Vidagdha-mādhava* (3.9) is spoken to Lord Kṛṣṇa by Paurṇamāsī, the grandmother of Śrīmatī Rādhārāṇī.

TEXT 156

রায় কহে,—"বৃন্দাবন, মুরলী-নিঃস্বন ।
কৃষ্ণ, রাধিকার কৈছে করিয়াছ বর্ণন ? ১৫৬ ॥

rāya kahe,——"vṛndāvana, muralī-niḥsvana
kṛṣṇa, rādhikāra kaiche kariyācha varṇana

SYNONYMS

rāya kahe—Rāmānanda Rāya says; *vṛndāvana*—the place named Vṛndāvana; *muralī-niḥsvana*—the vibration of Kṛṣṇa's flute; *kṛṣṇa*—Lord Kṛṣṇa; *rādhikāra*—of Śrīmatī Rādhārāṇī; *kaiche*—how; *kariyācha varṇana*—you have described.

TRANSLATION

Śrīla Rāmānanda Rāya further inquired: "How have you described Vṛndāvana, the vibration of the transcendental flute, and the relationship between Kṛṣṇa and Rādhikā?

TEXT 157

কহ, তোমার কবিত্ব শুনি' হয় চমৎকার ।"
ক্রমে রূপ-গোসাঞি কহে করি' নমস্কার ॥১৫৭॥

kaha, tomāra kavitva śuni' haya camatkāra"
krame rūpa-gosāñi kahe kari' namaskāra

SYNONYMS

kaha—kindly let me know; *tomāra kavitva śuni'*—by hearing your poetic ability; *haya*—there is; *camatkāra*—much astonishment; *krame*—gradually; *rūpa-gosāñi*—Śrīla Rūpa Gosvāmī; *kahe*—continues to speak; *kari' namaskāra*—offering obeisances.

TRANSLATION

"Please tell me all this, for your poetic ability is wonderful." After offering obeisances to Rāmānanda Rāya, Rūpa Gosvāmī gradually began answering his inquiries.

TEXT 158

সুগন্ধৌ মাকন্দপ্রকরমকরন্দস্য মধুরে
বিনিস্যন্দে বন্দীকৃতমধুপবৃন্দং মুহুরিদম্ ।
কৃতান্দোলং মন্দোন্নতিভিরনিলৈশ্চন্দনগিরে-
র্মমানন্দং বৃন্দা-বিপিনমতুলং তুন্দিলয়তি ॥ ১৫৮ ॥

sugandhau mākanda-prakara-makarandasya madhure
vinisyande vandī-kṛta-madhupa-vṛndaṁ muhur idam
kṛtāndolaṁ mandonnatibhir anilaiś candana-girer
mamānandaṁ vṛndā-vipinam atulaṁ tundilayati

SYNONYMS

su-gandhau—in the fragrance; *mākanda-prakara*—of the bunches of mango buds; *makarandasya*—of the honey; *madhure*—sweet; *vinisyande*—in the oozing; *vandī-kṛta*—grouped together; *madhupa-vṛndam*—bumblebees; *muhuḥ*—again and again; *idam*—this; *kṛta-andolam*—agitated; *manda-unnatibhiḥ*—moving softly; *anilaiḥ*—by the breezes; *candana-gireḥ*—from the Malaya Hills; *mama*—My; *ānandam*—pleasure; *vṛndā-vipinam*—the forest of Vṛndāvana; *atulam*—very much; *tundilayati*—increases more and more.

TRANSLATION

" 'The sweet, fragrant honey oozing from newly grown mango buds is again and again attracting groups of bumblebees, and this forest is trembling in the softly moving breezes from the Malaya Hills, which are full of sandalwood trees. Thus the forest of Vṛndāvana is increasing My transcendental pleasure.'

PURPORT

This verse from *Vidagdha-mādhava* (1.23) is spoken by Lord Kṛṣṇa Himself.

TEXT 159

বৃন্দাবনং দিব্যলতা-পরীতং
লতাশ্চ পুষ্পস্ফুরিতাগ্রভাজঃ ।
পুষ্পাণি চ স্ফীতমধুব্রতানি
মধুব্রতাশ্চ শ্রুতিহারিগীতাঃ ॥ ১৫৯ ॥

vṛndāvanaṁ divya-latā-parītaṁ
latāś ca puṣpa-sphuritāgra-bhājaḥ
puṣpāṇi ca sphīta-madhu-vratāni
madhu-vratāś ca śruti-hāri-gītāḥ

SYNONYMS

vṛndāvanam—the forest of Vṛndāvana; *divya-latā-parītam*—surrounded by transcendental creepers; *latāḥ ca*—and the creepers; *puṣpa*—by flowers; *sphurita*—distinguished; *agra-bhājaḥ*—possessing ends; *puṣpāṇi*—the flowers; *ca*—and; *sphīta-madhu-vratāni*—having many maddened bumblebees; *madhu-vratāḥ*—the bumblebees; *ca*—and; *śruti-hāri-gītāḥ*—whose songs defeat the Vedic hymns and are pleasing to the ear.

TRANSLATION

" 'My dear friend, see how this forest of Vṛndāvana is full of transcendental creepers and trees. The tops of the creepers are full of flowers, and intoxicated bumblebees are buzzing around them, humming songs that please the ear and surpass even the Vedic hymns.'

PURPORT

This verse from *Vidagdha-mādhava* (1.24) is spoken by Lord Balarāma to His friend Śrīdāmā.

TEXT 160

ক্বচিদ্‌ভৃঙ্গীগীতং ক্বচিদনিলভঙ্গী-শিশিরতা
ক্বচিদ্‌বল্লীলাস্যং ক্বচিদমলমল্লীপরিমলঃ ।
ক্বচিদ্ধারাশালী করকফলপালী-রসভরো
হৃষীকাণাং বৃন্দং প্রমদয়তি বৃন্দাবনমিদম্ ॥ ১৬০ ॥

kvacid bhṛṅgī-gītaṁ kvacid anila-bhaṅgī-śiśiratā
kvacid vallī-lāsyaṁ kvacid amala-mallī-parimalaḥ
kvacid dhārā-śālī karaka-phala-pālī-rasa-bharo
hṛṣīkāṇāṁ vṛndaṁ pramadayati vṛndāvanam idam

SYNONYMS

kvacit—somewhere; *bhṛṅgī-gītam*—the humming songs of the bumblebees; *kvacit*—somewhere; *anila-bhaṅgī-śiśiratā*—coolness from the waves of the mild breezes; *kvacit*—somewhere; *vallī-lāsyam*—the dancing of the creepers; *kvacit*—somewhere; *amala-mallī-parimalaḥ*—the pure fragrance of the *mallikā* flowers; *kvacit*—somewhere; *dhārā-śālī*—abounding in showers; *karaka-phala-pālī*—of pomegranate fruits; *rasa-bharaḥ*—overabundance of juice; *hṛṣīkāṇām*—of the senses; *vṛndam*—to the group; *pramadayati*—is giving pleasure; *vṛndāvanam*—the forest of Vṛndāvana; *idam*—this.

TRANSLATION

" 'My dear friend, this forest of Vṛndāvana is giving great pleasure to our senses in various ways. Somewhere bumblebees are singing in groups, and in some places mild breezes are cooling the entire atmosphere. Somewhere the creepers and tree twigs are dancing, the mallikā flowers are expanding their fragrance, and an overabundance of juice is constantly flowing in showers from pomegranate fruits.'

PURPORT

This verse from *Vidagdha-mādhava* (1.31) is spoken by Lord Kṛṣṇa to His cowherd friend Madhumaṅgala.

TEXT 161

পরামৃষ্টাঙ্গুষ্ঠত্রয়মসিতরত্নৈরুভয়তো
বহন্তী সংকীর্ণৌ মণিভিররুণৈস্তৎপরিসরৌ ।
তয়োর্মধ্যে হীরোজ্জ্বলবিমল-জাম্বূনদময়ী
করে কল্যাণীয়ং বিহরতি হরেঃ কেলিমুরলী ॥ ১৬১ ॥

parāmṛṣṭāṅguṣṭha-trayam asita-ratnair ubhayato
vahantī saṅkīrṇau maṇibhir aruṇais tat-parisarau
tayor madhye hīrojjvala-vimala-jāmbūnada-mayī
kare kalyāṇīyaṁ viharati hareḥ keli-muralī

SYNONYMS

parāmṛṣṭā—measured; *anguṣṭha-trayam*—a length of three fingers; *asita-ratnaiḥ*—with valuable *indra-nīla* jewels; *ubhayataḥ*—from both ends; *vahantī*—having; *saṅkīrṇau*—bedecked; *maṇibhiḥ*—by gems; *aruṇaiḥ*—rubies; *tat-parisarau*—the two ends of the flute; *tayoḥ madhye*—between them; *hīra*—with diamonds; *ujjvala*—blazing; *vimala*—pure; *jāmbūnada-mayī*—covered with gold plate; *kare*—in the hand; *kalyāṇī*—very auspicious; *iyam*—this; *viharati*—glitters; *hareḥ*—of Kṛṣṇa; *keli-muralī*—the pastime flute.

TRANSLATION

" 'The flute of Kṛṣṇa's pastimes measures three fingers in length, and it is bedecked with indra-nīla gems. At the ends of the flute are aruṇa gems [rubies], glittering beautifully, and in between the flute is plated with gold, set ablaze by diamonds. This auspicious flute, pleasing to Kṛṣṇa, is glittering in His hand with transcendental brilliance.'

PURPORT

This verse from *Vidagdha-mādhava* (3.1) is spoken to Lalitādevī by Paurṇamāsī, the grandmother of Rādhārāṇī.

TEXT 162

সদ্বংশতস্তব জনিঃ পুরুষোত্তমস্য
পাণৌ স্থিতির্মুরলিকে সরলাসি জাত্যা ।
কস্মাত্ত্বয়া সখি গুরোর্বিষমা গৃহীতা
গোপাঙ্গনাগণবিমোহনমন্ত্রদীক্ষা ॥ ১৬২ ॥

sad-vaṁśatas tava janiḥ puruṣottamasya
pāṇau sthitir muralike saralāsi jātyā
kasmāt tvayā sakhi guror viṣamā gṛhītā
gopāṅganā-gaṇa-vimohana-mantra-dīkṣā

SYNONYMS

sat-vaṁśataḥ—very respectable families; *tava*—your; *janiḥ*—birth; *puruṣottamasya*—of Lord Śrī Kṛṣṇa; *pāṇau*—in the hands; *sthitiḥ*—residence; *muralike*—O good flute; *saralā*—simple; *asi*—you are; *jātyā*—by birth; *kasmāt*—why; *tvayā*—by you; *sakhi*—O my dear friend; *guroḥ*—from the spiritual master; *viṣamā*—dangerous; *gṛhītā*—taken; *gopā-aṅganā-gaṇa-vimohana*—for bewildering the groups of the *gopīs*; *mantra-dīkṣā*—initiation in the *mantra*.

TRANSLATION

" 'My dear friend the flute, it appears that you have been born of a very good family, for your residence is in the hands of Śrī Kṛṣṇa. By birth you are simple and are not at all crooked. Why then have you taken initiation into this dangerous mantra that enchants the assembled gopīs?'

PURPORT

This verse (*Vidagdha-mādhava* 5.17) is spoken by Śrīmatī Rādhārāṇī.

TEXT 163

সখি মুরলি বিশালচ্ছিদ্রজালেন পূর্ণা
লঘুরতিকঠিনা ত্বং গ্রন্থিলা নীরসাসি ।
তদপি ভজসি শশ্বচ্চুম্বনানন্দসান্দ্রং
হরিকরপরিরম্ভং কেন পুণ্যোদয়েন ॥ ১৬৩ ॥

sakhi murali viśāla-cchidra-jālena pūrṇā
laghur atikaṭhinā tvaṁ granthilā nīrasāsi
tad api bhajasi śvaśvac cumbanānanda-sāndraṁ
hari-kara-parirambhaṁ kena puṇyodayena

SYNONYMS

sakhi murali—O dear friend the flute; *viśāla-chidra-jālena*—with so many big holes in your body (in other words, full of *chidra,* which also means "faults"); *pūrṇā*—full; *laghuḥ*—very light; *atikaṭhinā*—very hard in constitution; *tvam*—you; *granthilā*—full of knots; *nīrasā*—without juice; *asi*—are; *tat api*—therefore; *bhajasi*—you obtain through service; *śvaśvat*—continuously; *cumbana-ānanda*—the transcendental bliss of kissing by the Lord; *sāndram*—intense; *hari-kara-parirambham*—embracing by the hands of Śrī Kṛṣṇa; *kena*—by what; *puṇya-udayena*—means of pious activities.

TRANSLATION

" 'My dear friend the flute, you are actually full of many holes or faults. You are light, hard, juiceless and full of knots. But what kind of pious activities have engaged you in the service of being kissed by the Lord and embraced by His hands?'

PURPORT

This verse (*Vidagdha-mādhava* 4.7) is spoken by Candrāvalī-sakhī, the *gopī* competitor of Śrīmatī Rādhārāṇī.

TEXT 164

রুন্ধন্নম্বুভৃতশ্চমৎকৃতিপরং কুর্বন্মুহুস্তম্বুরুং
ধ্যানাদন্তরয়ন্ সনন্দনমুখান্ বিস্মাপয়ন্ বেধসম্ ।
ঔৎসুক্যাবলিভির্বলিং চটুলয়ন্ ভোগীন্দ্রমাঘূর্ণয়ন্
ভিন্দন্নণ্ডকটাহভিত্তিমভিতো বভ্রাম বংশীধ্বনিঃ ॥ ১৬৪ ॥

rundhann ambu-bhṛtaś camatkṛti-paraṁ kurvan muhus tumburuṁ
dhyānād antarayan sanandana-mukhān vismāpayan vedhasam
autsukyāvalibhir baliṁ caṭulayan bhogīndram āghūrṇayan
bhindann aṇḍa-kaṭāha-bhittim abhito babhrāma vaṁśī-dhvaniḥ

SYNONYMS

rundhan—blocking; *ambu-bhṛtaḥ*—the clouds bearing rain; *camatkṛti-param*—full of wonder; *kurvan*—making; *muhuḥ*—at every moment; *tumburum*—the King of the Gandharvas, Tumburu; *dhyānāt*—from meditation; *antarayan*—disturbing; *sanandana-mukhān*—the great saintly persons headed by Sanandana; *vismāpayan*—causing wonder; *vedhasam*—even to Lord Brahmā; *autsukya-āvalibhiḥ*—with thoughts of curiosity; *balim*—King Bali; *caṭulayan*—agitating; *bhogī-indram*—the King of the Nāgas; *āghūrṇayan*—whirling around; *bhindan*—penetrating; *aṇḍa-kaṭāha-bhittim*—the strong coverings of the universe; *abhitaḥ*—all around; *babhrāma*—circulated; *vaṁśī-dhvaniḥ*—the transcendental vibration of the flute.

TRANSLATION

" 'The transcendental vibration of Kṛṣṇa's flute blocked the movements of the rain clouds, struck the Gandharvas full of wonder, and agitated the meditation of great saintly persons like Sanaka and Sanandana. It created wonder in Lord Brahmā, wrought intense curiosity that agitated the mind of Bali Mahārāja, who was otherwise firmly fixed, made Mahārāja Ananta, the carrier of the planets, whirl around, and penetrated the strong coverings of the universe. Thus the sound of the flute in the hands of Kṛṣṇa created a wonderful situation.'

PURPORT

This verse (*Vidagdha-mādhava* 1.27) is spoken by Madhumaṅgala, a cowherd friend of Kṛṣṇa's.

TEXT 165

অয়ং নয়নদণ্ডিতপ্রবরপুণ্ডরীকপ্রভঃ
প্রভাতি নবজাগুড়-দ্যুতিবিড়ম্বি-পীতাম্বরঃ ।

অরণ্যজপরিষ্ক্রিয়া-দমিতদিব্যবেশাদরো
হরিন্মণিমনোহরদ্যুতিভিরুজ্জ্বলাঙ্গো হরিঃ ॥ ১৬৫ ॥

ayaṁ nayana-daṇḍita-pravara-puṇḍarīka-prabhaḥ
prabhāti nava-jāguḍa-dyuti-viḍambi-pītāmbaraḥ
araṇyaja-pariṣkriyā-damita-divya-veśādaro
harin-maṇi-manohara-dyutibhir ujjvalāṅgo hariḥ

SYNONYMS

ayam—this; *nayana*—by whose beautiful eyes; *daṇḍita*—defeated; *pravara*—best; *puṇḍarīka-prabhaḥ*—the luster of the white lotus flower; *prabhāti*—looks beautiful; *nava-jāguḍa-dyuti*—the brilliance of newly painted *kuṅkuma*; *viḍambi*—deriding; *pīta-ambaraḥ*—whose yellow dress; *araṇya-ja*—picked up from the forest; *pariṣkriyā*—by whose ornaments; *damita*—subdued; *divya-veśa-ādaraḥ*—the hankering for first-class dress; *harin-maṇi*—of emeralds; *manohara*—mind-attracting; *dyutibhiḥ*—with splendor; *ujjvala-aṅgaḥ*—whose beautiful body; *hariḥ*—the Supreme Personality of Godhead.

TRANSLATION

" 'The beauty of Kṛṣṇa's eyes surpasses the beauty of white lotus flowers, His yellow garments surpass the brilliance of fresh decorations of kuṅkuma, His ornaments of selected forest flowers surpass the hankering for the best of garments, and His bodily beauty possesses mind-attracting splendor greater than the jewels known as marakata-maṇi [emeralds].'

PURPORT

This verse from *Vidagdha-mādhava* (1.17) is spoken by Paurṇamāsī.

TEXT 166

জঙ্ঘাধস্তটসঙ্গিদক্ষিণপদং কিঞ্চিদ্বিভুগ্নত্রিকং
সাচিস্তম্ভিতকন্ধরং সখি তিরঃসঞ্চারিনেত্রাঞ্চলম্ ।
বংশীং কুট্‌মলিতে দধানমধরে লোলাঙ্গুলীসঙ্গতাং
রিঙ্গদ্‌ভ্রূভ্রমরং বরাঙ্গি পরমানন্দং পুরঃ স্বীকুরু ॥ ১৬৬ ॥

jaṅghādhas-taṭa-saṅgi-dakṣiṇa-padaṁ kiñcid vibhugna-trikaṁ
sāci-stambhita-kandharaṁ sakhi tiraḥ-sañcāri-netrāñcalam
vaṁśīṁ kuṭmalite dadhānam adhare lolāṅgulī-saṅgatāṁ
riṅgad-bhrū-bhramaraṁ varāṅgi paramānandaṁ puraḥ svīkuru

SYNONYMS

jaṅghā—of the shin; *adhaḥ-taṭa*—at the lower border; *saṅgi*—connected; *dakṣiṇa-padam*—the right foot; *kiñcit*—slightly; *vibhugna-trikam*—the middle of the body bent in three places; *sāci-stumbhita-kandharam*—whose neck is fixed in a curve to the side; *sakhi*—O friend; *tiraḥ-sañcāri*—roaming sideways; *netra-añcalam*—whose borders of the eyes; *vaṁśīm*—flute; *kuṭmalite*—shut like a flower bud; *dadhānam*—placing; *adhare*—on the lips; *lolā-aṅgulī-saṅgatām*—joined with fingers moving here and there; *riṅgat-bhrū*—whose slowly moving eyebrows; *bhramaram*—like bumblebees; *varāṅgi*—O most beautiful one; *paramānandam*—the personality of bliss; *puraḥ*—situated in front; *svī-kuru*—just accept.

TRANSLATION

" 'O most beautiful friend, please accept the Supreme Personality of Godhead, who is standing before you full of transcendental bliss. The borders of His eyes roam from side to side, and His eyebrows move slowly like bumblebees on His lotuslike face. Standing with His right foot placed below the knee of His left leg, the middle of His body curved in three places, and His neck gracefully tilted to the side, He takes His flute to His pursed lips and moves His fingers upon it here and there.'

PURPORT

This verse is from the *Lalita-mādhava-nāṭaka* (4.27), a ten-act play by Śrīla Rūpa Gosvāmī. The speaker here is Lalitādevī.

TEXT 167

কুলবরতনুধর্মগ্রাববৃন্দানি ভিন্দন্
সুমুখি নিশিতদীর্ঘাপাঙ্গটঙ্কচ্ছটাভিঃ ।
যুগপদয়মপূর্বঃ কঃ পুরো বিশ্বকর্মা
মরকতমণিলক্ষৈর্গোষ্ঠকক্ষাং চিনোতি ॥ ১৬৭ ॥

kula-varatanu-dharma-grāva-vṛndāni bhindan
sumukhi niśita-dīrghāpāṅga-ṭaṅka-cchaṭābhiḥ
yugapad ayam apūrvaḥ kaḥ puro viśva-karmā
marakata-maṇi-lakṣair goṣṭha-kakṣāṁ cinoti

SYNONYMS

kula-varatanu—of the family women; *dharma*—in the form of dedication to the husband, etc.; *grāva-vṛndāni*—the stones; *bhindan*—splitting; *sumukhi*—O beautiful-faced one; *niśita*—sharp; *dīrgha-apāṅga*—in the form of long outer corners of the eyes; *ṭaṅka-chaṭābhiḥ*—by chisels; *yugapat*—simultaneously; *ayam*—this; *apūrvaḥ*—unprecedented; *kaḥ*—who; *puraḥ*—in front; *viśva-karmā*—creative person; *marakata-maṇi-lakṣaiḥ*—with countless emeralds; *goṣṭha-kakṣām*—a private room for meeting; *cinoti*—He is constructing.

TRANSLATION

" 'O beautiful-faced one, who is this creative person standing before us? With the sharp chisels of His loving glances, He is splitting the hard stones of many women's devotion to their husbands. And with the luster of His body, surpassing the brilliance of countless emeralds, He is simultaneously constructing private meeting places for His pastimes.'

PURPORT

This verse (*Lalita-mādhava* 1.52) is spoken by Rādhārāṇī to Lalitādevī.

TEXT 168

মহেন্দ্রমণিমণ্ডলীমদবিড়ম্বিদেহদ্যুতি-
র্ব্রজেন্দ্রকুলচন্দ্রমাঃ স্ফুরতি কোঽপি নব্যো যুবা ।
সখি স্থিরকুলাঙ্গনা-নিকর-নীবি-বন্ধার্গল-
চ্ছিদাকরণ-কৌতুকী জয়তি যস্য বংশীধ্বনিঃ ॥ ১৬৮ ॥

mahendra-maṇi-maṇḍalī-mada-viḍambi-deha-dyutir
vrajendra-kula-candramāḥ sphurati ko 'pi navyo yuvā
sakhi sthira-kulāṅganā-nikara-nīvi-bandhārgala-
cchidākaraṇa-kautukī jayati yasya vaṁśī-dhvaniḥ

SYNONYMS

mahendra-maṇi—of jewels of the name *mahendra-maṇi*; *maṇḍalī*—of masses; *mada-viḍambi*—defeating the pride; *deha-dyutiḥ*—one whose bodily luster; *vrajendra-kula-candramāḥ*—the moon of the family of Vrajarāja (Nanda Mahārāja); *sphurati*—manifests; *kaḥ api*—some; *navyaḥ yuvā*—newly youthful person; *sakhi*—O my dear friend; *sthira*—steady; *kula-aṅganā*—of family ladies; *nikara*—of groups; *nīvi-bandha-argala*—of the impediments such as tightened dresses and belts; *chidā-karaṇa*—in causing the cutting; *kautukī*—very cunning; *jayati*—all glories; *yasya*—of whom; *vaṁśī-dhvaniḥ*—to the vibration of the flute.

TRANSLATION

" 'My dear friend, this newly youthful Lord Śrī Kṛṣṇa, the moon in the family of Nanda Mahārāja, is so beautiful that He defies the beauty of clusters of

valuable jewels. All glories to the vibration of His flute, for it is cunningly breaking the patience of chaste ladies by loosening their belts and tight dresses.'

PURPORT

This verse from *Lalita-mādhava* (1.49) is spoken by Lalitādevī to Rādhārāṇī.

TEXT 169

বলাদক্ষ্ণোর্লক্ষ্মীঃ কবলয়তি নব্যং কুবলয়ং
মুখোল্লাসঃ ফুল্লং কমলবনমুল্লঙ্ঘয়তি চ ।
দশাং কষ্টামষ্টাপদমপি নয়ত্যাঙ্গিকরুচি-
র্বিচিত্রং রাধায়াঃ কিমপি কিল রূপং বিলসতি ॥১৬৯॥

balād akṣṇor lakṣmīḥ kavalayati navyaṁ kuvalayaṁ
mukhollāsaḥ phullaṁ kamala-vanam ullaṅghayati ca
daśāṁ kaṣṭām aṣṭā-padam api nayaty āṅgika-rucir
vicitraṁ rādhāyāḥ kim api kila rūpaṁ vilasati

SYNONYMS

balāt—by force; *akṣṇoḥ*—of the two eyes; *lakṣmīḥ*—the beauty; *kavalayati*—devours; *navyam*—newly awakened; *kuvalayam*—lotus flower; *mukha-ullāsaḥ*—the beauty of the face; *phullam*—fructified; *kamala-vanam*—a forest of lotus flowers; *ullaṅghayati*—surpasses; *ca*—also; *daśām*—to a situation; *kaṣṭām*—painful; *aṣṭā-padam*—gold; *api*—even; *nayati*—brings; *āṅgika-ruciḥ*—the luster of the body; *vicitram*—wonderful; *rādhāyāḥ*—of Śrīmatī Rādhārāṇī; *kim api*—some; *kila*—certainly; *rūpam*—the beauty; *vilasati*—manifests.

TRANSLATION

" 'The beauty of Śrīmatī Rādhārāṇī's eyes forcibly devours the beauty of newly grown blue lotus flowers, and the beauty of Her face surpasses that of an entire forest of fully blossomed lotuses. Her bodily luster seems to place even gold in a painful situation. Thus the wonderful, unprecedented beauty of Śrīmatī Rādhārāṇī is awakening in Vṛndāvana.'

PURPORT

This verse is from *Vidagdha-mādhava* (1.32). It is spoken by Paurṇamāsī.

TEXT 170

বিধুরেতি দিবা বিরূপতাং
শতপত্রং বত শর্বরীমুখে ।

ইতি কেন সদাশ্রিয়োজ্জ্বলং
তুলনামর্হতি মৎপ্রিয়াননম্ ॥ ১৭০ ॥

vidhur eti divā virūpatāṁ
śata-patraṁ bata śarvarī-mukhe
iti kena sadā śriyojjvalaṁ
tulanām arhati mat-priyānanam

SYNONYMS

vidhuḥ—the moon; *eti*—becomes; *divā*—by daytime; *virūpatām*—faded away; *śata-patram*—the lotus flower; *bata*—alas; *śarvarī-mukhe*—in the beginning of evening; *iti*—thus; *kena*—with what; *sadā*—always; *śriyā-ujjvalam*—brilliant with beauty; *tulanām*—comparison; *arhati*—deserves; *mat*—of Me; *priyā*—of the dear one; *ānanam*—the face.

TRANSLATION

" 'Although the effulgence of the moon is brilliant initially at night, in the daytime it fades away. Similarly, although the lotus is beautiful during the daytime, at night it closes. But, O My friend, the face of My most dear Śrīmatī Rādhārāṇī is always bright and beautiful, both day and night. Therefore, to what can Her face be compared?'

PURPORT

This verse (*Vidagdha-mādhava* 5.20) is spoken by Śrī Kṛṣṇa to Madhumaṅgala.

TEXT 171

প্রমদরসতরঙ্গস্মেরগণ্ডস্থলায়াঃ
স্মরধনুরনুবন্ধিভ্রূলতা-লাস্যভাজঃ ।
মদকলচলভৃঙ্গীভ্রান্তিভঙ্গীং দধানো
হৃদয়মিদমদাঙ্ক্ষীৎ পক্ষ্মলাক্ষ্যাঃ কটাক্ষঃ ॥ ১৭১ ॥

pramada-rasa-taraṅga-smera-gaṇḍa-sthalāyāḥ
smara-dhanur anubandhi-bhrū-latā-lāsya-bhājaḥ
mada-kala-cala-bhṛṅgī-bhrānti-bhaṅgīṁ dadhāno
hṛdayam idam adāṅkṣīt pakṣmalākṣyāḥ kaṭākṣaḥ

SYNONYMS

pramada—of joy; *rasa-taraṅga*—by the continuous waves of the mellow; *smera*—mildly smiling; *gaṇḍa-sthalāyāḥ*—whose cheeks; *smara-dhanuḥ*—the bow of Cupid; *anubandhi*—related with; *bhrū-latā*—of the arched eyebrows; *lāsya*—dancing; *bhājaḥ*—of one who has; *mada-kala*—intoxicated; *cala*—unsteady; *bhṛṅgī-bhrānti*—the moving to and fro of bees; *bhaṅgīm*—the semblance of; *dadhānaḥ*—giving; *hṛdayam idam*—this heart; *adāṅkṣīt*—has bitten; *pakṣmala*—possessing exquisite eyelashes; *akṣyāḥ*—of whose two eyes; *kaṭa-akṣaḥ*—the glance.

TRANSLATION

" 'When Śrīmatī Rādhārāṇī smiles, waves of joy overtake Her cheeks, and Her arched eyebrows dance like the bow of Cupid. Her glance is so enchanting that it is like a dancing bumblebee, moving unsteadily due to intoxication. That bee has bitten the whorl of My heart.' "

PURPORT

This verse from *Vidagdha-mādhava* (2.51) is also spoken by Lord Kṛṣṇa.

TEXT 172

রায় কহে,—"তোমার কবিত্ব অমৃতের ধার।
দ্বিতীয় নাটকের কহ নান্দী-ব্যবহার ॥"১৭২ ॥

rāya kahe,——"tomāra kavitva amṛtera dhāra
dvitīya nāṭakera kaha nāndī-vyavahāra"

SYNONYMS

rāya kahe—Rāmānanda Rāya says; *tomāra*—you; *kavitva*—superexcellence in poetic presentation; *amṛtera dhāra*—a continuous shower of nectar; *dvitīya nāṭakera*—of the second drama; *kaha*—please tell; *nāndī-vyavahāra*—treatment of the introduction.

TRANSLATION

Having heard these verses recited by Rūpa Gosvāmī, Śrīla Rāmānanda Rāya said, "Your poetic expressions are like continuous showers of nectar. Kindly let me hear the introductory portion of the second drama."

TEXT 173

রূপ কহে,—"কাহাঁ তুমি সূর্যোপম ভাস।
মুঞি কোন্ ক্ষুদ্র,—যেন খদ্যোত-প্রকাশ ॥ ১৭৩ ॥

rūpa kahe,——"kāhāṅ tumi sūryopama bhāsa
muñi kon kṣudra,——yena khadyota-prakāśa

SYNONYMS

rūpa kahe—Rūpa Gosvāmī says; *kāhāṅ*—where; *tumi*—you; *sūrya-upama*—like the sun; *bhāsa*—brilliance; *muñi*—I; *kon*—some; *kṣudra*—insignificant; *yena*—exactly like; *khadyota-prakāśa*—the brilliance of the glowworm.

TRANSLATION

Śrīla Rūpa Gosvāmī said, "In your presence, which is just like brilliant sunshine, I am as insignificant as the light of a glowworm.

TEXT 174

তোমার আগে ধার্ষ্ট্য এই মুখ-ব্যাদান।"
এত বলি' নান্দী-শ্লোক করিলা ব্যাখ্যান ॥ ১৭৪ ॥

tomāra āge dhārṣṭya ei mukha-vyādāna"
eta bali' nāndī-śloka karilā vyākhyāna

SYNONYMS

tomāra āge—before you; *dhārṣṭya*—impudence; *ei*—this; *mukha-vyādāna*—simply opening the mouth; *eta bali'*—saying this; *nāndī-śloka*—the introductory verses; *karilā vyākhyāna*—explained.

TRANSLATION

"It is even impudent for me to open my mouth before you." Then, having said this, he recited the introductory verse of Lalita-mādhava.

TEXT 175

সুররিপুসুদৃশামুরোজকোকা-
ন্মুখকমলানি চ খেদয়ন্নখণ্ডঃ।
চিরমখিলসুহৃচ্চকোরনন্দী
দিশতু মুকুন্দযশঃশশী মুদং বঃ ॥ ১৭৫ ॥

sura-ripu-sudṛśām uroja-kokān
mukha-kamalāni ca khedayann akhaṇḍaḥ
ciram akhila-suhṛc-cakora-nandī
diśatu mukunda-yaśaḥ-śaśī mudaṁ vaḥ

SYNONYMS

sura-ripu—of the enemies of the demigods; *sudṛśām*—of the wives; *uroja*—the breasts; *kokān*—like birds known as *cakravāka* birds; *mukha*—faces;

kamalāni—like lotuses; *ca*—also; *khedayan*—distressing; *akhaṇḍaḥ*—completely without distortion; *ciram*—for a long time; *akhila*—of all; *suhṛt*—the friend; *cakora-nandī*—pleasing to the *cakora* birds; *diśatu*—let it give; *mukunda*—of Śrī Kṛṣṇa; *yaśaḥ*—the glories; *śaśī*—like the moon; *mudam*—pleasure; *vaḥ*—to all of you.

TRANSLATION

" 'The beautiful moonlike glories of Mukunda give distress to the lotuslike faces of the wives of the demons and to their raised breasts, which are like gleaming cakravāka birds. Those glories, however, are pleasing to all His devotees, who are like cakora birds. May those glories forever give pleasure to you all.' "

PURPORT

This is the first verse of Act One of *Lalita-mādhava.*

TEXT 176

'দ্বিতীয় নান্দী কহ দেখি ?'—রায় পুছিলা ।
সঙ্কোচ পাঞা রূপ পড়িতে লাগিলা ॥ ১৭৬ ॥

'dvitīya nāndī kaha dekhi?'——rāya puchilā
saṅkoca pāñā rūpa paḍite lāgilā

SYNONYMS

dvitīya nāndī—the second introductory verse; *kaha*—recite; *dekhi*—so that we can see; *rāya puchilā*—Śrīla Rāmānanda Rāya again inquired; *saṅkoca pāñā*—becoming a little hesitant; *rūpa*—Śrīla Rūpa Gosvāmī; *paḍite lāgilā*—began to read.

TRANSLATION

When Śrīla Rāmānanda Rāya further inquired about the second introductory verse, Śrīla Rūpa Gosvāmī was somewhat hesitant, but nevertheless he began to read.

TEXT 177

নিজপ্রণয়িতাং সুধামুদয়মাপ্নুবন্ যঃ ক্ষিতৌ
কিরত্যলমুরীকৃতদ্বিজকুলাধিরাজস্থিতিঃ ।
স লুঞ্চিত-তমস্ততির্মম শচীসুতাখ্যঃ শশী
বশীকৃতজগন্মনাঃ কিমপি শর্ম বিন্যস্তু ॥ ১৭৭ ॥

nija-praṇayitāṁ sudhām udayam āpnuvan yaḥ kṣitau
kiraty alam urīkṛta-dvija-kulādhirāja-sthitiḥ
sa luñcita-tamas-tatir mama śacī-sutākhyaḥ śaśī
vaśīkṛta-jagan-manāḥ kim api śarma vinyasyatu

SYNONYMS

nija-praṇayitām—own devotional love; *sudhām*—the nectar; *udayam*—appearance; *āpnuvan*—obtaining; *yaḥ*—one who; *kṣitau*—on the surface of the world; *kirati*—expands; *alam*—extensively; *urī-kṛta*—accepted; *dvija-kula-adhirāja-sthitiḥ*—the situation of the most exalted of the *brāhmaṇa* community; *saḥ*—He; *luñcita*—driven away; *tamaḥ*—of darkness; *tatiḥ*—mass; *mama*—my; *śacī-suta-ākhyaḥ*—known as Śacīnandana, the son of mother Śacī; *śaśī*—the moon; *vaśī-kṛta*—subdued; *jagat-manāḥ*—the minds of the whole world; *kim api*—somehow; *śarma*—auspiciousness; *vinyasyatu*—let it be bestowed.

TRANSLATION

" 'The moonlike Supreme Personality of Godhead, who is known as the son of mother Śacī, has now appeared on earth to spread devotional love of Himself. He is emperor of the brāhmaṇa community. He can drive away all the darkness of ignorance and control the mind of everyone in the world. May that rising moon bestow upon us all good fortune.' "

PURPORT

This is the third verse of Act One of *Vidagdha-mādhava*.

TEXT 178

শুনিয়া প্রভুর যদি অন্তরে উল্লাস ।
বাহিরে কহেন কিছু করি' রোষাভাস ॥ ১৭৮ ॥

śuniyā prabhura yadi antare ullāsa
bāhire kahena kichu kari' roṣābhāsa

SYNONYMS

śuniyā—hearing this; *prabhura*—of Lord Śrī Caitanya Mahāprabhu; *yadi*—although; *antare*—within; *ullāsa*—great jubilation; *bāhire*—externally; *kahena*—says; *kichu*—something; *kari'*—making; *roṣa-ābhāsa*—as if angry.

TRANSLATION

Although Śrī Caitanya Mahāprabhu was inwardly greatly pleased when He heard this verse, externally He spoke as if angry.

TEXT 179

**"কাঁহা তোমার কৃষ্ণরসকাব্য-সুধাসিন্ধু।
তার মধ্যে মিথ্যা কেনে স্তুতি-ক্ষারবিন্দু" ॥ ১৭৯ ॥**

*kāṅhā tomāra kṛṣṇa-rasa-kāvya-sudhā-sindhu
tāra madhye mithyā kene stuti-kṣāra-bindu*

SYNONYMS

kāṅhā—where; *tomāra*—your; *kṛṣṇa-rasa-kāvya*—of exalted poetry concerning the mellows of Lord Kṛṣṇa's pastimes; *sudhā-sindhu*—ocean of the nectar; *tāra madhye*—within that; *mithyā*—false; *kene*—why; *stuti*—prayer; *kṣāra-bindu*—like a drop of alkali.

TRANSLATION

"Your exalted poetic descriptions of the mellows of Lord Kṛṣṇa's pastimes are like an ocean of nectar. But why have you put in a false prayer about Me? It is like a drop of detestful alkali."

TEXT 180

**রায় কহে,—"রূপের কাব্য অমৃতের পূর।
তার মধ্যে এক বিন্দু দিয়াছে কর্পূর ॥"১৮০ ॥**

*rāya kahe,——"rūpera kāvya amṛtera pūra
tāra madhye eka bindu diyāche karpūra"*

SYNONYMS

rāya kahe—Śrīla Rāmānanda Rāya says; *rūpera kāvya*—the poetic expression of Śrīla Rūpa Gosvāmī; *amṛtera pūra*—filled with all nectar; *tāra madhye*—within that; *eka bindu*—one drop; *diyāche*—he has given; *karpūra*—camphor.

TRANSLATION

Śrīla Rāmānanda Rāya objected, "It is not alkali at all. It is a particle of camphor he has put into the nectar of his exalted poetic expression."

TEXT 181

**প্রভু কহে,—"রায়, তোমার ইহাতে উল্লাস।
শুনিতেই লজ্জা, লোকে করে উপহাস ॥"১৮১ ॥**

prabhu kahe,——"rāya, tomāra ihāte ullāsa
śunitei lajjā, loke kare upahāsa"

SYNONYMS

prabhu kahe—Śrī Caitanya Mahāprabhu says; *rāya*—Rāmānanda Rāya; *tomāra*—your; *ihāte*—in this; *ullāsa*—jubilation; *śunitei*—to hear; *lajjā*—ashamed; *loke*—the people in general; *kare*—do; *upahāsa*—joking.

TRANSLATION

Śrī Caitanya Mahāprabhu said, "My dear Rāmānanda Rāya, you are jubilant at hearing these poetic expressions, but I am ashamed to hear them, for people in general will joke about the subject of this verse."

TEXT 182

রায় কহে,—"লোকের সুখ ইহার শ্রবণে ।
অভীষ্ট-দেবের স্মৃতি মঙ্গলাচরণে ॥"১৮২ ॥

rāya kahe,——"lokera sukha ihāra śravaṇe
abhīṣṭa-devera smṛti maṅgalācaraṇe"

SYNONYMS

rāya kahe—Rāmānanda Rāya says; *lokera*—of the people in general; *sukha*—happiness; *ihāra śravaṇe*—in hearing such poetic expressions; *abhīṣṭa-devera*—of the worshipable Deity; *smṛti*—remembrance; *maṅgalācaraṇe*—in the performance of auspiciousness in the beginning.

TRANSLATION

Rāmānanda Rāya said, "Instead of joking, people in general will feel great pleasure in hearing such poetry, for the initial remembrance of the worshipable Deity invokes good fortune."

TEXT 183

রায় কহে,—"কোন্ অঙ্গে পাত্রের প্রবেশ ?"
তবে রূপ-গোসাঞি কহে তাহার বিশেষ ॥ ১৮৩ ॥

rāya kahe,——"kon aṅge pātrera praveśa?"
tabe rūpa-gosāñi kahe tāhāra viśeṣa

SYNONYMS

rāya kahe—Rāmānanda Rāya says; *kon*—what; *aṅge*—subdivision of style; *pātrera praveśa*—the entrance of the players; *tabe*—at that time; *rūpa-gosāñi*—Śrīla Rūpa Gosvāmī; *kahe*—continues to speak; *tāhāra viśeṣa*—specifically on this matter.

TRANSLATION

Rāmānanda Rāya inquired, "By which subdivision of style do the players enter?" Rūpa Gosvāmī then began to speak specifically about this subject.

TEXT 184

নটতা কিরাতরাজং নিহত্য রঙ্গস্থলে কলানিধিনা।
সময়ে তেন বিধেয়ং গুণবতি তারাকরগ্রহণম্ ॥ ১৮৪ ॥

naṭatā kirāta-rājaṁ
nihatya raṅga-sthale kalā-nidhinā
samaye tena vidheyaṁ
guṇavati tārā-kara-grahaṇam

SYNONYMS

naṭatā—dancing on the stage; *kirāta-rājam*—the ruler of the *kirāta* (uncivilized men), Kaṁsa; *nihatya*—killing; *raṅga-sthale*—on the stage; *kalā-nidhinā*—the master of all arts; *samaye*—at the time; *tena*—by Him; *vidheyam*—to be done; *guṇa-vati*—at the qualified moment; *tārā-kara*—of the hand of Tārā (Rādhā); *grahaṇam*—the acceptance.

TRANSLATION

" 'While dancing on the stage after having killed the ruler of uncivilized men [Kaṁsa], Lord Kṛṣṇa, master of all arts, will at the proper time accept the hand of Śrīmatī Rādhārāṇī, who is qualified with all transcendental attributes.'
(Lalita-mādhava 1.11)

TEXT 185

'উদ্‌ঘাত্যক' নাম এই 'আমুখ'—'বীথী' অঙ্গ।
তোমার আগে কহি—ইহা ধার্ষ্ট্যের তরঙ্গ ॥ ১৮৫ ॥

'udghātyaka' nāma ei 'āmukha'——'vīthī' aṅga
tomāra āge kahi——ihā dhārṣṭyera taraṅga

SYNONYMS

'udghātyaka' nāma—a dancing appearance of the player, technically known as *udghātyaka; ei āmukha*—this is the introduction; *vīthī aṅga*—the part is called *vīthī; tomāra āge*—before you; *kahi*—I say; *ihā*—this; *dhārṣṭyera taraṅga*—a wave of impudence.

TRANSLATION

"This introduction is technically called udghātyaka, and the whole scene is called vīthī. You are so expert in dramatic expression that each of my statements before you is like a wave from an ocean of impudence.

PURPORT

In this connection Śrīla Bhaktisiddhānta Sarasvatī Ṭhākura again quotes the following verse from the *Sāhitya-darpaṇa* (6.288):

udghātyakaḥ kathodghātaḥ
prayogātiśayas tathā
pravartakāvalagite
pañca prastāvanā-bhidāḥ

Thus the technical names for the five kinds of introductory scenes of the drama are listed as *udghātyaka, kathodghāta, prayogātiśaya, pravartaka* and *avalagita*. When Śrīla Rāmānanda Rāya inquired which of these five Śrīla Rūpa Gosvāmī had used to accomplish the technical introduction to his drama *Lalita-mādhava*, Rūpa Gosvāmī replied that he had used the introduction technically called *udghātyaka*. According to *Bhāratī-vṛtti,* three technical terms used are *prarocanā, vīthī* and *prahasanā*. Thus Rūpa Gosvāmī also mentioned *vīthī,* which is a technical term for a certain type of expression. According to the *Sāhitya-darpaṇa* (6.520):

vīthyām eko bhaved aṅkaḥ
kaścid eko 'tra kalpyate
ākāśa-bhāṣitair uktaiś
citrāṁ pratyuktim āśritaḥ

The *vīthī* beginning of a drama consists of only one scene. In that scene, one of the heroes enters the stage, and by means of opposing statements uttered by a voice from the sky (offstage), he introduces the abundant conjugal mellow and other mellows to some degree. In the course of the introduction, all the seeds of the play are planted. This introduction is called *udghātyaka* because the player dances on the stage. This term also indicates that the full moon enters the stage. In this case, when the word *naṭatā* ("dancing on the stage") is linked with the moon, its meaning is obscure, but because the meaning becomes very clear when the word *naṭatā* is linked with Kṛṣṇa, this type of introduction is called *udghātyaka.*

Śrīla Rāmānanda Rāya used highly technical terms when he discussed this with Śrīla Rūpa Gosvāmī. Rūpa Gosvāmī admitted that Śrīla Rāmānanda Rāya was a greatly learned scholar of bona fide dramatic composition. Thus although Śrīla Rūpa Gosvāmī was quite fit to answer Śrīla Rāmānanda Rāya's questions, due to his Vaiṣṇava humility he admitted that his words were impudent. Actually both Rūpa Gosvāmī and Rāmānanda Rāya were scholarly experts in composing poetry and presenting it strictly according to the *Sāhitya-darpaṇa* and other Vedic literatures.

TEXT 186

"পদানি ত্বগতার্থানি তদর্থগতয়ে নরাঃ ।
যোজয়ন্তি পদৈরন্যৈঃ স উদ্ঘাত্যক উচ্যতে ॥"১৮৬ ॥

padāni tv agatārthāni
tad-artha-gataye narāḥ
yojayanti padair anyaiḥ
sa udghātyaka ucyate

SYNONYMS

padāni—words; *tu*—but; *agata-arthāni*—having an unclear meaning; *tat*—that; *artha-gataye*—to understand the meaning; *narāḥ*—men; *yojayanti*—join; *padaiḥ*—with words; *anyaiḥ*—other; *saḥ*—that; *udghātyakaḥ*—*udghātyaka*; *ucyate*—is called.

TRANSLATION

" 'To explain an unclear word, men generally join it with other words. Such an attempt is called udghātyaka.' "

PURPORT

This verse is quoted from the *Sāhitya-darpaṇa* (6.289).

TEXT 187

রায় কহে,—"কহ আগে অঙ্গের বিশেষ" ।
শ্রীরূপ কহেন কিছু সংক্ষেপ-উদ্দেশ ॥ ১৮৭ ॥

rāya kahe,——"kaha āge aṅgera viśeṣa"
śrī-rūpa kahena kichu saṅkṣepa-uddeśa

SYNONYMS

rāya kahe—Śrīla Rāmānanda Rāya says; *kaha*—please tell me; *āge*—further; *aṅgera viśeṣa*—particular portions; *śrī-rūpa kahena*—Śrīla Rūpa Gosvāmī says; *kichu*—something; *saṅkṣepa*—in brief; *uddeśa*—reference.

TRANSLATION

When Rāmānanda Rāya requested Śrīla Rūpa Gosvāmī to speak further about various portions of the play, Śrīla Rūpa Gosvāmī briefly quoted his Lalita-mādhava.

TEXT 188

হরিমুদ্দিশতে রজোভরঃ, পুরতঃ সঙ্গময়ত্যমুং তমঃ ।
ব্রজবামদৃশাং ন পদ্ধতিঃ, প্রকটা সর্বদৃশঃ শ্রুতেরপি ॥ ১৮৮॥

harim uddiśate rajo-bharaḥ
purataḥ saṅgamayaty amuṁ tamaḥ
vrajavāma-dṛśāṁ na paddhatiḥ
prakaṭā sarva-dṛśaḥ śruter api

SYNONYMS

harim—Kṛṣṇa; *uddiśate*—it indicates; *rajaḥ-bharaḥ*—dust from the cows; *purataḥ*—in front; *saṅgamayati*—causes to meet; *amum*—Kṛṣṇa; *tamaḥ*—the darkness; *vrajavāma-dṛśām*—of the damsels of Vṛndāvana; *na*—not; *paddhatiḥ*—the course of activities; *prakaṭā*—manifested; *sarva-dṛśaḥ*—who know everything; *śruteḥ*—of the *Vedas*; *api*—as well as.

TRANSLATION

" 'The dust from cows and calves on the road creates a kind of darkness indicating that Kṛṣṇa is returning home from the pasture. Also, the darkness of evening provokes the gopīs to meet Kṛṣṇa. Thus the pastimes of Kṛṣṇa and the gopīs are covered by a kind of transcendental darkness and are therefore impossible for ordinary scholars of the Vedas to see.'

PURPORT

This verse from the *Lalita-mādhava* (1.23) is spoken by Paurṇamāsī in a conversation with Gārgī.

Kṛṣṇa stated in *Bhagavad-gītā, traiguṇya-viṣayā vedā nistraiguṇyo bhavārjuna.* Thus He advised Arjuna to rise above the modes of material nature, for the entire Vedic system is filled with descriptions involving *sattva-guṇa, rajo-guṇa* and *tamo-guṇa.* People are generally covered by the quality of *rajo-guṇa* and are therefore unable to understand the pastimes of Kṛṣṇa with the *gopīs* of Vraja. Moreover, the quality of *tamo-guṇa* further disturbs their understanding. In Vṛndāvana, however, although Kṛṣṇa is covered by the hazy darkness of the dust, the *gopīs* can nevertheless understand that within the dust storm is Kṛṣṇa. Because they are His topmost devotees, they can perceive His hand in everything. Thus even in the dark or in a hazy storm of dust, devotees can understand what Kṛṣṇa is doing. The purport of this verse is that Kṛṣṇa is never lost, under any circumstances, to the vision of exalted devotees like the *gopīs*.

TEXT 189

হ্রিয়মবগৃহ্য গৃহেভ্যঃ কর্ষতি রাধাং বনায় যা নিপুণা ।
সা জয়তি নিস্থষ্টার্থা বরবংশজকাকলী দূতী ॥ ১৮৯ ॥

hriyam avagṛhya gṛhebhyaḥ karṣati
rādhāṁ vanāya yā nipuṇā
sā jayati nisṛṣṭārthā
vara-vaṁśaja-kākalī dūtī

SYNONYMS

hriyam—bashfulness; *avagṛhya*—impeding; *gṛhebhyaḥ*—from private houses; *karṣati*—attracts; *rādhām*—Śrīmatī Rādhārāṇī; *vanāya*—to the forest; *yā*—which; *nipuṇā*—being expert; *sā*—that; *jayati*—let it be glorified; *nisṛṣṭa-arthā*—authorized; *vara-vaṁśaja*—of the bamboo flute; *kākalī*—the sweet tone; *dūtī*—the messenger.

TRANSLATION

" 'May the sweet sound of Lord Kṛṣṇa's flute, His authorized messenger, be glorified, for it expertly releases Śrīmatī Rādhārāṇī from Her shyness and attracts Her from Her home to the forest.'

PURPORT

This verse from *Lalita-mādhava* (1.24) is spoken by Gārgī, the daughter of Gargamuni.

TEXT 190

সহচরি নিরাতঙ্কঃ কোঽয়ং যুবা মুদিরদ্যুতি-
র্ব্রজভুবি কুতঃ প্রাপ্তো মাদ্যন্মতঙ্গজবিভ্রমঃ ।
অহহ চটুলৈরুৎসর্পদ্ভির্দৃগঞ্চলতস্করৈ-
র্মম ধৃতিধনং চেতঃকোষাদ্বিলুণ্ঠয়তীহ যঃ ॥ ১৯০ ॥

sahacari nirātaṅkaḥ ko 'yaṁ yuvā mudira-dyutir
vraja-bhuvi kutaḥ prāpto mādyan mataṅgaja-vibhramaḥ
ahaha caṭulair utsarpadbhir dṛg-añcala-taskarair
mama dhṛti-dhanaṁ cetaḥ-koṣād viluṇṭhayatīha yaḥ

SYNONYMS

saha-cari—O My dear friend; *nirātaṅkaḥ*—without fear; *kaḥ*—who; *ayam*—this; *yuvā*—young man; *mudira-dyutiḥ*—as effulgent as a lightning cloud; *vraja-bhuvi*—in the land of Vraja, Vṛndāvana; *kutaḥ*—from where; *prāptaḥ*—obtained; *mādyan*—being intoxicated; *mataṅgaja*—like an elephant; *vibhramaḥ*—whose pastimes; *ahaha*—alas; *caṭulaiḥ*—very unsteady; *utsarpadbhiḥ*—with wanderings in all directions; *dṛk-añcala-taskaraiḥ*—by the glances of His eyes like thieves; *mama*—My; *dhṛti-dhanam*—the treasure of My patience; *cetaḥ*—of the heart; *koṣāt*—from the core; *viluṇṭhayati*—plunders; *iha*—here in Vṛndāvana; *yaḥ*—the person who.

TRANSLATION

" 'My dear friend, who is this fearless young man? He is as bright as a lightning cloud, and He wanders in His pastimes like a maddened elephant. From where has He come to Vṛndāvana? Alas, by His restless movements and attractive glances He is plundering from the vault of My heart the treasure of My patience.'

PURPORT

This verse (*Lalita-mādhava* 2.11) is spoken by Śrīmatī Rādhārāṇī to Her friend Lalitādevī.

TEXT 191

বিহারস্থরদীর্ঘিকা মম মনঃকরীন্দ্রস্য যা
বিলোচন-চকোরয়োঃ শরদমন্দচন্দ্রপ্রভা ।
উরোঽম্বরতটস্য চাভরণচারুতারাবলী
ময়োন্নতমনোরথৈরিয়মলম্ভি সা রাধিকা ॥" ১৯১ ॥

vihāra-sura-dīrghikā mama manaḥ-karīndrasya yā
vilocana-cakorayoḥ śarad-amanda-candra-prabhā
uro 'mbara-taṭasya cābharaṇa-cāru-tārāvalī
mayonnata-manorathair iyam alambhi sā rādhikā

SYNONYMS

vihāra-sura-dīrghikā—the Ganges flowing in the heavenly planets; *mama*—My; *manaḥ-kari-indrasya*—of the elephant-like mind; *yā*—She who; *vilocana*—

glancing; *cakorayoḥ*—of My two eyes, which are like *cakora* birds; *śarat-amanda-candra-prabhā*—like the shine of the full moon in the autumn; *uraḥ*—of My chest; *ambara*—like the sky; *taṭasya*—on the edge; *ca*—also; *ābharaṇa*—ornaments; *cāru*—beautiful; *tārā-āvalī*—like the stars; *mayā*—by Me; *unnata*—highly elevated; *manorathaiḥ*—by mental desires; *iyam*—this; *alambhi*—attained; *sā*—She; *rādhikā*—Śrīmatī Rādhārāṇī.

TRANSLATION

" 'Śrīmatī Rādhārāṇī is the Ganges in which the elephant of My mind enjoys pastimes. She is the shining of the full autumn moon for the cakora birds of My eyes. She is the dazzling ornament, the bright and beautiful arrangement of stars, on the border of the sky of My chest. Now today I have gained Śrīmatī Rādhārāṇī because of the highly elevated state of My mind.' "

PURPORT

This verse from *Lalita-mādhava* (2.10) expresses the thoughts of Lord Kṛṣṇa in relation with Rādhārāṇī.

TEXT 192

এত শুনি' রায় কহে প্রভুর চরণে ।
রূপের কবিত্ব প্রশংসি' সহস্র-বদনে ॥ ১৯২ ॥

eta śuni' rāya kahe prabhura caraṇe
rūpera kavitva praśaṁsi' sahasra-vadane

SYNONYMS

eta śuni'—hearing this; *rāya*—Rāmānanda Rāya; *kahe*—says; *prabhura caraṇe*—at the lotus feet of Śrī Caitanya Mahāprabhu; *rūpera*—of Rūpa Gosvāmī; *kavitva*—poetic art; *praśaṁsi'*—glorifying; *sahasra-vadane*—as if with a thousand mouths.

TRANSLATION

After hearing this, Śrīla Rāmānanda Rāya submitted at the lotus feet of Śrī Caitanya Mahāprabhu the superexcellence of Śrīla Rūpa Gosvāmī's poetic expression and began to praise it as if he had thousands of mouths.

TEXT 193

"কবিত্ব না হয় এই অমৃতের ধার ।
নাটক-লক্ষণ সব সিদ্ধান্তের সার ॥ ১৯৩ ॥

"kavitva nā haya ei amṛtera dhāra
nāṭaka-lakṣaṇa saba siddhāntera sāra

SYNONYMS

kavitva—poetic art; *nā haya*—is not; *ei*—this; *amṛtera dhāra*—constant shower of nectar; *nāṭaka*—a drama; *lakṣana*—appearing as; *saba*—all; *siddhāntera sāra*—essences of ultimate realization.

TRANSLATION

Śrīla Rāmānanda Rāya said, "This is not a poetic presentation; it is a continuous shower of nectar. Indeed, it is the essence of all ultimate realizations, appearing in the form of plays.

TEXT 194

প্রেম-পরিপাটী এই অদ্ভুত বর্ণন ।
শুনি' চিত্ত-কর্ণের হয় আনন্দ-ঘূর্ণন ॥ ১৯৪ ॥

prema-paripāṭī ei adbhuta varṇana
śuni' citta-karṇera haya ānanda-ghūrṇana

SYNONYMS

prema-paripāṭī—a first-class arrangement to express loving affairs; *ei*—this; *adbhuta varṇana*—wonderful description; *śuni'*—hearing; *citta-karṇera*—of the heart and the ear; *haya*—there is; *ānanda-ghūrṇana*—a whirlpool of transcendental bliss.

TRANSLATION

"The wonderful descriptions of Rūpa Gosvāmī are superb arrangements to express loving affairs. Hearing them will plunge the heart and ears of everyone into a whirlpool of transcendental bliss.

TEXT 195

"কিং কাব্যেন কবেস্তস্য কিং কাণ্ডেন ধনুষ্মতঃ ।
পরস্য হৃদয়ে লগ্নং ন ঘূর্ণয়তি যচ্ছিরঃ ॥" ১৯৫ ॥

kiṁ kāvyena kaves tasya
kiṁ kāṇḍena dhanuṣ-mataḥ
parasya hṛdaye lagnaṁ
na ghūrṇayati yac chiraḥ

SYNONYMS

kim—what use; *kāvyena*—with poetry; *kaveḥ*—of the poet; *tasya*—that; *kim*—what use; *kāṇḍena*—with the arrow; *dhanuḥ-mataḥ*—of the bowman; *parasya*—of another; *hṛdaye*—in the heart; *lagnam*—penetrating; *na ghūrṇayati*—does not cause to roll about; *yat*—which; *śiraḥ*—the head.

TRANSLATION

" 'What is the use of a bowman's arrow or a poet's poetry if they penetrate the heart but do not cause the head to spin?'

TEXT 196

তোমার শক্তি বিনা জীবের নহে এই বাণী ।
তুমি শক্তি দিয়া কহাও,—হেন অনুমানি ॥ ১৯৬ ॥

tomāra śakti vinā jīvera nahe ei vāṇī
tumi śakti diyā kahāo,——hena anumāni"

SYNONYMS

tomāra śakti vinā—without Your special power; *jīvera*—of an ordinary living being; *nahe*—there is not; *ei vāṇī*—these words; *tumi*—You; *śakti diyā*—giving power; *kahāo*—make him say; *hena*—such; *anumāni*—I guess.

TRANSLATION

"Without Your mercy such poetic expressions would be impossible for an ordinary living being to write. My guess is that You have given him the power."

TEXT 197

প্রভু কহে,– "প্রয়াগে ইহার হইল মিলন ।
ইহার গুণে ইহাতে আমার তুষ্ট হৈল মন ॥ ১৯৭ ॥

prabhu kahe,——"prayāge ihāra ha-ila milana
ihāra guṇe ihāte āmāra tuṣṭa haila mana

SYNONYMS

prabhu kahe—Lord Śrī Caitanya Mahāprabhu says; *prayāge*—at Prayāga; *ihāra*—of him; *ha-ila*—there was; *milana*—meeting; *ihāra guṇe*—by his transcendental qualities; *ihāte*—in him; *āmāra*—of Me; *tuṣṭa*—satisfied; *haila*—became; *mana*—the mind.

TRANSLATION

Śrī Caitanya Mahāprabhu replied, "I met Śrīla Rūpa Gosvāmī at Prayāga. He attracted and satisfied Me because of his qualities."

PURPORT

The Supreme Personality of Godhead is not partial to some and neutral to others. One can actually draw the attention of the Supreme Personality of Godhead by service. Then one is further empowered by the Lord to act in such a way that everyone can appreciate his service. This is confirmed in *Bhagavad-gītā* (4.11): *ye yathā māṁ prapadyante tāṁs tathaiva bhajāmy aham.* Kṛṣṇa is responsive. If one tries to render his best service to the Lord, the Lord gives him the power to do so. Kṛṣṇa also says in *Bhagavad-gītā*:

teṣāṁ satata-yuktānāṁ
bhajatāṁ prīti-pūrvakam
dadāmi buddhi-yogaṁ taṁ
yena mām upayānti te

"To those who are constantly devoted and worship Me with love, I give the understanding by which they can come to Me." (Bg. 10.10) Śrī Caitanya Mahāprabhu bestowed His special favor upon Śrīla Rūpa Gosvāmī because Rūpa Gosvāmī wanted to serve the Lord to the best of his ability. Such is the reciprocation between the devotee and the Lord in the discharge of devotional duties.

TEXT 198

মধুর প্রসন্ন ইহার কাব্য সালঙ্কার ।
ঐছে কবিত্ব বিনু নহে রসের প্রচার ॥ ১৯৮ ॥

madhura prasanna ihāra kāvya sālaṅkāra
aiche kavitva vinu nahe rasera pracāra

SYNONYMS

madhura—sweet; *prasanna*—pleasing; *ihāra*—his; *kāvya*—poetry; *sa-alaṅkāra*—with metaphors and other ornaments; *aiche*—such as that; *kavitva*—poetic qualifications; *vinu*—without; *nahe*—there is not; *rasera*—of mellows; *pracāra*—preaching.

TRANSLATION

Śrī Caitanya Mahāprabhu praised the metaphors and other literary ornaments of Śrīla Rūpa Gosvāmī's transcendental poetry. Without such poetic attributes, He said, there is no possibility of preaching transcendental mellows.

TEXT 199

সবে কৃপা করি' ইঁহারে দেহ' এই বর।
ব্রজলীলা-প্রেমরস যেন বর্ণে নিরন্তর ॥ ১৯৯ ॥

sabe kṛpā kari' iṅhāre deha' ei vara
vraja-līlā-prema-rasa yena varṇe nirantara

SYNONYMS

sabe—all of you; *kṛpā kari'*—showing your mercy; *iṅhāre*—unto Śrīla Rūpa Gosvāmī; *deha'*—give; *ei vara*—this benediction; *vraja-līlā-prema-rasa*—transcendental mellows of the pastimes of Vṛndāvana; *yena*—so that; *varṇe*—he can describe; *nirantara*—without cessation.

TRANSLATION

Śrī Caitanya Mahāprabhu requested all His personal associates to bless Rūpa Gosvāmī so that he might continuously describe the pastimes of Vṛndāvana, which are full of emotional love of Godhead.

TEXT 200

ইঁহার যে জ্যেষ্ঠভ্রাতা, নাম—'সনাতন'।
পৃথিবীতে বিজ্ঞবর নাহি তাঁর সম ॥ ২০০ ॥

iṅhāra ye jyeṣṭha-bhrātā, nāma——'sanātana'
pṛthivīte vijña-vara nāhi tāṅra sama

SYNONYMS

iṅhāra—of Śrīla Rūpa Gosvāmī; *ye*—who; *jyeṣṭha-bhrātā*—the elder brother; *nāma*—named; *sanātana*—Sanātana Gosvāmī; *pṛthivīte*—on the surface of the world; *vijña-vara*—most learned; *nāhi*—there is none; *tāṅra sama*—equal to him.

TRANSLATION

Śrī Caitanya Mahāprabhu said, "Śrīla Rūpa Gosvāmī's elder brother, whose name is Sanātana Gosvāmī, is such a wise and learned scholar that no one is equal to him."

TEXT 201

তোমার যৈছে বিষয়ত্যাগ, তৈছে তাঁর রীতি।
দৈন্য-বৈরাগ্য-পাণ্ডিত্যের তাঁহাতেই স্থিতি ॥ ২০১ ॥

tomāra yaiche viṣaya-tyāga, taiche tāṅra rīti
dainya-vairāgya-pāṇḍityera tāṅhātei sthiti

SYNONYMS

tomāra—your; *yaiche*—just as; *viṣaya-tyāga*—renunciation of material connections; *taiche*—similarly; *tāṅra rīti*—his manner of activity; *dainya*—humbleness; *vairāgya*—renunciation; *pāṇḍityera*—of learned scholarship; *tāṅhātei*—in him; *sthiti*—existing.

TRANSLATION

Śrī Caitanya Mahāprabhu told Rāmānanda Rāya, "Sanātana Gosvāmī's renunciation of material connections is just like yours. Humility, renunciation and excellent learning exist in him simultaneously.

TEXT 202

এই দুই ভাইয়ে আমি পাঠাইলুঁ বৃন্দাবনে ।
শক্তি দিয়া ভক্তিশাস্ত্র করিতে প্রবর্তনে ॥ ২০২ ॥

ei dui bhāiye āmi pāṭhāiluṅ vṛndāvane
śakti diyā bhakti-śāstra karite pravartane

SYNONYMS

ei—these; *dui*—two; *bhāiye*—brothers; *āmi*—I; *pāṭhāiluṅ*—sent; *vṛndāvane*—to Vṛndāvana; *śakti diyā*—empowering them; *bhakti-śāstra*—transcendental literature regarding devotional service; *karite*—to do; *pravartane*—establishing.

TRANSLATION

"I empowered both of these brothers to go to Vṛndāvana to expand the literature of bhakti."

PURPORT

Śrī Caitanya Mahāprabhu informed Śrīla Rāmānanda Rāya that he and Sanātana Gosvāmī had engaged equally in devotional service after giving up all relationships with material activity. Such renunciation is a symptom of an unalloyed devotee engaged in the service of the Lord with no tinge of material contamination. According to Śrī Caitanya Mahāprabhu, this is the position of *tṛṇād api sunīcena taror api sahiṣṇunā.* A pure devotee, free from the reactions of the material modes of nature, executes devotional service with tolerance like that of a tree. He also feels humbler than the grass. Such a devotee, who is called *niṣkiñcana,* or free from all material possessions, is always absorbed in emotional love of Godhead. He is reluctant to perform any kind of sense gratification. In other words, such a devotee is free from all material bondage, but he engages in Kṛṣṇa conscious activities. Such expert devotional service is performed without hypocrisy. Humility, renunciation and learned scholarship were combined in Sanātana Gosvāmī, the ideal pure devotee, who was on the same level of understanding as Śrīla Rāmānanda Rāya. Like Rāmānanda Rāya, Sanātana Gosvāmī was a fully cognizant expert in the conclusions of devotional service and was therefore able to describe such transcendental knowledge.

TEXT 203

রায় কহে,—"ঈশ্বর তুমি যে চাহ করিতে ।
কাষ্ঠের পুতলী তুমি পার নাচাইতে ॥ ২০৩ ॥

rāya kahe,——"īśvara tumi ye cāha karite
kāṣṭhera putalī tumi pāra nācāite

SYNONYMS

rāya kahe—Śrīla Rāmānanda Rāya says; *īśvara tumi*—You are the Supreme Personality of Godhead; *ye*—whatever; *cāha*—You want; *karite*—to do; *kāṣṭhera*—of wood; *putalī*—a doll; *tumi*—You; *pāra*—are able; *nācāite*—to make dance.

TRANSLATION

Śrīla Rāmānanda Rāya replied to Śrī Caitanya Mahāprabhu, "My Lord, You are the Supreme Personality of Godhead. If You like, You can cause even a wooden doll to dance.

TEXT 204

মোর মুখে যে সব রস করিলা প্রচারণে ।
সেই রস দেখি এই ইহার লিখনে ॥ ২০৪ ॥

mora mukhe ye saba rasa karilā pracāraṇe
sei rasa dekhi ei ihāra likhane

SYNONYMS

mora mukhe—through my mouth; *ye*—whatever; *saba rasa*—all such transcendental mellows; *karilā*—You did; *pracāraṇe*—preaching; *sei rasa*—those same transcendental mellows; *dekhi*—I see; *ei*—this; *ihāra likhane*—in the writing of Śrīla Rūpa Gosvāmī.

TRANSLATION

"I see that the truths regarding transcendental mellow that You have expounded through my mouth are all explained in the writings of Śrīla Rūpa Gosvāmī.

TEXT 205

ভক্তে কৃপা-হেতু প্রকাশিতে চাহ ব্রজ-রস ।
যারে করাও, সেই করিবে জগৎ তোমার বশ ॥২০৫

bhakte kṛpā-hetu prakāśite cāha vraja-rasa
yāre karāo, sei karibe jagat tomāra vaśa

SYNONYMS

bhakte—unto the devotees; *kṛpā-hetu*—because of mercy; *prakāśite*—to show; *cāha*—You want; *vraja-rasa*—the transcendental mellows in Vṛndāvana; *yāre*—whomever; *karāo*—You may empower; *sei*—he; *karibe*—will make; *jagat*—the whole world; *tomāra vaśa*—under Your control.

TRANSLATION

"Because of Your causeless mercy toward Your devotees, You want to describe the transcendental pastimes in Vṛndāvana. Anyone empowered to do this can bring the entire world under Your influence."

PURPORT

This passage parallels the statement *kṛṣṇa-śakti vinā nahe tāra pravartana,* which means that unless empowered by the Supreme Personality of Godhead, Kṛṣṇa, one cannot spread the holy name of the Lord throughout the entire world (Cc. *Antya* 7.11). Under the protection of the Supreme Personality of Godhead, a pure devotee can preach the holy name of the Lord so that everyone may take advantage of this facility and thus become Kṛṣṇa conscious.

TEXT 206

তবে মহাপ্রভু কৈলা রূপে আলিঙ্গন ।
তাঁরে করাইলা সবার চরণ বন্দন ॥ ২০৬ ॥

tabe mahāprabhu kailā rūpe āliṅgana
tāṅre karāilā sabāra caraṇa vandana

SYNONYMS

tabe—at that time; *mahāprabhu*—Śrī Caitanya Mahāprabhu; *kailā*—did; *rūpe*—unto Rūpa Gosvāmī; *āliṅgana*—embracing; *tāṅre*—him; *karāilā*—induced to do; *sabāra*—of all of them; *caraṇa vandana*—worshiping the lotus feet.

TRANSLATION

Śrī Caitanya Mahāprabhu then embraced Rūpa Gosvāmī and asked him to offer prayers at the lotus feet of all the devotees present.

TEXT 207

অদ্বৈত-নিত্যানন্দাদি সব ভক্তগণ ।
কৃপা করি' রূপে সবে কৈলা আলিঙ্গন ॥ ২০৭ ॥

advaita-nityānandādi saba bhakta-gaṇa
kṛpā kari' rūpe sabe kailā āliṅgana

SYNONYMS

advaita—Advaita Ācārya; *nityānanda-ādi*—Śrī Nityānanda Prabhu and others; *saba*—all; *bhakta-gaṇa*—personal devotees; *kṛpā kari'*—being very merciful; *rūpe*—unto Rūpa Gosvāmī; *sabe*—all of them; *kailā āliṅgana*—embraced.

TRANSLATION

Advaita Ācārya, Nityānanda Prabhu and all the other devotees showed their causeless mercy to Rūpa Gosvāmī by embracing him in return.

TEXT 208

প্রভু-কৃপা রূপে, আর রূপের সদ্গুণ ।
দেখি' চমৎকার হৈল সবাকার মন ॥ ২০৮ ॥

prabhu-kṛpā rūpe, āra rūpera sad-guṇa
dekhi' camatkāra haila sabākāra mana

SYNONYMS

prabhu-kṛpā—Lord Caitanya's mercy; *rūpe*—upon Rūpa Gosvāmī; *āra*—and; *rūpera sat-guṇa*—the transcendental qualities of Śrīla Rūpa Gosvāmī; *dekhi'*—seeing; *camatkāra haila*—there was astonishment; *sabākāra*—of all of them; *mana*—in the minds.

TRANSLATION

Seeing Śrī Caitanya Mahāprabhu's special mercy toward Śrīla Rūpa Gosvāmī and seeing his personal qualities, all the devotees were struck with wonder.

TEXT 209

তবে মহাপ্রভু সব ভক্ত লঞা গেলা ।
হরিদাস-ঠাকুর রূপে আলিঙ্গন কৈলা ॥ ২০৯ ॥

tabe mahāprabhu saba bhakta lañā gelā
haridāsa-ṭhākura rūpe āliṅgana kailā

SYNONYMS

tabe—at that time; *mahāprabhu*—Śrī Caitanya Mahāprabhu; *saba*—all; *bhakta*—devotees; *lañā*—with; *gelā*—departed from the place; *hari-dāsa-ṭhākura*—of the name Haridāsa Ṭhākura; *rūpe*—unto Rūpa Gosvāmī; *āliṅgana kailā*—embraced.

TRANSLATION

Then, when Śrī Caitanya Mahāprabhu left with all of His devotees, Haridāsa Ṭhākura also embraced Śrīla Rūpa Gosvāmī.

TEXT 210

হরিদাস কহে,—"তোমার ভাগ্যের নাহি সীমা ।
যে সব বর্ণিলা, ইহার কে জানে মহিমা ?"২১০ ॥

haridāsa kahe,——"tomāra bhāgyera nāhi sīmā
ye saba varṇilā, ihāra ke jāne mahimā?"

SYNONYMS

hari-dāsa kahe—Haridāsa Ṭhākura says; *tomāra*—your; *bhāgyera*—of fortune; *nāhi sīmā*—there is no limit; *ye*—whatever; *saba*—all; *varṇilā*—you have described; *ihāra*—of this; *ke jāne*—who can understand; *mahimā*—the glories.

TRANSLATION

Haridāsa Ṭhākura told him: "There is no limit to your good fortune. No one can understand the glories of what you have described."

TEXT 211

শ্রীরূপ কহেন,—আমি কিছুই না জানি।
যেই মহাপ্রভু কহান, সেই কহি বাণী ॥"২১১ ॥

śrī-rūpa kahena,——āmi kichui nā jāni
yei mahāprabhu kahāna, sei kahi vāṇī

SYNONYMS

śrī-rūpa kahena—Śrīla Rūpa Gosvāmī replies; *āmi*—I; *kichui*—anything; *nā jāni*—do not know; *yei*—whatever; *mahāprabhu kahāna*—Śrī Caitanya Mahāprabhu makes me say or write; *sei*—that; *kahi*—I speak; *vāṇī*—transcendental words.

TRANSLATION

Śrī Rūpa Gosvāmī said, "I do not know anything. The only transcendental words I can utter are those which Śrī Caitanya Mahāprabhu makes me speak.

PURPORT

The poet or writer dealing with transcendental subject matters is not an ordinary writer or translator. Because he is empowered by the Supreme Personality of Godhead, whatever he writes becomes very effective. The principle of being empowered by the Supreme Personality of Godhead is essential. A materialistic poet who describes in his poetry the material activities of man and woman cannot describe the transcendental pastimes of the Lord or the transcendental conclusions of devotional service. Śrīla Sanātana Gosvāmī has therefore warned all neophyte devotees that one should not hear from the mouth of a non-Vaiṣṇava.

avaiṣṇava-mukhodgīrṇaṁ
pūtaṁ hari-kathāmṛtam
śravaṇaṁ naiva kartavyaṁ
sarpocchiṣṭaṁ yathā payaḥ (*Padma Purāṇa*)

Unless one is a fully unalloyed devotee of the Lord, one should not try to describe the pastimes of Kṛṣṇa in poetry, for it will be only mundane. There are many descriptions of Kṛṣṇa's *Bhagavad-gītā* written by persons whose consciousness is mundane and who are not qualified by pure devotion. Although they attempted to write transcendental literature, they could not fully engage even a single devotee in Kṛṣṇa's service. Such literature is mundane, and therefore, as warned by Śrī Sanātana Gosvāmī, one should not touch it.

TEXT 212

হৃদি যস্য প্রেরণয়া প্রবর্তিতোঽহং বরাকরূপোঽপি ।
তস্য হরেঃ পদকমলং বন্দে চৈতন্যদেবস্য ॥ ২১২ ॥

hṛdi yasya preraṇayā
pravartito 'haṁ varāka-rūpo 'pi
tasya hareḥ pada-kamalaṁ
vande caitanya-devasya

SYNONYMS

hṛdi—within the heart; *yasya*—of whom (the Supreme Personality of Godhead, who gives His pure devotees the intelligence to spread the Kṛṣṇa consciousness movement); *preraṇayā*—by the inspiration; *pravartitaḥ*—engaged; *aham*—I; *varāka*—insignificant and low; *rūpaḥ*—Rūpa Gosvāmī; *api*—although; *tasya*—of Him; *hareḥ*—of Hari, the Supreme Personality of Godhead; *pada-kamalam*—to the lotus feet; *vande*—let me offer my prayers; *caitanya-devasya*—of Śrī Caitanya Mahāprabhu.

TRANSLATION

" 'Although I am the lowest of men and have no knowledge, the Lord has mercifully bestowed upon me the inspiration to write transcendental literature about devotional service. Therefore I offer my obeisances at the lotus feet of Śrī Caitanya Mahāprabhu, the Supreme Personality of Godhead, who has given me the chance to write these books.' "

PURPORT

This verse is from *Bhakti-rasāmṛta-sindhu* (1.1.2).

TEXT 213

এইমত দুইজন কৃষ্ণকথারঙ্গে ।
সুখে কাল গোঙায় রূপ হরিদাস-সঙ্গে ॥ ২১৩ ॥

ei-mata dui-jana kṛṣṇa-kathā-raṅge
sukhe kāla goṅāya rūpa haridāsa-saṅge

SYNONYMS

ei-mata—in this way; *dui-jana*—Haridāsa Ṭhākura and Śrīla Rūpa Gosvāmī; *kṛṣṇa-kathā-raṅge*—in the pleasure of discussing topics about Kṛṣṇa; *sukhe*—in happiness; *kāla*—time; *goṅāya*—passes; *rūpa*—Śrīla Rūpa Gosvāmī; *hari-dāsa-saṅge*—in the company of Haridāsa Ṭhākura.

TRANSLATION

In this way Śrīla Rūpa Gosvāmī passed his time in close association with Haridāsa Ṭhakura by discussing the pastimes of Lord Kṛṣṇa in great happiness.

TEXT 214

চারি মাস রহি' সব প্রভুর ভক্তগণ ।
গোসাঞি বিদায় দিলা, গৌড়ে করিলা গমন ॥২১৪॥

cāri māsa rahi' saba prabhura bhakta-gaṇa
gosāñi vidāya dilā, gauḍe karilā gamana

SYNONYMS

cāri māsa—four months; *rahi'*—staying; *saba*—all; *prabhura*—of Śrī Caitanya Mahāprabhu; *bhakta-gaṇa*—the devotees; *gosāñi*—Caitanya Mahāprabhu; *vidāya dilā*—bade farewell; *gauḍe*—to Bengal; *karilā gamana*—they returned.

TRANSLATION

All the devotees of Śrī Caitanya Mahāprabhu thus spent four months with Him. Then the Lord bade them farewell, and they returned to Bengal.

TEXT 215

শ্রীরূপ প্রভুপদে নীলাচলে রহিলা ।
দোলযাত্রা প্রভুসঙ্গে আনন্দে দেখিলা ॥ ২১৫ ॥

śrī-rūpa prabhu-pade nīlācale rahilā
dola-yātrā prabhu-saṅge ānande dekhilā

SYNONYMS

śrī-rūpa—Śrīla Rūpa Gosvāmī; *prabhu-pade*—at the feet of Śrī Caitanya Mahāprabhu; *nīlācale*—at Jagannātha Purī; *rahilā*—remained; *dola-yātrā*—the festival of Dola-yātrā; *prabhu-saṅge*—with Śrī Caitanya Mahāprabhu; *ānande*—in great happiness; *dehilā*—saw.

TRANSLATION

Śrīla Rūpa Gosvāmī, however, stayed at the lotus feet of Śrī Caitanya Mahāprabhu, and when the Dola-yātrā festival took place, he saw it in great happiness with the Lord.

TEXT 216

দোল অনন্তরে প্রভু রূপে বিদায় দিলা ।
অনেক প্রসাদ করি' শক্তি সঞ্চারিলা ॥ ২১৬ ॥

dola anantare prabhu rūpe vidāya dilā
aneka prasāda kari' śakti sañcārilā

SYNONYMS

dola anantare—after the Dola-yātrā; *prabhu*—Śrī Caitanya Mahāprabhu; *rūpe*—unto Rūpa Gosvāmī; *vidāya dilā*—bade farewell; *aneka prasāda kari'*—endowing with all kinds of mercy; *śakti sañcārilā*—empowered him.

TRANSLATION

After the Dola-yātrā festival ended, Śrī Caitanya Mahāprabhu bade farewell to Rūpa Gosvāmī also. The Lord empowered him and bestowed upon him all kinds of mercy.

TEXT 217

"বৃন্দাবনে যাহ' তুমি, রহিহ বৃন্দাবনে ।
একবার ইহাঁ পাঠাইহ সনাতনে ॥ ২১৭ ॥

"vṛndāvane yāha' tumi, rahiha vṛndāvane
ekabāra ihāṅ pāṭhāiha sanātane

SYNONYMS

vṛndāvane—to Vṛndāvana; *yāha'*—now go; *tumi*—you; *rahiha*—stay; *vṛndāvane*—in Vṛndāvana; *eka-bāra*—once; *ihāṅ*—here; *pāṭhāiha*—send; *sanātane*—your elder brother, Sanātana Gosvāmī.

TRANSLATION

"Now go to Vṛndāvana and stay there," the Lord said. "You may send here your elder brother, Sanātana.

TEXT 218

ব্রজে যাই রসশাস্ত্র করিহ নিরূপণ ।
লুপ্ত-তীর্থ সব তাহাঁ করিহ প্রচারণ ॥ ২১৮ ॥

vraje yāi rasa-śāstra kariha nirūpaṇa
lupta-tīrtha saba tāhāṅ kariha pracāraṇa

SYNONYMS

vraje yāi—going to Vṛndāvana; *rasa-śāstra*—all transcendental literature concerning the pastimes of Lord Śrī Kṛṣṇa; *kariha nirūpaṇa*—write carefully; *lupta-tīrtha*—the lost holy places; *saba*—all; *tāhāṅ*—there; *kariha pracāraṇa*—make known.

TRANSLATION

"When you go to Vṛndāvana, stay there, preach transcendental literature and excavate the lost holy places.

TEXT 219

কৃষ্ণসেবা, রসভক্তি করিহ প্রচার ।
আমিহ দেখিতে তাহাঁ যাইমু একবার ॥ ২১৯ ॥

kṛṣṇa-sevā, rasa-bhakti kariha pracāra
āmiha dekhite tāhāṅ yāimu ekabāra"

SYNONYMS

kṛṣṇa-sevā—the service of Lord Kṛṣṇa; *rasa-bhakti*—devotional service; *kariha pracāra*—preach; *āmiha*—I also; *dekhite*—to see; *tāhāṅ*—there to Vṛndāvana; *yāimu*—I shall go; *eka-bāra*—once more.

TRANSLATION

"Establish the service of Lord Kṛṣṇa and preach the mellows of Lord Kṛṣṇa's devotional service. I shall also go to Vṛndāvana once more."

TEXT 220

এত বলি' প্রভু তাঁরে কৈলা আলিঙ্গন ।
রূপ গোসাঞি শিরে ধরে প্রভুর চরণ ॥ ২২০ ॥

eta bali' prabhu tāṅre kailā āliṅgana
rūpa gosāñi śire dhare prabhura caraṇa

SYNONYMS

eta bali'—saying this; *prabhu*—Śrī Caitanya Mahāprabhu; *tāṅre*—unto Rūpa Gosvāmī; *kailā āliṅgana*—embraced; *rūpa gosāñi*—Śrīla Rūpa Gosvāmī; *śire*—on the head; *dhare*—takes; *prabhura caraṇa*—the lotus feet of Śrī Caitanya Mahāprabhu.

TRANSLATION

Having thus spoken, Śrī Caitanya Mahāprabhu embraced Rūpa Gosvāmī, who then placed the lotus feet of the Lord upon his head.

TEXT 221

প্রভুর ভক্তগণ-পাশে বিদায় লইলা ।
পুনরপি গৌড়-পথে বৃন্দাবনে আইলা ॥ ২২১ ॥

prabhura bhakta-gaṇa-pāśe vidāya la-ilā
punarapi gauḍa-pathe vṛndāvane āilā

SYNONYMS

prabhura—of Śrī Caitanya Mahāprabhu; *bhakta-gaṇa-pāśe*—from the devotees; *vidāya la-ilā*—took leave; *punarapi*—again; *gauḍa-pathe*—on the way to Bengal; *vṛndāvane*—to Vṛndāvana; *āilā*—returned.

TRANSLATION

Śrīla Rūpa Gosvāmī took leave of all the devotees of Śrī Caitanya Mahāprabhu and returned to Vṛndāvana by the path to Bengal.

TEXT 222

এই ত' কহিলাঙ পুনঃ রূপের মিলন ।
ইহা যেই শুনে, পায় চৈতন্যচরণ ॥ ২২২ ॥

ei ta' kahilāṅa punaḥ rūpera milana
ihā yei śune, pāya caitanya-caraṇa

SYNONYMS

ei ta' kahilāṅa—thus I have said; *punaḥ*—again; *rūpera milana*—the meeting with Śrīla Rūpa Gosvāmī; *ihā*—this narration; *yei śune*—anyone who hears; *pāya*—gets; *caitanya-caraṇa*—the shelter of Śrī Caitanya Mahāprabhu.

TRANSLATION

Thus I have described the second meeting of Rūpa Gosvāmī and Śrī Caitanya Mahāprabhu. Anyone who hears of this incident will certainly attain the shelter of Śrī Caitanya Mahāprabhu.

TEXT 223

শ্রীরূপ-রঘুনাথ-পদে যার আশ।
চৈতন্যচরিতামৃত কহে কৃষ্ণদাস ॥ ২২৩ ॥

śrī-rūpa-raghunātha-pade yāra āśa
caitanya-caritāmṛta kahe kṛṣṇadāsa

SYNONYMS

śrī-rūpa—Śrīla Rūpa Gosvāmī; *raghunātha*—Śrīla Raghunātha dāsa Gosvāmī; *pade*—at the lotus feet; *yāra*—whose; *āśa*—expectation; *caitanya-caritāmṛta*—the book named *Caitanya-caritāmṛta; kahe*—describes; *kṛṣṇa-dāsa*—Śrīla Kṛṣṇadāsa Kavirāja Gosvāmī.

TRANSLATION

Praying at the lotus feet of Śrī Rūpa and Śrī Raghunātha, always desiring their mercy, I, Kṛṣṇadāsa, narrate Śrī Caitanya-caritāmṛta, following in their footsteps.

Thus end the Bhaktivedanta purports to the Śrī Caitanya-caritāmṛta, Antya-līlā, *First Chapter, describing the second meeting of Śrīla Rūpa Gosvāmī and Śrī Caitanya Mahāprabhu.*

CHAPTER 2

The Chastisement of Junior Haridāsa

The purport of this chapter is explained by Śrīla Bhaktivinoda Ṭhākura in his *Amṛta-prāvaha-bhāṣya* as follows. Kṛṣṇadāsa Kavirāja Gosvāmī, the author of *Śrī Caitanya-caritāmṛta,* wanted to explain direct meetings with Śrī Caitanya Mahāprabhu, meetings with those empowered by Him, and His *āvirbhāva* appearance. Thus he described the glories of Nṛsiṁhānanda and other devotees. A devotee named Bhagavān Ācārya was exceptionally faithful to the lotus feet of Śrī Caitanya Mahāprabhu. Nevertheless, his brother, Gopāla Bhaṭṭa Ācārya, discoursed upon the commentary of impersonalism (Māyāvāda). Śrīla Svarūpa Dāmodara Gosvāmī, the secretary of Śrī Caitanya Mahāprabhu, forbid Bhagavān Ācārya to indulge in hearing that commentary. Later, when Junior Haridāsa, following the order of Bhagavān Ācārya, went to collect alms from Mādhavīdevī, he committed an offense by talking intimately with a woman although he was in the renounced order. Because of this, Śrī Caitanya Mahāprabhu rejected Junior Haridāsa, and despite all the requests of the Lord's stalwart devotees, the Lord did not accept him again. One year after this incident, Junior Haridāsa went to the confluence of the Ganges and Yamunā and committed suicide. In his spiritual body, however, he continued to sing devotional songs, and Śrī Caitanya Mahāprabhu heard them. When the Vaiṣṇavas of Bengal went to see Śrī Caitanya Mahāprabhu, these incidents became known to Svarūpa Dāmodara and others.

TEXT 1

বন্দেঽহং শ্রীগুরোঃ শ্রীযুতপদকমলং শ্রীগুরূন্ বৈষ্ণবাংশ্চ
শ্রীরূপং সাগ্রজাতং সহগণরঘুনাথান্বিতং তং সজীবম্।
সাদ্বৈতং সাবধূতং পরিজনসহিতং কৃষ্ণচৈতন্যদেবং
শ্রীরাধাকৃষ্ণপাদান্ সহগণললিতা-শ্রীবিশাখান্বিতাংশ্চ ॥ ১ ॥

vande 'haṁ śrī-guroḥ śrī-yuta-pada-kamalaṁ śrī-gurūn vaiṣṇavāṁś ca
śrī-rūpaṁ sāgrajātaṁ saha-gaṇa-raghunāthānvitaṁ taṁ sa-jīvam
sādvaitaṁ sāvadhūtaṁ parijana-sahitaṁ kṛṣṇa-caitanya-devaṁ
śrī-rādhā-kṛṣṇa-pādān saha-gaṇa-lalitā-śrī-viśākhānvitāṁś ca

SYNONYMS

vande—offer my respectful obeisances; *aham*—I; *śrī-guroḥ*—of my initiating spiritual master or instructing spiritual master; *śrī-yuta-pada-kamalam*—unto the opulent lotus feet; *śrī-gurūn*—unto the spiritual masters in the *paramparā* system, beginning from Mādhavendra Purī down to Śrīla Bhaktisiddhānta Sarasvatī Ṭhākura Prabhupāda; *vaiṣṇavān*—unto all the Vaiṣṇavas, beginning from Lord Brahmā and others coming from the very start of the creation; *ca*—and; *śrī-rūpam*—unto Śrīla Rūpa Gosvāmī; *sa-agra-jātam*—with his elder brother, Śrī Sanātana Gosvāmī; *saha-gaṇa-raghunātha-anvitam*—with Raghunātha dāsa Gosvāmī and his associates; *tam*—unto him; *sa-jīvam*—with Jīva Gosvāmī; *sa-advaitam*—with Advaita Ācārya; *sa-avadhūtam*—with Nityānanda Prabhu; *pari-jana-sahitam*—and with Śrīvāsa Ṭhākura and all the other devotees; *kṛṣṇa-caitanya-devam*—unto Lord Śrī Caitanya Mahāprabhu; *śrī-rādhā-kṛṣṇa-pādān*—unto the lotus feet of the all-opulent Śrī Kṛṣṇa and Rādhārāṇī; *saha-gaṇa*—with associates; *lalitā-śrī-viśākhā-anvitān*—accompanied by Lalitā and Śrī Viśākhā; *ca*—also.

TRANSLATION

I offer my respectful obeisances unto the lotus feet of my spiritual master and of all the other preceptors on the path of devotional service. I offer my respectful obeisances unto all the Vaiṣṇavas and unto the six Gosvāmīs, including Śrīla Rūpa Gosvāmī, Śrīla Sanātana Gosvāmī, Raghunātha dāsa Gosvāmī, Jīva Gosvāmī and their associates. I offer my respectful obeisances unto Śrī Advaita Ācārya Prabhu, Śrī Nityānanda Prabhu, Śrī Caitanya Mahāprabhu, and all His devotees, headed by Śrīvāsa Ṭhākura. I then offer my respectful obeisances unto the lotus feet of Lord Kṛṣṇa, Śrīmatī Rādhārāṇī and all the gopīs, headed by Lalitā and Viśākhā.

TEXT 2

জয় জয় শ্রীচৈতন্য জয় নিত্যানন্দ ।
জয়াদ্বৈতচন্দ্র জয় গৌরভক্তবৃন্দ ॥ ২ ॥

jaya jaya śrī-caitanya jaya nityānanda
jayādvaita-candra jaya gaura-bhakta-vṛnda

SYNONYMS

jaya jaya—all glories; *śrī-caitanya*—to Śrī Caitanya; *jaya*—all glories; *nityānanda*—to Lord Nityānanda; *jaya advaita-candra*—all glories to Advaita Ācārya; *jaya*—all glories; *gaura-bhakta-vṛnda*—to the devotees of Lord Caitanya.

TRANSLATION

All glories to Śrī Caitanya Mahāprabhu! All glories to Nityānanda Prabhu! All glories to Advaita Ācārya! And all glories to all the devotees of Śrī Caitanya Mahāprabhu!

TEXT 3

সর্ব-লোক উদ্ধারিতে গৌর-অবতার ।
নিস্তারের হেতু তার ত্রিবিধ প্রকার ॥ ৩ ॥

sarva-loka uddhārite gaura-avatāra
nistārera hetu tāra trividha prakāra

SYNONYMS

sarva-loka—all the worlds; *uddhārite*—to deliver; *gaura-avatāra*—the incarnation of Lord Śrī Caitanya Mahāprabhu; *nistārera hetu*—causes of the deliverance of all people; *tāra*—His; *tri-vidha prakāra*—three kinds.

TRANSLATION

In His incarnation as Śrī Caitanya Mahāprabhu, Lord Śrī Kṛṣṇa descended to deliver all the living beings in the three worlds, from Brahmaloka down to Pātālaloka. He caused their deliverance in three ways.

TEXT 4

সাক্ষাৎ-দর্শন, আর যোগ্যভক্ত-জীবে ।
'আবেশ' করয়ে কাহাঁ, কাহাঁ 'আবির্ভাবে' ॥ ৪ ॥

sākṣāt-darśana, āra yogya-bhakta-jīve
'āveśa' karaye kāhāṅ, kāhāṅ 'āvirbhāve'

SYNONYMS

sākṣāt-darśana—direct meeting; *āra*—and; *yogya-bhakta*—perfect devotee; *jīve*—living beings; *āveśa karaye*—empowers with specific spiritual potencies; *kāhāṅ*—somewhere; *kāhāṅ*—in other places; *āvirbhāve*—by appearing Himself.

TRANSLATION

The Lord delivered the fallen souls in some places by meeting them directly, in other places by empowering a pure devotee, and in still other places by appearing before someone Himself.

TEXTS 5-6

'সাক্ষাৎ-দর্শনে' প্রায় সব নিস্তারিলা।
নকুল-ব্রহ্মচারীর দেহে 'আবিষ্ট' হইলা ॥ ৫ ॥
প্রদ্যুম্ন-নৃসিংহানন্দ আগে কৈলা 'আবির্ভাব'।
'লোক নিস্তারিব',—এই ঈশ্বর-স্বভাব ॥ ৬ ॥

'sākṣāt-darśane' prāya saba nistārilā
nakula-brahmacārīra dehe 'āviṣṭa' ha-ilā

pradyumna-nṛsiṁhānanda āge kailā 'āvirbhāva'
'loka nistāriba',——ei īśvara-svabhāva

SYNONYMS

sākṣāt-darśane—by direct meeting; *prāya*—almost; *saba*—all; *nistārilā*—delivered; *nakula-brahmacārīra*—of a *brahmacārī* named Nakula; *dehe*—in the body; *āviṣṭa ha-ilā*—entered; *pradyumna-nṛsiṁhānanda*—Pradyumna Nṛsiṁhānanda; *āge*—in front of; *kailā*—made; *āvirbhāva*—appearance; *loka nistāriba*—I shall deliver all the fallen souls; *ei*—this; *īśvara-svabhāva*—the characteristic of the Supreme Personality of Godhead.

TRANSLATION

Śrī Caitanya Mahāprabhu delivered almost all the fallen souls by directly meeting them. He delivered others by entering the body of Nakula Brahmacārī and by appearing before Nṛsiṁhānanda Brahmacārī. "I shall deliver the fallen souls." This statement characterizes the Supreme Personality of Godhead.

PURPORT

The Lord always manifested His *āvirbhāva* appearance in the following four places: (1) the house of Śrīmatī Śacīmātā, (2) wherever Nityānanda Prabhu danced in ecstasy, (3) the house of Śrīvāsa (when *kīrtana* was performed), and (4) the house of Rāghava Paṇḍita. Lord Caitanya Himself appeared in these four places. (In this connection, one may consult text 34.)

TEXT 7

সাক্ষাৎ-দর্শনে সব জগৎ তারিলা।
একবার যে দেখিলা, সে কৃতার্থ হইলা ॥ ৭ ॥

sākṣāt-darśane saba jagat tārilā
eka-bāra ye dekhilā, se kṛtārtha ha-ilā

SYNONYMS

sākṣāt-darśane—by direct meetings; *saba*—all; *jagat*—the universe; *tārilā*—He delivered; *eka-bāra*—once; *ye*—anyone who; *dekhilā*—saw; *se*—he; *kṛta-artha*—fully satisfied; *ha-ilā*—became.

TRANSLATION

When Śrī Caitanya Mahāprabhu was personally present, anyone in the world who met Him even once was fully satisfied and became spiritually advanced.

TEXT 8

গৌড়-দেশের ভক্তগণ প্রত্যব্দ আসিয়া।
পুনঃ গৌড়দেশে যায় প্রভুরে মিলিয়া ॥ ৮ ॥

gauḍa-deśera bhakta-gaṇa pratyabda āsiyā
punaḥ gauḍa-deśe yāya prabhure miliyā

SYNONYMS

gauḍa-deśera—of Bengal; *bhakta-gaṇa*—devotees; *prati-abda*—every year; *āsiyā*—coming; *punaḥ*—again; *gauḍa-deśe*—to Bengal; *yāya*—return; *prabhure*—Śrī Caitanya Mahāprabhu; *miliyā*—after meeting.

TRANSLATION

Every year, devotees from Bengal would go to Jagannātha Purī to meet Śrī Caitanya Mahāprabhu, and after the meeting they would return to Bengal.

TEXT 9

আর নানা-দেশের লোক আসি' জগন্নাথ।
চৈতন্য-চরণ দেখি' হইল কৃতার্থ ॥ ৯ ॥

āra nānā-deśera loka āsi' jagannātha
caitanya-caraṇa dekhi' ha-ila kṛtārtha

SYNONYMS

āra—again; *nānā-deśera*—of different provinces; *loka*—people; *āsi'*—coming; *jagannātha*—to Jagannātha Purī; *caitanya-caraṇa*—the lotus feet of Śrī Caitanya Mahāprabhu; *dekhi'*—seeing; *ha-ila*—became; *kṛta-artha*—fully satisfied.

TRANSLATION

Similarly, people who went to Jagannātha Purī from various provinces of India were fully satisfied after seeing the lotus feet of Śrī Caitanya Mahāprabhu.

TEXT 10

সপ্তদ্বীপের লোক আর নবখণ্ডবাসী।
দেব, গন্ধর্ব, কিন্নর মনুষ্য-বেশে আসি' ॥ ১০ ॥

sapta-dvīpera loka āra nava-khaṇḍa-vāsī
deva, gandharva, kinnara manuṣya-veśe āsi'

SYNONYMS

sapta-dvīpera loka—people from all of the seven islands within the universe; *āra*—and; *nava-khaṇḍa-vāsī*—the inhabitants of the nine *khaṇḍas*; *deva*—demigods; *gandharva*—the inhabitants of Gandharvaloka; *kinnara*—the inhabitants of Kinnaraloka; *manuṣya-veśe*—in the form of human beings; *āsi'*—coming.

TRANSLATION

People from all over the universe, including the seven islands, the nine khaṇḍas, the planets of the demigods, Gandharvaloka and Kinnaraloka, would go there in the forms of human beings.

PURPORT

For an explanation of *sapta-dvīpa*, see *Madhya-līlā*, Chapter Twenty, verse 218, and *Śrīmad-Bhāgavatam*, Fifth Canto, Chapters Sixteen and Twenty. In the *Siddhānta-śiromaṇi*, Chapter One (*Golādhyāya*), in the *Bhuvana-kośa* section, the nine *khaṇḍas* are mentioned as follows:

aindraṁ kaśeru sakalaṁ kila tāmraparṇam
anyad gabhastimad ataś ca kumārikākhyam
nāgaṁ ca saumyam iha vāruṇam antya-khaṇḍaṁ
gāndharva-saṁjñam iti bhārata-varṣa-madhye

"Within Bhārata-varṣa, there are nine *khaṇḍas*. They are known as (1) Aindra, (2) Kaśeru, (3) Tāmraparṇa, (4) Gabhastimat, (5) Kumārikā, (6) Nāga, (7) Saumya, (8) Vāruṇa and (9) Gāndharva."

TEXT 11

প্রভুরে দেখিয়া যায় 'বৈষ্ণব' হঞা।
কৃষ্ণ বলি' নাচে সব প্রেমাবিষ্ট হঞা ॥ ১১ ॥

prabhure dekhiyā yāya 'vaiṣṇava' hañā
kṛṣṇa bali' nāce saba premāviṣṭa hañā

SYNONYMS

prabhure dekhiyā—by seeing the Lord; *yāya*—they return; *vaiṣṇava hañā*—having become devotees of the Supreme Personality of Godhead, Kṛṣṇa; *kṛṣṇa bali'*—chanting Kṛṣṇa; *nāce*—dance; *saba*—all of them; *prema-āviṣṭa hañā*—overwhelmed by ecstatic love.

TRANSLATION

Having seen the Lord, they all became Vaiṣṇavas. Thus they danced and chanted the Hare Kṛṣṇa mantra in ecstatic love of Godhead.

TEXT 12

এইমত দর্শনে ত্রিজগৎ নিস্তারি।
যে কেহ আসিতে নারে অনেক সংসারী ॥ ১২ ॥

ei-mata darśane trijagat nistāri
ye keha āsite nāre aneka saṁsārī

SYNONYMS

ei-mata—in this way; *darśane*—by direct visits; *tri-jagat*—the three worlds; *nistāri*—delivering; *ye keha*—some who; *āsite nāre*—could not come; *aneka*—many; *saṁsārī*—persons entangled in this material world.

TRANSLATION

Thus by direct meetings, Śrī Caitanya Mahāprabhu delivered the three worlds. Some people, however, could not go and were entangled in material activities.

TEXT 13

তা-সবা তারিতে প্রভু সেই সব দেশে।
যোগ্যভক্ত জীবদেহে করেন 'আবেশে' ॥ ১৩ ॥

tā-sabā tārite prabhu sei saba deśe
yogya-bhakta jīva-dehe karena 'āveśe'

SYNONYMS

tā-sabā—all of them; *tārite*—to deliver; *prabhu*—Śrī Caitanya Mahāprabhu; *sei*—those; *saba*—all; *deśe*—in countries; *yogya-bhakta*—a suitable devotee; *jīva-dehe*—in the body of such a living entity; *karena*—does; *āveśe*—entrance.

TRANSLATION

To deliver people in regions throughout the universe who could not meet Him, Śrī Caitanya Mahāprabhu personally entered the bodies of pure devotees.

TEXT 14

সেই জীবে নিজ-ভক্তি করেন প্রকাশে ।
তাহার দর্শনে 'বৈষ্ণব' হয় সর্বদেশে ॥ ১৪ ॥

sei jīve nija-bhakti karena prakāśe
tāhāra darśane 'vaiṣṇava' haya sarva-deśe

SYNONYMS

sei jīve—in that living being; *nija-bhakti*—His own devotion; *karena prakāśe*—manifests directly; *tāhāra darśane*—by seeing such an empowered devotee; *vaiṣṇava*—devotees of Kṛṣṇa; *haya*—become; *sarva-deśe*—in all other countries.

TRANSLATION

Thus He empowered living beings [His pure devotees] by manifesting in them so much of His own devotion that people in all other countries became devotees by seeing them.

PURPORT

As stated in *Caitanya-caritāmṛta* (*Antya* 7.11):

kali-kālera dharma——kṛṣṇa-nāma-saṅkīrtana
kṛṣṇa-śakti vinā nahe tāra pravartana

Unless one is empowered by the Supreme Personality of Godhead, Śrī Caitanya Mahāprabhu, one cannot spread the holy names of the Hare Kṛṣṇa *mahā-mantra* throughout the world. Persons who do so are empowered. Therefore they are sometimes called *āveśa-avatāras* or incarnations, for they are endowed with the power of Śrī Caitanya Mahāprabhu.

TEXT 15

এইমত আবেশে তারিল ত্রিভুবন ।
গৌড়ে যৈছে আবেশ, করি দিগ্ দরশন ॥ ১৫ ॥

ei-mata āveśe tārila tribhuvana
gauḍe yaiche āveśa, kari dig daraśana

SYNONYMS

ei-mata—in this way; *āveśe*—by empowering; *tārila tri-bhuvana*—delivered the entire three worlds; *gauḍe*—in Bengal; *yaiche*—how; *āveśa*—empowering; *kari dik daraśana*—I shall describe in brief.

TRANSLATION

In this way Śrī Caitanya Mahāprabhu delivered the entire three worlds, not only by His personal presence but also by empowering others. I shall briefly describe how He empowered a living being in Bengal.

TEXT 16

আম্বুয়া-মুলুকে হয় নকুল-ব্রহ্মচারী ।
পরম-বৈষ্ণব তেঁহো বড় অধিকারী ॥ ১৬ ॥

āmbuyā-muluke haya nakula-brahmacārī
parama-vaiṣṇava teṅho baḍa adhikārī

SYNONYMS

āmbuyā-muluke—in the province known as Āmbuyā; *haya*—there is; *nakula-brahmacārī*—a person known as Nakula Brahmacārī; *parama-vaiṣṇava*—a perfectly pure devotee; *teṅho*—he; *baḍa adhikārī*—very advanced in devotional service.

TRANSLATION

In Āmbuyā-muluka there was a person named Nakula Brahmacārī, who was a perfectly pure devotee, greatly advanced in devotional service.

PURPORT

Śrīla Bhaktivinoda Ṭhākura says that Āmbuyā-muluka is the present Ambikā, a city in the Vardhamāna district of West Bengal. Formerly, during the Mohammedan regime, it was known as Āmbuyā-muluka. In this city there is a neighborhood called Pyārīgañja, and that is where Nakula Brahmacārī used to live.

TEXT 17

গৌড়দেশের লোক নিস্তারিতে মন হৈল ।
নকুল-হৃদয়ে প্রভু 'আবেশ' করিল ॥ ১৭ ॥

gauḍa-deśera loka nistārite mana haila
nakula-hṛdaye prabhu 'āveśa' karila

SYNONYMS

gauḍa-deśera loka—the people of Bengal; *nistārite*—to deliver; *mana haila*—wanted; *nakula-hṛdaye*—in the heart of Nakula Brahmacārī; *prabhu*—Śrī Caitanya Mahāprabhu; *āveśa karila*—entered.

TRANSLATION

Desiring to deliver all the people of Bengal, Śrī Caitanya Mahāprabhu entered the heart of Nakula Brahmacārī.

TEXT 18

গ্রহগ্রস্তপ্রায় নকুল প্রেমাবিষ্ট হঞা।
হাসে, কান্দে, নাচে, গায় উন্মত্ত হঞা ॥ ১৮ ॥

graha-grasta-prāya nakula premāviṣṭa hañā
hāse, kānde, nāce, gāya unmatta hañā

SYNONYMS

graha-grasta-prāya—exactly like one haunted by a ghost; *nakula*—Nakula Brahmacārī; *prema-āviṣṭa hañā*—being overwhelmed by ecstatic love of God; *hāse*—laughs; *kānde*—cries; *nāce*—dances; *gāya*—chants; *unmatta hañā*—just like a madman.

TRANSLATION

Nakula Brahmacārī became exactly like a man haunted by a ghost. Thus he sometimes laughed, sometimes cried, sometimes danced and sometimes chanted like a madman.

TEXT 19

অশ্রু, কম্প, স্তম্ভ, স্বেদ, সাত্ত্বিক বিকার।
নিরন্তর প্রেমে নৃত্য, সঘন হুঙ্কার ॥ ১৯ ॥

aśru, kampa, stambha, sveda, sāttvika vikāra
nirantara preme nṛtya, saghana huṅkāra

SYNONYMS

aśru—tears; *kampa*—trembling; *stambha*—becoming stunned; *sveda*—perspiration; *sāttvika vikāra*—all such transcendental transformations; *nirantara*—continuously; *preme nṛtya*—dancing in ecstatic love; *sa-ghana huṅkāra*—a sound like that of a cloud.

TRANSLATION

He continuously exhibited bodily transformations of transcendental love. Thus he cried, trembled, became stunned, perspired, danced in love of Godhead and made sounds like those of a cloud.

TEXT 20

তৈছে গৌরকান্তি, তৈছে সদা প্রেমাবেশ।
তাহা দেখিবারে আইসে সর্ব গৌড়দেশ ॥ ২০ ॥

taiche gaura-kānti, taiche sadā premāveśa
tāhā dekhibāre āise sarva gauḍa-deśa

SYNONYMS

taiche—in that way; *gaura-kānti*—a bodily luster like that of Lord Śrī Caitanya Mahāprabhu; *taiche*—similarly; *sadā*—always; *prema-āveśa*—absorbed in ecstatic love; *tāhā dekhibāre*—to see that; *āise*—come; *sarva*—all; *gauḍa-deśa*—people from all provinces of Bengal.

TRANSLATION

His body shone with the same luster as that of Śrī Caitanya Mahāprabhu, and he showed the same absorption in ecstatic love of Godhead. People came from all provinces of Bengal to see these symptoms.

TEXT 21

যারে দেখে তারে কহে,—'কহ কৃষ্ণনাম'।
তাঁহার দর্শনে লোক হয় প্রেমোদ্দাম ॥ ২১ ॥

yāre dekhe tāre kahe,——'kaha kṛṣṇa-nāma'
tāṅhāra darśane loka haya premoddāma

SYNONYMS

yāre dekhe—to whomever he saw; *tāre kahe*—he addresses him; *kaha kṛṣṇa-nāma*—my dear friend, chant Kṛṣṇa's holy name; *tāṅhāra darśane*—by seeing him; *loka haya*—people became; *prema-uddāma*—highly elevated in love of Godhead.

TRANSLATION

He advised whomever he met to chant the holy names Hare Kṛṣṇa. Thus upon seeing him, people were overwhelmed with love of Godhead.

TEXT 22

চৈতন্যের আবেশ হয় নকুলের দেহে।
শুনি' শিবানন্দ আইলা করিয়া সন্দেহে ॥ ২২ ॥

caitanyera āveśa haya nakulera dehe
śuni' śivānanda āilā kariyā sandehe

SYNONYMS

caitanyera—of Śrī Caitanya Mahāprabhu; *āveśa*—taking possession; *haya*—there is; *nakulera dehe*—in the body of Nakula Brahmacārī; *śuni'*—hearing; *śivānanda āilā*—Śivānanda Sena came; *kariyā sandehe*—doubting.

TRANSLATION

When Śivānanda Sena heard that Śrī Caitanya Mahāprabhu had entered the body of Nakula Brahmacārī, he went there with doubts in his mind.

TEXT 23

পরীক্ষা করিতে তাঁর যবে ইচ্ছা হৈল।
বাহিরে রহিয়া তবে বিচার করিল ॥ ২৩ ॥

parīkṣā karite tāṅra yabe icchā haila
bāhire rahiyā tabe vicāra karila

SYNONYMS

parīkṣā karite—to test; *tāṅra*—of Śivānanda Sena; *yabe*—when; *icchā*—desire; *haila*—there was; *bāhire rahiyā*—staying outside; *tabe*—at that time; *vicāra karila*—considered.

TRANSLATION

Desiring to test the authenticity of Nakula Brahmacārī, he stayed outside, thinking as follows.

TEXTS 24-25

"আপনে বোলান মোরে, ইহা যদি জানি।
আমার ইষ্ট-মন্ত্র জানি' কহেন আপনি ॥ ২৪ ॥
তবে জানি, ইঁহাতে হয় চৈতন্য-আবেশে।"
এত চিন্তি' শিবানন্দ রহিলা দূরদেশে ॥ ২৫ ॥

"āpane bolāna more, ihā yadi jāni
āmāra iṣṭa-mantra jāni' kahena āpani

tabe jāni, iṅhāte haya caitanya-āveśe"
eta cinti' śivānanda rahilā dūra-deśe

SYNONYMS

āpane—personally; *bolāna*—calls; *more*—me; *ihā*—this; *yadi*—if; *jāni*—I understand; *āmāra*—my; *iṣṭa-mantra*—worshipable *mantra; jāni'*—knowing; *kahena āpani*—he says himself; *tabe jāni*—then I shall understand; *iṅhāte*—in him; *haya*—there is; *caitanya-āveśe*—being possessed by Śrī Caitanya Mahāprabhu; *eta cinti'*—thinking this; *śivānanda*—Śivānanda Sena; *rahilā*—remained; *dūra-deśe*—a little far off.

TRANSLATION

"If Nakula Brahmacārī personally calls me and knows my worshipable mantra, then I shall understand that he is inspired by the presence of Śrī Caitanya Mahāprabhu." Thinking in this way, he stayed some distance apart.

TEXT 26

অসংখ্য লোকের ঘটা,—কেহ আইসে যায়।
লোকের সংঘট্টে কেহ দর্শন না পায়॥ ২৬॥

asaṅkhya lokera ghaṭā,——keha āise yāya
lokera saṅghaṭṭe keha darśana nā pāya

SYNONYMS

asaṅkhya lokera ghaṭā—a great crowd of people; *keha*—some; *āise*—come; *yāya*—go; *lokera saṅghaṭṭe*—in the great crowd of people; *keha*—some of them; *darśana nā pāya*—could not see Nakula Brahmacārī.

TRANSLATION

There was a large crowd of people, some coming and some going. Indeed, some people in that great crowd could not even see Nakula Brahmacārī.

TEXT 27

আবেশে ব্রহ্মচারী কহে,—'শিবানন্দ আছে দূরে।
জন দুই চারি যাহ, বোলাহ তাহারে॥' ২৭॥

āveśe brahmacārī kahe,——'śivānanda āche dūre
jana dui cāri yāha, bolāha tāhāre'

SYNONYMS

āveśe—in that state of possession; *brahmacārī kahe*—Nakula Brahmacārī said; *śivānanda*—Śivānanda Sena; *āche dūre*—is staying some distance off; *jana*—persons; *dui*—two; *cāri*—four; *yāha*—go; *bolāha tāhāre*—call him.

TRANSLATION

In his inspired state, Nakula Brahmacārī said, "Śivānanda Sena is staying some distance away. Two or four of you go call him."

TEXT 28

চারিদিকে ধায় লোকে 'শিবানন্দ' বলি ।
শিবানন্দ কোন্, তোমায় বোলায় ব্রহ্মচারী ॥ ২৮ ॥

cāri-dike dhāya loke 'śivānanda' bali
śivānanda kon, tomāya bolāya brahmacārī

SYNONYMS

cāri-dike—in four directions; *dhāya loke*—people began to run; *śivānanda bali*—calling loudly the name of Śivānanda; *śivānanda kon*—whoever is Śivānanda; *tomāya*—unto you; *bolāya*—calls; *brahmacārī*—Nakula Brahmacārī.

TRANSLATION

Thus people began running here and there, calling in all directions, "Śivānanda! Whoever is Śivānanda, please come. Nakula Brahmacārī is calling you."

TEXT 29

শুনি' শিবানন্দ সেন তাঁহা শীঘ্র আইল ।
নমস্কার করি' তাঁর নিকটে বসিল ॥ ২৯ ॥

śuni' śivānanda sena tāṅhā śīghra āila
namaskāra kari' tāṅra nikaṭe vasila

SYNONYMS

śuni'—hearing; *śivānanda sena*—of the name Śivānanda Sena; *tāṅhā*—there; *śīghra*—quickly; *āila*—came; *namaskāra kari'*—offering obeisances; *tāṅra nikaṭe*—near him; *vasila*—sat down.

TRANSLATION

Hearing these calls, Śivānanda Sena quickly went there, offered obeisances to Nakula Brahmacārī, and sat down near him.

TEXT 30

ব্রহ্মচারী বলে,—"তুমি করিলা সংশয়।
এক-মনা হঞা শুন তাহার নিশ্চয়॥ ৩০ ॥

brahmacārī bale,——"tumi karilā saṁśaya
eka-manā hañā śuna tāhāra niścaya

SYNONYMS

brahmacārī bale—Nakula Brahmacārī said; *tumi*—you; *karilā saṁśaya*—have doubted; *eka-manā hañā*—with great attention; *śuna*—please hear; *tāhāra*—for that; *niścaya*—settlement.

TRANSLATION

Nakula Brahmacārī said, "I know that you are doubtful. Now please hear this evidence with great attention.

TEXT 31

'গৌরগোপাল মন্ত্র' তোমার চারি অক্ষর।
অবিশ্বাস ছাড়, যেই করিয়াছ অন্তর॥" ৩১ ॥

'gaura-gopāla mantra' tomāra cāri akṣara
aviśvāsa chāḍa, yei kariyācha antara"

SYNONYMS

gaura-gopāla mantra—the Gaura-gopāla *mantra; tomāra*—your; *cāri akṣara*—composed of four syllables; *aviśvāsa chāḍa*—give up your doubts; *yei*—which; *kariyācha antara*—you have kept within your mind.

TRANSLATION

"You are chanting the Gaura-gopāla mantra composed of four syllables. Now please give up the doubts that have resided within you."

PURPORT

Śrīla Bhaktivinoda Ṭhākura explains the Gaura-gopāla *mantra* in his *Amṛta-pravāha-bhāṣya.* Worshipers of Śrī Gaurasundara accept the four syllables *gau-ra-aṅ-*

ga as the Gaura *mantra,* but pure worshipers of Rādhā and Kṛṣṇa accept the four syllables *rā-dhā kṛṣ-ṇa* as the Gaura-gopāla *mantra.* However, Vaiṣṇavas consider Śrī Caitanya Mahāprabhu nondifferent from Rādhā-Kṛṣṇa (*śrī-kṛṣṇa-caitanya rādhā-kṛṣṇa nahe anya*). Therefore one who chants the *mantra* Gaurāṅga and one who chants the names of Rādhā and Kṛṣṇa are on the same level.

TEXT 32

তবে শিবানন্দের মনে প্রতীতি হইল।
অনেক সম্মান করি' বহু ভক্তি কৈল ॥ ৩২ ॥

tabe śivānandera mane pratīti ha-ila
aneka sammāna kari' bahu bhakti kaila

SYNONYMS

tabe—thereupon; *śivānandera*—of Śivānanda Sena; *mane*—in the mind; *pratīti ha-ila*—there was confidence; *aneka sammāna kari'*—offering him much respect; *bahu bhakti kaila*—offered him devotional service.

TRANSLATION

Śivānanda Sena thereupon developed full confidence in his mind that Nakula Brahmacārī was filled with the presence of Śrī Caitanya Mahāprabhu. Śivānanda Sena then offered him respect and devotional service.

TEXT 33

এইমত মহাপ্রভুর অচিন্ত্য প্রভাব।
এবে শুন প্রভুর যৈছে হয় 'আবির্ভাব ॥' ৩৩ ॥

ei-mata mahāprabhura acintya prabhāva
ebe śuna prabhura yaiche haya 'āvirbhāva'

SYNONYMS

ei-mata—in this way; *mahāprabhura*—of Śrī Caitanya Mahāprabhu; *acintya prabhāva*—inconceivable influence; *ebe*—now; *śuna*—hear; *prabhura*—of Śrī Caitanya Mahāprabhu; *yaiche*—in which way; *haya*—there is; *āvirbhāva*—appearance.

TRANSLATION

In this way, one should understand the inconceivable potencies of Śrī Caitanya Mahāprabhu. Now please hear how His appearance [āvirbhāva] takes place.

TEXTS 34-35

শচীর মন্দিরে, আর নিত্যানন্দ-নর্তনে ।
শ্রীবাস-কীর্তনে, আর রাঘব-ভবনে ॥ ৩৪ ॥
এই চারি ঠাঞি প্রভুর সদা 'আবির্ভাব' ।
প্রেমাকৃষ্ট হয়,—প্রভুর সহজ স্বভাব ॥ ৩৫ ॥

śacīra mandire, āra nityānanda-nartane
śrīvāsa-kīrtane, āra rāghava-bhavane

ei cāri ṭhāñi prabhura sadā 'āvirbhāva'
premākṛṣṭa haya,——prabhura sahaja svabhāva

SYNONYMS

śacīra mandire—in the household temple of mother Śacī; *āra*—and; *nityānanda-nartane*—at the time of Śrī Nityānanda Prabhu's dancing; *śrīvāsa-kīrtane*—at the time of congregational chanting headed by Śrīvāsa Paṇḍita; *āra*—and; *rāghava-bhavane*—in the house of Rāghava; *ei cāri ṭhāñi*—in these four places; *prabhura*—of Śrī Caitanya Mahāprabhu; *sadā*—always; *āvirbhāva*—appearance; *prema-ākṛṣṭa haya*—is attracted by love; *prabhura*—of Śrī Caitanya Mahāprabhu; *sahaja sva-bhāva*—natural characteristic.

TRANSLATION

Śrī Caitanya Mahāprabhu always appeared in four places—in the household temple of mother Śacī, in the places where Śrī Nityānanda Prabhu danced, in the house of Śrīvāsa Paṇḍita during congregational chanting and in the house of Rāghava Paṇḍita. He appeared because of His attraction to the love of His devotees. That is His natural characteristic.

TEXT 36

নৃসিংহানন্দের আগে আবির্ভূত হঞা ।
ভোজন করিলা, তাহা শুন মন দিয়া ॥ ৩৬ ॥

nṛsiṁhānandera āge āvirbhūta hañā
bhojana karilā, tāhā śuna mana diyā

SYNONYMS

nṛsiṁhānandera—the *brahmacārī* known as Nṛsiṁhānanda; *āge*—before; *āvirbhūta hañā*—appearing; *bhojana karilā*—He accepted offerings of food; *tāhā*—that; *śuna*—hear; *mana diyā*—with attention.

TRANSLATION

Śrī Caitanya Mahāprabhu appeared before Nṛsiṁhānanda Brahmacārī and ate his offerings. Please hear about this with attention.

TEXT 37

শিবানন্দের ভাগিনা শ্রীকান্ত-সেন নাম।
প্রভুর কৃপাতে তেঁহো বড় ভাগ্যবান্ ॥ ৩৭ ॥

śivānandera bhāginā śrī-kānta-sena nāma
prabhura kṛpāte teṅho baḍa bhāgyavān

SYNONYMS

śivānandera—of Śivānanda Sena; *bhāginā*—nephew; *śrī-kānta-sena nāma*—named Śrīkānta Sena; *prabhura kṛpāte*—by the causeless mercy of Śrī Caitanya Mahāprabhu; *teṅho*—he; *baḍa*—very; *bhāgyavān*—fortunate.

TRANSLATION

Śivānanda Sena had a nephew named Śrīkānta Sena, who by the grace of Śrī Caitanya Mahāprabhu was extremely fortunate.

TEXT 38

এক বৎসর তেঁহো প্রথম একেশ্বর।
প্রভু দেখিবারে আইলা উৎকণ্ঠা-অন্তর ॥ ৩৮ ॥

eka vatsara teṅho prathama ekeśvara
prabhu dekhibāre āilā utkaṇṭhā-antara

SYNONYMS

eka vatsara—one year; *teṅho*—Śrīkānta Sena; *prathama*—first; *ekeśvara*—alone; *prabhu dekhibāre*—to see the Lord; *āilā*—came; *utkaṇṭhā-antara*—with great anxiety in the mind.

TRANSLATION

One year, Śrīkānta Sena came alone to Jagannātha Purī in great eagerness to see the Lord.

TEXT 39

মহাপ্রভু তারে দেখি' বড় কৃপা কৈলা।
মাস-দুই তেঁহো প্রভুর নিকটে রহিলা ॥ ৩৯ ॥

mahāprabhu tāre dekhi' baḍa kṛpā kailā
māsa-dui teṅho prabhura nikaṭe rahilā

SYNONYMS

mahāprabhu—Śrī Caitanya Mahāprabhu; *tāre*—him; *dekhi'*—seeing; *baḍa kṛpā kailā*—bestowed great mercy; *māsa-dui*—for two months; *teṅho*—Śrīkānta Sena; *prabhura nikaṭe*—near Śrī Caitanya Mahāprabhu; *rahilā*—stayed.

TRANSLATION

Seeing Śrīkānta Sena, Śrī Caitanya Mahāprabhu bestowed causeless mercy upon him. Śrīkānta Sena stayed near Śrī Caitanya Mahāprabhu for about two months at Jagannātha Purī.

TEXT 40

তবে প্রভু তাঁরে আজ্ঞা কৈলা গৌড়ে যাইতে।
"ভক্তগণে নিষেধিহ এথাকে আসিতে ॥ ৪০ ॥

tabe prabhu tāṅre ājñā kailā gauḍe yāite
"bhakta-gaṇe niṣedhiha ethāke āsite

SYNONYMS

tabe—then; *prabhu*—Śrī Caitanya Mahāprabhu; *tāṅre*—unto him; *ājñā kailā*—ordered; *gauḍe yāite*—returning to Bengal; *bhakta-gaṇe*—the devotees; *niṣedhiha*—forbid; *ethāke āsite*—to come to this place.

TRANSLATION

When he was about to return to Bengal, the Lord told him, "Forbid the devotees of Bengal to come to Jagannātha Purī this year.

TEXT 41

এ-বৎসর তাঁহা আমি যাইমু আপনে।
তাহাই মিলিমু সব অদ্বৈতাদি সনে ॥ ৪১ ॥

e-vatsara tāṅhā āmi yāimu āpane
tāhāi milimu saba advaitādi sane

SYNONYMS

e-vatsara—this year; *tāṅhā*—there (to Bengal); *āmi*—I; *yāimu*—shall go; *āpane*—personally; *tāhāi*—there; *milimu*—I shall meet; *saba*—all; *advaita-ādi*—beginning with Advaita Ācārya; *sane*—with.

TRANSLATION

"This year I shall personally go to Bengal and meet all the devotees there, headed by Advaita Ācārya.

TEXT 42

শিবানন্দে কহিহ,—আমি এই পৌষ-মাসে ।
আচম্বিতে অবশ্য আমি যাইব তাঁর পাশে ॥ ৪২ ॥

śivānande kahiha,——āmi ei pauṣa-māse
ācambite avaśya āmi yāiba tāṅra pāśe

SYNONYMS

śivānande kahiha—speak to Śivānanda Sena; *āmi*—I; *ei*—this; *pauṣa-māse*—in the month of December; *ācambite*—all of a sudden; *avaśya*—certainly; *āmi*—I; *yāiba*—shall go; *tāṅra pāśe*—to his place.

TRANSLATION

"Please inform Śivānanda Sena that this December I shall certainly go to his home.

TEXT 43

জগদানন্দ হয় তাহাঁ, তেঁহো ভিক্ষা দিবে ।
সবারে কহিহ,—এ বৎসর কেহ না আসিবে ॥" ৪৩ ॥

jagadānanda haya tāhāṅ, teṅho bhikṣā dibe
sabāre kahiha,——e vatsara keha nā āsibe"

SYNONYMS

jagadānanda—Jagadānanda; *haya*—is; *tāhāṅ*—there; *teṅho*—he; *bhikṣā dibe*—will give offerings of food; *sabāre kahiha*—inform all of them; *e vatsara*—this year; *keha nā āsibe*—no one should come.

TRANSLATION

"Jagadānanda is there, and he will give Me offerings of food. Inform them all that no one should come to Jagannātha Purī this year."

TEXT 44

শ্রীকান্ত আসিয়া গৌড়ে সন্দেশ কহিল ।
শুনি' ভক্তগণ-মনে আনন্দ হইল ॥ ৪৪ ॥

śrī-kānta āsiyā gauḍe sandeśa kahila
śuni' bhakta-gaṇa-mane ānanda ha-ila

SYNONYMS

śrī-kānta—Śrīkānta Sena; *āsiyā*—coming back; *gauḍe*—in Bengal; *sandeśa*—message; *kahila*—delivered; *śuni'*—hearing; *bhakta-gaṇa-mane*—in the minds of the devotees; *ānanda ha-ila*—there was great happiness.

TRANSLATION

When Śrīkānta Sena returned to Bengal and delivered this message, the minds of all the devotees were very pleased.

TEXT 45

চলিতেছিলা আচার্য, রহিলা স্থির হঞা।
শিবানন্দ, জগদানন্দ রহে প্রত্যাশা করিয়া ॥ ৪৫ ॥

calitechilā ācārya, rahilā sthira hañā
śivānanda, jagadānanda rahe pratyāśā kariyā

SYNONYMS

calitechilā—was ready to go; *ācārya*—Advaita Ācārya; *rahilā*—remained; *sthira hañā*—being without movement; *śivānanda*—Śivānanda; *jagadānanda*—Jagadānanda; *rahe*—remain; *pratyāśā kariyā*—expecting.

TRANSLATION

Advaita Ācārya was just about to go to Jagannātha Purī with the other devotees, but upon hearing this message, He waited. Śivānanda Sena and Jagadānanda also stayed back, awaiting the arrival of Śrī Caitanya Mahāprabhu.

TEXT 46

পৌষ-মাসে আইল দুঁহে সামগ্রী করিয়া।
সন্ধ্যা-পর্যন্ত রহে অপেক্ষা করিয়া ॥ ৪৬ ॥

pauṣa-māse āila duṅhe sāmagrī kariyā
sandhyā-paryanta rahe apekṣā kariyā

SYNONYMS

pauṣa-māse—the month of Pauṣa (December-January); *āila*—came; *duṅhe*—Śivānanda Sena and Jagadānanda; *sāmagrī kariyā*—making all arrangements; *sandhyā-paryanta*—until the evening; *rahe*—remain; *apekṣā kariyā*—waiting.

TRANSLATION

When the month of Pauṣa arrived, both Jagadānanda and Śivānanda collected all kinds of paraphernalia for the Lord's reception. Every day, they would wait until evening for the Lord to come.

TEXT 47

এইমত মাস গেল, গোসাঞি না আইলা।
জগদানন্দ, শিবানন্দ দুঃখিত হইলা॥ ৪৭॥

ei-mata māsa gela, gosāñi nā āilā
jagadānanda, śivānanda duḥkhita ha-ilā

SYNONYMS

ei-mata—in this way; *māsa gela*—the month passed; *gosāñi nā āilā*—Śrī Caitanya Mahāprabhu did not come; *jagadānanda*—Jagadānanda; *śivānanda*—Śivānanda; *duḥkhita ha-ilā*—became very unhappy.

TRANSLATION

As the month passed but Śrī Caitanya Mahāprabhu did not come, Jagadānanda and Śivānanda became most unhappy.

TEXTS 48-49

আচম্বিতে নৃসিংহানন্দ তাহাঁই আইলা।
দুঁহে তাঁরে মিলি' তবে স্থানে বসাইলা॥ ৪৮॥
দুঁহে দুঃখী দেখি' তবে কহে নৃসিংহানন্দ।
'তোমা দুহাঁকারে কেনে দেখি নিরানন্দ?' ৪৯॥

ācambite nṛsiṁhānanda tāhāṅi āilā
duṅhe tāṅre mili' tabe sthāne vasāilā

duṅhe duḥkhī dekhi' tabe kahe nṛsiṁhānanda
'tomā duṅhākāre kene dekhi nirānanda?'

SYNONYMS

ācambite—all of a sudden; *nṛsiṁhānanda*—Nṛsiṁhānanda; *tāhāṅi āilā*—came there; *duṅhe*—Śivānanda and Jagadānanda; *tāṅre*—him; *mili'*—meeting; *tabe*—then; *sthāne vasāilā*—caused to sit; *duṅhe*—both; *duḥkhī*—unhappy; *dekhi'*—seeing; *tabe*—then; *kahe nṛsiṁhānanda*—Nṛsiṁhānanda began to speak; *tomā duṅhākāre*—both of you; *kene*—why; *dekhi*—I see; *nirānanda*—unhappy.

TRANSLATION

Suddenly Nṛsiṁhānanda arrived, and Jagadānanda and Śivānanda arranged for him to sit near them. Seeing them both so unhappy, Nṛsiṁhānanda inquired, "Why do I see that you are both despondent?"

TEXT 50

তবে শিবানন্দ তাঁরে সকল কহিলা ।
'আসিব আজ্ঞা দিলা প্রভু কেনে না আইলা ?' ৫০ ॥

tabe śivānanda tāṅre sakala kahilā
'āsiba ājñā dilā prabhu kene nā āilā?'

SYNONYMS

tabe—thereupon; *śivānanda*—Śivānanda; *tāṅre*—unto Nṛsiṁhānanda; *sakala kahilā*—said everything; *āsiba*—I shall come; *ājñā dilā*—promised; *prabhu*—Śrī Caitanya Mahāprabhu; *kene*—why; *nā āilā*—has He not come.

TRANSLATION

Then Śivānanda Sena told him, "Śrī Caitanya Mahāprabhu promised that He would come. Why, then, has He not arrived?"

TEXT 51

শুনি' ব্রহ্মচারী কহে,—'করহ সন্তোষে ।
আমি ত' আনিব তাঁরে তৃতীয় দিবসে ॥' ৫১ ॥

śuni' brahmacārī kahe,—'karaha santoṣe
āmi ta' āniba tāṅre tṛtīya divase'

SYNONYMS

śuni'—hearing; *brahmacārī*—Nṛsiṁhānanda Brahmacārī; *kahe*—said; *karaha santoṣe*—become happy; *āmi*—I; *ta'*—certainly; *āniba*—shall bring; *tāṅre*—Him (Śrī Caitanya Mahāprabhu); *tṛtīya divase*—on the third day.

TRANSLATION

Hearing this, Nṛsiṁhānanda Brahmacārī replied, "Please be satisfied. I assure you that I shall bring Him here three days from now."

TEXT 52

তাঁহার প্রভাব-প্রেম জানে দুইজনে ।
আনিবে প্রভুরে এবে নিশ্চয় কৈলা মনে ॥ ৫২ ॥

tāṅhāra prabhāva-prema jāne dui-jane
ānibe prabhure ebe niścaya kailā mane

SYNONYMS

tāṅhāra—his; *prabhāva*—influence; *prema*—love of Godhead; *jāne*—know; *dui-jane*—both of them; *ānibe prabhure*—he will bring Śrī Caitanya Mahāprabhu; *ebe*—now; *niścaya kailā mane*—they were greatly assured within their minds.

TRANSLATION

Śivānanda and Jagadānanda knew of Nṛsiṁhānanda Brahmacārī's influence and love of Godhead. Therefore they now felt assured that he would certainly bring Śrī Caitanya Mahāprabhu.

TEXT 53

'প্রদ্যুম্ন ব্রহ্মচারী'-- তাঁর নিজ-নাম ।
'নৃসিংহানন্দ' নাম তাঁর কৈলা গৌরধাম ॥ ৫৩ ॥

'pradyumna brahmacārī'——tāṅra nija-nāma
'nṛsiṁhānanda' nāma tāṅra kailā gaura-dhāma

SYNONYMS

pradyumna brahmacārī—Pradyumna Brahmacārī; *tāṅra*—his; *nija-nāma*—real name; *nṛsiṁhānanda*—Nṛsiṁhānanda; *nāma*—name; *tāṅra*—his; *kailā gaura-dhāma*—was given by Śrī Caitanya Mahāprabhu.

TRANSLATION

His real name was Pradyumna Brahmacārī. The name Nṛsiṁhānanda had been given to him by Lord Gaurasundara Himself.

TEXT 54

দুই দিন ধ্যান করি' শিবানন্দেরে কহিল ।
"পাণিহাটি গ্রামে আমি প্রভুরে আনিল ॥ ৫৪ ॥

dui dina dhyāna kari' śivānandere kahila
"pāṇihāṭi grāme āmi prabhure ānila

SYNONYMS

dui dina—for two days; *dhyāna kari'*—after meditating; *śivānandere kahila*—he said to Śivānanda Sena; *pāṇihāṭi grāme*—to the village called Pāṇihāṭi; *āmi*—I; *prabhure ānila*—have brought Śrī Caitanya Mahāprabhu.

TRANSLATION

After meditating for two days, Nṛsiṁhānanda Brahmacārī told Śivānanda Sena, "I have already brought Śrī Caitanya Mahāprabhu to the village known as Pāṇihāṭi.

TEXT 55

কালি মধ্যাহ্নে তেঁহো আসিবেন তোমার ঘরে ।
পাক-সামগ্রী আনহ, আমি ভিক্ষা দিমু তাঁরে ॥ ৫৫ ॥

kāli madhyāhne teṅho āsibena tomāra ghare
pāka-sāmagrī ānaha, āmi bhikṣā dimu tāṅre

SYNONYMS

kāli madhyāhne—tomorrow at noon; *teṅho*—He; *āsibena*—will come; *tomāra ghare*—to your place; *pāka-sāmagrī ānaha*—please bring everything necessary for cooking; *āmi*—I; *bhikṣā dimu*—shall cook and offer food; *tāṅre*—to Him.

TRANSLATION

"Tomorrow at noon He will come to your home. Therefore please bring all kinds of cooking ingredients. I shall personally cook and offer Him food.

TEXT 56

তবে তাঁরে এথা আমি আনিব সত্বর ।
নিশ্চয় কহিলাঙ, কিছু সন্দেহ না কর ॥ ৫৬ ॥

tabe tāṅre ethā āmi āniba satvara
niścaya kahilāṅa, kichu sandeha nā kara

SYNONYMS

tabe—in this way; *tāṅre*—Him; *ethā*—here; *āmi*—I; *āniba satvara*—shall bring very soon; *niścaya*—with certainty; *kahilāṅa*—I spoke; *kichu sandeha nā kara*—do not be doubtful.

TRANSLATION

"In this way I shall bring Him here very soon. Be assured that I am telling you the truth. Do not be doubtful.

TEXT 57

যে চাহিয়ে, তাহা কর হঞা তৎপর ।
অতি ত্বরায় করিব পাক, শুন অতঃপর ॥ ৫৭ ॥

ye cāhiye, tāhā kara hañā tat-para
ati tvarāya kariba pāka, śuna ataḥpara

SYNONYMS

ye cāhiye—whatever I want; *tāhā kara*—arrange for that; *hañā tat-para*—being intent; *ati tvarāya*—very soon; *kariba pāka*—I shall begin cooking; *śuna ataḥpara*—just hear.

TRANSLATION

"Bring all the ingredients very soon, for I want to begin cooking immediately. Please do what I say."

TEXT 58

পাক-সামগ্রী আনহ, আমি যাহা চাই ।'
যে মাগিল, শিবানন্দ আনি' দিলা তাই ॥ ৫৮ ॥

pāka-sāmagrī ānaha, āmi yāhā cāi'
ye māgila, śivānanda āni' dilā tāi

SYNONYMS

pāka-sāmagrī ānaha—bring all cooking ingredients; *āmi yāhā cāi*—whatever I want; *ye māgila*—whatever he wanted; *śivānanda*—Śivānanda Sena; *āni'*—bringing; *dilā tāi*—delivered everything.

TRANSLATION

Nṛsiṁhānanda Brahmacārī said to Śivānanda, "Please bring whatever cooking ingredients I want." Thus Śivānanda Sena immediately brought whatever he asked for.

TEXT 59

প্রাতঃকাল হৈতে পাক করিলা অপার ।
নানা ব্যঞ্জন, পিঠা, ক্ষীর নানা উপহার ॥ ৫৯ ॥

prātaḥ-kāla haite pāka karilā apāra
nānā vyañjana, piṭhā, kṣīra nānā upahāra

SYNONYMS

prātaḥ-kāla haite—beginning from the morning; *pāka karilā apāra*—cooked many varieties of food; *nānā vyañjana*—varieties of vegetables; *piṭhā*—cakes; *kṣīra*—sweet rice; *nānā*—various; *upahāra*—offerings of food.

TRANSLATION

Beginning early in the morning, Nṛsiṁhānanda Brahmacārī cooked many varieties of food, including vegetables, cakes, sweet rice and other preparations.

TEXT 60

জগন্নাথের ভিন্ন ভোগ পৃথক্ বাড়িল ।
চৈতন্য প্রভুর লাগি' আর ভোগ কৈল ॥ ৬০ ॥

jagannāthera bhinna bhoga pṛthak bāḍila
caitanya prabhura lāgi' āra bhoga kaila

SYNONYMS

jagannāthera—of Lord Jagannātha; *bhinna*—separate; *bhoga*—offerings; *pṛthak*—separately; *bāḍila*—arranged; *caitanya prabhura lāgi'*—for Śrī Caitanya Mahāprabhu; *āra*—other; *bhoga*—offerings of food; *kaila*—made.

TRANSLATION

After he finished cooking, he brought separate dishes for Jagannātha and Śrī Caitanya Mahāprabhu.

TEXT 61

ইষ্টদেব নৃসিংহ লাগি' পৃথক্ বাড়িল ।
তিন-জনে সমর্পিয়া বাহিরে ধ্যান কৈল ॥ ৬১ ॥

iṣṭa-deva nṛsiṁha lāgi' pṛthak bāḍila
tina-jane samarpiyā bāhire dhyāna kaila

SYNONYMS

iṣṭa-deva—the worshipable Deity; *nṛsiṁha*—Lord Nṛsiṁhadeva; *lāgi'*—for; *pṛthak*—separately; *bāḍila*—arranged; *tina-jane*—to the three Deities; *samarpiyā*—offering; *bāhire*—outside; *dhyāna kaila*—meditated.

TRANSLATION

He also separately offered dishes to Nṛsiṁhadeva, his worshipable Deity. Thus he divided all the food into three offerings. Then, outside the temple, he began to meditate upon the Lord.

TEXT 62

দেখে, শীঘ্র আসি' বসিলা চৈতন্য-গোসাঞি ।
তিন ভোগ খাইলা, কিছু অবশিষ্ট নাই ॥ ৬২ ॥

dekhe, śīghra āsi' vasilā caitanya-gosāñi
tina bhoga khāilā, kichu avaśiṣṭa nāi

SYNONYMS

dekhe—he sees; *śīghra āsi'*—coming quickly; *vasilā*—sat down; *caitanya-gosāñi*—Śrī Caitanya Mahāprabhu; *tina bhoga*—the three separate offerings; *khāilā*—He ate; *kichu avaśiṣṭa nāi*—there were no remnants left.

TRANSLATION

In his meditation he saw Śrī Caitanya Mahāprabhu quickly come, sit down and eat all three offerings, leaving behind no remnants.

TEXT 63

আনন্দে বিহ্বল প্রদ্যুম্ন, পড়ে অশ্রুধার ।
"হাহা কিবা কর" বলি' করয়ে ফুৎকার ॥ ৬৩ ॥

ānande vihvala pradyumna, paḍe aśru-dhāra
"hāhā kibā kara" bali' karaye phutkāra

SYNONYMS

ānande vihvala—overwhelmed by transcendental ecstasy; *pradyumna*—Pradyumna Brahmacārī; *paḍe aśru-dhāra*—tears fell from his eyes; *hāhā*—alas, alas; *kibā kara*—what are You doing; *bali'*—saying; *karaye phut-kāra*—began to express disappointment.

TRANSLATION

Pradyumna Brahmacārī was overwhelmed by transcendental ecstasy upon seeing Caitanya Mahāprabhu eating everything. Thus tears flowed from his eyes. Nevertheless, he expressed dismay, saying, "Alas, alas! My dear Lord, what are You doing? You are eating everyone's food!

TEXT 64

'জগন্নাথে-তোমায় ঐক্য, খাও তাঁর ভোগ ।
নৃসিংহের ভোগ কেনে কর উপযোগ ? ৬৪ ॥

'jagannāthe-tomāya aikya, khāo tāṅra bhoga
nṛsiṁhera bhoga kene kara upayoga?

SYNONYMS

jagannāthe—with Lord Jagannātha; *tomāya*—and You; *aikya*—oneness; *khāo tāṅra bhoga*—You may eat His offering; *nṛsiṁhera bhoga*—the offering of Nṛsiṁhadeva; *kene kara upayoga*—why are You eating.

TRANSLATION

"My dear Lord, You are one with Jagannātha; therefore I have no objection to Your eating His offering. But why are You touching the offering to Lord Nṛsiṁhadeva?

TEXT 65

নৃসিংহের হৈল জানি আজি উপবাস ।
ঠাকুর উপবাসী রহে, জিয়ে কৈছে দাস ?' ৬৫ ॥

nṛsiṁhera haila jāni āji upavāsa
ṭhākura upavāsī rahe, jiye kaiche dāsa?'

SYNONYMS

nṛsiṁhera—of Lord Nṛsiṁha; *haila*—there was; *jāni*—I understand; *āji*—today; *upavāsa*—fasting; *ṭhākura upavāsī rahe*—the master remains fasting; *jiye kaiche dāsa*—how can the servant sustain his life.

TRANSLATION

"I think that Nṛsiṁhadeva could not eat anything today, and therefore He is fasting. If the master fasts, how can the servant live?"

TEXT 66

ভোজন দেখি' যদ্যপি তাঁর হৃদয়ে উল্লাস ।
নৃসিংহ লক্ষ্য করি' বাহ্যে কিছু করে দুঃখাভাস ॥৬৬॥

bhojana dekhi' yadyapi tāṅra hṛdaye ullāsa
nṛsiṁha lakṣya kari' bāhye kichu kare duḥkhābhāsa

SYNONYMS

bhojana dekhi'—seeing the eating; *yadyapi*—although; *tāṅra hṛdaye*—within his heart; *ullāsa*—jubilation; *nṛsiṁha*—Lord Nṛsiṁhadeva; *lakṣya kari'*—for the sake of; *bāhye*—externally; *kichu*—some; *kare*—does; *duḥkha-ābhāsa*—expression of disappointment.

TRANSLATION

Although Nṛsiṁha Brahmacārī felt jubilation within his heart to see Śrī Caitanya Mahāprabhu eating everything, for the sake of Lord Nṛsiṁhadeva he externally expressed disappointment.

TEXT 67

স্বয়ং ভগবান্ কৃষ্ণচৈতন্য-গোসাঞি ।
জগন্নাথ-নৃসিংহ-সহ কিছু ভেদ নাই ॥ ৬৭ ॥

svayaṁ bhagavān kṛṣṇa-caitanya-gosāñi
jagannātha-nṛsiṁha-saha kichu bheda nāi

SYNONYMS

svayam—personally; *bhagavān*—the Supreme Personality of Godhead; *kṛṣṇa-caitanya-gosāñi*—Lord Śrī Kṛṣṇa Caitanya Mahāprabhu; *jagannātha-nṛsiṁha-saha*—with Lord Jagannātha and Nṛsiṁhadeva; *kichu bheda*—any difference; *nāi*—there is not.

TRANSLATION

Śrī Caitanya Mahāprabhu is the Supreme Personality of Godhead Himself. Therefore there is no difference between Him, Lord Jagannātha and Lord Nṛsiṁhadeva.

TEXT 68

ইহা জানিবারে প্রদ্যুম্নের গূঢ় হৈত মন ।
তাহা দেখাইলা প্রভু করিয়া ভোজন ॥ ৬৮ ॥

ihā jānibāre pradyumnera gūḍha haita mana
tāhā dekhāilā prabhu kariyā bhojana

SYNONYMS

ihā—this fact; *jānibāre*—to know; *pradyumnera*—of Pradyumna Brahmacārī; *gūḍha*—deeply; *haita mana*—was eager; *tāhā*—that; *dekhāilā*—exhibited; *prabhu*—Śrī Caitanya Mahāprabhu; *kariyā bhojana*—by eating.

TRANSLATION

Pradyumna Brahmacārī was deeply eager to understand this fact. Therefore Śrī Caitanya Mahāprabhu revealed it to him by a practical demonstration.

TEXT 69

ভোজন করিয়া প্রভু গেলা পাণিহাটি ।
সন্তোষ পাইলা দেখি' ব্যঞ্জন-পরিপাটী ॥ ৬৯ ॥

bhojana kariyā prabhu gelā pāṇihāṭi
santoṣa pāilā dekhi' vyañjana-paripāṭī

SYNONYMS

bhojana kariyā—after eating all the offerings; *prabhu*—Śrī Caitanya Mahāprabhu; *gelā pāṇihāṭi*—started for Pāṇihāṭi; *santoṣa pāilā*—He became very satisfied; *dekhi'*—seeing; *vyañjana-paripāṭī*—arrangement of vegetables.

TRANSLATION

After eating all the offerings, Śrī Caitanya Mahāprabhu started for Pāṇihāṭi. There, He was greatly satisfied to see the different varieties of vegetables prepared in the house of Rāghava.

TEXT 70

শিবানন্দ কহে,—'কেনে করহ ফুৎকার ?'
তেঁহ কহে,—"দেখ তোমার প্রভুর ব্যবহার ॥ ৭০ ॥

śivānanda kahe,——'kene karaha phutkāra?'
teṅha kahe,——"dekha tomāra prabhura vyavahāra

SYNONYMS

śivānanda kahe—Śivānanda Sena said; *kene karaha phut-kāra*—why are you expressing dismay; *teṅha kahe*—he replied; *dekha*—see; *tomāra prabhura*—of your Lord; *vyayahāra*—the behavior.

TRANSLATION

Śivānanda said to Nṛsiṁhānanda, "Why are you expressing dismay?" Nṛsiṁhānanda replied, "Just see the behavior of your Lord Śrī Caitanya Mahāprabhu.

TEXT 71

তিন জনার ভোগ তেঁহো একেলা খাইলা ।
জগন্নাথ-নৃসিংহ উপবাসী হইলা ॥" ৭১ ॥

tina janāra bhoga teṅho ekelā khāilā
jagannātha-nṛsiṁha upavāsī ha-ilā"

SYNONYMS

tina janāra—of the three Deities; *bhoga*—offerings; *teṅho*—He; *ekelā*—alone; *khāilā*—ate; *jagannātha-nṛsiṁha*—Lord Jagannātha and Lord Nṛsiṁhadeva; *upavāsī ha-ilā*—remained fasting.

TRANSLATION

"He alone has eaten the offerings for all three Deities. Because of this, both Jagannātha and Nṛsiṁhadeva remain fasting."

TEXT 72

শুনি শিবানন্দের চিত্তে হইল সংশয়।
কিবা প্রেমাবেশে কহে, কিবা সত্য হয় ॥ ৭২ ॥

śuni śivānandera citte ha-ila saṁśaya
kibā premāveśe kahe, kibā satya haya

SYNONYMS

śuni—hearing; *śivānandera*—of Śivānanda; *citte*—in the mind; *ha-ila saṁśaya*—there was some doubt; *kibā*—whether; *prema-āveśe kahe*—was speaking something in ecstatic love; *kibā*—or; *satya haya*—it was a fact.

TRANSLATION

When Śivānanda Sena heard this statement, he was unsure whether Nṛsiṁhānanda Brahmacārī was speaking that way because of ecstatic love or because it was actually a fact.

TEXT 73

তবে শিবানন্দে কিছু কহে ব্রহ্মচারী।
সামগ্রী আন নৃসিংহ লাগি পুনঃ পাক করি' ॥ ৭৩ ॥

tabe śivānande kichu kahe brahmacārī
sāmagrī āna nṛsiṁha lāgi punaḥ pāka kari'

SYNONYMS

tabe—upon this; *śivānande*—unto Śivānanda; *kichu*—something; *kahe*—says; *brahmacārī*—Nṛsiṁhānanda Brahmacārī; *sāmagrī āna*—bring more ingredients; *nṛsiṁha lāgi'*—for Lord Nṛsiṁhadeva; *punaḥ*—again; *pāka kari'*—let me cook.

TRANSLATION

When Śivānanda Sena was thus perplexed, Nṛsiṁhānanda Brahmacārī said to him, "Bring more food. Let me cook again for Lord Nṛsiṁhadeva."

TEXT 74

তবে শিবানন্দ ভোগ-সামগ্রী আনিলা ।
পাক করি' নৃসিংহের ভোগ লাগাইলা ॥ ৭৪ ॥

tabe śivānanda bhoga-sāmagrī ānilā
pāka kari' nṛsiṁhera bhoga lāgāilā

SYNONYMS

tabe—thereupon; *śivānanda*—Śivānanda Sena; *bhoga-sāmagrī*—ingredients for preparing food; *ānilā*—brought; *pāka kari'*—after cooking; *nṛsiṁhera*—of Lord Nṛsiṁhadeva; *bhoga lāgāilā*—offered the food.

TRANSLATION

Then Śivānanda Sena again brought the ingredients with which to cook, and Pradyumna Brahmacārī again cooked and offered the food to Nṛsiṁhadeva.

TEXT 75

বর্ষান্তরে শিবানন্দ লঞা ভক্তগণ ।
নীলাচলে দেখে যাঞা প্রভুর চরণ ॥ ৭৫ ॥

varṣāntare śivānanda lañā bhakta-gaṇa
nīlācale dekhe yāñā prabhura caraṇa

SYNONYMS

varṣa-antare—the next year; *śivānanda*—Śivānanda Sena; *lañā*—taking; *bhakta-gaṇa*—all the devotees; *nīlācale*—at Jagannātha Purī; *dekhe*—sees; *yāñā*—going; *prabhura caraṇa*—the lotus feet of the Lord.

TRANSLATION

The next year, Śivānanda went to Jagannātha Purī with all the other devotees to see the lotus feet of Śrī Caitanya Mahāprabhu.

TEXT 76

একদিন সভাতে প্রভু বাত চালাইলা ।
নৃসিংহানন্দের গুণ কহিতে লাগিলা ॥ ৭৬ ॥

eka-dina sabhāte prabhu vāta cālāilā
nṛsiṁhānandera guṇa kahite lāgilā

SYNONYMS

eka-dina—one day; *sabhāte*—in the presence of all the devotees; *prabhu*—Śrī Caitanya Mahāprabhu; *vāta cālāilā*—raised the topic (of eating at Nṛsiṁhānanda's house); *nṛsiṁhānandera*—of Nṛsiṁhānanda Brahmacārī; *guṇa*—transcendental qualities; *kahite lāgilā*—began to speak.

TRANSLATION

One day, in the presence of all the devotees, the Lord raised these topics concerning Nṛsiṁhānanda Brahmacārī and praised his transcendental qualities.

TEXT 77

'গতবর্ষ পৌষে মোরে করাইল ভোজন ।
কভু নাহি খাই ঐছে মিষ্টান্ন-ব্যঞ্জন ॥' ৭৭ ॥

'gata-varṣa pauṣe more karāila bhojana
kabhu nāhi khāi aiche miṣṭānna-vyañjana'

SYNONYMS

gata-varṣa—last year; *pauṣe*—in the month of Pauṣa (December-January); *more*—unto Me; *karāila bhojana*—offered many foodstuffs; *kabhu nāhi khāi*—I never tasted; *aiche*—such; *miṣṭānna*—sweetmeats; *vyañjana*—vegetables.

TRANSLATION

The Lord said, "Last year in the month of Pauṣa, when Nṛsiṁhānanda gave me varieties of sweetmeats and vegetables to eat, they were so good that I had never before eaten such preparations."

TEXT 78

শুনি' ভক্তগণ মনে আশ্চর্য মানিল ।
শিবানন্দের মনে তবে প্রত্যয় জন্মিল ॥ ৭৮ ॥

śuni' bhakta-gaṇa mane āścarya mānila
śivānandera mane tabe pratyaya janmila

SYNONYMS

śuni'—hearing; *bhakta-gaṇa*—all the devotees; *mane*—in the mind; *āścarya mānila*—felt wonder; *śivānandera*—of Śivānanda Sena; *mane*—in the mind; *tabe*—thereupon; *pratyaya janmila*—there was confidence.

TRANSLATION

Hearing this, all the devotees were struck with wonder, and Śivānanda became confident that the incident was true.

TEXT 79

এইমত শচীগৃহে সতত ভোজন ।
শ্রীবাসের গৃহে করেন কীর্তন-দর্শন ॥ ৭৯ ॥

ei-mata śacī-gṛhe satata bhojana
śrīvāsera gṛhe karena kīrtana-darśana

SYNONYMS

ei-mata—in this way; *śacī-gṛhe*—at the house of Śacīmātā; *satata*—always; *bhojana*—eating; *śrīvāsera gṛhe*—in the house of Śrīvāsa Ṭhākura; *karena*—performs; *kīrtana-darśana*—visiting the *kīrtana* performances.

TRANSLATION

In this way Śrī Caitanya Mahāprabhu used to eat at the temple of Śacīmātā every day and also visit the house of Śrīvāsa Ṭhākura when kīrtana was performed.

TEXT 80

নিত্যানন্দের নৃত্য দেখেন আসি' বারে বারে ।
'নিরন্তর আবির্ভাব' রাঘবের ঘরে ॥ ৮০ ॥

nityānandera nṛtya dekhena āsi' bāre bāre
'nirantara āvirbhāva' rāghavera ghare

SYNONYMS

nityānandera nṛtya—the dancing of Śrī Nityānanda Prabhu; *dekhena*—He sees; *āsi'*—coming; *bāre bāre*—again and again; *nirantara āvirbhāva*—constant appearance; *rāghavera ghare*—in the house of Rāghava.

TRANSLATION

Similarly, He was always present when Nityānanda Prabhu danced, and He regularly appeared at the house of Rāghava.

TEXT 81

প্রেমবশ গৌরপ্রভু, যাহাঁ প্রেমোত্তম ।
প্রেমবশ হঞা তাহা দেন দরশন ॥ ৮১ ॥

prema-vaśa gaura-prabhu, yāhāṅ premottama
prema-vaśa hañā tāhā dena daraśana

SYNONYMS

prema-vaśa—subdued by loving service; *gaura-prabhu*—Śrī Caitanya Mahāprabhu, Gaurasundara; *yāhāṅ prema-uttama*—wherever there is pure love; *prema-vaśa hañā*—being subdued by such love; *tāhā*—there; *dena daraśana*—appears personally.

TRANSLATION

Lord Gaurasundara is greatly influenced by the love of His devotees. Therefore wherever there is pure devotion to the Lord, the Lord Himself, subdued by such love, appears, and His devotees see Him.

TEXT 82

শিবানন্দের প্রেমসীমা কে কহিতে পারে ?
যাঁর প্রেমে বশ প্রভু আইসে বারে বারে ॥ ৮২ ॥

śivānandera prema-sīmā ke kahite pāre?
yāṅra preme vaśa prabhu āise bāre bāre

SYNONYMS

śivānandera—of Śivānanda Sena; *prema-sīmā*—the limit of love; *ke*—who; *kahite pāre*—can estimate; *yāṅra*—whose; *preme*—by loving affairs; *vaśa*—influenced; *prabhu*—Śrī Caitanya Mahāprabhu; *āise*—comes; *bāre bāre*—again and again.

TRANSLATION

Influenced by the loving affairs of Śivānanda Sena, Śrī Caitanya Mahāprabhu came again and again. Therefore who can estimate the limits of his love?

TEXT 83

এই ত' কহিলু গৌরের 'আবির্ভাব' ।
ইহা যেই শুনে, জানে চৈতন্য-প্রভাব ॥ ৮৩ ॥

ei ta' kahilu gaurera 'āvirbhāva'
ihā yei śune, jāne caitanya-prabhāva

SYNONYMS

ei ta'—thus; *kahilu*—I have described; *gaurera*—of Śrī Caitanya Mahāprabhu; *āvirbhāva*—appearance; *ihā*—this incident; *yei śune*—whoever hears; *jāne*—knows; *caitanya-prabhāva*—the opulence of Śrī Caitanya Mahāprabhu.

TRANSLATION

Thus I have described the appearance of Śrī Caitanya Mahāprabhu. Anyone who hears about these incidents can understand the transcendental opulence of the Lord.

TEXT 84

পুরুষোত্তমে প্রভু-পাশে ভগবান্ আচার্য ।
পরম বৈষ্ণব তেঁহো সুপণ্ডিত আর্য ॥ ৮৪ ॥

puruṣottame prabhu-pāśe bhagavān ācārya
parama vaiṣṇava teṅho supaṇḍita ārya

SYNONYMS

puruṣottame—at Jagannātha Purī; *prabhu-pāśe*—in the association of Śrī Caitanya Mahāprabhu; *bhagavān ācārya*—Bhagavān Ācārya; *parama vaiṣṇava*—pure devotee; *teṅho*—he; *su-paṇḍita*—very learned scholar; *ārya*—gentleman.

TRANSLATION

At Jagannātha Purī, in the association of Śrī Caitanya Mahāprabhu, lived Bhagavān Ācārya, who was certainly a gentleman, a learned scholar and a great devotee.

PURPORT

For a description of Bhagavān Ācārya, one may refer to the *Ādi-līlā,* Tenth Chapter, verse 136.

TEXT 85

সখ্যভাবাক্রান্ত-চিত্ত, গোপ-অবতার ।
স্বরূপ-গোসাঞি-সহ সখ্য-ব্যবহার ॥ ৮৫ ॥

sakhya-bhāvākrānta-citta, gopa-avatāra
svarūpa-gosāñi-saha sakhya-vyavahāra

SYNONYMS

sakhya-bhāva—by fraternal love; *ākrānta*—overwhelmed; *citta*—heart; *gopa-avatāra*—an incarnation of one of the cowherd boys; *svarūpa-gosāñi-saha*—with Svarūpa Dāmodara; *sakhya-vyavahāra*—dealings just like those of a friend.

TRANSLATION

He was fully absorbed in thoughts of fraternal relationships with God. He was an incarnation of a cowherd boy, and thus his dealings with Svarūpa Dāmodara Gosvāmī were very friendly.

TEXT 86

একান্তভাবে আশ্রিয়াছেন চৈতন্যচরণ ।
মধ্যে মধ্যে প্রভুর তেঁহো করেন নিমন্ত্রণ ॥ ৮৬ ॥

ekānta-bhāve āśriyāchena caitanya-caraṇa
madhye madhye prabhura teṅho karena nimantraṇa

SYNONYMS

ekānta-bhāve—with full attention; *āśriyāchena*—has taken shelter of; *caitanya-caraṇa*—the lotus feet of Lord Caitanya; *madhye madhye*—sometimes; *prabhura*—of Śrī Caitanya Mahāprabhu; *teṅho*—he; *karena*—does; *nimantraṇa*—invitation.

TRANSLATION

He sought the shelter of Śrī Caitanya Mahāprabhu with full surrender. Sometimes he would invite the Lord to dine at his home.

TEXT 87

ঘরে ভাত করি' করেন বিবিধ ব্যঞ্জন ।
একলে গোসাঞি লঞা করান ভোজন ॥ ৮৭ ॥

ghare bhāta kari' karena vividha vyañjana
ekale gosāñi lañā karāna bhojana

SYNONYMS

ghare—at home; *bhāta kari'*—preparing rice; *karena*—prepares; *vividha vyañjana*—varieties of vegetables; *ekale*—alone; *gosāñi lañā*—taking Śrī Caitanya Mahāprabhu; *karāna bhojana*—makes to eat.

TRANSLATION

Bhagavān Ācārya prepared varieties of rice and vegetables at home and brought the Lord there alone to eat.

PURPORT

Generally those who invited Śrī Caitanya Mahāprabhu for dinner used to offer Him the remnants of food that had first been offered to Lord Jagannātha. Bhagavān Ācārya, however, instead of giving Him the remnants of Jagannātha's food, prepared dinner at his home. In Orissa, food offered to Lord Jagannātha is called *prasādī*, and that which is not offered to Lord Jagannātha is known as *āmānī* or *ghara-bhāta*, rice prepared at home.

TEXT 88

তাঁর পিতা 'বিষয়ী' বড় শতানন্দ-খাঁন ।
'বিষয়বিমুখ' আচার্য—'বৈরাগ্যপ্রধান' ॥ ৮৮ ॥

tāṅra pitā 'viṣayī' baḍa śatānanda-khāṅna
'viṣaya-vimukha' ācārya——'vairāgya-pradhāna'

SYNONYMS

tāṅra pitā—his father; *viṣayī*—a statesman; *baḍa*—expert; *śatānanda-khāṅna*—named Śatānanda Khān; *viṣaya-vimukha*—not interested in state management; *ācārya*—Bhagavān Ācārya; *vairāgya-pradhāna*—mostly in the renounced order of life.

TRANSLATION

Bhagavān Ācārya's father, whose name was Śatānanda Khān, was an expert statesman, whereas Bhagavān Ācārya was not at all interested in the management of the state. Indeed, he was almost in the renounced order of life.

TEXT 89

'গোপাল-ভট্টাচার্য' নাম তাঁর ছোট-ভাই ।
কাশীতে বেদান্ত পড়ি' গেলা তাঁর ঠাঞি ॥ ৮৯ ॥

'gopāla-bhaṭṭācārya' nāma tāṅra choṭa-bhāi
kāśīte vedānta paḍi' gelā tāṅra ṭhāñi

SYNONYMS

gopāla-bhaṭṭācārya—Gopāla Bhaṭṭācārya; *nāma*—named; *tāṅra*—his; *choṭa-bhāi*—younger brother; *kāśīte*—at Benares; *vedānta paḍi'*—studying Vedānta philosophy; *gelā*—went; *tāṅra ṭhāñi*—to his place.

TRANSLATION

Bhagavān Ācārya's brother, whose name was Gopāla Bhaṭṭācārya, had studied Vedānta philosophy at Benares and had then returned to Bhagavān Ācārya's home.

PURPORT

During those days and also at the present, Vedānta philosophy is understood through the commentary of Śaṅkarācārya, which is known as *Śārīraka-bhāṣya.* Thus it appears that Gopāla Bhaṭṭācārya, the younger brother of Bhagavān Ācārya, had studied Vedānta according to the way of the *Śārīraka-bhāṣya,* which expounds the Māyāvāda philosophy of the impersonalists.

TEXT 90

আচার্য তাহারে প্রভুপদে মিলাইলা ।
অন্তর্যামী প্রভু চিত্তে সুখ না পাইলা ॥ ৯০ ॥

ācārya tāhāre prabhu-pade milāilā
antaryāmī prabhu citte sukha nā pāilā

SYNONYMS

ācārya—Bhagavān Ācārya; *tāhāre*—him (his brother); *prabhu-pade milāilā*—got to meet Śrī Caitanya Mahāprabhu; *antaryāmī prabhu*—Lord Śrī Caitanya Mahāprabhu, who could study anyone's heart; *citte*—within Himself; *sukha*—happiness; *nā pāilā*—could not get.

TRANSLATION

Bhagavān Ācārya took his brother to meet Śrī Caitanya Mahāprabhu, but the Lord, knowing that Gopāla Bhaṭṭācārya was a Māyāvādī philosopher, could not get much happiness from meeting him.

TEXT 91

আচার্য-সম্বন্ধে বাহ্যে করে প্রীত্যাভাস ।
কৃষ্ণভক্তি বিনা প্রভুর না হয় উল্লাস ॥ ৯১ ॥

ācārya-sambandhe bāhye kare prītyābhāsa
kṛṣṇa-bhakti vinā prabhura nā haya ullāsa

SYNONYMS

ācārya-sambandhe—because he was related with Bhagavān Ācārya; *bāhye*—externally; *kare*—does; *prīti-ābhāsa*—appearance of pleasure; *kṛṣṇa-bhakti*—devotional service to Lord Kṛṣṇa; *vinā*—without; *prabhura*—of Śrī Caitanya Mahāprabhu; *nā haya*—there is no; *ullāsa*—jubilation.

TRANSLATION

Śrī Caitanya Mahāprabhu derives no happiness from meeting one who is not a pure devotee of Kṛṣṇa. Thus because Gopāla Bhaṭṭācārya was a Māyāvādī scholar, the Lord felt no jubilation in meeting him. Nevertheless, because Gopāla Bhaṭṭācārya was related to Bhagavān Ācārya, Śrī Caitanya Mahāprabhu feigned pleasure in seeing him.

TEXT 92

স্বরূপ গোসাঞিরে আচার্য কহে আর দিনে।
'বেদান্ত পড়িয়া গোপাল আইসাছে এখানে ॥ ৯২ ॥

svarūpa gosāñire ācārya kahe āra dine
'vedānta paḍiyā gopāla āisāche ekhāne

SYNONYMS

svarūpa gosāñire—unto Svarūpa Dāmodara Gosvāmī; *ācārya*—Bhagavān Ācārya; *kahe*—says; *āra dine*—the next day; *vedānta paḍiyā*—after studying Vedānta; *gopāla*—Gopāla; *āisāche*—has come back; *ekhāne*—here.

TRANSLATION

Bhagavān Ācārya said to Svarūpa Dāmodara, "Gopāla, my younger brother, has returned to my home, having concluded his study of Vedānta philosophy."

TEXT 93

সবে মেলি' আইস, শুনি 'ভাষ্য' ইহার স্থানে'।
প্রেম-ক্রোধ করি' স্বরূপ বলয় বচনে ॥ ৯৩ ॥

sabe meli' āisa, śuni 'bhāṣya' ihāra sthāne'
prema-krodha kari' svarūpa balaya vacane

SYNONYMS

sabe meli'—all together; *āisa*—come; *śuni*—let us hear; *bhāṣya*—the commentary; *ihāra sthāne*—from him; *prema-krodha kari'*—in an angry mood of love; *svarūpa*—Svarūpa Dāmodara; *balaya vacane*—said these words.

TRANSLATION

Bhagavān Ācārya requested Svarūpa Dāmodara to hear from Gopāla the commentary upon Vedānta. Svarūpa Dāmodara Gosvāmī, however, somewhat angry because of love, spoke as follows.

TEXT 94

"বুদ্ধি ভ্রষ্ট হৈল তোমার গোপালের সঙ্গে ।
মায়াবাদ শুনিবারে উপজিল রঙ্গে ॥ ৯৪ ॥

"buddhi bhraṣṭa haila tomāra gopālera saṅge
māyāvāda śunibāre upajila raṅge

SYNONYMS

buddhi—intelligence; *bhraṣṭa*—lost; *haila*—has been; *tomāra*—your; *gopālera saṅge*—in the association of Gopāla; *māyāvāda śunibāre*—to hear the commentary of Māyāvāda philosophy; *upajila raṅge*—has awakened the propensity.

TRANSLATION

"You have lost your intelligence in the association of Gopāla, and therefore you are eager to hear the Māyāvāda philosophy.

TEXT 95

বৈষ্ণব হঞা যেবা শারীরক-ভাষ্য শুনে ।
সেব্য-সেবক-ভাব ছাড়ি' আপনারে 'ঈশ্বর' মানে ॥৯৫॥

vaiṣṇava hañā yebā śārīraka-bhāṣya śune
sevya-sevaka-bhāva chāḍi' āpanāre 'īśvara' māne

SYNONYMS

vaiṣṇava hañā—being a Vaiṣṇava; *yebā*—anyone who; *śārīraka-bhāṣya*—the Māyāvāda commentary *Śārīraka-bhāṣya*; *śune*—listens to; *sevya-sevaka-bhāva*—the Kṛṣṇa conscious attitude that the Lord is the master and the living entity is His servant; *chāḍi'*—giving up; *āpanāre*—himself; *īśvara*—the Supreme Lord; *māne*—considers.

TRANSLATION

"When a Vaiṣṇava listens to the Śārīraka-bhāṣya, the Māyāvāda commentary upon Vedānta-sūtra, he gives up the Kṛṣṇa conscious attitude that the Lord is the master and the living entity is His servant. Instead, he considers himself the Supreme Lord.

PURPORT

The philosophers known as *kevalādvaita-vādīs* generally occupy themselves with hearing the *Śārīraka-bhāṣya,* a commentary by Śaṅkarācārya advocating that one impersonally consider oneself the Supreme Lord. Such Māyāvāda philosophical commentaries upon Vedānta are simply imaginary, but there are other commentaries on Vedānta philosophy. The commentary by Śrīla Rāmānujācārya, known as *Śrī-bhāṣya,* establishes the *viśiṣṭādvaita-vāda* philosophy. Similarly, in the Brahma-sampradāya, Madhvācārya's *Pūrṇaprajña-bhāṣya* establishes *śuddha-dvaita-vāda.* In the Kumāra-sampradāya, or Nimbārka-sampradāya, Śrī Nimbārka establishes the philosophy of *dvaitādvaita-vāda* in the *Pārijāta-saurabha-bhāṣya.* And in the Viṣṇusvāmi-sampradāya, or Rudra-samprādaya, which comes from Lord Śiva, Viṣṇusvāmī has written a commentary called *Sarvajña-bhāṣya,* which establishes *śuddhādvaita-vāda.*

A Vaiṣṇava should study the commentaries on *Vedānta-sūtra* written by the four *sampradāya-ācāryas,* namely Śrī Rāmānujācārya, Madhvācārya, Viṣṇusvāmī and Nimbārka, for these commentaries are based upon the philosophy that the Lord is the master and that all living entities are His eternal servants. One interested in studying Vedānta philosophy properly must study these commentaries, especially if he is a Vaiṣṇava. These commentaries are always adored by Vaiṣṇavas. The commentary by Śrīla Bhaktisiddhānta Sarasvatī is elaborately given in the *Ādi-līlā,* Chapter Seven, text 101. The Māyāvāda commentary *Śārīraka-bhāṣya* is like poison for a Vaiṣṇava. It should not be touched at all. Śrīla Bhaktivinoda Ṭhākura remarks that even a *mahā-bhāgavata,* or highly elevated devotee who has surrendered himself unto the lotus feet of Kṛṣṇa, sometimes falls down from pure devotional service if he hears the Māyāvāda philosophy of *Śārīraka-bhāṣya.* This commentary should therefore be shunned by all Vaiṣṇavas.

TEXT 96

মহাভাগবত যেই, কৃষ্ণ প্রাণধন যার ।
মায়াবাদ-শ্রবণে চিত্ত অবশ্য ফিরে তাঁর ॥" ৯৬ ॥

mahā-bhāgavata yei, kṛṣṇa prāṇa-dhana yāra
māyāvāda-śravaṇe citta avaśya phire tāṅra"

SYNONYMS

mahā-bhāgavata yei—one who is a highly elevated devotee; *kṛṣṇa*—Lord Kṛṣṇa; *prāṇa-dhana yāra*—whose life and soul; *māyāvāda-śravaṇe*—by hearing the Māyāvāda philosophy; *citta*—the heart; *avaśya*—certainly; *phire*—changes; *tāṅra*—his.

TRANSLATION

"The Māyāvāda philosophy presents such a jugglery of words that even a highly elevated devotee who has accepted Kṛṣṇa as his life and soul changes his decision when he reads the Māyāvāda commentary on Vedānta-sūtra."

TEXT 97

আচার্য কহে, - 'আমা সবার কৃষ্ণনিষ্ঠ-চিত্তে ।
আমা সবার মন ভাষ্য নারে ফিরাইতে ॥' ৯৭ ॥

ācārya kahe,——'āmā sabāra kṛṣṇa-niṣṭha-citte
āmā sabāra mana bhāṣya nāre phirāite'

SYNONYMS

ācārya kahe—Bhagavān Ācārya replied; *āmā sabāra*—of all of us; *kṛṣṇa-niṣṭha*—devoted to Kṛṣṇa; *citte*—hearts; *āmā sabāra*—of all of us; *mana*—minds; *bhāṣya*—*Śārīraka-bhāṣya*; *nāre phirāite*—cannot change.

TRANSLATION

In spite of Svarūpa Dāmodara's protest, Bhagavān Ācārya continued, "We are all fixed at the lotus feet of Kṛṣṇa with our hearts and souls. Therefore the Śārīraka-bhāṣya cannot change our minds."

TEXT 98

স্বরূপ কহে, "তথাপি মায়াবাদ-শ্রবণে ।
'চিৎ, ব্রহ্ম, মায়া, মিথ্যা'—এইমাত্র শুনে ॥ ৯৮ ॥

svarūpa kahe, "tathāpi māyāvāda-śravaṇe
'cit, brahma, māyā, mithyā'——ei-mātra śune

SYNONYMS

svarūpa kahe—Svarūpa Dāmodara replied; *tathāpi*—still; *māyāvāda-śravaṇe*—by hearing the Māyāvāda commentary; *cit*—knowledge; *brahma*—the Absolute Truth; *māyā*—external energy; *mithyā*—false; *ei-mātra*—only these; *śune*—hears.

TRANSLATION

Svarūpa Dāmodara replied, "Nevertheless, when we hear the Māyāvāda philosophy, we hear that Brahman is knowledge and that the universe of māyā is false, but we gain no spiritual understanding.

TEXT 99

জীবাজ্ঞান-কল্পিত ঈশ্বরে, সকলই অজ্ঞান ।
যাহার শ্রবণে ভক্তের ফাটে মন প্রাণ ॥" ৯৯ ॥

jīvājñāna-kalpita īśvare, sakala-i ajñāna
yāhāra śravaṇe bhaktera phāṭe mana prāṇa"

SYNONYMS

jīva—the ordinary living being; *ajñāna*—by ignorance; *kalpita*—imagined; *īśvare*—in the Supreme Lord; *sakala-i ajñāna*—all ignorance; *yāhāra śravaṇe*—hearing of which; *bhaktera*—of the devotee; *phāṭe*—breaks; *mana prāṇa*—mind and life.

TRANSLATION

"The Māyāvādī philosopher tries to establish that the living entity is only imaginary and that the Supreme Personality of Godhead is under the influence of māyā. Hearing this kind of commentary breaks the heart and life of a devotee."

PURPORT

Śrīla Svarūpa Dāmodara Gosvāmī wanted to impress upon Bhagavān Ācārya that even though someone firmly fixed in devotion to Kṛṣṇa's service might not be deviated by hearing the Māyāvāda *bhāṣya,* that *bhāṣya* is nevertheless full of impersonal words and ideas such as Brahman which represent knowledge but which are impersonal. The Māyāvādīs say that the world created by *māyā* is false, and that actually there is no living entity but only one spiritual effulgence. They further say that God is imaginary, that people think of God only because of ignorance, and that when the Supreme Absolute Truth is befooled by the external energy, *māyā,* He becomes a *jīva,* or living entity. Upon hearing all these nonsensical ideas from the nondevotee, a devotee is greatly afflicted, as if his heart and soul were broken.

TEXT 100

লজ্জা-ভয় পাঞা আচার্য মৌন হইলা ।
আর দিন গোপালেরে দেশে পাঠাইলা ॥ ১০০ ॥

lajjā-bhaya pāñā ācārya mauna ha-ilā
āra dina gopālere deśe pāṭhāilā

SYNONYMS

lajjā-bhaya—fear and shame; *pāñā*—getting; *ācārya*—Bhagavān Ācārya; *mauna ha-ilā*—became silent; *āra dina*—the next day; *gopālere*—Gopāla Bhaṭṭācārya; *deśe*—to his own country; *pāṭhāilā*—sent.

TRANSLATION

Thus Bhagavān Ācārya, greatly ashamed and fearful, remained silent. The next day, he asked Gopāla Bhaṭṭācārya to return to his own district.

TEXT 101

একদিন আচার্য প্রভুরে কৈলা নিমন্ত্রণ ।
ঘরে ভাত করি' করে বিবিধ ব্যঞ্জন ॥ ১০১ ॥

eka-dina ācārya prabhure kailā nimantraṇa
ghare bhāta kari' kare vividha vyañjana

SYNONYMS

eka-dina—one day; *ācārya*—Bhagavān Ācārya; *prabhure*—unto Śrī Caitanya Mahāprabhu; *kailā nimantraṇa*—made an invitation for dinner; *ghare*—at home; *bhāta kari'*—cooking rice; *kare*—prepares; *vividha vyañjana*—varieties of vegetable preparations.

TRANSLATION

One day Bhagavān Ācārya invited Śrī Caitanya Mahāprabhu to dine at his home. Thus he was preparing rice and various types of vegetables.

TEXT 102

'ছোট-হরিদাস' নাম প্রভুর কীর্তনীয়া ।
তাহারে কহেন আচার্য ডাকিয়া আনিয়া ॥ ১০২ ॥

'choṭa-haridāsa' nāma prabhura kīrtanīyā
tāhāre kahena ācārya ḍākiyā āniyā

SYNONYMS

choṭa-haridāsa nāma—a devotee named Choṭa Haridāsa; *prabhura kīrtanīyā*—a chanter of songs for Śrī Caitanya Mahāprabhu; *tāhāre*—unto him; *kahena*—says; *ācārya*—the *ācārya;* *ḍākiyā āniyā*—calling him to his place.

TRANSLATION

A devotee named Choṭa Haridāsa used to sing for Śrī Caitanya Mahāprabhu. Bhagavān Ācārya called him to his home and spoke as follows.

TEXT 103

'মোর নামে শিখি-মাহিতির ভগিনী-স্থানে গিয়া।
শুক্লচাউল এক মান আনহ মাগিয়া ॥' ১০৩ ॥

'mora nāme śikhi-māhitira bhaginī-sthāne giyā
śukla-cāula eka māna ānaha māgiyā'

SYNONYMS

mora nāme—in my name; *śikhi-māhitira*—of Śikhi Māhiti; *bhaginī-sthāne*—at the place of the sister; *giyā*—going; *śukla-cāula*—white rice; *eka māna*—the measurement of one *māna*; *ānaha*—please bring; *māgiyā*—requesting.

TRANSLATION

"Please go to the sister of Śikhi Māhiti. In my name, ask her for a māna of white rice and bring it here."

PURPORT

In India *śukla-cāula* (white rice) is also called *ātapa-cāula,* or rice that has not been boiled before being threshed. Another kind of rice, called *siddha-cāula* (brown rice), is boiled before being threshed. Generally, first-class fine white rice is required for offerings to the Deity. Thus Bhagavān Ācārya asked Choṭa Haridāṣa, or Junior Haridāsa, a singer in the assembly of Śrī Caitanya Mahāprabhu, to get some of this rice from the sister of Śikhi Māhiti. A *māna* is a standard of measurement in Orissa for rice and other food grains.

TEXT 104

মাহিতির ভগিনী সেই, নাম—মাধবী-দেবী।
বৃদ্ধা তপস্বিনী আর পরমা বৈষ্ণবী ॥ ১০৪ ॥

māhitira bhaginī sei, nāma——mādhavī-devī
vṛddhā tapasvinī āra paramā vaiṣṇavī

SYNONYMS

māhitira bhaginī—sister of Śikhi Māhiti; *sei*—that; *nāma*—named; *mādhavī-devī*—of the name Mādhavīdevī; *vṛddhā*—an elderly lady; *tapasvinī*—very strict in executing devotional service; *āra*—and; *paramā vaiṣṇavī*—a first-class devotee.

TRANSLATION

Śikhi Māhiti's sister was named Mādhavīdevī. She was an elderly lady who always performed austerities. She was very advanced in devotional service.

TEXT 105

প্রভু লেখা করে যারে—রাধিকার 'গণ'।
জগতের মধ্যে 'পাত্র'—সাড়ে তিন জন ॥ ১০৫ ॥

prabhu lekhā kare yāre——rādhikāra 'gaṇa'
jagatera madhye 'pātra'——sāḍe tina jana

SYNONYMS

prabhu—Śrī Caitanya Mahāprabhu; *lekhā kare*—accepts; *yāre*—whom; *rādhikāra gaṇa*—as one of the associates of Śrīmatī Rādhārāṇī; *jagatera madhye*—throughout the whole world; *pātra*—most confidential devotees; *sāḍe tina*—three and a half; *jana*—persons.

TRANSLATION

Śrī Caitanya Mahāprabhu accepted her as having formerly been an associate of Śrīmatī Rādhārāṇī. In the entire world, three and a half people were His intimate devotees.

TEXT 106

স্বরূপ গোসাঞি, আর রায় রামানন্দ।
শিখি-মাহিতি—তিন, তাঁর ভগিনী—অর্ধজন ॥ ১০৬ ॥

svarūpa gosāñi, āra rāya rāmānanda
śikhi-māhiti——tina, tāṅra bhaginī——ardha-jana

SYNONYMS

svarūpa gosāñi—of the name Svarūpa Gosvāmī; *āra*—and; *rāya rāmānanda*—Rāmānanda Rāya; *śikhi-māhiti*—Śikhi Māhiti; *tina*—three; *tāṅra bhaginī*—his sister; *ardha-jana*—half a person.

TRANSLATION

The three were Svarūpa Dāmodara Gosvāmī, Rāmānanda Rāya and Śikhi Māhiti, and the half a person was Śikhi Māhiti's sister.

TEXT 107

তাঁর ঠাঞি তণ্ডুল মাগি' আনিল হরিদাস ।
তণ্ডুল দেখি' আচার্যের অধিক উল্লাস ॥ ১০৭ ॥

tāṅra ṭhāñi taṇḍula māgi' ānila haridāsa
taṇḍula dekhi' ācāryera adhika ullāsa

SYNONYMS

tāṅra ṭhāñi—from her; *taṇḍula māgi'*—begging rice; *ānila haridāsa*—Haridāsa brought; *taṇḍula dekhi'*—seeing the rice; *ācāryera*—of Bhagavān Ācārya; *adhika ullāsa*—very great satisfaction.

TRANSLATION

After begging the rice from her, Junior Haridāsa brought it to Bhagavān Ācārya, who was very pleased to see its quality.

TEXT 108

স্নেহে রান্ধিল প্রভুর প্রিয় যে ব্যঞ্জন ।
দেউল প্রসাদ, আদা-চাকি, লেম্বু-সলবণ ॥ ১০৮ ॥

snehe rāndhila prabhura priya ye vyañjana
deula prasāda, ādā-cāki, lembu-salavaṇa

SYNONYMS

snehe—in great affection; *rāndhila*—cooked; *prabhura*—of Śrī Caitanya Mahāprabhu; *priya*—dear; *ye*—whatever; *vyañjana*—vegetables; *deula prasāda*—remnants from the temple of Jagannātha; *ādā-cāki*—ground ginger; *lembu*—lime; *sa-lavaṇa*—with salt.

TRANSLATION

In great affection, Bhagavān Ācārya cooked varieties of vegetables and other preparations dear to Śrī Caitanya Mahāprabhu. He also obtained remnants of food from Lord Jagannātha and digestive aids such as ground ginger and also lime with salt.

TEXT 109

মধ্যাহ্নে আসিয়া প্রভু ভোজনে বসিলা ।
শাল্যন্ন দেখি' প্রভু আচার্যে পুছিলা ॥ ১০৯ ॥

madhyāhne āsiyā prabhu bhojane vasilā
śālyanna dekhi' prabhu ācārye puchilā

SYNONYMS

madyāhne—at noon; *āsiyā*—coming; *prabhu*—Śrī Caitanya Mahāprabhu; *bhojane vasilā*—sat down to eat; *śāli-anna*—the rice of fine quality; *dekhi'*—seeing; *prabhu*—Śrī Caitanya Mahāprabhu; *ācārye puchilā*—inquired from Bhagavān Ācārya.

TRANSLATION

At noon, when Śrī Caitanya Mahāprabhu came to eat the offerings of Bhagavān Ācārya, He first appreciated the fine rice and therefore questioned him.

TEXT 110

উত্তম অন্ন এত তণ্ডুল কাঁহাতে পাইলা ?
আচার্য কহে,—মাধবী-পাশ মাগিয়া আনিলা ॥ ১১০ ॥

uttama anna eta taṇḍula kāṅhāte pāilā?
ācārya kahe,——mādhavī-pāśa māgiyā ānilā

SYNONYMS

uttama anna—fine rice; *eta*—such; *taṇḍula*—rice; *kāṅhāte pāilā*—where did you get; *ācārya kahe*—Bhagavān Ācārya replied; *mādhavī-pāśa*—from Mādhavīdevī; *māgiyā*—begging; *ānilā*—have brought.

TRANSLATION

"Where did you get such fine rice?" the Lord asked. Bhagavān Ācārya replied, "I got it by begging from Mādhavīdevī."

TEXT 111

প্রভু কহে,—'কোন্ যাই' মাগিয়া আনিল ?'
ছোট-হরিদাসের নাম আচার্য কহিল ॥ ১১১ ॥

prabhu kahe,——'kon yāi' māgiyā ānila?'
choṭa-haridāsera nāma ācārya kahila

SYNONYMS

prabhu kahe—Śrī Caitanya Mahāprabhu said; *kon yāi'*—who went; *māgiyā*—begging; *ānila*—brought; *choṭa-haridāsera*—of Junior Haridāsa; *nāma*—the name; *ācārya kahila*—Bhagavān Ācārya informed.

TRANSLATION

When Śrī Caitanya Mahāprabhu asked who had begged the rice and brought it back, Bhagavān Ācārya mentioned the name of Junior Haridāsa.

TEXT 112

অন্ন প্রশংসিয়া প্রভু ভোজন করিলা ।
নিজগৃহে আসি' গোবিন্দেরে আজ্ঞা দিলা ॥ ১১২ ॥

anna praśaṁsiyā prabhu bhojana karilā
nija-gṛhe āsi' govindere ājñā dilā

SYNONYMS

anna praśaṁsiyā—praising the rice; *prabhu*—Śrī Caitanya Mahāprabhu; *bhojana karilā*—partook of the *prasāda*; *nija-gṛhe*—to His own residence; *āsi'*—coming back; *govindere*—to Govinda; *ājñā dilā*—He gave order.

TRANSLATION

Praising the quality of the rice, Śrī Caitanya Mahāprabhu partook of the prasāda. Then, after returning to His residence, He gave the following order to Govinda, His personal assistant.

TEXT 113

'আজি হৈতে এই মোর আজ্ঞা পালিবা ।
ছোট হরিদাসে ইহাঁ আসিতে না দিবা ॥' ১১৩ ॥

'āji haite ei mora ājñā pālibā
choṭa haridāse ihāṅ āsite nā dibā'

SYNONYMS

āji haite—from today; *ei*—this; *mora*—My; *ājñā*—order; *pālibā*—you should carry out; *choṭa haridāse*—Choṭa Haridāsa; *ihāṅ*—here; *āsite*—to come; *nā dibā*—do not allow.

TRANSLATION

"From this day forward, do not allow Choṭa Haridāsa to come here."

TEXT 114

দ্বার মানা হৈল, হরিদাস দুঃখী হৈল মনে ।
কি লাগিয়া দ্বার-মানা কেহ নাহি জানে ॥ ১১৪ ॥

dvāra mānā haila, haridāsa duḥkhī haila mane
ki lāgiyā dvāra-mānā keha nāhi jāne

SYNONYMS

dvāra mānā—closed door; *haila*—there was; *haridāsa*—Choṭa Haridāsa; *duḥkhī*—very unhappy; *haila mane*—became within his mind; *ki lāgiyā*—for what reason; *dvāra-mānā*—the door was closed; *keha nāhi jāne*—no one could understand.

TRANSLATION

When Junior Haridāsa heard that he had been ordered not to approach Śrī Caitanya Mahāprabhu, he was very unhappy. No one could understand why he had been ordered not to come.

TEXT 115

তিনদিন হৈল হরিদাস করে উপবাস ।
স্বরূপাদি আসি, পুছিলা মহাপ্রভুর পাশ ॥ ১১৫ ॥

tina-dina haila haridāsa kare upavāsa
svarūpādi āsi, puchilā mahāprabhura pāśa

SYNONYMS

tina-dina haila—for three days; *haridāsa*—Junior Haridāsa; *kare upavāsa*—was fasting; *svarūpa-ādi*—Svarūpa Dāmodara and other confidential devotees; *āsi*—coming; *puchilā*—inquired; *mahāprabhura pāśa*—from Śrī Caitanya Mahāprabhu.

TRANSLATION

Haridāsa fasted continuously for three days. Then Svarūpa Dāmodara Gosvāmī and other confidential devotees approached Śrī Caitanya Mahāprabhu to inquire from Him.

TEXT 116

"কোন্ অপরাধ, প্রভু, কৈল হরিদাস ?
কি লাগিয়া দ্বার-মানা, করে উপবাস ?" ১১৬ ॥

"kon aparādha, prabhu, kaila haridāsa?
ki lāgiyā dvāra-mānā, kare upavāsa?"

SYNONYMS

kon aparādha—what great offense; *prabhu*—O Lord; *kaila haridāsa*—has Haridāsa committed; *ki lāgiyā*—for what reason; *dvāra-mānā*—the closed door; *kare upavāsa*—he is now fasting.

TRANSLATION

"What great offense has Junior Haridāsa committed? Why has he been forbidden to come to Your door? He has now been fasting for three days."

TEXT 117

প্রভু কহে,—"বৈরাগী করে প্রকৃতি সম্ভাষণ।
দেখিতে না পারোঁ। আমি তাহার বদন ॥ ১১৭ ॥

prabhu kahe,——"vairāgī kare prakṛti sambhāṣaṇa
dekhite nā pāroṅ āmi tāhāra vadana

SYNONYMS

prabhu kahe—Śrī Caitanya Mahāprabhu replied; *vairāgī*—a person in the renounced order of life; *kare*—does; *prakṛti sambhāṣaṇa*—intimate talking with a woman; *dekhite nā pāroṅ*—cannot see; *āmi*—I; *tāhāra vadana*—his face.

TRANSLATION

The Lord replied, "I cannot tolerate seeing the face of a person who has accepted the renounced order of life but who still talks intimately with a woman.

PURPORT

Śrīla Bhaktisiddhānta Sarasvatī Ṭhākura comments that *saralatā,* or simplicity, is the first qualification of a Vaiṣṇava, whereas duplicity or cunning behavior is a great offense against the principles of devotional service. As one advances in Kṛṣṇa consciousness, one must gradually become disgusted with material attachment and thus become more and more attached to the service of the Lord. If one is not factually detached from material activities but still proclaims himself advanced in devotional service, he is cheating. No one will be happy to see such behavior.

TEXT 118

দুর্বার ইন্দ্রিয় করে বিষয়-গ্রহণ।
দারবী প্রকৃতি হরে মুনেরপি মন ॥ ১১৮ ॥

durvāra indriya kare viṣaya-grahaṇa
dāravī prakṛti hare munerapi mana

SYNONYMS

durvāra—uncontrollable; *indriya*—the senses; *kare*—do; *viṣaya-grahaṇa*—accepting sense objects; *dāravī prakṛti*—a wooden statue of a woman; *hare*—attracts; *munerapi*—even of a great sage; *mana*—the mind.

TRANSLATION

"So strongly do the senses adhere to the objects of their enjoyment that indeed a wooden statue of a woman attracts the mind of even a great saintly person.

PURPORT

The senses and the sense objects are so intimately connected that the mind of even a great saintly person is attracted to a wooden doll if it is attractively shaped like a young woman. The sense objects, namely form, sound, smell, taste and touch, are always attractive for the eyes, ears, nose, tongue and skin. Since the senses and sense objects are naturally intimately related, sometimes even a person claiming control over his senses remains always subject to the control of sense objects. The senses are impossible to control unless purified and engaged in the service of the Lord. Thus even though a saintly person vows to control his senses, the senses are still sometimes perturbed by sense objects.

TEXT 119

মাত্রা স্বস্রা দুহিত্রা বা নাবিবিক্তাসনো ভবেৎ ।
বলবানিন্দ্রিয়গ্রামো বিদ্বাংসমপি কর্ষতি ॥ ১১৯ ॥

mātrā svasrā duhitrā vā
nā viviktāsano bhavet
balavān indriya-grāmo
vidvāṁsam api karṣati

SYNONYMS

mātrā—with one's mother; *svasrā*—with one's sister; *duhitrā*—with one's daughter; *vā*—or; *nā*—not; *vivikta-āsanaḥ*—sitting together; *bhavet*—there should be; *balavān*—very strong; *indriya-grāmaḥ*—the group of senses; *vidvāṁsam*—a person with knowledge of liberation; *api*—even; *karṣati*—attract.

TRANSLATION

" 'One should not sit closely with one's mother, sister or daughter, for the senses are so strong that they may attract even a person advanced in knowledge.'

PURPORT

This verse appears in the *Manu-saṁhitā* (2.215) and *Śrīmad-Bhāgavatam* (9.19.17).

TEXT 120

ক্ষুদ্রজীব সব মর্কট-বৈরাগ্য করিয়া ।
ইন্দ্রিয় চরাঞা বুলে 'প্রকৃতি' সম্ভাষিয়া ॥"১২০ ॥

kṣudra-jīva saba markaṭa-vairāgya kariyā
indriya carāñā bule 'prakṛti' sambhāṣiyā"

SYNONYMS

kṣudra-jīva—poor living entities; *saba*—all; *markaṭa vairāgya*—a renounced life like that of a monkey; *kariyā*—accepting; *indriya carāñā*—satisfying the senses; *bule*—wander here and there; *prakṛti sambhāṣiyā*—talking intimately with women.

TRANSLATION

"There are many persons with little in their possession who accept the renounced order of life like monkeys. They go here and there engaging in sense gratification and speaking intimately with women."

PURPORT

One should strictly follow the regulative principles, namely no illicit sex, no meat-eating, no intoxication and no gambling, and in this way one should make progress in spiritual life. If an unfit person sentimentally accepts *vairāgya* or takes *sannyāsa* but at the same time remains attached to women, he is in a very dangerous position. His renunciation is called *markaṭa-vairāgya,* or renunciation like that of a monkey. The monkey lives in the forest, eats fruit and does not even cover itself with a cloth. In this way it resembles a saint, but the monkey always thinks of female monkeys and sometimes keeps dozens of them for sexual intercourse. This is called *markaṭa-vairāgya.* Therefore one who is unfit should not accept the renounced order of life. One who accepts the order of *sannyāsa* but again becomes agitated by sensual disturbances and talks privately with women is called *dharma-dhvajī* or *dharma-kalaṅka,* which means that he brings condemnation upon the religious order. Therefore one should be extremely careful in this connection. Śrīla Bhaktisiddhānta Sarasvatī Ṭhākura explains the word *markaṭa* to mean "restless." A restless person cannot be steady; therefore he simply wanders about, gratifying his senses. Just to get praise from others, to get cheap adoration from his followers or people in general, such a person sometimes accepts the dress of a *sannyāsī* or *bābājī* in the renounced order, but he cannot give up desires for sense gratification, especially for the association of women. Such a person cannot make advancement in spiritual life. There are eight different kinds of sensual enjoyment with women, including talking about them and thinking about them. Thus for a *sannyāsī,* a person in the renounced order, talking intimately with women is a great offense. Śrī Rāmānanda Rāya and Śrīla Narottama dāsa Ṭhākura actually achieved the most elevated stage of the renounced order, but those who imitate them, accepting them as ordinary human beings, fall under the influence of the material energy, for that is a great misunderstanding.

TEXT 121

এত কহি' মহাপ্রভু অভ্যন্তরে গেলা ।
গোসাঞিির আবেশ দেখি' সবে মৌন হৈলা ॥১২১॥

eta kahi' mahāprabhu abhyantare gelā
gosāñira āveśa dekhi' sabe mauna hailā

SYNONYMS

eta kahi'—saying this; *mahāprabhu*—Śrī Caitanya Mahāprabhu; *abhyantare gelā*—entered His room; *gosāñira*—of Śrī Caitanya Mahāprabhu; *āveśa*—absorption in anger; *dekhi'*—seeing; *sabe*—all the devotees; *mauna hailā*—became silent.

TRANSLATION

After saying this, Śrī Caitanya Mahāprabhu entered His room. Seeing Him in such an angry mood, all the devotees fell silent.

TEXT 122

আর দিনে সবে মেলি' প্রভুর চরণে ।
হরিদাস লাগি, কিছু কৈলা নিবেদনে ॥ ১২২ ॥

āra dine sabe meli' prabhura caraṇe
haridāsa lāgi, kichu kailā nivedane

SYNONYMS

āra dine—the next day; *sabe meli'*—all the devotees, coming together; *prabhura caraṇe*—unto the lotus feet of Śrī Caitanya Mahāprabhu; *haridāsa lāgi*—on behalf of Junior Haridāsa; *kichu*—some; *kailā nivedane*—submitted petition.

TRANSLATION

The next day, all the devotees together approached the lotus feet of Śrī Caitanya Mahāprabhu to submit an appeal on behalf of Junior Haridāsa.

TEXT 123

“অল্প অপরাধ, প্রভু করহ প্রসাদ ।
এবে শিক্ষা হইল না করিবে অপরাধ” ॥ ১২৩ ॥

"alpa aparādha, prabhu karaha prasāda
ebe śikṣā ha-ila nā karibe aparādha"

SYNONYMS

alpa aparādha—the offense is not very great; *prabhu*—O Lord; *karaha prasāda*—be merciful; *ebe*—now; *śikṣā ha-ila*—he has gotten a sufficient lesson; *nā karibe*—he will not do; *aparādha*—offense.

TRANSLATION

"Haridāsa has committed a small offense," they said. "Therefore, O Lord, please be merciful to him. Now he has received a sufficient lesson. In the future he will not commit such an offense."

TEXT 124

প্রভু কহে,—“মোর বশ নহে মোর মন ।
প্রকৃতিসম্ভাষী বৈরাগী না করে দর্শন ॥ ১২৪ ॥

prabhu kahe,——"mora vaśa nahe mora mana
prakṛti-sambhāṣī vairāgī nā kare darśana

SYNONYMS

prabhu kahe—Śrī Caitanya Mahāprabhu said; *mora vaśa*—under My control; *nahe*—is not; *mora*—My; *mana*—mind; *prakṛti-sambhāṣī*—one who talks with women; *vairāgī*—a person in the renounced order; *nā kare darśana*—does not see.

TRANSLATION

Śrī Caitanya Mahāprabhu said, "My mind is not under My control. It does not like to see anyone in the renounced order who talks intimately with women.

TEXT 125

নিজ কার্যে যাহ সবে, ছাড় বৃথা কথা।
পুনঃ যদি কহ আমা না দেখিবে হেথা॥" ১২৫॥

nija kārye yāha sabe, chāḍa vṛthā kathā
punaḥ yadi kaha āmā nā dekhibe hethā"

SYNONYMS

nija kārye—your own business; *yāha sabe*—you can all go about; *chāḍa*—give up; *vṛthā kathā*—useless talk; *punaḥ*—again; *yadi kaha*—if you speak; *āmā*—Me; *nā dekhibe*—you will not see; *hethā*—here.

TRANSLATION

"You should all tend to your respective engagements. Give up this useless talk. If you speak this way again, I shall go away, and you will no longer see Me here."

TEXT 126

এত শুনি' সবে নিজ-কর্ণে হস্ত দিয়া।
নিজ নিজ কার্যে সবে গেল ত' উঠিয়া॥ ১২৬॥

eta śuni' sabe nija-karṇe hasta diyā
nija nija kārye sabe gela ta' uṭhiyā

SYNONYMS

eta śuni'—hearing this; *sabe*—all the devotees; *nija-karṇe*—over their ears; *hasta diyā*—putting their hands; *nija nija kārye*—to their respective duties; *sabe*—all of them; *gela*—went; *ta'*—certainly; *uṭhiyā*—getting up.

TRANSLATION

Hearing this, all the devotees covered their ears with their hands, got up and went about their respective duties.

TEXT 127

মহাপ্রভু মধ্যাহ্ন করিতে চলি, গেলা ।
বুঝন না যায় এই মহাপ্রভুর লীলা ॥ ১২৭ ॥

mahāprabhu madhyāhna karite cali, gelā
bujhana nā yāya ei mahāprabhura līlā

SYNONYMS

mahāprabhu—Śrī Caitanya Mahāprabhu; *madhyāhna karite*—to execute His noon activities; *cali*—walking; *gelā*—left; *bujhana nā yāya*—no one could understand; *ei*—this; *mahāprabhura līlā*—pastime of Śrī Caitanya Mahāprabhu.

TRANSLATION

Śrī Caitanya Mahāprabhu also left that place to perform His noon duties. No one could understand His pastimes.

TEXT 128

আর দিন সবে পরমানন্দপুরী-স্থানে ।
'প্রভুকে প্রসন্ন কর'—কৈলা নিবেদনে ॥ ১২৮ ॥

āra dina sabe paramānanda-purī-sthāne
'prabhuke prasanna kara'——kailā nivedane

SYNONYMS

āra dina—the next day; *sabe*—all the devotees; *paramānanda-purī-sthāne*—at the place of Paramānanda Purī; *prabhuke*—Śrī Caitanya Mahāprabhu; *prasanna kara*—please try to pacify; *kailā nivedane*—submitted.

TRANSLATION

The next day, all the devotees went to Śrī Paramānanda Purī and requested him to pacify the Lord.

TEXT 129

তবে পুরী-গোসাঞি একা প্রভুস্থানে আইলা ।
নমস্করি' প্রভু তাঁরে সম্ভ্রমে বসাইলা ॥ ১২৯ ॥

tabe purī-gosāñi ekā prabhu-sthāne āilā
namaskari' prabhu tāṅre sambhrame vasāilā

SYNONYMS

tabe—thereupon; *purī-gosāñi*—Paramānanda Purī; *ekā*—alone; *prabhu-sthāne*—to the place of Śrī Caitanya Mahāprabhu; *āilā*—came; *namaskari'*—after offering obeisances; *prabhu*—Śrī Caitanya Mahāprabhu; *tāṅre*—him; *sambhrame*—with great respect; *vasāilā*—got to sit down.

TRANSLATION

Paramānanda Purī thereupon went alone to the residence of Śrī Caitanya Mahāprabhu. The Lord, after offering him obeisances, seated him by His side with great respect.

TEXT 130

পুছিলা,— কি আজ্ঞা, কেনে হৈল আগমন ?
হরিদাসে প্রসাদ লাগি' কৈলা নিবেদন ॥ ১৩০ ॥

puchilā,——ki ājñā, kene haila āgamana?
'haridāse prasāda lāgi' kailā nivedana

SYNONYMS

puchilā—the Lord inquired; *ki ājñā*—what is your order; *kene haila āgamana*—what is the reason you have come; *haridāse prasāda lāgi'*—for a favor to Junior Haridāsa; *kailā nivedana*—he made a request.

TRANSLATION

The Lord inquired, "What is your order? For what purpose have you come here?" Paramānanda Purī then submitted his prayer that the Lord show favor to Junior Haridāsa.

TEXT 131

শুনিয়া কহেন প্রভু,—"শুনহ, গোসাঞি।
সব বৈষ্ণব লঞা তুমি রহ এই ঠাঞি ॥ ১৩১ ॥

śuniyā kahena prabhu,——"śunaha, gosāñi
saba vaiṣṇava lañā tumi raha ei ṭhāñi

SYNONYMS

śuniyā—hearing; *kahena prabhu*—Śrī Caitanya Mahāprabhu said; *śunaha*—please hear; *gosāñi*—my lord; *saba vaiṣṇava*—all the Vaiṣṇavas; *lañā*—taking; *tumi*—your lordship; *raha*—stay; *ei ṭhāñi*—in this place.

TRANSLATION

Hearing this request, Śrī Caitanya Mahāprabhu replied, "My dear lord, please hear me. It is better for you to stay here with all the Vaiṣṇavas.

TEXT 132

মোরে আজ্ঞা হয়, মুঞি যাঙ আলালনাথ ।
একলে রহিব তাহাঁ, গোবিন্দ-মাত্র সাথ ॥"১৩২ ॥

more ājñā haya, muñi yāṅa ālālanātha
ekale rahiba tāhāṅ, govinda-mātra sātha"

SYNONYMS

more—to Me; *ājñā haya*—please give permission; *muñi*—I; *yāṅa*—go; *ālālanātha*—to the place known as Ālālanātha; *ekale rahiba*—I shall remain alone; *tāhāṅ*—there; *govinda-mātra sātha*—with only Govinda.

TRANSLATION

"Please give Me permission to go to Ālālanātha. I shall remain there alone; only Govinda will go with Me."

TEXT 133

এত বলি' প্রভু যদি গোবিন্দে বোলাইলা ।
পুরীরে নমস্কার করি' উঠিয়া চলিলা ॥ ১৩৩ ॥

eta bali' prabhu yadi govinde bolāilā
purīre namaskāra kari' uṭhiyā calilā

SYNONYMS

eta bali'—saying this; *prabhu*—Śrī Caitanya Mahāprabhu; *yadi*—when; *govinde bolāilā*—called for Govinda; *purīre*—to Paramānanda Purī; *namaskāra kari'*—offering respect; *uṭhiyā calilā*—got up and began to go away.

TRANSLATION

After saying this, the Lord called for Govinda. Offering obeisances to Paramānanda Purī, He got up and began to leave.

TEXT 134

আস্তে-ব্যস্তে পুরী-গোসাঞি প্রভু আগে গেলা ।
অনুনয় করি' প্রভুরে ঘরে বসাইলা ॥ ১৩৪ ॥

āste-vyaste purī-gosāñi prabhu āge gelā
anunaya kari' prabhure ghare vasāilā

SYNONYMS

āste-vyaste—with great haste; *purī-gosāñi*—Paramānanda Purī; *prabhu āge*—in front of Śrī Caitanya Mahāprabhu; *gelā*—went; *anunaya kari'*—with great humility; *prabhure*—Śrī Caitanya Mahāprabhu; *ghare*—in His room; *vasāilā*—got to sit down.

TRANSLATION

In great haste Paramānanda Purī Gosāñi went before Him and with great humility persuaded Him to sit down in His own room.

TEXT 135

"তোমার যে ইচ্ছা, কর, স্বতন্ত্র ঈশ্বর।
কেবা কি বলিতে পারে তোমার উপর? ১৩৫॥

"tomāra ye icchā, kara, svatantra īśvara
kebā ki balite pāre tomāra upara?

SYNONYMS

tomāra ye icchā—whatever is Your desire; *kara*—You can do; *svatantra īśvara*—the independent Supreme Personality of Godhead; *kebā*—who; *ki balite pāre*—can speak; *tomāra upara*—above You.

TRANSLATION

Paramānanda Purī said, "My dear Lord Caitanya, You are the independent Personality of Godhead. You can do whatever You like. Who can say anything above You?

TEXT 136

লোক-হিত লাগি' তোমার সব ব্যবহার।
আমি সব না জানি গম্ভীর হৃদয় তোমার॥" ১৩৬॥

loka-hita lāgi' tomāra saba vyavahāra
āmi saba nā jāni gambhīra hṛdaya tomāra"

SYNONYMS

loka-hita lāgi'—for the benefit of people in general; *tomāra*—Your; *saba*—all; *vyavahāra*—activities; *āmi saba*—all of us; *nā jāni*—cannot understand; *gambhīra*—very deep and grave; *hṛdaya*—heart; *tomāra*—Your.

TRANSLATION

"All Your activities are for the benefit of people in general. We cannot understand them, for Your intentions are deep and grave."

TEXT 137

এত বলি' পুরী-গোসাঞি গেলা নিজ-স্থানে।
হরিদাস-স্থানে গেলা সব ভক্তগণে ॥ ১৩৭ ॥

eta bali' purī-gosāñi gelā nija-sthāne
haridāsa-sthāne gelā saba bhakta-gaṇe

SYNONYMS

eta bali'—saying this; *purī-gosāñi*—Paramānanda Gosāñi; *gelā*—left; *nija-sthāne*—for his own place; *haridāsa-sthāne*—unto the place of Junior Haridāsa; *gelā*—went; *saba bhakta-gaṇe*—all the other devotees.

TRANSLATION

After saying this, Paramānanda Purī Gosāñi left for his own home. Then all the devotees went to see Junior Haridāsa.

TEXT 138

স্বরূপ-গোসাঞি কহে,—"শুন, হরিদাস।
সবে তোমার হিত বাঞ্ছি, করহ বিশ্বাস ॥ ১৩৮ ॥

svarūpa-gosāñi kahe,—"śuna, haridāsa
sabe tomāra hita vāñchi, karaha viśvāsa

SYNONYMS

svarūpa-gosāñi kahe—Svarūpa Dāmodara Gosāñi said; *śuna haridāsa*—just hear, Haridāsa; *sabe*—all of us; *tomāra hita vāñchi*—wish well for you; *karaha viśvāsa*—just believe it.

TRANSLATION

Svarūpa Dāmodara Gosāñi said, "Please hear us, Haridāsa, for we all wish you well. Please believe this.

TEXT 139

প্রভু হঠে পড়িয়াছে স্বতন্ত্র ঈশ্বর।
কভু কৃপা করিবেন যাতে দয়ালু অন্তর ॥ ১৩৯ ॥

prabhu haṭhe paḍiyāche svatantra īśvara
kabhu kṛpā karibena yāte dayālu antara

SYNONYMS

prabhu—Śrī Caitanya Mahāprabhu; *haṭhe paḍiyāche*—has taken up a persistently angry mood; *svatantra īśvara*—the independent Personality of Godhead; *kabhu*—some time; *kṛpā karibena*—He will be merciful (to you); *yāte*—because; *dayālu*—merciful; *antara*—at heart.

TRANSLATION

"At present Śrī Caitanya Mahāprabhu is persisting in His mood of anger because He is the independent Supreme Personality of Godhead. At some time, however, He will surely be merciful, for at heart He is very kind.

TEXT 140

তুমি হঠ কৈলে তাঁর হঠ সে বাড়িবে।
স্নান ভোজন কর, আপনে ক্রোধ যাবে ॥"১৪০॥

tumi haṭha kaile tāṅra haṭha se bāḍibe
snāna bhojana kara, āpane krodha yābe"

SYNONYMS

tumi haṭha kaile—if you go on persisting; *tāṅra*—His; *haṭha*—persistence; *se*—that; *bāḍibe*—will increase; *snāna bhojana kara*—take your bath and take *prasāda; āpane krodha yābe*—automatically His anger will subside.

TRANSLATION

"The Lord is persisting, and if you also persist, His persistence will increase. It is better for you to bathe and take prasāda. In due course, His anger will automatically subside."

TEXT 141

এত বলি তারে স্নান ভোজন করাঞা।
আপন ভবন আইলা তারে আশ্বাসিয়া ॥ ১৪১ ॥

eta bali tāre snāna bhojana karāñā
āpana bhavana āilā tāre āśvāsiyā

SYNONYMS

eta bali—saying this; *tāre*—him; *snāna bhojana karāñā*—inducing to bathe and take *prasāda*; *āpana bhavana*—to his own place; *āilā*—returned; *tāre āśvāsiyā*—assuring him.

TRANSLATION

Having said this, Svarūpa Dāmodara Gosvāmī induced Haridāsa to bathe and take prasāda. After thus reassuring him, he returned home.

TEXT 142

প্রভু যদি যান জগন্নাথ-দরশনে ।
দূরে রহি' হরিদাস করেন দর্শনে ॥ ১৪২ ॥

prabhu yadi yāna jagannātha-daraśane
dūre rahi' haridāsa karena darśane

SYNONYMS

prabhu—Śrī Caitanya Mahāprabhu; *yadi*—when; *yāna*—goes; *jagannātha-daraśane*—to see Lord Jagannātha; *dūre rahi'*—remaining in a distant place; *haridāsa*—Junior Haridāsa; *karena darśane*—sees.

TRANSLATION

When Śrī Caitanya Mahāprabhu went to see Lord Jagannātha in the temple, Haridāsa would stay a long distance away and see Him.

TEXT 143

মহাপ্রভু—কৃপাসিন্ধু, কে পারে বুঝিতে ?
প্রিয় ভক্তে দণ্ড করেন ধর্ম বুঝাইতে ॥ ১৪৩ ॥

mahāprabhu——kṛpā-sindhu, ke pāre bujhite?
priya bhakte daṇḍa karena dharma bujhāite

SYNONYMS

mahāprabhu—Śrī Caitanya Mahāprabhu; *kṛpā-sindhu*—the ocean of mercy; *ke pāre bujhite*—who can understand; *priya bhakte*—unto His dear devotees; *daṇḍa karena*—makes chastisement; *dharma bujhāite*—to establish principles of religion or duty.

TRANSLATION

Śrī Caitanya Mahāprabhu is the ocean of mercy. Who can understand Him? When He chastises His dear devotees, He certainly does so to reestablish the principles of religion or duty.

PURPORT

Śrīla Bhaktisiddhānta Sarasvatī Ṭhākura says in this connection that Śrī Caitanya Mahāprabhu, the ocean of mercy, chastised Junior Haridāsa, although Junior Haridāsa was His dear devotee, to establish that one in the devotional line, engaged in pure devotional service, should not be a hypocrite. For a person engaged in devotional service in the renounced order, having intimate relationships with women is certainly hypocrisy. This chastisement was given to Junior Haridāsa as an example to future *sahajiyās* who might adopt the dress of the renounced order to imitate Rūpa Gosvāmī and other bona fide *sannyāsīs* but secretly have illicit connections with women. To teach such men, Śrī Caitanya Mahāprabhu chastised His dear devotee Haridāsa for a slight deviation from the regulative principles. Śrīmatī Mādhavīdevī was a highly elevated devotee; therefore approaching her to ask for some rice to serve Śrī Caitanya Mahāprabhu was certainly not very offensive. Nevertheless, just to preserve the regulative principles for the future, Śrī Caitanya Mahāprabhu enforced the hard-and-fast rule that no one in the renounced order should intimately mix with women. Had Śrī Caitanya Mahāprabhu not chastised Junior Haridāsa for this slight deviation, so-called devotees of the Lord would have exploited the example of Junior Haridāsa to continue their habit of illicit connections with women unrestrictedly. Indeed, they still preach that such behavior is allowed for a Vaiṣṇava. But it is strictly not allowed. Śrī Caitanya Mahāprabhu is the teacher of the entire world, and therefore He enforced this exemplary punishment to establish that illicit sexual connections are never allowed by Vaiṣṇava philosophy. This was His purpose in chastising Junior Haridāsa. Śrī Caitanya Mahāprabhu is in fact the most magnanimous incarnation of the Supreme Personality of Godhead, but He strictly prohibited illicit sex.

TEXT 144

দেখি' ত্রাস উপজিল সব ভক্তগণে ।
স্বপ্নেহ ছাড়িল সবে স্ত্রী-সম্ভাষণে ॥ ১৪৪ ॥

dekhi' trāsa upajila saba bhakta-gaṇe
svapne-ha chāḍila sabe strī-sambhāṣaṇe

SYNONYMS

dekhi'—seeing; *trāsa*—an atmosphere of fear; *upajila*—grew; *saba bhakta-gaṇe*—among all the devotees; *svapne-ha*—even in dreams; *chāḍila*—gave up; *sabe*—all; *strī-sambhāṣaṇe*—talk with women.

TRANSLATION

After all the devotees saw this example, a mentality of fear grew among them. Therefore they all stopped talking with women, even in dreams.

PURPORT

In connection with *strī-sambhāṣaṇa,* talking with women, Śrīla Bhaktisiddhānta Sarasvatī Ṭhākura says that talking with women for the purpose of mingling with them for sense gratification, subtle or gross, is strictly prohibited. Cāṇakya Paṇḍita, the great moral instructor, says, *mātṛvat para-dāreṣu.* Thus not only a person in the renounced order or one engaged in devotional service but everyone should avoid mingling with women. One should consider another's wife his mother.

TEXT 145

এইমতে হরিদাসের এক বৎসর গেল ।
তবু মহাপ্রভুর মনে প্রসাদ নহিল ॥ ১৪৫ ॥

ei-mate haridāsera eka vatsara gela
tabu mahāprabhura mane prasāda nahila

SYNONYMS

ei-mate—in this way; *haridāsera*—of Junior Haridāsa; *eka vatsara*—one year; *gela*—passed; *tabu*—still; *mahāprabhura*—of Śrī Caitanya Mahāprabhu; *mane*—in the mind; *prasāda nahila*—there were no symptoms of mercy.

TRANSLATION

In this way a complete year passed for Junior Haridāsa, but still there was not a sign of Śrī Caitanya Mahāprabhu's mercy toward him.

TEXT 146

রাত্রি অবশেষে প্রভুরে দণ্ডবৎ হঞা ।
প্রয়াগেতে গেল কারেহ কিছু না বলিয়া ॥ ১৪৬ ॥

rātri avaśeṣe prabhure daṇḍavat hañā
prayāgete gela kāreha kichu nā baliyā

SYNONYMS

rātri avaśeṣe—at the end of one night; *prabhure*—unto Śrī Caitanya Mahāprabhu; *daṇḍavat hañā*—offering obeisances; *prayāgete*—to the holy place known as Prayāga (Allahabad); *gela*—went; *kāreha*—to anyone; *kichu*—anything; *nā baliyā*—not saying.

TRANSLATION

Thus at the end of one night, Junior Haridāsa, after offering Śrī Caitanya Mahāprabhu his respectful obeisances, departed for Prayāga without saying anything to anyone.

TEXT 147

প্রভুপদপ্রাপ্তি লাগি' সঙ্কল্প করিল ।
ত্রিবেণী প্রবেশ করি' প্রাণ ছাড়িল ॥ ১৪৭ ॥

prabhu-pada-prāpti lāgi' saṅkalpa karila
triveṇī praveśa kari' prāṇa chāḍila

SYNONYMS

prabhu-pada—the lotus feet of Śrī Caitanya Mahāprabhu; *prāpti lāgi'*—with a view to getting; *saṅkalpa karila*—decided definitely; *tri-veṇī praveśa kari'*—entering into the water at the confluence of the Ganges and Yamunā at Prayāga; *prāṇa chāḍila*—give up his life.

TRANSLATION

Junior Haridāsa had conclusively decided to attain shelter at the lotus feet of Śrī Caitanya Mahāprabhu. Thus he entered deep into the water at Triveṇī, the confluence of the Ganges and Yamunā at Prayāga, and in this way gave up his life.

TEXT 148

সেইক্ষণে দিব্যদেহে প্রভুস্থানে আইলা ।
প্রভুকৃপা পাঞা অন্তর্ধানেই রহিলা ॥ ১৪৮ ॥

sei-kṣaṇe divya-dehe prabhu-sthāne āilā
prabhu-kṛpā pāñā antardhānei rahilā

SYNONYMS

sei-kṣaṇe—immediately thereupon; *divya-dehe*—in a spiritual body; *prabhu-sthāne āilā*—came to Śrī Caitanya Mahāprabhu; *prabhu-kṛpā*—the mercy of Śrī Caitanya Mahāprabhu; *pāñā*—getting; *antardhānei rahilā*—remained invisible.

TRANSLATION

Immediately after committing suicide in this way, he went in his spiritual body to Śrī Caitanya Mahāprabhu and received the mercy of the Lord. However, he still remained invisible.

TEXT 149

গন্ধর্ব-দেহে গান করেন অন্তর্ধানে ।
রাত্র্যে প্রভুরে শুনায় গীত, অন্যে নাহি জানে ॥১৪৯॥

gandharva-dehe gāna karena antardhāne
rātrye prabhure śunāya gīta, anye nāhi jāne

SYNONYMS

gandharva-dehe—in the body of a Gandharva; *gāna karena*—he sings; *antardhāne*—without being visible; *rātrye*—at night; *prabhure*—unto Śrī Caitanya Mahāprabhu; *śunāya gīta*—he was singing; *anye*—others; *nāhi jāne*—could not understand.

TRANSLATION

In a spiritual body resembling that of a Gandharva, Junior Haridāsa, although invisible, would sing at night for Śrī Caitanya Mahāprabhu to hear. No one but the Lord, however, knew of this.

TEXT 150

একদিন মহাপ্রভু পুছিলা ভক্তগণে ।
'হরিদাস কাঁহা ? তারে আনহ এখানে' ॥ ১৫০ ॥

eka-dina mahāprabhu puchilā bhakta-gaṇe
'haridāsa kāṅhā? tāre ānaha ekhāne'

SYNONYMS

eka-dina—one day; *mahāprabhu*—Śrī Caitanya Mahāprabhu; *puchilā bhakta-gaṇe*—inquired from the devotees; *haridāsa kāṅhā*—where is Haridāsa; *tāre*—him; *ānaha ekhāne*—bring here.

TRANSLATION

One day Śrī Caitanya Mahāprabhu inquired from the devotees, "Where is Haridāsa? Now you may bring him here."

TEXT 151

সবে কহে,—'হরিদাস বর্ষপূর্ণ দিনে ।
রাত্রে উঠি কাঁহা গেলা, কেহ নাহি জানে ॥"১৫১ ॥

sabe kahe,——'haridāsa varṣa-pūrṇa dine
rātre uṭhi kāṅhā gelā, keha nāhi jāne"

SYNONYMS

sabe kahe—everyone spoke; *haridāsa*—Haridāsa; *varṣa-pūrṇa dine*—at the end of one full year; *rātre*—at night; *uṭhi*—getting up; *kāṅhā gelā*—where he went; *keha nāhi jāne*—no one knows.

TRANSLATION

The devotees all replied, "One night at the end of a full year, Junior Haridāsa got up and went away. No one knows where he has gone."

TEXT 152

শুনি' মহাপ্রভু ঈষৎ হাসিয়া রহিলা ।
সব ভক্তগণ মনে বিস্ময় হইলা ॥ ১৫২ ॥

śuni' mahāprabhu īṣat hāsiyā rahilā
saba bhakta-gaṇa mane vismaya ha-ilā

SYNONYMS

śuni'—hearing; *mahāprabhu*—Śrī Caitanya Mahāprabhu; *īṣat*—slightly; *hāsiyā rahilā*—remained smiling; *saba bhakta-gaṇa*—all the devotees; *mane*—in the minds; *vismaya ha-ilā*—became surprised.

TRANSLATION

While hearing the devotees lament, Śrī Caitanya Mahāprabhu was mildly smiling. Thus all the devotees were very astonished.

TEXTS 153-154

একদিন জগদানন্দ, স্বরূপ, গোবিন্দ ।
কাশীশ্বর, শঙ্কর, দামোদর, মুকুন্দ ॥ ১৫৩ ॥
সমুদ্রস্নানে গেলা সবে, শুনে কথো দূরে ।
হরিদাস গায়েন, যেন ডাকি' কণ্ঠস্বরে ॥ ১৫৪ ॥

eka-dina jagadānanda, svarūpa, govinda
kāśīśvara, śaṅkara, dāmodara, mukunda

samudra-snāne gelā sabe, śune katho dūre
haridāsa gāyena, yena ḍāki' kaṇṭha-svare

SYNONYMS

eka-dina—one day; *jagadānanda*—Jagadānanda; *svarūpa*—Svarūpa; *govinda*—Govinda; *kāśīśvara*—Kāśīśvara; *śaṅkara*—Śaṅkara; *dāmodara*—Dāmodara; *mukunda*—Mukunda; *samudra-snāne*—bathing in the sea; *gelā*—went; *sabe*—all of them; *śune*—could hear; *katho dūre*—from a distant place; *haridāsa gāyena*—Junior Haridāsa was singing; *yena*—as if; *ḍāki'*—calling; *kaṇṭha-svare*—in his original voice.

TRANSLATION

One day Jagadānanda, Svarūpa, Govinda, Kāśīśvara, Śaṅkara, Dāmodara and Mukunda all went to bathe in the sea. They could hear Haridāsa singing from a distant place as if calling them in his original voice.

TEXT 155

মনুষ্য না দেখে—মধুর গীতমাত্র শুনে।
গোবিন্দাদি সবে মেলি' কৈল অনুমানে ॥ ১৫৫ ॥

manuṣya nā dekhe——madhura gīta-mātra śune
govindādi sabe meli' kaila anumāne

SYNONYMS

manuṣya—a man; *nā dekhe*—could not see; *madhura*—very sweet; *gīta*—singing; *mātra*—only; *śune*—one could hear; *govinda-ādi sabe*—all the devotees, headed by Govinda; *meli'*—coming together; *kaila anumāne*—guessed.

TRANSLATION

No one could see him, but they could hear him singing in a sweet voice. Therefore all the devotees, headed by Govinda, made this guess.

TEXT 156

'বিষাদি খাঞা হরিদাস আত্মঘাত কৈল।
সেই পাপে জানি 'ব্রহ্মরাক্ষস' হৈল ॥ ১৫৬ ॥

'viṣādi khāñā haridāsa ātma-ghāta kaila
sei pāpe jāni 'brahma-rākṣasa' haila

SYNONYMS

viṣa-ādi khāñā—by drinking poison; *haridāsa*—Junior Haridāsa; *ātma-ghāta kaila*—has committed suicide; *sei pāpe*—on account of that sinful activity; *jāni*—we understand; *brahma-rākṣasa*—a *brāhmaṇa* ghost; *haila*—he has become.

TRANSLATION

"Haridāsa must have committed suicide by drinking poison, and because of this sinful act, he has now become a brāhmaṇa ghost.

TEXT 157

আকার না দেখি, মাত্র শুনি তার গান।'
স্বরূপ কহেন,—"এই মিথ্যা অনুমান ॥ ১৫৭ ॥

ākāra nā dekhi, mātra śuni tāra gāna'
svarūpa kahena,——"ei mithyā anumāna

SYNONYMS

ākāra—form; *nā dekhi*—we cannot see; *mātra*—only; *śuni*—we hear; *tāra*—his; *gāna*—singing; *svarūpa kahena*—Svarūpa Dāmodara said; *ei*—this; *mithyā*—false; *anumāna*—guess.

TRANSLATION

"We cannot see his material form," they said, "but still we hear his sweet singing. Therefore he must have become a ghost." Svarūpa Dāmodara, however, protested, "This is a false guess.

TEXT 158

আজন্ম কৃষ্ণকীর্তন, প্রভুর সেবন।
প্রভু-কৃপাপাত্র, আর ক্ষেত্রের মরণ ॥ ১৫৮ ॥

ājanma kṛṣṇa-kīrtana, prabhura sevana
prabhu-kṛpā-pātra, āra kṣetrera maraṇa

SYNONYMS

ājanma—throughout the whole life; *kṛṣṇa-kīrtana*—chanting of the Hare Kṛṣṇa *mantra*; *prabhura sevana*—service to Śrī Caitanya Mahāprabhu; *prabhu-kṛpā-pātra*—very dear to the Lord; *āra*—and; *kṣetrera maraṇa*—his death in a holy place.

TRANSLATION

"Junior Haridāsa chanted the Hare Kṛṣṇa mantra throughout his entire life and served the Supreme Lord Śrī Caitanya Mahāprabhu. Moreover, he is dear to the Lord and has died in a holy place.

TEXT 159

দুর্গতি না হয় তার, সদ্গতি সে হয় ।
প্রভু-ভঙ্গী এই, পাছে জানিবা নিশ্চয় ॥"১৫৯ ॥

durgati nā haya tāra, sad-gati se haya
prabhu-bhaṅgī ei, pāche jānibā niścaya"

SYNONYMS

durgati—a bad result; *nā haya tāra*—is not his; *sat-gati se haya*—he must have achieved liberation; *prabhu-bhaṅgī*—a sport of Śrī Caitanya Mahāprabhu; *ei*—this; *pāche*—later; *jānibā*—you will understand; *niścaya*—the real fact.

TRANSLATION

"Haridāsa cannot have been degraded; he must have attained liberation. This is a pastime of Śrī Caitanya Mahāprabhu. You will all understand it later."

TEXT 160

প্রয়াগ হইতে এক বৈষ্ণব নবদ্বীপ আইল ।
হরিদাসের বার্তা তেঁহো সবারে কহিল ॥ ১৬০ ॥

prayāga ha-ite eka vaiṣṇava navadvīpa āila
haridāsera vārtā teṅho sabāre kahila

SYNONYMS

prayāga ha-ite—from Prayāga; *eka*—one; *vaiṣṇava*—devotee of Lord Kṛṣṇa; *navadvīpa āila*—came to Navadvīpa; *haridāsera vārtā*—the news of Haridāsa; *teṅho*—he; *sabāre kahila*—informed everyone.

TRANSLATION

A devotee returned to Navadvīpa from Prayāga and told everyone the details of Junior Haridāsa's suicide.

TEXT 161

যৈছে সংকল্প, যৈছে ত্রিবেণী প্রবেশিল ।
শুনি' শ্রীবাসাদির মনে বিস্ময় হইল ॥ ১৬১ ॥

yaiche saṅkalpa, yaiche triveṇī praveśila
śuni' śrīvāsādira mane vismaya ha-ila

SYNONYMS

yaiche saṅkalpa—how he was determined; *yaiche*—how; *triveṇī praveśila*—he entered into Triveṇī; *śuni'*—hearing; *śrīvāsa-ādira*—of Śrīvāsa Ṭhākura and others; *mane*—in the minds; *vismaya ha-ila*—there was surprise.

TRANSLATION

He explained how Junior Haridāsa had made his resolution and had thus entered the waters at the confluence of the Yamunā and Ganges. Hearing these details, Śrīvāsa Ṭhākura and the other devotees were very surprised.

TEXT 162

বর্ষান্তরে শিবানন্দ সব ভক্ত লঞা।
প্রভুরে মিলিলা আসি' আনন্দিত হঞা॥ ১৬২॥

varṣāntare śivānanda saba bhakta lañā
prabhure mililā āsi' ānandita hañā

SYNONYMS

varṣa-antare—at the end of the year; *śivānanda*—Śivānanda Sena; *saba*—all; *bhakta lañā*—taking the devotees; *prabhure mililā*—met Śrī Caitanya Mahāprabhu; *āsi'*—coming; *ānandita hañā*—becoming greatly happy.

TRANSLATION

At the end of the year, Śivānanda Sena came to Jagannātha Purī as usual, accompanied by the other devotees, and thus in great happiness met Śrī Caitanya Mahāprabhu.

TEXT 163

'হরিদাস কাঁহা?' যদি শ্রীবাস পুছিলা।
"স্বকর্মফলভুক্ পুমান্"—প্রভু উত্তর দিলা॥ ১৬৩॥

'haridāsa kāṅhā?' yadi śrīvāsa puchilā
"sva-karma-phala-bhuk pumān"——prabhu uttara dilā

SYNONYMS

haridāsa kāṅhā—where is Junior Haridāsa; *yadi*—when; *śrīvāsa puchilā*—Śrīvāsa Ṭhākura inquired; *sva-karma-phala-bhuk*—sure to accept the resultant action of his fruitive activities; *pumān*—a person; *prabhu*—Śrī Caitanya Mahāprabhu; *uttara dilā*—replied.

TRANSLATION

When Śrīvāsa Ṭhākura inquired from Śrī Caitanya Mahāprabhu, "Where is Junior Haridāsa?" The Lord replied, "A person is sure to achieve the results of his fruitive activities."

TEXT 164

তবে শ্রীবাস তার বৃত্তান্ত কহিল ।
যৈছে সংকল্প, যৈছে ত্রিবেণী প্রবেশিল ॥ ১৬৪ ॥

tabe śrīvāsa tāra vṛttānta kahila
yaiche saṅkalpa, yaiche triveṇī praveśila

SYNONYMS

tabe—at that time; *śrīvāsa*—Śrīvāsa Ṭhākura; *tāra*—of Junior Haridāsa; *vṛttānta*—story; *kahila*—spoke; *yaiche*—how; *saṅkalpa*—he decided; *yaiche*—how; *triveṇī praveśila*—he entered the waters at the confluence of the Ganges and Yamunā.

TRANSLATION

Then Śrīvāsa Ṭhākura related the details of Haridāsa's decision and his entering the waters at the confluence of the Ganges and Yamunā.

TEXT 165

শুনি' প্রভু হাসি' কহে সুপ্রসন্ন চিত্ত ।
'প্রকৃতি দর্শন কৈলে এই প্রায়শ্চিত্ত' ॥ ১৬৫ ॥

śuni' prabhu hāsi' kahe suprasanna citta
'prakṛti darśana kaile ei prāyaścitta'

SYNONYMS

śuni'—hearing; *prabhu*—Śrī Caitanya Mahāprabhu; *hāsi'*—smiling; *kahe*—replied; *su-prasanna citta*—being in a happy mood; *prakṛti darśana kaile*—if someone sees women with a sensual propensity; *ei prāyaścitta*—this is the atonement.

TRANSLATION

When Śrī Caitanya Mahāprabhu heard these details, He smiled in a pleased mood and said, "If with sensual intentions one looks at women, this is the only process of atonement."

TEXT 166

স্বরূপাদি মিলি' তবে বিচার করিলা।
ত্রিবেণী-প্রভাবে হরিদাস প্রভুপদ পাইলা ॥ ১৬৬ ॥

svarūpādi mili' tabe vicāra karilā
triveṇī-prabhāve haridāsa prabhu-pada pāilā

SYNONYMS

svarūpa-ādi—devotees headed by Svarūpa Dāmodara; *mili'*—coming together; *tabe*—then; *vicāra karilā*—discussed; *triveṇī-prabhāve*—by the influence of the holy place at the confluence of the Ganges and Yamunā; *haridāsa*—Junior Haridāsa; *prabhu-pada pāilā*—achieved the shelter of the lotus feet of Śrī Caitanya Mahāprabhu.

TRANSLATION

Then all the devotees, headed by Svarūpa Dāmodara Gosvāmī, concluded that because Haridāsa had committed suicide at the confluence of the rivers Ganges and Yamunā, he must have ultimately attained shelter at the lotus feet of Śrī Caitanya Mahāprabhu.

PURPORT

Śrīla Bhaktivinoda Ṭhākura remarks that after one adopts the renounced order and accepts the dress of either a *sannyāsī* or a *bābājī,* if he entertains the idea of sense gratification, especially in relationship with a woman, the only atonement is to commit suicide in the confluence of the Ganges and Yamunā. Only by such atonement can his sinful life be purified. If such a person is thus punished, it is possible for him to attain the shelter of Śrī Caitanya Mahāprabhu. Without such punishment, however, the shelter of Śrī Caitanya Mahāprabhu is very difficult to regain.

TEXT 167

এইমত লীলা করে শচীর নন্দন।
যাহা শুনি' ভক্তগণের যুড়ায় কর্ণ-মন ॥ ১৬৭ ॥

ei-mata līlā kare śacīra nandana
yāhā śuni' bhakta-gaṇera yuḍāya karṇa-mana

SYNONYMS

ei-mata—in this way; *līlā kare*—continues to execute pastimes; *śacīra nandana*—the son of mother Śacī; *yāhā śuni'*—hearing which; *bhakta-gaṇera*—of the devotees; *yuḍāya*—satisfies; *karṇa-mana*—the ears and the mind.

TRANSLATION

In this way, Śrī Caitanya Mahāprabhu, the son of mother Śacī, performs His pastimes, which greatly satisfy the ears and minds of pure devotees who hear about them.

TEXT 168

আপন কারুণ্য, লোকে বৈরাগ্য-শিক্ষণ ।
স্বভক্তের গাঢ়-অনুরাগ-প্রকটীকরণ ॥ ১৬৮ ॥

āpana kāruṇya, loke vairāgya-śikṣaṇa
sva-bhaktera gāḍha-anurāga-prakaṭī-karaṇa

SYNONYMS

āpana—personal; *kāruṇya*—favor; *loke*—to the people in general; *vairāgya-śikṣaṇa*—teaching about the order of renunciation; *sva-bhaktera*—of His devotees; *gāḍha*—deep; *anurāga*—of attachment; *prakaṭī*—manifestation; *karaṇa*—causing.

TRANSLATION

This incident manifests the mercy of Śrī Caitanya Mahāprabhu, His teaching that a sannyāsī should remain in the renounced order, and the deep attachment to Him felt by His faithful devotees.

TEXT 169

তীর্থের মহিমা, নিজ ভক্তে আত্মসাৎ ।
এক লীলায় করেন প্রভু কার্য পাঁচ-সাত ॥ ১৬৯ ॥

tīrthera mahimā, nija bhakte ātmasāt
eka līlāya karena prabhu kārya pāṅca-sāta

SYNONYMS

tīrthera mahimā—the glories of a holy place; *nija bhakte ātmasāt*—accepting His devotee again; *eka līlāya*—by one pastime; *karena*—executes; *prabhu*—Śrī Caitanya Mahāprabhu; *kārya pāṅca-sāta*—five to seven different purposes.

TRANSLATION

It also demonstrates the glories of holy places and shows how the Lord accepts His faithful devotee. Thus the Lord fulfilled five or seven purposes by performing one pastime.

TEXT 170

মধুর চৈতন্যলীলা—সমুদ্র-গম্ভীর ।
লোকে নাহি বুঝে, বুঝে যেই 'ভক্ত' 'ধীর' ॥ ১৭০ ॥

madhura caitanya-līlā——samudra-gambhīra
loke nāhi bujhe, bujhe yei 'bhakta' 'dhīra'

SYNONYMS

madhura—sweet; *caitanya-līlā*—pastimes of Lord Śrī Caitanya Mahāprabhu; *samudra-gambhīra*—as deep as the ocean; *loke nāhi bujhe*—people in general cannot understand; *bujhe*—can understand; *yei*—one who; *bhakta*—devotee; *dhīra*—sober.

TRANSLATION

The pastimes of Śrī Caitanya Mahāprabhu are like nectar, and they are deep like the ocean. People in general cannot understand them, but a sober devotee can.

TEXT 171

বিশ্বাস করিয়া শুন চৈতন্যচরিত ।
তর্ক না করিহ, তর্কে হবে বিপরীত ॥ ১৭১ ॥

viśvāsa kariyā śuna caitanya-carita
tarka nā kariha, tarke habe viparīta

SYNONYMS

viśvāsa kariyā—with faith and confidence; *śuna*—just hear; *caitanya-carita*—the pastimes of Śrī Caitanya Mahāprabhu; *tarka nā kariha*—do not uselessly argue; *tarke*—by argument; *habe viparīta*—will get the opposite result.

TRANSLATION

Please hear the pastimes of Śrī Caitanya Mahāprabhu with faith and confidence. Do not argue, for arguments will produce a contrary result.

TEXT 172

শ্রীরূপ-রঘুনাথ-পদে যার আশ ।
চৈতন্যচরিতামৃত কহে কৃষ্ণদাস ॥ ১৭২ ॥

śrī-rūpa-raghunātha-pade yāra āśa
caitanya-caritāmṛta kahe kṛṣṇadāsa

SYNONYMS

śrī-rūpa—Śrīla Rūpa Gosvāmī; *raghunātha*—Śrīla Raghunātha dāsa Gosvāmī; *pade*—at the lotus feet; *yāra*—whose; *āśa*—expectation; *caitanya-caritāmṛta*—the book named *Caitanya-caritāmṛta; kahe*—describes; *kṛṣṇa-dāsa*—Śrīla Kṛṣṇadāsa Kavirāja Gosvāmī.

TRANSLATION

Praying at the lotus feet of Śrī Rūpa and Śrī Raghunātha, always desiring their mercy, I, Kṛṣṇadāsa, narrate Śrī Caitanya-caritāmṛta, following in their footsteps.

Instructions from this Chapter

Summarizing this chapter, Śrīla Bhaktisiddhānta Sarasvatī Ṭhākura says that one should derive from it the following lessons. (1) Although Śrī Caitanya Mahāprabhu, the Supreme Personality of Godhead, is an incarnation of mercy, He nevertheless gave up the company of one of His personal associates, namely Junior Haridāsa, for if He had not done so, pseudo-devotees would have taken advantage of Junior Haridāsa's fault by using it as an excuse to live as devotees and at the same time have illicit sexual connections. Such activities would have demoralized the cult of Śrī Caitanya Mahāprabhu, and as a result, devotees would surely have gone to a hellish life in the name of Śrī Caitanya Mahāprabhu. (2) By chastising Junior Haridāsa, the Lord set the standard for *ācāryas,* or the heads of institutions propagating the Caitanya cult, and for all actual devotees. Śrī Caitanya Mahāprabhu wanted to maintain the highest standard. (3) Śrī Caitanya Mahāprabhu instructed that a pure devotee should be simple and free from sinful activities, for thus one can be His bona fide servant. Śrī Caitanya Mahāprabhu taught His followers how to observe the renounced order strictly. (4) Śrī Caitanya Mahāprabhu wanted to prove that His devotees are exalted and that their character is ideal. He kindly accepts His faithful devotees and teaches them how much tribulation and disturbance can be produced by even a slight deviation from the strict principles of devotional life. (5) By chastising Junior Haridāsa, Śrī Caitanya Mahāprabhu exhibited His mercy toward him, thus showing how elevated was Junior Haridāsa's devotion for Him. Because of this transcendental relationship, the Lord corrected even a slight offense committed by His pure devotee. Therefore one who wants to be a pure devotee of Śrī Caitanya Mahāprabhu should give up all material sense gratification; otherwise, the lotus feet of Śrī

Caitanya Mahāprabhu are very difficult to attain. (6) If one dies in such a celebrated holy place as Prayāga, Mathurā or Vṛndāvana, one can be relieved of the reactions to sinful life and then attain the shelter of the Supreme Personality of Godhead. (7) Although a pure or faithful devotee may fall down, he nevertheless ultimately gets the chance to go back home, back to Godhead, by the mercy of the Lord.

Thus end the Bhaktivedanta purports to the Śrī Caitanya-caritāmṛta, Antya-līlā, *Second Chapter, describing the chastisement of Junior Haridāsa.*

CHAPTER 3

The Glories of Śrīla Haridāsa Ṭhākura

A summary of this Third Chapter of *Antya-līlā* is given by Śrīla Bhaktivinoda Ṭhākura as follows. A beautiful young *brāhmaṇa* girl in Jagannātha Purī had a very handsome son who was coming every day to Śrī Caitanya Mahāprabhu. This was not very much to the liking of Dāmodara Paṇḍita, however, who therefore told Śrī Caitanya Mahāprabhu, "If You display so much love for this boy, people will doubt Your character." Hearing these words from Dāmodara Paṇḍita, the Lord sent him to Navadvīpa to supervise the affairs of His mother, Śacīdevī. He also especially requested Dāmodara Paṇḍita to remind His mother that He was sometimes going to her home to accept the food she offered. Thus, following the order of Śrī Caitanya Mahāprabhu, Dāmodara Paṇḍita went to Navadvīpa, taking with him all kinds of *prasāda* from Lord Jagannātha.

On another occasion, Śrī Caitanya Mahāprabhu once inquired from Haridāsa Ṭhākura, who was known as Brahma Haridāsa, how the *yavanas,* or persons bereft of Vedic culture, would be delivered in Kali-yuga. Haridāsa Ṭhākura replied that their deliverance would be possible if they very loudly chanted the Hare Kṛṣṇa *mantra,* for hearing the Hare Kṛṣṇa *mantra* chanted loudly, even with but little realization, would help them.

After describing this incident, the author of *Caitanya-caritāmṛta* also describes how Haridāsa Ṭhākura was tested at Benāpola, a village near Śāntipura. A person named Rāmacandra Khān, who was envious of Haridāsa Ṭhākura, sent a professional prostitute to attempt to defame him, but by the mercy of Haridāsa Ṭhākura, even the prostitute was delivered. Because of offending a pure Vaiṣṇava, Rāmacandra Khān was later cursed by Nityānanda Prabhu and ruined.

From Benāpola, Haridāsa Ṭhākura went to the village known as Cāndapura, where he lived at the house of Balarāma Ācārya. Thereafter, Haridāsa Ṭhākura was received by two brothers known as Hiraṇya and Govardhana Majumadāra, but in the course of a discussion he was offended by a caste *brāhmaṇa* known as Gopāla Cakravartī. Because of this offense, Gopāla Cakravartī was punished by being afflicted with leprosy.

Haridāsa Ṭhākura later left Cāndapura and went to the house of Advaita Ācārya, where he was tested by Māyādevī, the personification of the external energy. She also received his favor by being blessed with the chanting of the Hare Kṛṣṇa *mahā-mantra.*

TEXT 1

বন্দেহহং শ্রীগুরোঃ শ্রীযুতপদকমলং শ্রীগুরূন্ বৈষ্ণবাংশ্চ
শ্রীরূপং সাগ্রজাতং সহগণরঘুনাথান্বিতং তং সজীবম্ ।
সাদ্বৈতং সাবধূতং পরিজনসহিতং কৃষ্ণচৈতন্যদেবং
শ্রীরাধাকৃষ্ণপাদান্ সহগণললিতা-শ্রীবিশাখান্বিতাংশ্চ ॥ ১ ॥

vande 'haṁ śrī-guroḥ śrī-yuta-pada-kamalaṁ śrī-gurūn vaiṣṇavāṁś ca
śrī-rūpaṁ sāgrajātaṁ saha-gaṇa-raghunāthānvitaṁ taṁ sa-jīvam
sādvaitaṁ sāvadhūtaṁ parijana-sahitaṁ kṛṣṇa-caitanya-devaṁ
śrī-rādhā-kṛṣṇa-pādān saha-gaṇa-lalitā-śrī-viśākhānvitāṁś ca

SYNONYMS

vande—offer my respectful obeisances; *aham*—I; *śrī-guroḥ*—of my spiritual master; *śrī-yuta-pada-kamalam*—unto the opulent lotus feet; *śrī-gurūn*—unto the spiritual masters in the *paramparā* system, beginning from Mādhavendra Purī down to Śrīla Bhaktisiddhānta Sarasvatī Ṭhākura Prabhupāda; *vaiṣṇavān*—unto all the Vaiṣṇavas, beginning from Lord Brahmā and others coming from the very point of creation; *ca*—and; *śrī-rūpam*—unto Śrīla Rūpa Gosvāmī; *sa-agra-jātam*—with his elder brother, Śrī Sanātana Gosvāmī; *saha-gaṇa*—with associates; *raghunātha-anvitaṁ*—with Raghunātha dāsa Gosvāmī; *taṁ*—unto him; *sa-jīvam*—with Jīva Gosvāmī; *sa-advaitam*—with Advaita Ācārya; *sa-avadhūtam*—with Nityānanda Prabhu; *parijana-sahitam*—and with Śrīvāsa Ṭhākura and all the other devotees; *kṛṣṇa-caitanya-devam*—unto Lord Śrī Caitanya Mahāprabhu; *śrī-rādhā-kṛṣṇa-pādān*—unto the lotus feet of the all-opulent Śrī Kṛṣṇa and Rādhārāṇī; *saha-gaṇa*—with Their associates; *lalitā-śrī-viśākhā-anvitān*—accompanied by Lalitā and Śrī Viśākhā; *ca*—also.

TRANSLATION

I offer my respectful obeisances unto the lotus feet of my spiritual master and of all the other preceptors on the path of devotional service, unto all the Vaiṣṇavas and unto the six Gosvāmīs, including Śrīla Rūpa Gosvāmī, Śrīla Sanātana Gosvāmī, Raghunātha dāsa Gosvāmī, Jīva Gosvāmī and their associates. I offer my respectful obeisances unto Śrī Advaita Ācārya Prabhu, Śrī Nityānanda Prabhu and Śrī Caitanya Mahāprabhu, as well as all His devotees, headed by Śrīvāsa Ṭhākura. I then offer my respectful obeisances unto the lotus feet of Lord Kṛṣṇa and Śrīmatī Rādhārāṇī and all the gopīs, headed by Lalitā and Viśākhā.

TEXT 2

জয় জয় গৌরচন্দ্র জয় নিত্যানন্দ ।
জয়াদ্বৈতচন্দ্র জয় গৌরভক্তবৃন্দ ॥ ২ ॥

jaya jaya gauracandra jaya nityānanda
jayādvaita-candra jaya gaura-bhakta-vṛnda

SYNONYMS

jaya jaya—all glories; *gaura-candra*—to Śrī Caitanya; *jaya*—all glories; *nityānanda*—to Lord Nityānanda; *jaya advaita-candra*—all glories to Advaita Ācārya; *jaya*—all glories; *gaura-bhakta-vṛnda*—to the devotees of Lord Caitanya.

TRANSLATION

All glories to Śrī Caitanya Mahāprabhu! All glories to Nityānanda Prabhu! All glories to Advaita Ācārya! And all glories to all the devotees of Śrī Caitanya Mahāprabhu!

TEXT 3

পুরুষোত্তমে এক উড়িয়া-ব্রাহ্মণকুমার ।
পিতৃশূন্য, মহাসুন্দর, মৃদুব্যবহার ॥ ৩ ॥

puruṣottame eka uḍiyā-brāhmaṇa-kumāra
pitṛ-śūnya, mahā-sundara, mṛdu-vyavahāra

SYNONYMS

puruṣottame—in Jagannātha Purī; *eka*—one; *uḍiyā-brāhmaṇa-kumāra*—young son of a *brāhmaṇa* from Orissa; *pitṛ-śūnya*—without his father; *mahā-sundara*—possessing very beautiful bodily features; *mṛdu-vyavahāra*—having very gentle behavior.

TRANSLATION

In Jagannātha Purī there was a young boy who had been born of an Orissan brāhmaṇa but had later lost his father. The boy's features were very beautiful, and his behavior was extremely gentle.

TEXTS 4-5

প্রভু-স্থানে নিত্য আইসে, করে নমস্কার ।
প্রভু-সনে বাত্ কহে প্রভু-'প্রাণ' তার ॥ ৪ ॥

প্রভুতে তাহার প্রীতি, প্রভু দয়া করে।
দামোদর তার প্রীতি সহিতে না পারে ॥ ৫ ॥

prabhu-sthāne nitya āise, kare namaskāra
prabhu-sane vāt kahe prabhu-'prāṇa' tāra

prabhute tāhāra prīti, prabhu dayā kare
dāmodara tāra prīti sahite nā pāre

SYNONYMS

prabhu-sthāne—to the place of Śrī Caitanya Mahāprabhu; *nitya*—daily; *āise*—comes; *kare namaskāra*—offers respectful obeisances; *prabhu-sane*—with the Lord; *vāt kahe*—talks; *prabhu-prāṇa tāra*—his life and soul was Śrī Caitanya Mahāprabhu; *prabhute*—unto the Lord; *tāhāra prīti*—his affection; *prabhu*—the Lord; *dayā kare*—reciprocates His mercy; *dāmodara*—Dāmodara Paṇḍita; *tāra*—his; *prīti*—love of Lord Śrī Caitanya Mahāprabhu; *sahite nā pāre*—could not tolerate.

TRANSLATION

The boy came daily to Śrī Caitanya Mahāprabhu and offered Him respectful obeisances. He was free to talk with Śrī Caitanya Mahāprabhu because the Lord was his life and soul, but the boy's intimacy with the Lord and the Lord's mercy toward him were intolerable to Dāmodara Paṇḍita.

TEXT 6

বার বার নিষেধ করে ব্রাহ্মণকুমারে।
প্রভুরে না দেখিলে সেই রহিতে না পারে ॥ ৬ ॥

bāra bāra niṣedha kare brāhmaṇa-kumāre
prabhure nā dekhile sei rahite nā pāre

SYNONYMS

bāra bāra—again and again; *niṣedha kare*—forbids; *brāhmaṇa-kumāre*—the son of the *brāhmaṇa*; *prabhure*—Śrī Caitanya Mahāprabhu; *nā dekhile*—without seeing; *sei*—that boy; *rahite nā pāre*—could not stay.

TRANSLATION

Dāmodara Paṇḍita again and again forbade the son of the brāhmaṇa to visit the Lord, but the boy could not bear staying home and not seeing Śrī Caitanya Mahāprabhu.

TEXT 7

নিত্য আইসে, প্রভু তারে করে মহাপ্রীত ।
যাঁহা প্রীতি তাঁহা আইসে,—বালকের রীত ॥ ৭ ॥

nitya āise, prabhu tāre kare mahā-prīta
yāṅhā prīti tāṅhā āise,——bālakera rīta

SYNONYMS

nitya āise—he comes daily; *prabhu*—Lord Śrī Caitanya Mahāprabhu; *tāre*—to him; *kare*—does; *mahā-prīta*—very affectionate behavior; *yāṅhā prīti*—wherever there is love; *tāṅhā āise*—one comes there; *bālakera rīta*—the nature of a small boy.

TRANSLATION

The boy came every day to Śrī Caitanya Mahāprabhu, who treated him with great affection. It is the nature of any boy to go see a man who loves him.

TEXT 8

তাহা দেখি' দামোদর দুঃখ পায় মনে ।
বলিতে না পারে, বালক নিষেধ না মানে ॥ ৮ ॥

tāhā dekhi' dāmodara duḥkha pāya mane
balite nā pāre, bālaka niṣedha nā māne

SYNONYMS

tāhā dekhi'—seeing that; *dāmodara*—Dāmodara Paṇḍita; *duḥkha pāya*—gets unhappiness; *mane*—in his mind; *balite nā pāre*—could not say anything; *bālaka*—the boy; *niṣedha*—prohibition; *nā māne*—would not care for.

TRANSLATION

This was intolerable for Dāmodara Paṇḍita. He became greatly unhappy, but there was nothing he could say, for the boy would ignore his restrictions.

TEXT 9

আর দিন সেই বালক প্রভুস্থানে আইলা ।
গোসাঞি তারে প্রীতি করি' বার্তা পুছিলা ॥ ৯ ॥

āra dina sei bālaka prabhu-sthāne āilā
gosāñi tāre prīti kari' vārtā puchilā

SYNONYMS

āra dina—one day; *sei bālaka*—that boy; *prabhu-sthāne āilā*—came to Lord Śrī Caitanya Mahāprabhu; *gosāñi*—Lord Śrī Caitanya Mahāprabhu; *tāre*—unto him; *prīti kari'*—with great affection; *vārtā*—news; *puchilā*—inquired.

TRANSLATION

One day when the boy came to Śrī Caitanya Mahāprabhu, the Lord very affectionately inquired from him about all kinds of news.

TEXT 10

কতক্ষণে সে বালক উঠি' যবে গেলা ।
সহিতে না পারে, দামোদর কহিতে লাগিলা ॥ ১০ ॥

kata-kṣaṇe se bālaka uṭhi' yabe gelā
sahite nā pāre, dāmodara kahite lāgilā

SYNONYMS

kata-kṣaṇe—after some time; *se bālaka*—that boy; *uṭhi'*—standing up; *yabe*—when; *gelā*—left; *sahite nā pāre*—could not tolerate; *dāmodara*—Dāmodara Paṇḍita; *kahite lāgilā*—began to say.

TRANSLATION

After some time, when the boy stood up and left, the intolerant Dāmodara Paṇḍita began to speak.

TEXT 11

অন্যোপদেশে পণ্ডিত – কহে গোসাঞির ঠাঞি ।
'গোসাঞি' 'গোসাঞি' এবে জানিমু 'গোসাঞি' ॥১১॥

anyopadeśe paṇḍita——kahe gosāñira ṭhāñi
'gosāñi' 'gosāñi' ebe jānimu 'gosāñi'

SYNONYMS

anya-upadeśe—by instructing others; *paṇḍita*—learned teacher; *kahe*—says; *gosāñira ṭhāñi*—in front of Śrī Caitanya Mahāprabhu; *gosāñi gosāñi*—Lord Śrī Caitanya Mahāprabhu, the supreme teacher; *ebe*—now; *jānimu*—we shall know; *gosāñi*—what kind of teacher.

TRANSLATION

Dāmodara Paṇḍita impudently said to the Lord, "Everyone says that You are a great teacher because of Your instructions to others, but now we shall find out what kind of teacher You are.

PURPORT

Dāmodara Paṇḍita was a great devotee of Śrī Caitanya Mahāprabhu. Sometimes, however, a person in such a position becomes impudent, being influenced by the external energy and material considerations. Thus a devotee mistakenly dares to criticize the activities of the spiritual master or the Supreme Personality of Godhead. Despite the logic that "Caesar's wife must be above suspicion," a devotee should not be disturbed by the activities of his spiritual master and should not try to criticize him. A devotee should be fixed in the conclusion that the spiritual master cannot be subject to criticism and should never be considered equal to a common man. Even if there appears to be some discrepancy according to an imperfect devotee's estimation, the devotee should be fixed in the conviction that even if his spiritual master goes to a liquor shop, he is not a drunkard; rather, he must have some purpose in going there. It is said in a Bengali poem:

yadyapi nityānanda surā-bāḍi yāya
tathāpio haya nityānanda-rāya

"Even if I see that Lord Nityānanda has entered a liquor shop, I shall not be diverted from my conclusion that Nityānanda Rāya is the Supreme Personality of Godhead."

TEXT 12

এবে গোসাঞির গুণ-যশ সব লোকে গাইবে ।
তবে গোসাঞির প্রতিষ্ঠা পুরুষোত্তমে হইবে ॥ ১২ ॥

ebe gosāñira guṇa-yaśa saba loke gāibe
tabe gosāñira pratiṣṭhā puruṣottame ha-ibe

SYNONYMS

ebe—now; *gosāñira*—of Lord Śrī Caitanya Mahāprabhu; *guṇa-yaśa*—attributes and reputation; *saba loke*—everyone; *gāibe*—will talk about; *tabe*—at that time; *gosāñira*—of the Lord; *pratiṣṭhā*—the position; *puruṣottame*—in Puruṣottama (Jagannātha Purī); *ha-ibe*—will be.

TRANSLATION

"You are known as Gosāñi [teacher or ācārya], but now talk about Your attributes and reputation will spread throughout the city of Puruṣottama. How Your position will be impaired!"

TEXT 13

শুনি' প্রভু কহে,—'ক্যা কহ, দামোদর ?'
দামোদর কহে,—"তুমি স্বতন্ত্র 'ঈশ্বর' ॥ ১৩ ॥

śuni' prabhu kahe,——'kyā kaha, dāmodara?'
dāmodara kahe,——"tumi svatantra 'īśvara'

SYNONYMS

śuni'—hearing; *prabhu kahe*—Śrī Caitanya Mahāprabhu said; *kyā kaha*—what nonsense are you speaking; *dāmodara*—My dear Dāmodara; *dāmodara kahe*—Dāmodara Paṇḍita replied; *tumi*—You; *svatantra*—independent; *īśvara*—the Supreme Personality of Godhead.

TRANSLATION

Although Śrī Caitanya Mahāprabhu knew that Dāmodara Paṇḍita was a pure and simple devotee, upon hearing this impudent talk the Lord said, "My dear Dāmodara, what nonsense are you speaking?" Dāmodara Paṇḍita replied, "You are the independent Personality of Godhead, beyond all criticism.

TEXT 14

স্বচ্ছন্দে আচার কর, কে পারে বলিতে ?
মুখর জগতের মুখ পার আচ্ছাদিতে ? ১৪ ॥

svacchande ācāra kara, ke pāre balite?
mukhara jagatera mukha pāra ācchādite?

SYNONYMS

svacchande—without restriction; *ācāra kara*—You behave; *ke pāre balite*—who can talk; *mukhara*—talkative; *jagatera*—of the whole world; *mukha*—mouth; *pāra acchādite*—can You cover.

TRANSLATION

"My dear Lord, You can act as You please. No one can say anything to restrict You. Nevertheless, the entire world is impudent. People can say anything. How can You stop them?

TEXT 15

পণ্ডিত হঞা মনে কেনে বিচার না কর ?
রাণ্ডী ব্রাহ্মণীর বালকে প্রীতি কেনে কর ? ১৫ ॥

paṇḍita hañā mane kene vicāra nā kara?
rāṇḍī brāhmaṇīra bālake prīti kene kara?

SYNONYMS

paṇḍita hañā—being a learned teacher; *mane*—in the mind; *kene*—why; *vicāra nā kara*—do You not consider; *rāṇḍī brāhmaṇīra*—of a widowed wife of a *brāhmaṇa*; *bālake*—unto the son; *prīti*—affection; *kene kara*—why do You show.

TRANSLATION

"Dear Lord, You are a learned teacher. Why then don't You consider that this boy is the son of a widowed brāhmaṇī? Why are You so affectionate to him?

TEXT 16

যদ্যপি ব্রাহ্মণী সেই তপস্বিনী সতী ।
তথাপি তাহার দোষ—সুন্দরী যুবতী ॥ ১৬ ॥

yadyapi brāhmaṇī sei tapasvinī satī
tathāpi tāhāra doṣa——sundarī yuvatī

SYNONYMS

yadyapi—although; *brāhmaṇī*—wife of a *brāhmaṇa*; *sei*—that; *tapasvinī*—austere; *satī*—chaste; *tathāpi*—still; *tāhāra*—her; *doṣa*—fault; *sundarī*—very beautiful; *yuvatī*—young girl.

TRANSLATION

"Although the boy's mother is completely austere and chaste, she has one natural fault—she is a very beautiful young girl.

TEXT 17

তুমিহ—পরম যুবা, পরম সুন্দর ।
লোকের কাণাকাণি-বাতে দেহ অবসর ॥" ১৭ ॥

tumi-ha——parama yuvā, parama sundara
lokera kāṇākāṇi-vāte deha avasara"

SYNONYMS

tumi-ha—You also; *parama yuvā*—young man; *parama sundara*—very beautiful; *lokera*—of the people in general; *kāṇākāṇi*—whispering; *vāte*—talks; *deha avasara*—You are giving an opportunity for.

TRANSLATION

"And You, my dear Lord, are a handsome, attractive young man. Therefore certainly people will whisper about You. Why should You give them such an opportunity?"

PURPORT

As a simple and staunch devotee of Lord Śrī Caitanya Mahāprabhu, Dāmodara Paṇḍita could not tolerate criticism of the Lord, but unfortunately he himself was criticizing Lord Śrī Caitanya Mahāprabhu in his own way. The Lord could understand that it was because of Dāmodara Paṇḍita's simplicity that he impudently dared criticize Him. Nevertheless, such behavior by a devotee is not very good.

TEXT 18

এত বলি' দামোদর মৌন হইলা ।
অন্তরে সন্তোষ প্রভু হাসি' বিচারিলা ॥ ১৮ ॥

eta bali' dāmodara mauna ha-ilā
antare santoṣa prabhu hāsi' vicārilā

SYNONYMS

eta bali'—saying this; *dāmodara*—Dāmodara Paṇḍita; *mauna ha-ilā*—became silent; *antare*—within Himself; *santoṣa*—pleased; *prabhu*—Śrī Caitanya Mahāprabhu; *hāsi'*—smiling; *vicāralā*—considered.

TRANSLATION

Having said this, Dāmodara Paṇḍita became silent. Śrī Caitanya Mahāprabhu smiled, pleased within Himself, and considered the impudence of Dāmodara Paṇḍita.

TEXT 19

"ইহারে কহিয়ে শুদ্ধপ্রেমের তরঙ্গ ।
দামোদর-সম মোর নাহি 'অন্তরঙ্গ' ॥" ১৯ ॥

"ihāre kahiye śuddha-premera taraṅga
dāmodara-sama mora nāhi 'antaraṅga' "

SYNONYMS

ihāre—such behavior; *kahiye*—I can say; *śuddha-premera taraṅga*—waves of pure devotional service; *dāmodara-sama*—like Dāmodara; *mora*—My; *nāhi*—there is not; *antaraṅga*—intimate friend.

TRANSLATION

"This impudence is also a sign of pure love for Me. I have no other intimate friend like Dāmodara Paṇḍita."

TEXT 20

এতেক বিচারি' প্রভু মধ্যাহ্নে চলিলা ।
আর দিনে দামোদরে নিভৃতে বোলাইলা ॥ ২০ ॥

eteka vicāri' prabhu madhyāhne calilā
āra dine dāmodare nibhṛte bolāilā

SYNONYMS

eteka vicāri'—considering like this; *prabhu*—Śrī Caitanya Mahāprabhu; *madhyāhne calilā*—went to perform His noon duties; *āra dine*—the next day; *dāmodare*—unto Dāmodara Paṇḍita; *nibhṛte*—in a solitary place; *bolāilā*—called.

TRANSLATION

Thinking in this way, Śrī Caitanya Mahāprabhu went to perform His noon duties. The next day, He called Dāmodara Paṇḍita to a solitary place.

TEXT 21

প্রভু কহে,—"দামোদর, চলহ নদীয়া ।
মাতার সমীপে তুমি রহ তাঁহা যাঞা ॥ ২১ ॥

prabhu kahe,—"dāmodara, calaha nadīyā
mātāra samīpe tumi raha tāṅhā yāñā

SYNONYMS

prabhu kahe—Śrī Caitanya Mahāprabhu said; *dāmodara*—My dear friend Dāmodara; *calaha nadīyā*—you had better go to Nadia (Navadvīpa); *mātāra samīpe*—in the care of My mother; *tumi*—you; *raha*—stay; *tāṅhā*—there; *yāñā*—going.

TRANSLATION

The Lord said, "My dear friend Dāmodara, you had better go to Nadia and stay with My mother.

TEXT 22

তোমা বিনা তাঁহার রক্ষক নাহি দেখি আন।
আমাকেহ যাতে তুমি কৈলা সাবধান ॥ ২২ ॥

tomā vinā tāṅhāra rakṣaka nāhi dekhi āna
āmāke-ha yāte tumi kailā sāvadhāna

SYNONYMS

tomā vinā—besides you; *tāṅhāra*—of mother Śacīdevī; *rakṣaka*—protector; *nāhi*—not; *dekhi*—I see; *āna*—anyone else; *āmāke-ha*—even unto Me; *yāte*—by which; *tumi*—you; *kailā*—did; *sāvadhāna*—care.

TRANSLATION

"I see no one but you to protect her, for you are so careful that you can caution even Me.

TEXT 23

তোমা সম 'নিরপেক্ষ' নাহি মোর গণে।
'নিরপেক্ষ' নহিলে 'ধর্ম' না যায় রক্ষণে ॥ ২৩ ॥

tomā sama 'nirapekṣa' nāhi mora gaṇe
'nirapekṣa' nahile 'dharma' nā yāya rakṣaṇe

SYNONYMS

tomā sama—like you; *nirapekṣa*—neutral; *nāhi*—there is not; *mora gaṇe*—among My associates; *nirapekṣa*—neutral; *nahile*—without being; *dharma*—religious principles; *nā yāya rakṣaṇe*—cannot be protected.

TRANSLATION

"You are the most neutral among My associates. This is very good, for without being neutral one cannot protect religious principles.

TEXT 24

আমা হৈতে যে না হয়, সে তোমা হৈতে হয়।
আমারে করিলা দণ্ড, আন কেবা হয় ॥ ২৪ ॥

āmā haite ye nā haya, se tomā haite haya
āmāre karilā daṇḍa, āna kebā haya

SYNONYMS

āmā haite—from Me; *ye*—whatever; *nā haya*—is not; *se*—that; *tomā haite*—from you; *haya*—becomes possible; *āmāre*—Me; *karilā daṇḍa*—punished; *āna*—others; *kebā haya*—what to speak of.

TRANSLATION

"You can do whatever I cannot. Indeed, you can chastise even Me, not to speak of others.

TEXT 25

মাতার গৃহে রহ যাই মাতার চরণে।
তোমার আগে নহিবে কারো স্বচ্ছন্দাচরণে ॥ ২৫ ॥

mātāra gṛhe raha yāi mātāra caraṇe
tomāra āge nahibe kāro svacchandācaraṇe

SYNONYMS

mātāra—of My mother; *gṛhe*—at the home; *raha*—stay; *yāi*—going; *mātāra caraṇe*—at the shelter of My mother's lotus feet; *tomāra āge*—in front of you; *nahibe*—there will not be; *kāro*—of anyone; *svacchanda-ācaraṇe*—independent activities.

TRANSLATION

"It is best for you to go to the shelter of My mother's lotus feet, for no one will be able to behave independently in front of you.

TEXT 26

মধ্যে মধ্যে আসিবা কভু আমার দরশনে।
শীঘ্র করি' পুনঃ তাহাঁ করহ গমনে ॥ ২৬ ॥

madhye madhye āsibā kabhu āmāra daraśane
śīghra kari' punaḥ tāhāṅ karaha gamane

SYNONYMS

madhye madhye—at intervals; *āsibā*—you will come; *kabhu*—sometimes; *āmāra daraśane*—to see Me; *śīghra kari'*—very soon; *punaḥ*—again; *tāhāṅ*—there; *karaha gamane*—arrange to go.

TRANSLATION

"At intervals you may come see Me here and then soon again go there.

TEXT 27

মাতারে কহিহ মোর কোটী নমস্কারে ।
মোর সুখ-কথা কহি' সুখ দিহ' তাঁরে ॥ ২৭ ॥

mātāre kahiha mora koṭī namaskāre
mora sukha-kathā kahi' sukha diha' tāṅre

SYNONYMS

mātāre—to My mother; *kahiha*—inform; *mora*—My; *koṭī*—ten million; *namaskāre*—obeisances; *mora*—My; *sukha*—of happiness; *kathā*—topics; *kahi'*—saying; *sukha*—happiness; *diha' tāṅre*—give to her.

TRANSLATION

"Offer My mother millions of My obeisances. Please speak to her about My happiness here and thus give her happiness.

TEXT 28

'নিরন্তর নিজ-কথা তোমারে শুনাইতে ।
এই লাগি' প্রভু মোরে পাঠাইলা ইহাঁতে'॥ ২৮ ॥

'nirantara nija-kathā tomāre śunāite
ei lāgi' prabhu more pāṭhāilā ihāṅte'

SYNONYMS

nirantara—constantly; *nija-kathā*—personal activities; *tomāre śunāite*—to inform you; *ei lāgi'*—for this reason; *prabhu*—Śrī Caitanya Mahāprabhu; *more*—me; *pāṭhāilā*—has sent; *ihāṅte*—here.

TRANSLATION

"Tell her that I sent you to inform her of My personal activities so that she may share in My happiness.

TEXT 29

এত কহি' মাতার মনে সন্তোষ জন্মাইহ ।
আর গুহ্যকথা তাঁরে স্মরণ করাইহ ॥ ২৯ ॥

eta kahi' mātāra mane santoṣa janmāiha
āra guhya-kathā tāṅre smaraṇa karāiha

SYNONYMS

eta kahi'—saying this; *mātāra mane*—in the mind of My mother; *santoṣa janmāiha*—give satisfaction; *āra*—another; *guhya-kathā*—very confidential message; *tāṅre*—her; *smaraṇa karāiha*—make to remember.

TRANSLATION

"Speaking in this way, satisfy the mind of mother Śacī. Also, remind her of one most confidential incident with this message from Me.

TEXT 30

'বারে বারে আসি' আমি তোমার ভবনে ।
মিষ্টান্ন ব্যঞ্জন সব করিয়ে ভোজনে ॥ ৩০ ॥

'bāre bāre āsi' āmi tomāra bhavane
miṣṭānna vyañjana saba kariye bhojane

SYNONYMS

bāre bāre—again and again; *āsi'*—coming; *āmi*—I; *tomāra bhavane*—at your place; *miṣṭānna*—sweetmeats; *vyañjana*—vegetables; *saba*—all; *kariye*—do; *bhojane*—eating.

TRANSLATION

" 'I come to your home again and again to eat all the sweetmeats and vegetables you offer.

TEXT 31

ভোজন করিয়ে আমি, তুমি তাহা জান ।
বাহ্য বিরহে তাহা স্বপ্ন করি মান ॥ ৩১ ॥

bhojana kariye āmi, tumi tāhā jāna
bāhya virahe tāhā svapna kari māna

SYNONYMS

bhojana—dining; *kariye*—do; *āmi*—I; *tumi*—you; *tāhā*—that; *jāna*—know; *bāhya*—externally; *virahe*—in separation; *tāhā*—that; *svapna*—dream; *kari*—as; *māna*—you accept.

TRANSLATION

" 'You know that I come and eat the offerings, but because of external separation, you consider this a dream.

PURPORT

Because mother Śacī was feeling separation from Śrī Caitanya Mahāprabhu, she thought she was dreaming that her son had come to her. Śrī Caitanya Mahāprabhu, however, wanted to inform her that actually it was not a dream. He actually came there and ate whatever His mother offered Him. Such are the dealings of advanced devotees with the Supreme Personality of Godhead. As stated in the *Brahma-saṁhitā:*

premāñjana-cchurita-bhakti-vilocanena
santaḥ sadaiva hṛdayeṣu vilokayanti
yaṁ śyāmasundaram acintya-guṇa-svarūpaṁ
govindam ādi-puruṣaṁ tam ahaṁ bhajāmi

"I worship the primeval Lord, Govinda, who is always seen by the devotee whose eyes are anointed with the pulp of love. He is seen in His eternal form of Śyāmasundara, situated within the heart of the devotee." (Bs. 5.38) Pure devotees realize dealings with the Lord on the transcendental plane, but because the devotees are still in the material world, they think that these are dreams. The Lord, however, talks with the advanced devotee, and the advanced devotee also sees Him. It is all factual; it is not a dream.

TEXT 32

এই মাঘ-সংক্রান্ত্যে তুমি রন্ধন করিলা ।
নানা ব্যঞ্জন, ক্ষীর, পিঠা, পায়স রান্ধিলা ॥ ৩২ ॥

ei māgha-saṅkrāntye tumi randhana karilā
nānā vyañjana, kṣīra, piṭhā, pāyasa rāndhilā

SYNONYMS

ei—this; *māgha-saṅkrāntye*—on the occasion of the Māgha-saṅkrānti festival; *tumi*—you; *randhana karilā*—cooked; *nānā vyañjana*—varieties of vegetables; *kṣīra*—condensed milk; *piṭhā*—cakes; *pāyasa*—sweet rice; *rāndhilā*—cooked.

TRANSLATION

" 'During the last Māgha-saṅkrānti festival, you cooked varieties of vegetables, condensed milk, cakes and sweet rice for Me.

TEXT 33

কৃষ্ণে ভোগ লাগাঞা যবে কৈলা ধ্যান ।
আমার স্ফূর্তি হৈল, অশ্রু ভরিল নয়ন ॥ ৩৩ ॥

kṛṣṇe bhoga lāgāñā yabe kailā dhyāna
āmāra sphūrti haila, aśru bharila nayana

SYNONYMS

kṛṣṇe—unto Lord Kṛṣṇa; *bhoga*—offering; *lāgāñā*—giving; *yabe*—when; *kailā dhyāna*—you meditated; *āmāra*—My; *sphūrti*—sudden appearance; *haila*—there was; *aśru*—tears; *bharila*—filled; *nayana*—your eyes.

TRANSLATION

" 'You offered the food to Lord Kṛṣṇa, and while you were in meditation I suddenly appeared, and your eyes filled with tears.

TEXT 34

আস্তে-ব্যস্তে আমি গিয়া সকলি খাইল ।
আমি খাই,—দেখি' তোমার সুখ উপজিল ॥ ৩৪ ॥

āste-vyaste āmi giyā sakali khāila
āmi khāi,——dekhi' tomāra sukha upajila

SYNONYMS

āste-vyaste—in great haste; *āmi*—I; *giyā*—going; *sakali khāila*—ate everything; *āmi khāi*—I eat; *dekhi'*—seeing; *tomāra*—your; *sukha*—happiness; *upajila*—grew.

TRANSLATION

" 'I went there in great haste and ate everything. When you saw Me eating, you felt great happiness.

TEXT 35

ক্ষণেকে অশ্রু মুছিয়া শূন্য দেখি' পাত ।
স্বপন দেখিলুঁ, 'যেন নিমাঞি খাইল ভাত' ॥ ৩৫ ॥

kṣaṇeke aśru muchiyā śūnya dekhi' pāta
svapana dekhiluṅ, 'yena nimāñi khāila bhāta'

SYNONYMS

kṣaṇeke—in a moment; *aśru*—tears; *muchiyā*—wiping; *śūnya*—vacant; *dekhi'*—seeing; *pāta*—the plate; *svapana dekhiluṅ*—I saw a dream; *yena*—as if; *nimāñi*—Śrī Caitanya Mahāprabhu; *khāila bhāta*—ate the food.

TRANSLATION

" 'In a moment, after you had wiped your eyes, you saw that the plate you had offered Me was empty. Then you thought, "I dreamt as if Nimāi were eating everything."

TEXT 36

বাহ্য-বিরহ-দশায় পুনঃ ভ্রান্তি হৈল ।
'ভোগ না লাগাইলুঁ',—এই জ্ঞান হৈল ॥ ৩৬ ॥

bāhya-viraha-daśāya punaḥ bhrānti haila
'bhoga nā lāgāiluṅ',——ei jñāna haila

SYNONYMS

bāhya-viraha—of external separation; *daśāya*—by the condition; *punaḥ*—again; *bhrānti haila*—there was illusion; *bhoga*—offering to the Deity; *nā lāgāiluṅ*—I have not given; *ei*—this; *jñāna haila*—you thought.

TRANSLATION

" 'In the condition of external separation, you were again under illusion, thinking that you had not offered the food to Lord Viṣṇu.

TEXT 37

পাকপাত্রে দেখিলা সব অন্ন আছে ভরি' ।
পুনঃ ভোগ লাগাইলা স্থান-সংস্কার করি' ॥ ৩৭ ॥

pāka-pātre dekhilā saba anna āche bhari'
punaḥ bhoga lāgāilā sthāna-saṁskāra kari'

SYNONYMS

pāka-pātre—the cooking pots; *dekhilā*—she saw; *saba*—all; *anna*—food; *āche bhari'*—were filled with; *punaḥ*—again; *bhoga lāgāilā*—offered the food; *sthāna*—the place for offering; *saṁskāra kari'*—cleansing.

TRANSLATION

" 'Then you went to see the cooking pots and found that every pot was filled with food. Therefore you again offered the food, after cleansing the place for the offering.

TEXT 38

এইমত বার বার করিয়ে ভোজন ।
তোমার শুদ্ধপ্রেমে মোরে করে আকর্ষণ ॥ ৩৮ ॥

ei-mata bāra bāra kariye bhojana
tomāra śuddha-preme more kare ākarṣaṇa

SYNONYMS

ei-mata—in this way; *bāra bāra*—again and again; *kariye bhojana*—I eat; *tomāra*—your; *śuddha-preme*—pure love; *more*—Me; *kare ākarṣaṇa*—attracts.

TRANSLATION

" 'Thus I again and again eat everything you offer Me, for I am attracted by your pure love.

TEXT 39

তোমার আজ্ঞাতে আমি আছি নীলাচলে ।
নিকটে লঞা যাও আমা তোমার প্রেমবলে'॥ ৩৯ ॥

tomāra ājñāte āmi āchi nīlācale
nikaṭe lañā yāo āmā tomāra prema-bale'

SYNONYMS

tomāra ājñāte—on your order; *āmi*—I; *āchi*—reside; *nīlācale*—at Jagannātha Purī; *nikaṭe*—nearby; *lañā yāo*—you take away; *āmā*—Me; *tomāra*—your; *prema*—transcendental love; *bale*—on the strength of.

TRANSLATION

" 'Only by your order am I living in Nīlācala [Jagannātha Purī]. Nevertheless, you still pull Me near you because of your great love for Me.' "

TEXT 40

এইমত বার বার করাইহ স্মরণ ।
মোর নাম লঞা তাঁর বন্দিহ চরণ ॥" ৪০ ॥

ei-mata bāra bāra karāiha smaraṇa
mora nāma lañā tāṅra vandiha caraṇa"

SYNONYMS

ei-mata—in this way; *bāra bāra*—again and again; *karāiha*—cause; *smaraṇa*—remembrance; *mora*—My; *nāma*—name; *lañā*—taking; *tāṅra*—her; *vandiha*—worship; *caraṇa*—feet.

TRANSLATION

Śrī Caitanya Mahāprabhu told Dāmodara Paṇḍita, "Remind mother Śacī in this way again and again and worship her lotus feet in My name."

TEXT 41

এত কহি' জগন্নাথের প্রসাদ আনাইল ।
মাতাকে বৈষ্ণবে দিতে পৃথক্ পৃথক্ দিল ॥ ৪১ ॥

eta kahi' jagannāthera prasāda ānāila
mātāke vaiṣṇave dite pṛthak pṛthak dila

SYNONYMS

eta kahi'—saying this; *jagannāthera*—of Jagannātha; *prasāda*—remnants of food; *ānāila*—ordered to be brought; *mātāke*—to His mother; *vaiṣṇave*—and all the Vaiṣṇavas; *dite*—to deliver; *pṛthak pṛthak*—separately; *dila*—he gave.

TRANSLATION

After saying this, Śrī Caitanya Mahāprabhu ordered that varieties of prasāda offered to Lord Jagannātha be brought. The Lord then gave him the prasāda, separately packed, to offer to various Vaiṣṇavas and His mother.

TEXT 42

তবে দামোদর চলি' নদীয়া আইলা ।
মাতারে মিলিয়া তাঁর চরণে রহিলা ॥ ৪২ ॥

tabe dāmodara cali' nadīyā āilā
mātāre miliyā tāṅra caraṇe rahilā

SYNONYMS

tabe—then; *dāmodara*—Dāmodara Paṇḍita; *cali'*—walking; *nadīyā āilā*—reached Nadia (Navadvīpa); *mātāre miliyā*—just after meeting Śacīmātā; *tāṅra caraṇe*—at her lotus feet; *rahilā*—remained.

TRANSLATION

In this way Dāmodara Paṇḍita went to Nadia [Navadvīpa]. After meeting mother Śacī, he stayed under the care of her lotus feet.

TEXT 43

আচার্যাদি বৈষ্ণবেরে মহাপ্রসাদ দিলা ।
প্রভুর যৈছে আজ্ঞা, পণ্ডিত তাহা আচরিলা ॥ ৪৩ ॥

ācāryādi vaiṣṇavere mahā-prasāda dilā
prabhura yaiche ājñā, paṇḍita tāhā ācarilā

SYNONYMS

ācārya-ādi—headed by Advaita Ācārya; *vaiṣṇavere*—to all the Vaiṣṇavas; *mahā-prasāda dilā*—delivered all the *prasāda* of Lord Jagannātha; *prabhura*—of Śrī Caitanya Mahāprabhu; *yaiche*—as; *ājñā*—the order; *paṇḍita*—Dāmodara Paṇḍita; *tāhā*—that; *ācarilā*—performed.

TRANSLATION

He delivered all the prasāda to such great Vaiṣṇavas as Advaita Ācārya. Thus he stayed there and behaved according to the order of Śrī Caitanya Mahāprabhu.

TEXT 44

দামোদর আগে স্বাতন্ত্র্য না হয় কাহার ।
তার ভয়ে সবে করে সঙ্কোচ ব্যবহার ॥ ৪৪ ॥

dāmodara āge svātantrya nā haya kāhāra
tāra bhaye sabe kare saṅkoca vyavahāra

SYNONYMS

dāmodara āge—in front of Dāmodara Paṇḍita; *svātantrya*—independent behavior; *nā haya kāhāra*—no one dares to do; *tāra bhaye*—due to fear of him; *sabe*—all of them; *kare*—do; *saṅkoca vyavahāra*—dealings with great care.

TRANSLATION

Everyone knew that Dāmodara Paṇḍita was strict in practical dealings. Therefore everyone was afraid of him and dared not do anything independent.

TEXT 45

প্রভুগণে যাঁর দেখে অল্পমর্যাদা-লঙ্ঘন ।
বাক্যদণ্ড করি' করে মর্যাদা স্থাপন ॥ ৪৫ ॥

prabhu-gaṇe yāṅra dekhe alpa-maryādā-laṅghana
vākya-daṇḍa kari' kare maryādā sthāpana

SYNONYMS

prabhu-gaṇe—in the associates of Śrī Caitanya Mahāprabhu; *yāṅra*—whose; *dekhe*—sees; *alpa-maryādā-laṅghana*—a slight deviation from the standard etiquette and behavior; *vākya-daṇḍa kari'*—chastising with words; *kare*—does; *maryādā*—etiquette; *sthāpana*—establishing.

TRANSLATION

Dāmodara Paṇḍita would verbally chastise every devotee of Śrī Caitanya Mahāprabhu whom he found deviating even slightly from proper behavior. Thus he established the standard etiquette.

TEXT 46

এইত কহিল দামোদরের বাক্যদণ্ড ।
যাহার শ্রবণে ভাগে 'অজ্ঞান পাষণ্ড' ॥ ৪৬ ॥

ei-ta kahila dāmodarera vākya-daṇḍa
yāhāra śravaṇe bhāge 'ajñāna pāṣaṇḍa'

SYNONYMS

ei-ta—in this way; *kahila*—I have described; *dāmodarera*—of Dāmodara Paṇḍita; *vākya-daṇḍa*—chastisement by words; *yāhāra śravaṇe*—by hearing which; *bhāge*—goes away; *ajñāna pāṣaṇḍa*—the atheist of ignorance.

TRANSLATION

In this way I have described Dāmodara Paṇḍita's verbal chastisements. As one hears about this, atheistic principles and ignorance depart.

TEXT 47

চৈতন্যের লীলা—গম্ভীর, কোটিসমুদ্র হৈতে ।
কি লাগি' কি করে, কেহ না পারে বুঝিতে ॥ ৪৭ ॥

caitanyera līlā——gambhīra, koṭi-samudra haite
ki lāgi' ki kare, keha nā pāre bujhite

SYNONYMS

caitanyera līlā—the pastimes of Śrī Caitanya Mahāprabhu; *gambhīra*—very deep; *koṭi-samudra haite*—more than millions of seas; *ki lāgi'*—for what reason; *ki kare*—what He does; *keha*—anyone; *nā*—not; *pāre bujhite*—can understand.

TRANSLATION

The pastimes of Śrī Caitanya Mahāprabhu are deeper than millions of seas and oceans. Therefore no one can understand what He does nor why He does it.

TEXT 48

অতএব গূঢ় অর্থ কিছুই না জানি ।
বাহ্য অর্থ করিবারে করি টানাটানি ॥ ৪৮ ॥

ataeva gūḍha artha kichui nā jāni
bāhya artha karibāre kari ṭānāṭāni

SYNONYMS

ataeva—therefore; *gūḍha artha*—deep meaning; *kichui*—any; *nā jāni*—I do not know; *bāhya artha karibāre*—to explain the external meanings; *kari*—I make; *ṭānāṭāni*—hard endeavor.

TRANSLATION

I do not know the deep meaning of Śrī Caitanya Mahāprabhu's activities. As far as possible I shall try to explain them externally.

TEXT 49

একদিন প্রভু হরিদাসেরে মিলিলা ।
তাঁহা লঞা গোষ্ঠী করি' তাঁহারে পুছিলা ॥ ৪৯ ॥

eka-dina prabhu haridāsere mililā
tāṅhā lañā goṣṭhī kari' tāṅhāre puchilā

SYNONYMS

eka-dina—one day; *prabhu*—Śrī Caitanya Mahāprabhu; *haridāsere*—with Haridāsa Ṭhākura; *mililā*—met; *tāṅhā lañā*—taking him; *goṣṭhī kari'*—making a discussion; *tāṅhāre puchilā*—the Lord inquired from him.

TRANSLATION

One day Śrī Caitanya Mahāprabhu met Haridāsa Ṭhākura as usual, and in the course of discussion He inquired as follows.

TEXT 50

"হরিদাস, কলিকালে যবন অপার ।
গো-ব্রাহ্মণে হিংসা করে মহা দুরাচার ॥ ৫০ ॥

"haridāsa, kali-kāle yavana apāra
go-brāhmaṇe hiṁsā kare mahā durācāra

SYNONYMS

haridāsa—My dear Haridāsa; *kali-kāle*—in this age of Kali; *yavana*—demons against the Vedic principles; *apāra*—unlimited; *go-brāhmaṇe*—cows and brahminical culture; *hiṁsā kare*—do violence against; *mahā durācāra*—extremely fallen.

TRANSLATION

"My dear Ṭhākura Haridāsa, in this age of Kali most people are bereft of Vedic culture, and therefore they are called yavanas. They are concerned only with killing cows and brahminical culture. In this way they all engage in sinful acts.

PURPORT

From this statement by Śrī Caitanya Mahāprabhu we can clearly understand that the word *yavana* does not refer only to a particular class of men. Anyone who is against the behavior of the Vedic principles is called a *yavana.* Such a *yavana* may be in India or outside of India. As described here, the symptom of *yavanas* is that they are violent killers of cows and brahminical culture. We offer our prayers to the Lord by saying, *namo brahmaṇya-devāya go-brāhmaṇa-hitāya ca.* The Lord is the maintainer of brahminical culture. His first concern is to see to the benefit of cows and *brāhmaṇas.* As soon as human civilization turns against brahminical culture and allows unrestricted killing of cows, we should understand that men are no longer under the control of the Vedic culture but are all *yavanas* and *mlecchas.* It is said that the Kṛṣṇa consciousness movement will be prominent within the next ten thousand years, but after that people will all become *mlecchas* and *yavanas.* Thus at the end of the *yuga,* Kṛṣṇa will appear as the Kalki *avatāra* and kill them without consideration.

TEXT 51

ইহা-সবার কোন্ মতে হইবে নিস্তার ?
তাহার হেতু না দেখিয়ে,—এ দুঃখ অপার ॥"৫১ ॥

ihā-sabāra kon mate ha-ibe nistāra?
tāhāra hetu nā dekhiye,——e duḥkha apāra"

SYNONYMS

ihā-sabāra—of all these *yavanas; kon mate*—by which way; *ha-ibe nistāra*—will be deliverance; *tāhāra hetu*—the cause of such deliverance; *nā dekhiye*—I do not see; *e duḥkha apāra*—it is My great unhappiness.

TRANSLATION

"How will these yavanas be delivered? To My great unhappiness, I do not see any way."

PURPORT

This verse reveals the significance of Lord Śrī Caitanya's appearance as *patita-pāvana,* the deliverer of all the fallen souls. Śrīla Narottama dāsa Ṭhākura sings, *patita-pāvana-hetu tava avatāra:* "O my Lord, You have appeared just to deliver all the fallen souls." *mo-sama patita prabhu nā pāibe āra:* "And among all the fallen souls, I am the lowest." How Śrī Kṛṣṇa Caitanya Mahāprabhu was always thinking about the deliverance of the fallen souls is shown by the statement *e duḥkha apāra* ("It is My great unhappiness"). This statement indicates that Śrī Caitanya Mahāprabhu, who is the Supreme Personality of Godhead Kṛṣṇa Himself, is always very unhappy to see the fallen souls in the material world. Therefore He Himself comes as He is, or He comes as a devotee in the form of Śrī Caitanya Mahāprabhu, to deliver love of Kṛṣṇa directly to the fallen souls. *Namo mahā-vadānyāya kṛṣṇa-prema-pradāya te.* Śrī Caitanya Mahāprabhu is so merciful that He not only gives knowledge of Kṛṣṇa but by His practical activities teaches everyone how to love Kṛṣṇa (*kṛṣṇa-prema-pradāya te*).

Those who are following in the footsteps of Śrī Caitanya Mahāprabhu should take the Lord's mission most seriously. In this age of Kali, people are gradually becoming less than animals. Nevertheless, although they are eating the flesh of cows and are envious of brahminical culture, Śrī Caitanya Mahāprabhu is considering how to deliver them from this horrible condition of life. Thus He asks all Indians to take up His mission.

bhārata-bhūmite haila manuṣya-janma yāra
janma sārthaka kari' kara para-upakāra

"One who has taken his birth as a human being in the land of India [Bhārata-varṣa] should make his life successful and work for the benefit of all other people." (Cc. *Ādi-līlā* 9.41) It is therefore the duty of every advanced and cultured Indian to take this cause very seriously. All Indians should help the Kṛṣṇa consciousness movement in its progress, to the best of their ability. Then they will be considered real followers of Śrī Caitanya Mahāprabhu.

Unfortunately, even some so-called Vaiṣṇavas enviously refuse to cooperate with this movement but instead condemn it in so many ways. We are very sorry to say that these people try to find fault with us, being unnecessarily envious of our activities, although we are trying to the best of our ability to introduce the Kṛṣṇa consciousness movement directly into the countries of the *yavanas* and *mlecchas*. Such *yavanas* and *mlecchas* are coming to us and becoming purified Vaiṣṇavas who follow in the footsteps of Śrī Caitanya Mahāprabhu. One who identifies himself as a follower of Śrī Caitanya Mahāprabhu should feel like Śrī Caitanya Mahāprabhu, who said, *ihā-sabāra kon mate ha-ibe nistāra*: "How will all these *yavanas* be delivered?" Śrī Caitanya Mahāprabhu was always anxious to deliver the fallen souls because their fallen condition gave Him great unhappiness. That is the platform on which one can propagate the mission of Śrī Caitanya Mahāprabhu.

TEXT 52

হরিদাস কহে,—"প্রভু, চিন্তা না করিহ ।
যবনের সংসার দেখি' দুঃখ না ভাবিহ ॥ ৫২ ॥

haridāsa kahe,——"prabhu, cintā nā kariha
yavanera saṁsāra dekhi' duḥkha nā bhāviha

SYNONYMS

haridāsa kahe—Haridāsa replied; *prabhu*—my dear Lord; *cintā nā kariha*—do not be in anxiety; *yavanera saṁsāra*—the material condition of the *yavanas*; *dekhi'*—seeing; *duḥkha nā bhāviha*—do not be sorry.

TRANSLATION

Haridāsa Ṭhākura replied, "My dear Lord, do not be in anxiety. Do not be unhappy to see the condition of the yavanas in material existence.

PURPORT

These words of Haridāsa Ṭhākura are just befitting a devotee who has dedicated his life and soul to the service of the Lord. When the Lord is unhappy because of the condition of the fallen souls, the devotee consoles Him, saying, "My dear Lord, do not be in anxiety." This is service. Everyone should adopt the cause of Śrī Caitanya Mahāprabhu to try to relieve Him from the anxiety He feels. This is actually service to the Lord. One who tries to relieve Śrī Caitanya Mahāprabhu's anxiety for the fallen souls is certainly a most dear and confidential devotee of the Lord. To blaspheme such a devotee who is trying his best to spread the cult of Śrī Caitanya Mahāprabhu is the greatest offense. One who does so is simply awaiting punishment for his envy.

TEXT 53

যবনসকলের 'মুক্তি' হবে অনায়াসে।
'হা রাম, হা রাম' বলি' কহে নামাভাসে ॥ ৫৩ ॥

yavana-sakalera 'mukti' habe anāyāse
'hā rāma, hā rāma' bali' kahe nāmābhāse

SYNONYMS

yavana-sakalera—of all the *yavanas; mukti*—liberation; *habe*—there will be; *anāyāse*—very easily; *hā rāma hā rāma*—O Lord Rāma, O Lord Rāma; *bali'*—saying; *kahe*—they say; *nāma-ābhāse*—almost chanting the holy name of the Lord without offenses.

TRANSLATION

"Because the yavanas are accustomed to saying, 'hā rāma, hā rāma' [O Lord Rāmacandra], they will very easily be delivered by this nāmābhāsa.

TEXT 54

মহাপ্রেমে ভক্ত কহে,—'হা রাম, হা রাম'।
যবনের ভাগ্য দেখ, লয় সেই নাম ॥ ৫৪ ॥

mahā-preme bhakta kahe,—'hā rāma, hā rāma'
yavanera bhāgya dekha, laya sei nāma

SYNONYMS

mahā-preme—in great ecstatic love; *bhakta kahe*—a devotee says; *hā rāma hā rāma*—O Lord Rāmacandra, O Lord Rāmacandra; *yavanera*—of the *yavanas; bhāgya*—fortune; *dekha*—just see; *laya sei nāma*—they are also chanting the same holy name.

TRANSLATION

"A devotee in advanced ecstatic love exclaims, 'O my Lord Rāmacandra! O my Lord Rāmacandra!' But the yavanas also chant, 'hā rāma, hā rāma!' Just see their good fortune!"

PURPORT

If a child touches fire, the fire will burn him, and if an elderly man touches fire, it will burn him also. Haridāsa Ṭhākura says that a great devotee of the Lord exclaims, "*hā rāma, hā rāma,*" but although *yavanas* do not know the transcendental meaning of *"hā rāma, hā rāma,"* they say those words in the course of their ordinary life. For the *yavanas* the words *"hā rāma"* mean "abominable," whereas the devotee exclaims the words *"hā rāma"* in ecstatic love. Nevertheless, because the words *"hā rāma"* are the spiritual *summum bonum,* the fact is the same, whether they are uttered by *yavanas* or by great devotees, just as fire is the same both for a child and for an elderly man. In other words, the holy name of the Lord, *"hā rāma,"* always acts, even when the holy names are chanted without reference to the Supreme Lord. *Yavanas* utter the holy name in a different attitude than devotees, but the holy name *"hā rāma"* is so powerful spiritually that it acts anywhere, whether one knows it or not. This is explained as follows.

TEXT 55

যদ্যপি অন্য সঙ্কেতে অন্য হয় নামাভাস ।
তথাপি নামের তেজ না হয় বিনাশ ॥ ৫৫ ॥

yadyapi anya saṅkete anya haya nāmābhāsa
tathāpi nāmera teja nā haya vināśa

SYNONYMS

yadyapi—although; *anya*—another; *saṅkete*—by intimation; *anya*—that other; *haya*—is; *nāma-ābhāsa*—almost equal to the holy name; *tathāpi*—still; *nāmera teja*—the transcendental power of the holy name; *nā haya vināśa*—is not destroyed.

TRANSLATION

Nāmācārya Haridāsa Ṭhākura, the authority on the chanting of the holy name, said, "The chanting of the Lord's holy name to indicate something other than the Lord is an instance of nāmābhāsa. Even when the holy name is chanted in this way, its transcendental power is not destroyed.

TEXT 56

দংষ্ট্রিদংষ্ট্রাহতো ম্লেচ্ছো হা রামেতি পুনঃ পুনঃ ।
উক্ত্বাপি মুক্তিমাপ্নোতি কিং পুনঃ শ্রদ্ধয়া গৃণন্ ॥৫৬॥

daṁṣṭri-daṁṣṭrāhato mleccho
hā rāmeti punaḥ punaḥ
uktvāpi muktim āpnoti
kiṁ punaḥ śraddhayā gṛṇan

SYNONYMS

daṁṣṭri—of a boar; *daṁṣṭra*—by the teeth; *āhataḥ*—killed; *mlecchaḥ*—a meateater; *hā*—O; *rāma*—my Lord Rāma; *iti*—thus; *punaḥ punaḥ*—again and again; *uktvā*—saying; *api*—even; *muktim*—liberation; *āpnoti*—gets; *kim*—what; *punaḥ*—again; *śraddhayā*—with faith and veneration; *gṛṇan*—chanting.

TRANSLATION

" 'Even a mleccha who is being killed by the tusk of a boar and who cries in distress again and again, "hā rāma, hā rāma" attains liberation. What then to speak of those who chant the holy name with veneration and faith?'

PURPORT

This refers to an instance in which a meateater being killed by a boar uttered the words "*hā rāma, hā rāma*" again and again at the time of his death. Since this is a quotation from the *Nṛsiṁha Purāṇa,* this indicates that in the purāṇic age there must also have been *mlecchas* and *yavanas* (meateaters), and the words "*hā rāma,*" meaning "condemned," were also uttered in those days. Thus Haridāsa Ṭhākura gives evidence that even a meateater who condemns something by uttering the words "*hā rāma*" gets the benefit of chanting the holy name that the devotee chants to mean "O my Lord Rāma."

TEXT 57

অজামিল পুত্রে বোলায় বলি 'নারায়ণ'।
বিষ্ণুদূত আসি' ছাড়ায় তাহার বন্ধন ॥ ৫৭ ॥

ajāmila putre bolāya bali 'nārāyaṇa'
viṣṇu-dūta āsi' chāḍāya tāhāra bandhana

SYNONYMS

ajāmila—Ajāmila; *putre*—unto his son; *bolāya*—calls; *bali*—saying; *nārāyaṇa*—the holy name of Nārāyaṇa; *viṣṇu-dūta*—the attendants of Lord Viṣṇu; *āsi'*—coming; *chāḍāya*—remove; *tāhāra*—of him; *bandhana*—the bonds.

TRANSLATION

"Ajāmila was a great sinner during his life, but at the time of death he accidentally called for his youngest son, whose name was Nārāyaṇa, and the attendants of Lord Viṣṇu came to relieve him from the bonds of Yamarāja, the superintendent of death.

TEXT 58

'রাম' দুই অক্ষর ইহা নহে ব্যবহিত।
প্রেমবাচী 'হা'-শব্দ তাহাতে ভূষিত ॥ ৫৮ ॥

'rāma' dui akṣara ihā nahe vyavahita
prema-vācī 'hā'-śabda tāhāte bhūṣita

SYNONYMS

rāma—the holy name of the Lord; *dui*—two; *akṣara*—syllables; *ihā*—these; *nahe*—are not; *vyavahita*—separated; *prema-vācī*—a word indicating love; *hā*—"O"; *śabda*—the word; *tāhāte*—by that; *bhūṣita*—decorated.

TRANSLATION

"The word 'rāma' consists of the two syllables, 'rā' and 'ma.' These are unseparated and are decorated with the loving word 'hā,' meaning 'O.'

TEXT 59

নামের অক্ষর-সবের এই ত' স্বভাব।
ব্যবহিত হৈলে না ছাড়ে আপন-প্রভাব ॥ ৫৯ ॥

nāmera akṣara-sabera ei ta' svabhāva
vyavahita haile nā chāḍe āpana-prabhāva

SYNONYMS

nāmera—of the holy name; *akṣara*—letters; *sabera*—of all; *ei*—this; *ta'*—certainly; *sva-bhāva*—the characteristic; *vyavahita haile*—even when improperly uttered; *nā*—do not; *chāḍe*—give up; *āpana-prabhāva*—their own spiritual influence.

TRANSLATION

"The letters of the holy name have so much spiritual potency that they act even when uttered improperly.

PURPORT

Śrīla Bhaktisiddhānta Sarasvatī Ṭhākura states that the word *vyavahita* ("improperly uttered") is not used here to refer to the mundane vibration of the letters of the alphabet. Such negligent utterance for the sense gratification of materialistic persons is not a vibration of transcendental sound. Utterance of the holy name while one engages in sense gratification is an impediment on the path toward achieving ecstatic love for Kṛṣṇa. On the other hand, if one who is eager for devotional service utters the holy name even partially or improperly, the holy name, who is identical with the Supreme Personality of Godhead, exhibits its spiritual potency because of that person's offenseless utterance. Thus one is relieved from all unwanted practices, and one gradually awakens his dormant love for Kṛṣṇa.

TEXT 60

নামৈকং যস্য বাচি স্মরণপথগতং শ্রোত্রমূলং গতং বা
শুদ্ধং বাশুদ্ধবর্ণং ব্যবহিত-রহিতং তারয়ত্যেব সত্যম্ ।
তচ্চেদ্দেহ-দ্রবিণ-জনতা-লোভ-পাষণ্ড-মধ্যে
নিক্ষিপ্তং স্যান্ন ফলজনকং শীঘ্রমেবাত্র বিপ্র ॥ ৬০ ॥

nāmaikaṁ yasya vāci smaraṇa-patha-gataṁ śrotra-mūlaṁ gataṁ vā
śuddhaṁ vāśuddha-varṇaṁ vyavahita-rahitaṁ tārayaty eva satyam
tac ced deha-draviṇa-janatā-lobha-pāṣaṇḍa-madhye
nikṣiptaṁ syān na phala-janakaṁ śīghram evātra vipra

SYNONYMS

nāma—the holy name; *ekam*—once; *yasya*—whose; *vāci*—in the mouth; *smaraṇa-patha-gatam*—entered the path of remembrance; *śrotra-mūlam gatam*—entered the roots of the ears; *vā*—or; *śuddham*—pure; *vā*—or; *aśuddha-varṇam*—impurely uttered; *vyavahita-rahitam*—without offenses or without being separated; *tārayati*—delivers; *eva*—certainly; *satyam*—truly; *tat*—that name; *cet*—if; *deha*—the material body; *draviṇa*—material opulence; *janatā*—public support; *lobha*—greed; *pāṣaṇḍa*—atheism; *madhye*—toward; *nikṣiptam*—directed; *syāt*—may be; *na*—not; *phala-janakam*—producing the results; *śīghram*—quickly; *eva*—certainly; *atra*—in this matter; *vipra*—O *brāhmaṇa*.

TRANSLATION

" 'If a devotee once utters the holy name of the Lord, or if it penetrates his mind or enters his ear, which is the channel of aural reception, that holy name will certainly deliver him from material bondage, whether vibrated properly or improperly, with correct or incorrect grammar, and properly joined or vibrated in separate parts. O brāhmaṇa, the potency of the holy name is therefore certainly great. However, if one uses the vibration of the holy name for the benefit of the material body, for material wealth and followers, or under the influence of greed or atheism—in other words, if one utters the

name with offenses—such chanting will not produce the desired result very soon. Therefore one should diligently avoid offenses in chanting the holy name of the Lord.' "

PURPORT

This verse from the *Padma Purāṇa* is included in the *Hari-bhakti-vilāsa* (11.527) by Sanātana Gosvāmī. Therein Śrīla Sanātana Gosvāmī gives the following explanation:

vāci gataṁ prasaṅgād vāṅ-madhye pravṛttam api, smaraṇa-patha-gataṁ kathañcin manaḥ-spṛṣṭam api, śrotra-mūlaṁ gataṁ kiñcit śrutam api; śuddha-varṇaṁ vā aśuddha-varṇam api vā; 'vyavahitaṁ' śabdāntareṇa yad-vyavadhānaṁ vakṣyamāṇa-nārāyaṇa-śabdasya kiñcid uccāraṇānantaraṁ prasaṅgād āpatitaṁ śabdāntaraṁ tena rahitaṁ sat.

This means that if one somehow or other hears, utters or remembers the holy name, or if it catches his mind while coming near his ears, that holy name, even if vibrated in separate words, will act. An example of such separation is given as follows:

yadvā, yadyapi 'halaṁ riktam' ity ādy-uktau hakāra-rikārayor vṛttyā harīti-nāmāsty eva, tathā 'rāja-mahiṣī' ity atra rāma-nāmāpi, evam anyad apy ūhyam, tathāpi tat-tan-nāma-madhye vyavadhāyakam akṣarāntaram astīty etādṛśa-vyavadhāna-rahitam ity arthaḥ; yad-vā, vyavahitaṁ ca tad-rahitaṁ cāpi vā; tatra 'vyavahitaṁ'—nāmnaḥ kiñcid uccāraṇānantaraṁ kathañcid āpatitaṁ śabdāntaraṁ samādhāya paścān nāmāvaśiṣṭākṣara-grahaṇam ity evaṁ rūpaṁ, madhye śabdāntareṇāntaritam ity arthaḥ, 'rahitaṁ' paścād avaśiṣṭākṣara-grahaṇa-varjitaṁ, kenacid aṁśena hīnam ity arthaḥ, tathāpi tārayaty eva.

Suppose one is using the two words "*halaṁ riktam.*" Now the syllable *ha* in the word "*halam*" and the syllable *ri* in "*riktam*" are separately pronounced, but nevertheless it will act because one somehow or other utters the word "*hari.*" Similarly, in the word "*rāja-mahiṣī,*" the syllables *rā* and *ma* appear in two separate words, but because they somehow or other appear together, the holy name *rāma* will act, provided there are no offenses.

sarvebhyaḥ pāpebhyo 'parādhebhyaś ca saṁsārād apy uddhārayaty eveti satyam eva; kintu nāma-sevanasya mukhyaṁ yat phalaṁ, tan na sadyaḥ sampadyate. tathā deha-bharaṇādy-artham api nāma-sevanena mukhyaṁ phalam āśu na sidhyatīty āha—tac ced iti.

The holy name has so much spiritual potency that it can deliver one from all sinful reactions and material entanglements, but utterance of the holy name will not be very soon fruitful if done to facilitate sinning.

tan nāma ced yadi dehādi-madhye nikṣiptaṁ——deha-bharaṇādy-artham eva vinyastam, tadāpi phala-janakaṁ na bhavati kim? api tu bhavaty eva, kintu atra iha loke śīghraṁ na bhavati, kintu vilambenaiva bhavatīty arthaḥ.

The holy name is so powerful that it must act, but when one utters the holy name with offenses, its action will be delayed, not immediate, although in favorable circumstances the holy names of the Lord act very quickly.

TEXT 61

নামাভাস হৈতে হয় সর্বপাপক্ষয় ॥ ৬১ ॥

nāmābhāsa haite haya sarva-pāpa-kṣaya

SYNONYMS

nāma-ābhāsa haite—from the vibration of *nāmābhāsa*; *haya*—is; *sarva-pāpa*—of all reactions to sins; *kṣaya*—destruction.

TRANSLATION

Nāmācārya Haridāsa Ṭhakura continued, "If one offenselessly utters the holy name even imperfectly, one can be freed from all the results of sinful life.

TEXT 62

তং নির্ব্যাজং ভজ গুণনিধে পাবনং পাবনানাং
শ্রদ্ধা-রজ্যন্মতিরতিতরামুত্তমঃশ্লোকমৌলিম্ ।
প্রোদ্যন্নন্তঃকরণকুহরে হন্ত যন্নামভানো-
রাভাসোঽপি ক্ষপয়তি মহাপাতকধ্বান্তরাশিম্ ॥ ৬২ ॥

taṁ nirvyājaṁ bhaja guṇa-nidhe pāvanaṁ pāvanānāṁ
śraddhā-rajyan-matir atitarām uttamaḥ-śloka-maulim
prodyann antaḥ-karaṇa-kuhare hanta yan-nāma-bhānor
ābhāso 'pi kṣapayati mahā-pātaka-dhvānta-rāśim

SYNONYMS

tam—Him; *nirvyājam*—without duplicity; *bhaja*—worship; *guṇa-nidhe*—O reservoir of all good qualities; *pāvanam*—purifier; *pāvanānām*—of all other purifiers; *śraddhā*—with faith; *rajyat*—being enlivened; *matiḥ*—mind; *atitarām*—exceedingly; *uttamaḥ-śloka-maulim*—the best of the personalities who are worshiped by choice poetry or who are transcendental to all material positions;

prodyan—manifesting; *antaḥ-karaṇa-kuhare*—in the core of the heart; *hanta*—alas; *yat-nāma*—whose holy name; *bhānoḥ*—of the sun; *ābhāsaḥ*—slight appearance; *api*—even; *kṣapayati*—eradicates; *mahā-pātaka*—the resultant actions of greatly sinful activities; *dhvānta*—of ignorance; *rāśim*—the mass.

TRANSLATION

" 'O reservoir of all good qualities, just worship Śrī Kṛṣṇa, the purifier of all purifiers, the most exalted of the personalities worshiped by choice poetry. Worship Him with a faithful, unflinching mind, without duplicity and in a highly elevated manner. Thus worship the Lord, whose name is like the sun, for just as a slight appearance of the sun dissipates the darkness of night, so a slight appearance of the holy name of Kṛṣṇa can drive away all the darkness of ignorance that arises in the heart due to greatly sinful activities performed in previous lives.'

PURPORT

This verse is found in *Bhakti-rasāmṛta-sindhu* (2.1.103).

TEXT 63

নামাভাস হৈতে হয় সংসারের ক্ষয় ॥ ৬৩ ॥

nāmābhāsa haite haya saṁsārera kṣaya

SYNONYMS

nāma-ābhāsa haite—even on account of *nāmābhāsa*; *haya*—there is; *saṁsārera kṣaya*—deliverance from material bondage.

TRANSLATION

"Even a faint light from the holy name of the Lord can eradicate all the reactions of sinful life.

TEXT 64

ম্রিয়মাণো হরের্নাম গৃণন্ পুত্রোপচারিতম্ ।
অজামিলোঽপ্যগাদ্ধাম কিমুত শ্রদ্ধয়া গৃণন্ ॥ ৬৪ ॥

mriyamāṇo harer nāma
gṛṇan putropacāritam
ajāmilo 'py agād dhāma
kim uta śraddhayā gṛṇan

SYNONYMS

mriyamāṇaḥ—dying; *hareḥ nāma*—the holy name of the Supreme Lord; *gṛṇan*—chanting; *putra-upacāritam*—though spoken for his son; *ajāmilaḥ*—Ajāmila; *api*—also; *agāt*—attained; *dhāma*—the spiritual world; *kim uta*—what to speak of; *śraddhayā*—with faith and reverence; *gṛṇan*—chanting.

TRANSLATION

" 'While dying, Ajāmila chanted the holy name of the Lord, intending to call his son Nārāyaṇa. Nevertheless, he attained the spiritual world. What then to speak of those who chant the holy name with faith and reverence?'

PURPORT

This is a verse from *Śrīmad-Bhāgavatam* (6.2.49).

TEXT 65

নামাভাসে 'মুক্তি' হয় সর্বশাস্ত্রে দেখি।
শ্রীভাগবতে তাতে অজামিল – সাক্ষী ॥"৬৫॥

nāmābhāse 'mukti' haya sarva-śāstre dekhi
śrī-bhāgavate tāte ajāmila——sākṣī"

SYNONYMS

nāma-ābhāse—simply by a glimpse of the rays of the holy name; *mukti*—liberation; *haya*—there is; *sarva-śāstre*—in all the revealed scriptures; *dekhi*—I find; *śrī-bhāgavate*—in *Śrīmad-Bhāgavatam*; *tāte*—to that; *ajāmila*—Ajāmilạ; *sākṣī*—witness.

TRANSLATION

"Because of even the faintest rays of the effulgence of the Lord's holy name, one can attain liberation. We can see this in all the revealed scriptures. The evidence appears in the story of Ajāmila in Śrīmad-Bhāgavatam."

TEXT 66

শুনিয়া প্রভুর সুখ বাড়য়ে অন্তরে।
পুনরপি ভঙ্গী করি' পুছয়ে তাঁহারে ॥ ৬৬ ॥

śuniyā prabhura sukha bāḍaye antare
punarapi bhaṅgī kari' puchaye tāṅhāre

SYNONYMS

śuniyā—hearing; *prabhura*—of Śrī Caitanya Mahāprabhu; *sukha*—happiness; *bāḍaye*—increased; *antare*—within the heart; *punarapi*—still; *bhaṅgī kari'*—as a matter of course; *puchaye tāṅhāre*—inquires from Haridāsa Ṭhākura.

TRANSLATION

As Śrī Caitanya Mahāprabhu heard this from Haridāsa Ṭhākura, the happiness within His heart increased, but as a matter of course, He still inquired further.

TEXT 67

"পৃথিবীতে বহুজীব—স্থাবর-জঙ্গম ।
ইহা-সবার কি প্রকারে হইবে মোচন ?"৬৭ ॥

"pṛthivīte bahu-jīva——sthāvara-jaṅgama
ihā-sabāra ki prakāre ha-ibe mocana?"

SYNONYMS

pṛthivīte—on this earth; *bahu-jīva*—many living entities; *sthāvara*—not moving; *jaṅgama*—moving; *ihā-sabāra*—of all of these; *ki prakāre*—how; *ha-ibe mocana*—there will be deliverance.

TRANSLATION

"On this earth there are many living entities," the Lord said, "some moving and some not moving. What will happen to the trees, plants, insects and other living entities? How will they be delivered from material bondage?"

TEXT 68

হরিদাস কহে,—"প্রভু, সে কৃপা তোমার ।
স্থাবর-জঙ্গম আগে করিয়াছ নিস্তার ॥ ৬৮ ॥

haridāsa kahe,——"prabhu, se kṛpā tomāra
sthāvara-jaṅgama āge kariyācha nistāra

SYNONYMS

haridāsa kahe—Haridāsa replied; *prabhu*—my dear Lord; *se*—that; *kṛpā*—mercy; *tomāra*—Your; *sthāvara-jaṅgama*—nonmoving and moving living entities; *āge*—previously; *kariyācha nistāra*—You have delivered.

TRANSLATION

Haridāsa Ṭhākura replied, "My dear Lord, the deliverance of all moving and nonmoving living entities takes place only by Your mercy. You have already granted this mercy and delivered them.

TEXT 69

তুমি যে করিয়াছ এই উচ্চ সঙ্কীর্তন।
স্থাবর-জঙ্গমের সেই হয়ত' শ্রবণ ॥ ৬৯ ॥

tumi ye kariyācha ei ucca saṅkīrtana
sthāvara-jaṅgamera sei hayata' śravaṇa

SYNONYMS

tumi—You; *ye*—what; *kariyācha*—have executed; *ei*—this; *ucca*—loud; *saṅkīrtana*—chanting; *sthāvara-jaṅgamera*—of all living entities, moving and non-moving; *sei*—they; *hayata'*—there is; *śravaṇa*—hearing.

TRANSLATION

"You have loudly chanted the Hare Kṛṣṇa mantra, and everyone, moving or not moving, has benefited by hearing it.

TEXT 70

শুনিয়া জঙ্গমের হয় সংসার-ক্ষয়।
স্থাবরে সে শব্দ লাগে, প্রতিধ্বনি হয় ॥ ৭০ ॥

śuniyā jaṅgamera haya saṁsāra-kṣaya
sthāvare se śabda lāge, pratidhvani haya

SYNONYMS

śuniyā—hearing; *jaṅgamera*—of the living entities who can move; *haya*—there is; *saṁsāra-kṣaya*—annihilation of bondage to the material world; *sthāvare*—unto the nonmoving living entities; *se śabda*—that transcendental vibration; *lāge*—touches; *prati-dhvani*—echo; *haya*—there is.

TRANSLATION

"My Lord, the moving entities who have heard Your loud saṅkīrtana have already been delivered from bondage to the material world, and after the non-moving living entities like trees hear it, there is an echo.

TEXT 71

'প্রতিধ্বনি' নহে, সেই করয়ে 'কীর্তন'।
তোমার কৃপার এই অকথ্য কথন ॥ ৭১ ॥

'pratidhvani' nahe, sei karaye 'kīrtana'
tomāra kṛpāra ei akathya kathana

SYNONYMS

prati-dhvani nahe—that sound vibration is not an echo; *sei*—they; *karaye kīrtana*—are chanting; *tomāra kṛpāra*—of Your mercy; *ei*—this; *akathya kathana*—inconceivable incident.

TRANSLATION

"Actually, however, it is not an echo; it is the kīrtana of the nonmoving living entities. All this, although inconceivable, is possible by Your mercy.

TEXT 72

সকল জগতে হয় উচ্চ সঙ্কীর্তন।
শুনিয়া প্রেমাবেশে নাচে স্থাবর-জঙ্গম ॥ ৭২ ॥

sakala jagate haya ucca saṅkīrtana
śuniyā premāveśe nāce sthāvara-jaṅgama

SYNONYMS

sakala jagate—all over the universe; *haya*—there is; *ucca saṅkīrtana*—loud chanting of the Hare Kṛṣṇa *mantra*; *śuniyā*—hearing; *prema-āveśe*—in ecstatic emotional love; *nāce*—dance; *sthāvara-jaṅgama*—all living entities, nonmoving and moving.

TRANSLATION

"When loud chanting of the Hare Kṛṣṇa mantra is performed all over the world by those who follow in Your footsteps, all living entities, moving and nonmoving, dance in ecstatic devotional love.

TEXT 73

যৈছে কৈলা ঝারিখণ্ডে বৃন্দাবন যাইতে।
বলভদ্র-ভট্টাচার্য কহিয়াছেন আমাতে ॥ ৭৩ ॥

yaiche kailā jhārikhaṇḍe vṛndāvana yāite
balabhadra-bhaṭṭācārya kahiyāchena āmāte

SYNONYMS

yaiche—as; *kailā*—You have performed; *jhārikhaṇḍe*—in the forest known as Jhārikhaṇḍa; *vṛndāvana yāite*—while going to Vṛndāvana; *balabhadra-bhaṭṭācārya*—Your servant Balabhadra Bhaṭṭācārya; *kahiyāchena āmāte*—has said to me.

TRANSLATION

"My dear Lord, all the incidents that took place while You were going to Vṛndāvana through the forest known as Jhārikhaṇḍa have been related to me by Your servant Balabhadra Bhaṭṭācārya.

TEXT 74

বাসুদেব জীব লাগি' কৈল নিবেদন ।
তবে অঙ্গীকার কৈলা জীবের মোচন ॥ ৭৪ ॥

vāsudeva jīva lāgi' kaila nivedana
tabe aṅgīkāra kailā jīvera mocana

SYNONYMS

vāsudeva—the Lord's devotee named Vāsudeva; *jīva lāgi'*—for all living entities; *kaila nivedana*—submitted his appeal; *tabe*—at that time; *aṅgīkāra kailā*—You accepted; *jīvera mocana*—the deliverance of all living entities.

TRANSLATION

"When Your devotee Vāsudeva Datta submitted his plea at Your lotus feet for the deliverance of all living entities, You accepted that request.

TEXT 75

জগৎ নিস্তারিতে এই তোমার অবতার ।
ভক্তভাব আগে তাতে কৈলা অঙ্গীকার ॥ ৭৫ ॥

jagat nistārite ei tomāra avatāra
bhakta-bhāva āge tāte kailā aṅgīkāra

SYNONYMS

jagat nistārite—to deliver the whole world; *ei*—this; *tomāra avatāra*—Your incarnation; *bhakta-bhāva*—the mood of a devotee; *āge*—previously; *tāte*—therefore; *kailā aṅgīkāra*—You accepted.

TRANSLATION

"My dear Lord, You have accepted the form of a devotee just to deliver all the fallen souls of this world.

TEXT 76

উচ্চ সঙ্কীর্তন তাতে করিলা প্রচার।
স্থিরচর জীবের সব খণ্ডাইলা সংসার ॥"৭৬ ॥

ucca saṅkīrtana tāte karilā pracāra
sthira-cara jīvera saba khaṇḍāilā saṁsāra"

SYNONYMS

ucca saṅkīrtana—loud chanting of the Hare Kṛṣṇa *mantra*; *tāte*—therefore; *karilā pracāra*—You have spread; *sthira-cara*—nonmoving and moving; *jīvera*—of the living entities; *saba*—all; *khaṇḍāilā*—You finished; *saṁsāra*—the bondage to material existence.

TRANSLATION

"You have preached the loud chanting of the Hare Kṛṣṇa mahā-mantra and in this way freed all moving and nonmoving living entities from material bondage."

TEXT 77

প্রভু কহে,—"সব জীব মুক্তি যবে পাবে।
এই ত' ব্রহ্মাণ্ড তবে জীবশূন্য হবে!" ৭৭ ॥

prabhu kahe,——"saba jīva mukti yabe pābe
ei ta' brahmāṇḍa tabe jīva-śūnya habe!"

SYNONYMS

prabhu kahe—the Lord replied; *saba jīva*—all living entities; *mukti*—liberation; *yabe*—when; *pābe*—will achieve; *ei*—this; *ta'*—certainly; *brahmāṇḍa*—universe; *tabe*—then; *jīva-śūnya*—devoid of living entities; *habe*—will be.

TRANSLATION

Śrī Caitanya Mahāprabhu replied, "If all living entities were liberated, the entire universe would be devoid of living beings."

TEXTS 78-79

হরিদাস বলে,– "তোমার যাবৎ মর্ত্যে স্থিতি।
তাবৎ স্থাবর-জঙ্গম, সর্ব জীব-জাতি ॥ ৭৮ ॥
সব মুক্ত করি' তুমি বৈকুণ্ঠে পাঠাইবা।
সূক্ষ্মজীবে পুনঃ কর্মে উদ্বুদ্ধ করিবা ॥ ৭৯ ॥

haridāsa bale,——"tomāra yāvat martye sthiti
tāvat sthāvara-jaṅgama, sarva jīva-jāti

saba mukta kari' tumi vaikuṇṭhe pāṭhāibā
sūkṣma-jīve punaḥ karme udbuddha karibā

SYNONYMS

haridāsa bale—Haridāsa Ṭhākura said; *tomāra*—Your; *yāvat*—as long as; *martye*—in this material world; *sthiti*—situation; *tāvat*—for that duration of time; *sthāvara-jaṅgama*—nonmoving and moving; *sarva*—all; *jīva-jāti*—species of living entities; *saba*—all; *mukta kari'*—liberating; *tumi*—You; *vaikuṇṭhe*—to the spiritual world; *pāṭhāibā*—will send; *sūkṣma-jīve*—the undeveloped living entities; *punaḥ*—again; *karme*—in their activities; *udbuddha karibā*—You will awaken.

TRANSLATION

Haridāsa said, "My Lord, as long as You are situated within the material world, You will send to the spiritual sky all the developed moving and nonmoving living entities in different species. Then again You will awaken the living entities who are not yet developed and engage them in activities.

TEXT 80

সেই জীব হবে ইহাঁ স্থাবর-জঙ্গম।
তাহাতে ভরিবে ব্রহ্মাণ্ড যেন পূর্ব-সম ॥ ৮০ ॥

sei jīva habe ihāṅ sthāvara-jaṅgama
tāhāte bharibe brahmāṇḍa yena pūrva-sama

SYNONYMS

sei jīva—such living entities; *habe*—will be; *ihāṅ*—in this material world; *sthāvara-jaṅgama*—nonmoving and moving living entities; *tāhāte*—in that way; *bharibe*—You will fill; *brahmāṇḍa*—the entire universe; *yena*—as; *pūrva-sama*—the same as previously.

TRANSLATION

"In this way all moving and nonmoving living entities will come into existence, and the entire universe will be filled as it was previously.

PURPORT

While we are preaching, opposing elements sometimes argue, "If all living entities were delivered by the Kṛṣṇa consciousness movement, what would happen then? The universe would be devoid of living entities." In answer to this, we may say that in a prison there are many prisoners, but if one thinks that the prison would be empty if all the prisoners adopted good behavior, he is incorrect. Even if all the prisoners within a jail are freed, other criminals will fill it again. A prison will never be vacant, for there are many prospective criminals who will fill the prison cells, even if the present criminals are freed by the government. As confirmed in *Bhagavad-gītā, kāraṇaṁ guṇa-saṅgo 'sya sad-asad-yoni-janmasu:* "Because of the living entity's association with material nature, he meets with good and evil among various species." (Bg. 13.22) There are many unmanifested living entities covered by the mode of ignorance who will gradually come to the mode of passion. Most of them will become criminals because of their fruitive activities and again fill the prisons.

TEXT 81

পূর্বে যেন রঘুনাথ সব আযোধ্যা লঞা ।
বৈকুণ্ঠকে গেলা, অন্যজীবে অযোধ্যা ভরাঞা ॥ ৮১ ॥

pūrve yena raghunātha saba āyodhyā lañā
vaikuṇṭhake gelā, anya-jīve āyodhyā bharāñā

SYNONYMS

pūrve—previously; *yena*—as; *raghunātha*—Rāmacandra; *saba*—all; *āyodhyā*—the population of Āyodhyā; *lañā*—taking with Him; *vaikuṇṭhake gelā*—went back to Vaikuṇṭhaloka; *anya-jīve*—other living entities; *āyodhyā*—Āyodhyā; *bharāñā*—filling.

TRANSLATION

"Previously, when Lord Rāmacandra left this world, He took with Him all the living entities of Āyodhyā. Then He filled Āyodhyā again with other living entities.

TEXT 82

অবতরি' তুমি ঐছে পাতিয়াছ হাট ।
কেহ না বুঝিতে পারে তোমার গূঢ় নাট ॥ ৮২ ॥

avatari' tumi aiche pātiyācha hāṭa
keha nā bujhite pāre tomāra gūḍha nāṭa

SYNONYMS

avatari'—descending; *tumi*—You; *aiche*—like that; *pātiyācha hāṭa*—have set up a market; *keha nā bujhite pāre*—no one can understand; *tomāra*—Your; *gūḍha nāṭa*—deep acting.

TRANSLATION

"My dear Lord, You have set a plan in motion by descending on the material world, but no one can understand how You are acting.

TEXT 83

পূর্বে যেন ব্রজে কৃষ্ণ করি' অবতার ।
সকল ব্রহ্মাণ্ড-জীবের খণ্ডাইলা সংসার ॥ ৮৩ ॥

pūrve yena vraje kṛṣṇa kari' avatāra
sakala brahmāṇḍa-jīvera khaṇḍāilā saṁsāra

SYNONYMS

pūrve—previously; *yena*—as; *vraje*—in Vṛndāvana; *kṛṣṇa*—Lord Kṛṣṇa; *kari' avatāra*—descending as an incarnation; *sakala*—all; *brahmāṇḍa-jīvera*—of living entities within this universe; *khaṇḍāilā*—destroyed; *saṁsāra*—the material existence.

TRANSLATION

"Formerly, when Lord Kṛṣṇa descended in Vṛndāvana, He freed all living entities in the universe from material existence in the same way.

TEXT 84

ন চৈবং বিস্ময়ঃ কার্যো ভবতা ভগবত্যজে ।
যোগেশ্বরেশ্বরে কৃষ্ণে যত এতদ্বিমুচ্যতে ॥ ৮৪ ॥

na caivaṁ vismayaḥ kāryo
bhavatā bhagavaty aje
yogeśvareśvare kṛṣṇe
yata etad vimucyate

SYNONYMS

na—not; *ca*—also; *evam*—thus; *vismayaḥ*—wonder; *kāryaḥ*—to be done; *bhavatā*—by You; *bhagavati*—unto the Supreme Personality of Godhead; *aje*—the unborn; *yoga-īśvara-īśvare*—the master of all masters of mystic power; *kṛṣṇe*—unto Lord Kṛṣṇa; *yataḥ*—by whom; *etat*—all living entities; *vimucyate*—are delivered.

TRANSLATION

" 'Kṛṣṇa, the unborn Supreme Personality of Godhead, master of all of the masters of mystic power, delivers all living entities, moving and nonmoving. Nothing is astonishing in the activities of the Lord.'

PURPORT

This is a quotation from *Śrīmad-Bhāgavatam* (10.29.16).

TEXT 85

"অয়ং হি ভগবান্ দৃষ্টঃ কীর্তিতঃ সংস্মৃতশ্চ
দ্বেষানুবন্ধেনাপ্যখিলসুরাসুরাদি-
দুর্লভং ফলং প্রযচ্ছতি, কিমুত সম্যগ্
ভক্তিমতাম্" ইতি ॥ ৮৫ ॥

"ayaṁ hi bhagavān dṛṣṭaḥ kīrtitaḥ saṁsmṛtaś ca
dveṣānubandhenāpy akhila-surāsurādi-durlabhaṁ
phalaṁ prayacchati, kim uta samyag bhaktimatām" iti

SYNONYMS

ayam—this; *hi*—certainly; *bhagavān*—Supreme Personality of Godhead; *dṛṣṭaḥ*—seen; *kīrtitaḥ*—glorified; *saṁsmṛtaḥ*—remembered; *ca*—and; *dveṣa*—of envy; *anubandhena*—with the conception; *api*—although; *akhila-sura-asura-ādi*—by all demigods and demons; *durlabham*—very rarely achieved; *phalam*—result; *prayacchati*—awards; *kim uta*—what to speak of; *samyak*—fully; *bhakti-matām*—of those engaged in devotional service; *iti*—thus.

TRANSLATION

" 'Although the Supreme Personality of Godhead may be seen, glorified or remembered with an attitude of envy, He nevertheless awards the most confidential liberation, which is rarely achieved by the demigods and demons. What, then, can be said of those who are already fully engaged in devotional service to the Lord?'

PURPORT

This is a quotation from the *Viṣṇu Purāṇa* (4.15.17).

TEXT 86

তৈছে তুমি নবদ্বীপে করি' অবতার ।
সকল-ব্রহ্মাণ্ড-জীবের করিলা নিস্তার ॥ ৮৬ ॥

taiche tumi navadvīpe kari' avatāra
sakala-brahmāṇḍa-jīvera karilā nistāra

SYNONYMS

taiche—in that way; *tumi*—You; *navadvīpe*—at Navadvīpa; *kari' avatāra*—descending as an incarnation; *sakala*—all; *brahmāṇḍa*—of the universe; *jīvera*—the living entities; *karilā nistāra*—have delivered.

TRANSLATION

"By descending as an incarnation at Navadvīpa, You, just like Kṛṣṇa, have already delivered all the living entities of the universe.

TEXT 87

যে কহে,—'চৈতন্য-মহিমা মোর গোচর হয়' ।
সে জানুক, মোর পুনঃ এই ত' নিশ্চয় ॥ ৮৭ ॥

ye kahe,—'caitanya-mahimā mora gocara haya'
se jānuka, mora punaḥ ei ta' niścaya

SYNONYMS

ye kahe—whoever says; *caitanya-mahimā*—the glories of Śrī Caitanya Mahāprabhu; *mora gocara*—known to me; *haya*—are; *se jānuka*—he may know; *mora*—of me; *punaḥ*—again; *ei ta' niścaya*—this is the decision.

TRANSLATION

"One may say that he understands the glories of Śrī Caitanya Mahāprabhu. He may know whatever he may know, but as far as I am concerned, this is my conclusion.

TEXT 88

তোমার যে লীলা মহা-অমৃতের সিন্ধু ।
মোর মনোগোচর নহে তার এক বিন্দু ॥"৮৮ ॥

tomāra ye līlā mahā-amṛtera sindhu
mora mano-gocara nahe tāra eka bindu"

SYNONYMS

tomāra—Your; *ye*—whatever; *līlā*—pastimes; *mahā-amṛtera sindhu*—a great ocean of nectar; *mora*—for me; *manaḥ-gocara nahe*—it is not possible to conceive; *tāra*—of it; *eka bindu*—one drop.

TRANSLATION

"My dear Lord, Your pastimes are just like an ocean of nectar. It is not possible for me to conceive how great that ocean is or even to understand a drop of it."

TEXT 89

এত শুনি' প্রভুর মনে চমৎকার হৈল ।
'মোর গূঢ়লীলা হরিদাস কেমনে জানিল ?' ৮৯ ॥

eta śuni' prabhura mane camatkāra haila
'mora gūḍha-līlā haridāsa kemane jānila?'

SYNONYMS

eta śuni'—hearing this; *prabhura*—of Śrī Caitanya Mahāprabhu; *mane*—in the mind; *camatkāra haila*—there was astonishment; *mora*—My; *gūḍha-līlā*—confidential pastimes; *haridāsa*—Haridāsa; *kemane*—how; *jānila*—has understood.

TRANSLATION

Hearing all this, Śrī Caitanya Mahāprabhu was astonished. "These are actually My confidential pastimes," He thought. "How could Haridāsa have understood them?"

TEXT 90

মনের সন্তোষে তাঁরে কৈলা আলিঙ্গন ।
বাহ্যে প্রকাশিতে এ-সব করিলা বর্জন ॥ ৯০ ॥

manera santoṣe tāṅre kailā āliṅgana
bāhye prakāśite e-saba karilā varjana

SYNONYMS

manera santoṣe—with complete satisfaction of the mind; *tāṅre*—him; *kailā āliṅgana*—He embraced; *bāhye*—externally; *prakāśite*—to disclose; *e-saba*—all this; *karilā varjana*—He avoided.

TRANSLATION

Greatly satisfied by the statements of Haridāsa Ṭhākura, Śrī Caitanya Mahāprabhu embraced him. Outwardly, however, He avoided further discussions of these matters.

TEXT 91

ঈশ্বর-স্বভাব,—ঐশ্বর্য চাহে আচ্ছাদিতে ।
ভক্ত-ঠাঞি লুকাইতে নারে, হয় ত' বিদিতে ॥ ৯১ ॥

īśvara-svabhāva,——aiśvarya cāhe ācchādite
bhakta-ṭhāñi lukāite nāre, haya ta' vidite

SYNONYMS

īśvara-svabhāva—the characteristic of the Supreme Personality of Godhead; *aiśvarya*—opulence; *cāhe*—wants; *ācchādite*—to cover; *bhakta-ṭhāñi*—before His devotee; *lukāite nāre*—He cannot cover; *haya ta' vidite*—is well-known.

TRANSLATION

This is a characteristic of the Supreme Personality of Godhead. Although He wants to cover His opulence, He cannot do so before His devotees. This is well-known everywhere.

TEXT 92

উল্লঙ্ঘিতত্রিবিধসীমসমাতিশায়ি-
সম্ভাবনং তব পরিব্রঢ়িমস্বভাবম্ ।
মায়াবলেন ভবতাপি নিগুহ্যমানং
পশ্যন্তি কেচিদনিশং ত্বদনন্যভাবাঃ ॥ ৯২ ॥

ullaṅghita-trividha-sīma-samātiśāyi-
sambhāvanaṁ tava parivraḍhima-svabhāvam

māyā-balena bhavatāpi niguhyamānaṁ
paśyanti kecid aniśaṁ tvad-ananya-bhāvāḥ

SYNONYMS

ullaṅghita—passed over; *tri-vidha*—three kinds; *sīma*—the limitations; *sama*—of equal; *atiśāyi*—and of excelling; *sambhāvanam*—by which the adequacy; *tava*—Your; *parivraḍhima*—of supremacy; *sva-bhāvam*—the real nature; *māyā-balena*—by the strength of the illusory energy; *bhavatā*—Your; *api*—although; *niguhyamānam*—being hidden; *paśyanti*—they see; *kecit*—some; *aniśam*—always; *tvat*—to You; *ananya-bhāvāḥ*—those who are exclusively devoted.

TRANSLATION

"O my Lord, everything within material nature is limited by time, space and thought. Your characteristics, however, being unequaled and unsurpassed, are always transcendental to such limitations. You sometimes cover such characteristics by Your own energy, but nevertheless Your unalloyed devotees are always able to see You under all circumstances."

PURPORT

This is a verse from the *Stotra-ratna* of Yāmunācārya.

TEXT 93

তবে মহাপ্রভু নিজভক্তপাশে যাঞা ।
হরিদাসের গুণ কহে শতমুখ হঞা ॥ ৯৩ ॥

tabe mahāprabhu nija-bhakta-pāśe yāñā
haridāsera guṇa kahe śata-mukha hañā

SYNONYMS

tabe—after this; *mahāprabhu*—Śrī Caitanya Mahāprabhu; *nija-bhakta-pāśe*—to His personal devotees; *yāñā*—going; *haridāsera guṇa*—the transcendental qualities of Haridāsa Ṭhākura; *kahe*—explains; *śata-mukha*—as if with hundreds of mouths; *hañā*—becoming.

TRANSLATION

Then Śrī Caitanya Mahāprabhu went to His personal devotees and began speaking about Haridāsa Ṭhākura's transcendental qualities as if He had hundreds of mouths.

TEXT 94

ভক্তের গুণ কহিতে প্রভুর বাড়য়ে উল্লাস।
ভক্তগণ-শ্রেষ্ঠ তাতে শ্রীহরিদাস ॥ ৯৪ ॥

bhaktera guṇa kahite prabhura bāḍaye ullāsa
bhakta-gaṇa-śreṣṭha tāte śrī-haridāsa

SYNONYMS

bhaktera—of the devotees; *guṇa*—qualities; *kahite*—speaking; *prabhura*—of Śrī Caitanya Mahāprabhu; *bāḍaye*—increases; *ullāsa*—jubilation; *bhakta-gaṇa*—of all devotees; *śreṣṭha*—topmost; *tāte*—in that; *śrī-haridāsa*—Haridāsa Ṭhākura.

TRANSLATION

Śrī Caitanya Mahāprabhu derives great pleasure from glorifying His devotees, and among the devotees, Haridāsa Ṭhākura is the foremost.

TEXT 95

হরিদাসের গুণগণ—অসংখ্য, অপার।
কেহ কোন অংশে বর্ণে, নাহি পায় পার ॥ ৯৫ ॥

haridāsera guṇa-gaṇa——asaṅkhya, apāra
keha kona aṁśe varṇe, nāhi pāya pāra

SYNONYMS

haridāsera guṇa-gaṇa—the stock of transcendental qualities of Haridāsa Ṭhākura; *asaṅkhya*—innumerable; *apāra*—unfathomed; *keha*—someone; *kona aṁśe*—some part; *varṇe*—describes; *nāhi pāya pāra*—cannot reach the limit.

TRANSLATION

The transcendental qualities of Haridāsa Ṭhākura are innumerable and unfathomable. One may describe a portion of them, but to count them all is impossible.

TEXT 96

চৈতন্যমঙ্গলে শ্রীবৃন্দাবন-দাস।
হরিদাসের গুণ কিছু করিয়াছেন প্রকাশ ॥ ৯৬ ॥

caitanya-maṅgale śrī-vṛndāvana-dāsa
haridāsera guṇa kichu kariyāchena prakāśa

SYNONYMS

caitanya-maṅgale—in the book known as *Caitanya-maṅgala* (*Caitanya-bhāgavata*); *śrī-vṛndāvana-dāsa*—Śrī Vṛndāvana dāsa Ṭhākura; *haridāsera*—of Haridāsa Ṭhākura; *guṇa*—qualities; *kichu*—some; *kariyāchena prakāśa*—manifested.

TRANSLATION

In Caitanya-maṅgala, Śrīla Vṛndāvana dāsa Ṭhākura has described the attributes of Haridāsa Ṭhākura to some extent.

TEXT 97

সব কহা না যায় হরিদাসের চরিত্র ।
কেহ কিছু কহে করিতে আপনা পবিত্র ॥ ৯৭ ॥

saba kahā nā yāya haridāsera caritra
keha kichu kahe karite āpanā pavitra

SYNONYMS

saba—all; *kahā*—to speak; *nā yāya*—is not possible; *haridāsera caritra*—the characteristics of Haridāsa Ṭhākura; *keha kichu kahe*—someone says something; *karite*—just to make; *āpanā*—himself; *pavitra*—purified.

TRANSLATION

No one can describe all the qualities of Haridāsa Ṭhākura. One may say something about them just to purify himself.

TEXT 98

বৃন্দাবন-দাস যাহা না কৈল বর্ণন ।
হরিদাসের গুণ কিছু শুন, ভক্তগণ ॥ ৯৮ ॥

vṛndāvana-dāsa yāhā nā kaila varṇana
haridāsera guṇa kichu śuna, bhakta-gaṇa

SYNONYMS

vṛndāvana-dāsa—Śrīla Vṛndāvana dāsa Ṭhākura; *yāhā*—whatever; *nā*—not; *kaila varṇana*—described; *haridāsera guṇa*—qualities of Haridāsa Ṭhākura; *kichu*—something; *śuna*—hear; *bhakta-gaṇa*—O devotees of Śrī Caitanya Mahāprabhu.

TRANSLATION

O devotees of Śrī Caitanya Mahāprabhu, please hear something about the qualities of Haridāsa Ṭhākura that Śrīla Vṛndāvana dāsa Ṭhākura has not described in detail.

TEXT 99

হরিদাস যবে নিজ-গৃহ ত্যাগ কৈলা ।
বেনাপোলের বন-মধ্যে কতদিন রহিলা ॥ ৯৯ ॥

haridāsa yabe nija-gṛha tyāga kailā
benāpolera vana-madhye kata-dina rahilā

SYNONYMS

haridāsa—Haridāsa Ṭhākura; *yabe*—when; *nija-gṛha*—his own residence; *tyāga kailā*—gave up; *benāpolera*—of the village known as Benāpola; *vana-madhye*—in the forest; *kata-dina*—for some time; *rahilā*—stayed.

TRANSLATION

After leaving his home, Haridāsa Ṭhākura stayed for some time in the forest of Benāpola.

TEXT 100

নির্জন-বনে কুটির করি' তুলসী সেবন ।
রাত্রি-দিনে তিন লক্ষ নাম-সঙ্কীর্তন ॥ ১০০ ॥

nirjana-vane kuṭira kari' tulasī sevana
rātri-dine tina lakṣa nāma-saṅkīrtana

SYNONYMS

nirjana-vane—in a solitary forest; *kuṭira*—a cottage; *kari'*—making; *tulasī*—the *tulasī* plant; *sevana*—worshiping; *rātri-dine*—throughout the entire day and night; *tina*—three; *lakṣa*—hundred thousand; *nāma-saṅkīrtana*—chanting of the holy name.

TRANSLATION

Haridāsa Ṭhākura constructed a cottage in a solitary forest. There he planted a tulasī plant, and in front of the tulasī he would chant the holy name of the Lord 300,000 times daily. He chanted throughout the entire day and night.

PURPORT

The village of Benāpola is situated in the district of Yaśohara, which is now in Bangladesh. Benāpola is near the Banagāṅo station, which is at the border of Bangladesh and may be reached by the eastern railway from Shelda Station in Calcutta. Haridāsa Ṭhākura, being the *ācārya* of chanting the Hare Kṛṣṇa *mahā-mantra,* is called Nāmācārya Haridāsa Ṭhākura. From his personal example we can understand that chanting the Hare Kṛṣṇa *mantra* and becoming highly elevated in Kṛṣṇa consciousness is very simple. Without difficulty one can sit down anywhere, especially on the bank of the Ganges, Yamunā or any sacred river, devise a sitting place or cottage, plant a *tulasī,* and before the *tulasī* chant the Hare Kṛṣṇa *mahā-mantra* undisturbed.

Haridāsa Ṭhākura used to chant the holy name on his beads 300,000 times daily. Throughout the entire day and night, he would chant the sixteen names of the Hare Kṛṣṇa *mahā-mantra.* One should not, however, imitate Haridāsa Ṭhākura, for no one else can chant the Hare Kṛṣṇa *mahā-mantra* 300,000 times a day. Such chanting is for the *mukta-puruṣa,* or liberated soul. We can follow his example, however, by chanting sixteen rounds of the Hare Kṛṣṇa *mahā-mantra* on beads every day and offering respect to the *tulasī* plant. This is not at all difficult for anyone, and the process of chanting the Hare Kṛṣṇa *mahā-mantra* with a vow before the *tulasī* plant has such great spiritual potency that simply by doing this one can become spiritually strong. Therefore we request the members of the Hare Kṛṣṇa movement to follow Haridāsa Ṭhākura's example rigidly. Chanting sixteen rounds does not take much time, nor is offering respects to the *tulasī* plant difficult. The process has immense spiritual potency. One should not miss this opportunity.

TEXT 101

ব্রাহ্মণের ঘরে করে ভিক্ষা নির্বাহণ ।
প্রভাবে সকল লোক করয়ে পূজন ॥ ১০১ ॥

brāhmaṇera ghare kare bhikṣā nirvāhaṇa
prabhāve sakala loka karaye pūjana

SYNONYMS

brāhmaṇera ghare—in the house of a *brāhmaṇa; kare*—does; *bhikṣā nirvāhaṇa*—asking alms of food; *prabhāve*—by spiritual potency; *sakala loka*—all people; *karaye pūjana*—worship.

TRANSLATION

For his bodily maintenance he would go to a brāhmaṇa's house and beg some food. He was spiritually so influential that all the neighboring people worshiped him.

PURPORT

In the days of Haridāsa Ṭhākura, all the *brāhmaṇas* worshiped Nārāyaṇa in the form of the *śālagrama-śilā.* Therefore begging from a *brāhmaṇa's* house meant taking *kṛṣṇa-prasāda,* which is transcendental (*nirguṇa*). If we take food from the house of others, such as *karmīs,* we shall have to share the qualities of those from whom we take alms. Therefore Śrī Caitanya Mahāprabhu took *prasāda* in the houses of Vaiṣṇavas. This is the general process. The members of the Kṛṣṇa consciousness movement are advised not to take food from anywhere but a Vaiṣṇava's or *brāhmaṇa's* house where Deity worship is performed. Śrī Caitanya Mahāprabhu has said, *viṣayīra anna khāile duṣṭa haya mana:* if a devotee takes alms or food from the house of a *karmī* who is simply interested in money, his mind will be unclean. We must always remember that a devotee's life is one of *vairāgya-vidyā,* or renunciation and knowledge. Therefore all devotees are warned not to live unnecessarily luxurious lives at the cost of others. *Gṛhasthas* living within the jurisdiction of the temple must be especially careful not to imitate *karmīs* by acquiring opulent clothing, food and conveyances. As far as possible, these should be avoided. A member of the temple, whether *gṛhastha, brahmacārī* or *sannyāsī,* must practice a life of renunciation, following in the footsteps of Haridāsa Ṭhākura and the six Gosvāmīs. Otherwise, because *māyā* is very strong, at any time one may become a victim of *māyā* and fall down from spiritual life.

TEXT 102

সেই দেশাধ্যক্ষ নাম—রামচন্দ্র খাঁন ।
বৈষ্ণববিদ্বেষী সেই পাষণ্ড-প্রধান ॥ ১০২ ॥

sei deśādhyakṣa nāma——rāmacandra khāṅna
vaiṣṇava-vidveṣī sei pāṣaṇḍa-pradhāna

SYNONYMS

sei—that; *deśa-adhyakṣa*—landholder; *nāma*—whose name; *rāmacandra khāṅna*—Rāmacandra Khān; *vaiṣṇava-vidveṣī*—envious of Vaiṣṇavas; *sei*—that; *pāṣaṇḍa-pradhāna*—chief of the atheists.

TRANSLATION

A landholder named Rāmacandra Khān was the zamindar of that district. He was envious of Vaiṣṇavas and was therefore a great atheist.

TEXT 103

হরিদাসে লোকে পূজে, সহিতে না পারে ।
তাঁর অপমান করিতে নানা উপায় করে ॥ ১০৩ ॥

haridāse loke pūje, sahite nā pāre
tāṅra apamāna karite nānā upāya kare

SYNONYMS

haridāse—unto Haridāsa Ṭhākura; *loke*—people; *pūje*—offer respect; *sahite nā pāre*—he could not tolerate; *tāṅra*—his; *apamāna*—dishonor; *karite*—to do; *nānā*—various; *upāya*—means; *kare*—plans.

TRANSLATION

Unable to tolerate that such respect was being offered to Haridāsa Ṭhākura, Rāmacandra Khān planned in various ways to dishonor him.

TEXT 104

কোনপ্রকারে হরিদাসের ছিদ্র নাহি পায়।
বেশ্যাগণে আনি' করে ছিদ্রের উপায় ॥ ১০৪ ॥

kona-prakāre haridāsera chidra nāhi pāya
veśyā-gaṇe āni' kare chidrera upāya

SYNONYMS

kona-prakāre—by any means; *haridāsera*—of Haridāsa Ṭhākura; *chidra*—fault; *nāhi*—not; *pāya*—gets; *veśyā-gaṇe*—prostitutes; *āni'*—bringing; *kare*—makes; *chidrera upāya*—a means to find some fault.

TRANSLATION

By no means could he find any fault in the character of Haridāsa Ṭhākura. Therefore he called for local prostitutes and began a plan to discredit His Holiness.

PURPORT

This is typical of atheistic men, but even among so-called religionists, *sādhus,* mendicants, *sannyāsīs* and *brahmacārīs,* there are many enemies of the Kṛṣṇa consciousness movement who always try to find faults in it, not considering that the movement is spreading automatically by the grace of Lord Śrī Caitanya Mahāprabhu, who wanted it spread all over the world, in every town and village. We are trying to fulfill the Lord's desire, and our attempt has become fairly successful, but the enemies of this movement unnecessarily try to find faults in it, exactly like the old rascal Rāmacandra Khān, who opposed Haridāsa Ṭhākura.

TEXT 105

বেশ্যাগণে কহে,—"এই বৈরাগী হরিদাস।
তুমি-সব কর ইহার বৈরাগ্য-ধর্ম নাশ॥" ১০৫॥

veśyā-gaṇe kahe,——"ei vairāgī haridāsa
tumi-saba kara ihāra vairāgya-dharma nāśa"

SYNONYMS

veśyā-gaṇe—unto the prostitutes; *kahe*—said; *ei*—this; *vairāgī*—mendicant; *haridāsa*—Haridāsa Ṭhākura; *tumi-saba*—all of you; *kara*—cause; *ihāra*—his; *vairāgya-dharma*—from the life of a mendicant; *nāśa*—deviation.

TRANSLATION

Rāmacandra Khān said to the prostitutes, "There is a mendicant named Haridāsa Ṭhākura. All of you devise a way to deviate him from his vows of austerity."

PURPORT

Devotional service is the path of *vairāgya-vidyā* (renunciation and knowledge). Haridāsa Ṭhākura was following this path, but Rāmacandra Khān planned to induce him to break his vows. Renunciation means renunciation of sensual pleasure, especially the pleasure of sex. Therefore a *brahmacārī, sannyāsī* or *vānaprastha* is strictly prohibited from having relationships with women. Haridāsa Ṭhākura was strictly renounced, and thus Rāmacandra Khān called for prostitutes because prostitutes know how to break a man's vow of celibacy by their feminine influence and thus pollute a mendicant or a person engaged in devotional life. It was impossible for Rāmacandra Khān to induce any other women to break Haridāsa Ṭhākura's vow, and therefore he called for prostitutes. Free mingling with women has never been possible in India, but for one who wanted to associate with society girls, they were available in a district of prostitutes. There were prostitutes in human society even in Lord Kṛṣṇa's time, for it is said that the prostitutes of Dvārakā City came forth to receive the Lord. Although they were prostitutes, they were also devotees of Kṛṣṇa.

TEXT 106

বেশ্যাগণ-মধ্যে এক সুন্দরী যুবতী।
সে কহে,—"তিনদিনে হরিব তাঁর মতি"॥ ১০৬॥

veśyā-gaṇa-madhye eka sundarī yuvatī
se kahe,——"tina-dine hariba tāṅra mati"

SYNONYMS

veśyā-gaṇa-madhye—among the prostitutes; *eka*—one; *sundarī*—attractive; *yuvatī*—young; *se*—she; *kahe*—said; *tina-dine*—in three days; *hariba*—I shall attract; *tāṅra*—his; *mati*—mind.

TRANSLATION

Among the prostitutes, one attractive young girl was selected. "I shall attract the mind of Haridāsa Ṭhākura," she promised, "within three days."

TEXT 107

খাঁন কহে,—"মোর পাইক যাউক তোমার সনে।
তোমার সহিত একত্র তারে ধরি' যেন আনে॥"১০৭॥

khāṅna kahe,——"mora pāika yāuka tomāra sane
tomāra sahita ekatra tāre dhari' yena āne"

SYNONYMS

khāṅna kahe—Rāmacandra Khān said; *mora pāika*—my constable; *yāuka*—let him go; *tomāra sane*—with you; *tomāra sahita*—with you; *ekatra*—together; *tāre*—him; *dhari'*—arresting; *yena*—so that; *āne*—can bring.

TRANSLATION

Rāmacandra Khān said to the prostitute, "My constable will go with you so that as soon as he sees you with Haridāsa Ṭhākura, immediately he will arrest him and bring both of you to me."

TEXT 108

বেশ্যা কহে,—"মোর সঙ্গ হউক একবার।
দ্বিতীয়বারে ধরিতে পাইক লইমু তোমার॥"১০৮॥

veśyā kahe,——"mora saṅga ha-uka eka-bāra
dvitīya-bāre dharite pāika la-imu tomāra"

SYNONYMS

veśyā kahe—the prostitute said; *mora saṅga*—union with me; *ha-uka*—let there be; *eka-bāra*—one time; *dvitīya-bāre*—the second time; *dharite*—to arrest; *pāika*—constable; *la-imu*—I shall take; *tomāra*—your.

TRANSLATION

The prostitute replied, "First let me have union with him once; then the second time I shall take your constable with me to arrest him."

TEXT 109

রাত্রিকালে সেই বেশ্যা সুবেশ ধরিয়া।
হরিদাসের বাসায় গেল উল্লসিত হঞা॥ ১০৯॥

rātri-kāle sei veśyā suveśa dhariyā
haridāsera vāsāya gela ullasita hañā

SYNONYMS

rātri-kāle—at night; *sei*—that; *veśyā*—prostitute; *su-veśa dhariyā*—dressing herself very nicely; *haridāsera*—of Haridāsa Ṭhākura; *vāsāya*—to the place; *gela*—went; *ullasita hañā*—with great jubilation.

TRANSLATION

At night the prostitute, after dressing herself most attractively, went to the cottage of Haridāsa Ṭhākura with great jubilation.

TEXT 110

তুলসী নমস্করি' হরিদাসের দ্বারে যাঞা।
গোসাঞিরে নমস্করি' রহিলা দাণ্ডাঞা॥ ১১০॥

tulasī namaskari' haridāsera dvāre yāñā
gosāñire namaskari' rahilā dāṇḍāñā

SYNONYMS

tulasī namaskari'—after offering obeisances to the *tulasī* plant; *haridāsera*—of Ṭhākura Haridāsa; *dvāre*—at the door; *yāñā*—going; *gosāñire*—unto the *ācārya*; *namaskari'*—offering obeisances; *rahilā dāṇḍāñā*—remained standing.

TRANSLATION

After offering obeisances to the tulasī plant, she went to the door of Haridāsa Ṭhākura, offered him obeisances and stood there.

TEXT 111

অঙ্গ উঘাড়িয়া দেখাই বসিলা দুয়ারে।
কহিতে লাগিলা কিছু সুমধুর স্বরে॥ ১১১॥

aṅga ughāḍiyā dekhāi vasilā duyāre
kahite lāgilā kichu sumadhura svare

SYNONYMS

aṅga ughāḍiyā—exposing part of her body; *dekhāi*—visible; *vasilā*—sat down; *duyāre*—on the threshold of the door; *kahite lāgilā*—began to speak; *kichu*—something; *su-madhura svare*—in very sweet language.

TRANSLATION

Exposing part of her body to his view, she sat down on the threshold of the door and spoke to him in very sweet words.

TEXT 112

"ঠাকুর, তুমি—পরমসুন্দর, প্রথম যৌবন।
তোমা দেখি' কোন্ নারী ধরিতে পারে মন?১১২॥

"ṭhākura, tumi——parama-sundara, prathama yauvana
tomā dekhi' kon nārī dharite pāre mana?

SYNONYMS

ṭhākura—O great devotee *ācārya*; *tumi*—you; *parama-sundara*—very beautifully constructed; *prathama yauvana*—the beginning of youth; *tomā dekhi'*—seeing you; *kon nārī*—what woman; *dharite pāre*—can control; *mana*—her mind.

TRANSLATION

"My dear Ṭhākura, O great preacher, great devotee, you are so beautifully built, and your youth is just beginning. Who is the woman who could control her mind after seeing you?

TEXT 113

তোমার সঙ্গম লাগি' লুব্ধ মোর মন।
তোমা না পাইলে প্রাণ না যায় ধারণ॥" ১১৩॥

tomāra saṅgama lāgi' lubdha mora mana
tomā nā pāile prāṇa nā yāya dhāraṇa"

SYNONYMS

tomāra saṅgama—union with you; *lāgi'*—for the sake of; *lubdha*—greedy; *mora mana*—my mind; *tomā*—you; *nā pāile*—if I do not get; *prāṇa*—my life; *nā*—not; *yāya*—can be; *dhāraṇa*—maintained.

TRANSLATION

"I am eager to be united with you. My mind is greedy for this. If I don't obtain you, I shall not be able to keep my body and soul together."

TEXTS 114-115

হরিদাস কহে,—"তোমা করিমু অঙ্গীকার।
সংখ্যা-নাম-সমাপ্তি যাবৎ না হয় আমার ॥ ১১৪ ॥
তাবৎ তুমি বসি' শুন নাম-সঙ্কীর্তন।
নাম-সমাপ্তি হৈলে করিমু যে তোমার মন ॥"১১৫ ॥

haridāsa kahe,——"tomā karimu aṅgīkāra
saṅkhyā-nāma-samāpti yāvat nā haya āmāra

tāvat tumi vasi' śuna nāma-saṅkīrtana
nāma-samāpti haile karimu ye tomāra mana"

SYNONYMS

haridāsa kahe—Haridāsa Ṭhākura said; *tomā*—you; *karimu aṅgīkāra*—I shall accept; *saṅkhyā-nāma*—the number of holy names; *samāpti*—finishing; *yāvat*—as long as; *nā*—not; *haya*—it is; *āmāra*—my; *tāvat*—so long; *tumi*—you; *vasi'*—sitting; *śuna*—hear; *nāma-saṅkīrtana*—chanting of the holy name; *nāma*—of the holy name; *samāpti*—finishing; *haile*—when there is; *karimu*—I shall do; *ye*—what; *tomāra*—your; *mana*—mind.

TRANSLATION

Haridāsa Ṭhākura replied, "I shall accept you without fail, but you will have to wait until I have finished chanting my regular rounds on my beads. Until that time, please sit and listen to the chanting of the holy name. As soon as I am finished, I shall fulfill your desire."

TEXT 116

এত শুনি' সেই বেশ্যা বসিয়া রহিলা।
কীর্তন করে হরিদাস প্রাতঃকাল হৈলা ॥ ১১৬ ॥

eta śuni' sei veśyā vasiyā rahilā
kīrtana kare haridāsa prātaḥ-kāla hailā

SYNONYMS

eta śuni'—hearing this; *sei veśyā*—that prostitute; *vasiyā rahilā*—stayed there sitting; *kīrtana*—chanting; *kare*—performs; *haridāsa*—Haridāsa Ṭhākura; *prātaḥ-kāla hailā*—there was the light of morning.

TRANSLATION

Hearing this, the prostitute remained sitting there while Haridāsa Ṭhākura chanted on his beads until the light of morning appeared.

TEXT 117

প্রাতঃকাল দেখি' বেশ্যা উঠিয়া চলিলা ।
সব সমাচার যাই খাঁনেরে কহিলা ॥ ১১৭ ॥

prātaḥ-kāla dekhi' veśyā uṭhiyā calilā
saba samācāra yāi khāṅnere kahilā

SYNONYMS

prātaḥ-kāla dekhi'—seeing the morning; *veśyā*—the prostitute; *uṭhiyā calilā*—stood up and left; *saba samācāra*—all information; *yāi*—going; *khāṅnere kahilā*—she spoke to Rāmacandra Khān.

TRANSLATION

When she saw that it was morning, the prostitute stood up and left. Coming before Rāmacandra Khān, she informed him of all the news.

TEXT 118

'আজি আমা অঙ্গীকার করিয়াছে বচনে ।
কালি অবশ্য তাহার সঙ্গে হইবে সঙ্গমে ॥' ১১৮ ॥

'āji āmā aṅgīkāra kariyāche vacane
kāli avaśya tāhāra saṅge ha-ibe saṅgame'

SYNONYMS

āji—today; *āmā*—me; *aṅgīkāra*—acceptance; *kariyāche*—he has done; *vacane*—by word; *kāli*—tomorrow; *avaśya*—certainly; *tāhāra saṅge*—with him; *ha-ibe*—there will be; *saṅgame*—union.

TRANSLATION

"Today Haridāsa Ṭhākura has promised to enjoy with me. Tomorrow certainly I shall have union with him."

TEXT 119

আর দিন রাত্রি হৈলে বেশ্যা আইল।
হরিদাস তারে বহু আশ্বাস করিল ॥ ১১৯ ॥

āra dina rātri haile veśyā āila
haridāsa tāre bahu āśvāsa karila

SYNONYMS

āra dina—the next day; *rātri*—night; *haile*—when there was; *veśyā*—the prostitute; *āila*—came; *haridāsa*—Haridāsa Ṭhākura; *tāre*—unto her; *bahu*—many; *āśvāsa karila*—gave assurances.

TRANSLATION

The next night, when the prostitute came again, Haridāsa Ṭhākura gave her many assurances.

TEXT 120

'কালি দুঃখ পাইলা, অপরাধ না লইবা মোর।
অবশ্য করিমু আমি তোমায় অঙ্গীকার ॥ ১২০ ॥

'kāli duḥkha pāilā, aparādha nā la-ibā mora
avaśya karimu āmi tomāya aṅgīkāra

SYNONYMS

kāli—yesterday; *duḥkha pāilā*—you were disappointed; *aparādha*—offense; *nā la-ibā*—please do not take; *mora*—my; *avaśya*—certainly; *karimu*—shall do; *āmi*—I; *tomāya*—unto you; *aṅgīkāra*—acceptance.

TRANSLATION

"Last night you were disappointed. Please excuse my offense. I shall certainly accept you.

TEXT 121

তাবৎ ইহাঁ বসি' শুন নাম-সঙ্কীর্তন।
নাম পূর্ণ হৈলে, পূর্ণ হবে তোমার মন ॥' ১২১ ॥

tāvat ihāṅ vasi' śuna nāma-saṅkīrtana
nāma pūrṇa haile, pūrṇa habe tomāra mana'

SYNONYMS

tāvat—until that time; *ihāṅ*—here; *vasi'*—sitting; *śuna*—hear; *nāma-saṅkīrtana*—chanting of the holy name of the Lord; *nāma pūrṇa haile*—as soon as the regular chanting is fulfilled; *pūrṇa*—satisfied; *habe*—will be; *tomāra mana*—your mind.

TRANSLATION

"Please sit down and hear the chanting of the Hare Kṛṣṇa mahā-mantra until my regular chanting is finished. Then your desire will surely be fulfilled."

TEXT 122

তুলসীরে তাঁকে বেশ্যা নমস্কার করি' ।
দ্বারে বসি' নাম শুনে বলে 'হরি' 'হরি' ॥ ১২২ ॥

tulasīre tāṅke veśyā namaskāra kari'
dvāre vasi' nāma śune bale 'hari' 'hari'

SYNONYMS

tulasīre—unto the *tulasī* plant; *tāṅke*—unto Haridāsa Ṭhākura; *veśyā*—the prostitute; *namaskāra kari'*—offering obeisances; *dvāre vasi'*—sitting at the door; *nāma*—the holy name; *śune*—hears; *bale*—says; *hari hari*—O my Lord Hari, O my Lord Hari.

TRANSLATION

After offering her obeisances to the tulasī plant and Haridāsa Ṭhākura, she sat down at the door. Hearing Haridāsa Ṭhākura chanting the Hare Kṛṣṇa mantra, she also chanted, "O my Lord Hari, O my Lord Hari."

PURPORT

Herein one can clearly see how a Vaiṣṇava delivers a fallen soul by a transcendental trick. The prostitute came to pollute Haridāsa Ṭhākura, but he took it as his duty to deliver the prostitute. As clearly demonstrated here, the process of deliverance is very simple. With faith and reverence the prostitute associated with Haridāsa Ṭhākura, who personally treated her material disease by chanting the Hare Kṛṣṇa *mahā-mantra.* Although the prostitute had an ulterior motive, somehow or other she got the association of a Vaiṣṇava and satisfied him by occasionally chanting in imitation, "O my Lord Hari, O my Lord Hari." The conclusion is that associating with a Vaiṣṇava, chanting the holy name of the Lord and offering obeisances to the *tulasī* plant or a Vaiṣṇava all lead one to become a transcendental devotee who is completely cleansed of all material contamination.

TEXT 123

**রাত্রি-শেষ হৈল, বেশ্যা উসিমিসি করে।
তার রীতি দেখি' হরিদাস কহেন তাহারে ॥ ১২৩ ॥**

rātri-śeṣa haila, veśyā usimisi kare
tāra rīti dekhi' haridāsa kahena tāhāre

SYNONYMS

rātri—night; *śeṣa haila*—came to an end; *veśyā*—the prostitute; *usimisi*—restless; *kare*—became; *tāra*—her; *rīti*—activities; *dekhi'*—seeing; *haridāsa*—Haridāsa Ṭhākura; *kahena*—says; *tāhāre*—unto her.

TRANSLATION

When the night came to an end, the prostitute was restless. Seeing this, Haridāsa Ṭhākura spoke to her as follows.

TEXT 124

**"কোটিনামগ্রহণ-যজ্ঞ করি একমাসে।
এই দীক্ষা করিয়াছি, হৈল আসি' শেষে ॥ ১২৪ ॥**

"koṭi-nāma-grahaṇa-yajña kari eka-māse
ei dīkṣā kariyāchi, haila āsi' śeṣe

SYNONYMS

koṭi-nāma-grahaṇa—chanting ten million names; *yajña*—such a sacrifice; *kari*—I perform; *eka-māse*—in one month; *ei*—this; *dīkṣā*—vow; *kariyāchi*—I have taken; *haila*—it was; *āsi'*—nearing; *śeṣe*—the end.

TRANSLATION

"I have vowed to chant ten million names in a month. I have taken this vow, but now it is nearing its end.

PURPORT

If one regularly chants 333,333 times daily for a month and then chants one time more, he will thus chant ten million times. In this way a devotee worships the Supreme Personality of Godhead. Such worship is called *yajña. Yajñaiḥ saṅkīrtana-prāyair yajanti hi sumedhasaḥ:* those whose intelligence is brilliant accept this *hari-nāma-yajña,* the *yajña* of chanting the holy name of the Lord. By performing this *yajña,* one satisfies the Supreme Personality of Godhead and thus attains perfection in spiritual life.

According to external vision, Haridāsa Ṭhākura belonged to a Mohammedan family. Nevertheless, because he engaged himself in performing the *yajña* of chanting the Hare Kṛṣṇa *mahā-mantra,* he became a regularly initiated *brāhmaṇa.* As stated in *Śrīmad-Bhāgavatam* (3.33.6):

yan-nāmadheya-śravaṇānukīrtanād
yat-prahvaṇād yat-smaraṇād api kvacit
śvādo 'pi sadyaḥ savanāya kalpate
kutaḥ punas te bhagavan nu darśanāt

Even if a devotee comes from a family of dog-eaters, if he surrenders to the Personality of Godhead he immediately becomes a qualified *brāhmaṇa* and is immediately fit to perform *yajña,* whereas a person born in a family of *brāhmaṇas* has to wait until completing the reformatory processes before he may be called *saṁskṛta,* purified. It is further said in *Śrīmad-Bhāgavatam* (12.1.42):

asaṁskṛtāḥ kriyā-hīnā
rajasā tamasāvṛtāḥ
prajās te bhakṣayiṣyanti
mlecchā rājanya-rūpiṇaḥ

"In the age of Kali, *mlecchas,* or lowborn people who have not undergone the purifying process of *saṁskāra,* who do not know how to apply that process in actual life and who are covered by the modes of passion and ignorance, will take the posts of administrators. They will devour the citizens with their atheistic activities." A person who is not purified by the prescribed process of *saṁskāra* is called *asaṁskṛta,* but if one remains *kriyā-hīna* even after being purified by initiation—in other words, if one fails to actually apply the principles of purity in his life—he remains an unpurified *mleccha* or *yavana.* On the other hand, we find that Haridāsa Ṭhākura, although born in a *mleccha* or *yavana* family, became Nāmācārya Haridāsa Ṭhākura because he performed the *nāma-yajña* a minimum of 300,000 times every day.

Herein we find that Haridāsa Ṭhākura strictly followed his regulative principle of chanting 300,000 times. Thus when the prostitute became restless, he informed her that first he had to finish his chanting and then he would be able to satisfy her. Actually Haridāsa Ṭhākura chanted the holy name of the Lord for three nights continuously and gave the prostitute a chance to hear him. Thus she became purified, as will be seen in the following verses.

TEXT 125

আজি সমাপ্ত হইবে,—হেন জ্ঞান ছিল ।
সমস্ত রাত্রি নিলুঁ নাম সমাপ্ত না হৈল ॥ ১২৫ ॥

āji samāpta ha-ibe,——hena jñāna chila
samasta rātri niluṅ nāma samāpta nā haila

SYNONYMS

āji—today; *samāpta ha-ibe*—will be finished; *hena jñāna chila*—I thought that; *samasta rātri*—all night; *niluṅ*—I took; *nāma*—the holy name of the Lord; *samāpta*—finished; *nā haila*—was not.

TRANSLATION

"I thought that today I would be able to finish my performance of yajña, my chanting of the Hare Kṛṣṇa mantra. I tried my best to chant the holy name all night, but I still did not finish.

TEXT 126

কালি সমাপ্ত হবে, তবে হবে ব্রতভঙ্গ ।
স্বচ্ছন্দে তোমার সঙ্গে হইবেক সঙ্গ ॥" ১২৬ ॥

kāli samāpta habe, tabe habe vrata-bhaṅga
svacchande tomāra saṅge ha-ibeka saṅga"

SYNONYMS

kāli—tomorrow; *samāpta habe*—it will end; *tabe*—at that time; *habe*—there will be; *vrata-bhaṅga*—the end of my vow; *svacchande*—in full freedom; *tomāra saṅge*—with you; *ha-ibeka*—there will be; *saṅga*—union.

TRANSLATION

"Tomorrow I will surely finish, and my vow will be fulfilled. Then it will be possible for me to enjoy with you in full freedom."

PURPORT

Haridāsa Ṭhākura never wanted to enjoy the prostitute, but he tricked her to deliver her by giving her a chance to hear the holy name of the Lord while he chanted. Pure devotees chant the Hare Kṛṣṇa *mantra,* and simply by hearing this chanting from a purified transcendental person, one is purified of all sinful activities, no matter how lowborn or fallen one may be. As soon as one is thus completely free from the reactions of sinful activities, he is eligible to render devotional service to the Lord. This is the process for engaging the fallen souls in devotional service. As Lord Kṛṣṇa says in *Bhagavad-gītā* (7.28):

yeṣāṁ tv anta-gataṁ pāpaṁ
janānāṁ puṇya-karmaṇām
te dvandva-moha-nirmuktā
bhajante māṁ dṛḍha-vratāḥ

"Persons who have acted piously in previous lives and in this life, whose sinful actions are completely eradicated and who are freed from the duality of delusion, engage themselves in My service with determination."

TEXT 127

বেশ্যা গিয়া সমাচার খাঁনেরে কহিল ।
আর দিন সন্ধ্যা হইতে ঠাকুর-ঠাঞি আইল ॥ ১২৭ ॥

veśyā giyā samācāra khāṅnere kahila
āra dina sandhyā ha-ite ṭhākura-ṭhāñi āila

SYNONYMS

veśyā—the prostitute; *giyā*—returning; *samācāra*—information; *khāṅnere kahila*—spoke to Rāmacandra Khān; *āra dina*—the next day; *sandhyā ha-ite*—beginning from the evening; *ṭhākura-ṭhāñi āila*—she came and remained at the residence of Haridāsa Ṭhākura.

TRANSLATION

The prostitute returned to Rāmacandra Khān and informed him of what had happened. The next day she came earlier, at the beginning of the evening, and stayed with Haridāsa Ṭhākura.

TEXT 128

তুলসীকে, ঠাকুরকে নমস্কার করি' ।
দ্বারে বসি' নাম শুনে, বলে 'হরি' 'হরি' ॥ ১২৮ ॥

tulasīke, ṭhākurake namaskāra kari'
dvāre vasi' nāma śune, bale 'hari' 'hari'

SYNONYMS

tulasīke—unto the *tulasī* plant; *ṭhākurake*—and unto Haridāsa Ṭhākura; *namaskāra kari'*—offers her obeisances; *dvāre vasi'*—sitting at the door; *nāma śune*—hears the holy name; *bale*—chants; *hari hari*—the holy name of the Lord.

TRANSLATION

After offering obeisances to the tulasī plant and Haridāsa Ṭhākura, she sat down on the threshold of the room. Thus she began to hear Haridāsa Ṭhākura's chanting, and she also personally chanted "Hari, Hari," the holy name of the Lord.

TEXT 129

'নাম পূর্ণ হবে আজি',—বলে হরিদাস ।
'তবে পূর্ণ করিমু আজি তোমার অভিলাষ' ॥ ১২৯ ॥

'nāma pūrṇa habe āji',——bale haridāsa
'tabe pūrṇa karimu āji tomāra abhilāṣa'

SYNONYMS

nāma—chanting of the holy name; *pūrṇa*—complete; *habe*—will be; *āji*—today; *bale haridāsa*—Haridāsa Ṭhākura said; *tabe*—then; *pūrṇa karimu*—I shall satisfy; *āji*—today; *tomāra abhilāṣa*—your desires.

TRANSLATION

"Today it will be possible for me to finish my chanting," Haridāsa Ṭhākura informed her. "Then I shall satisfy all your desires."

TEXT 130

কীর্তন করিতে ঐছে রাত্রি-শেষ হৈল ।
ঠাকুরের সনে বেশ্যার মন ফিরি' গেল ॥ ১৩০ ॥

kīrtana karite aiche rātri-śeṣa haila
ṭhākurera sane veśyāra mana phiri' gela

SYNONYMS

kīrtana karite—chanting and chanting; *aiche*—in that way; *rātri-śeṣa haila*—the night ended; *ṭhākurera sane*—by the association of Haridāsa Ṭhākura; *veśyāra*—of the prostitute; *mana*—mind; *phiri' gela*—was converted.

TRANSLATION

The night ended while Haridāsa Ṭhākura was chanting, but by his association the mind of the prostitute had changed.

TEXT 131

দণ্ডবৎ হঞা পড়ে ঠাকুর-চরণে ।
রামচন্দ্র-খাঁনের কথা কৈল নিবেদনে ॥ ১৩১ ॥

daṇḍavat hañā paḍe ṭhākura-caraṇe
rāmacandra-khāṅnera kathā kaila nivedane

SYNONYMS

daṇḍavat hañā—offering obeisances; *paḍe*—she fell down; *ṭhākura-caraṇe*—at the lotus feet of Haridāsa Ṭhākura; *rāmacandra-khāṅnera*—of Rāmacandra Khān; *kathā*—policy; *kaila*—did; *nivedane*—submission.

TRANSLATION

The prostitute, now purified, fell at the lotus feet of Haridāsa Ṭhākura and confessed that Rāmacandra Khān had appointed her to pollute him.

TEXT 132

"বেশ্যা হঞা মুঞি পাপ করিয়াছোঁ অপার ।
কৃপা করি' কর মো-অধমে নিস্তার ॥" ১৩২ ॥

"veśyā hañā muñi pāpa kariyāchoṅ apāra
kṛpā kari' kara mo-adhame nistāra"

SYNONYMS

veśyā hañā—being a prostitute; *muñi*—I; *pāpa*—sinful activities; *kariyāchoṅ*—have done; *apāra*—unlimited; *kṛpā kari'*—being merciful; *kara*—please do; *mo-adhame*—unto me, the most fallen; *nistāra*—deliverance.

TRANSLATION

"Because I have taken the profession of a prostitute," she said, "I have performed unlimited sinful acts. My lord, be merciful to me. Deliver my fallen soul."

TEXT 133

ঠাকুর কহে,—খাঁনের কথা সব আমি জানি ।
অজ্ঞ মূর্খ সেই, তারে দুঃখ নাহি মানি ॥ ১৩৩ ॥

ṭhākura kahe,——khāṅnera kathā saba āmi jāni
ajña mūrkha sei, tāre duḥkha nāhi māni

SYNONYMS

ṭhākura kahe—Haridāsa Ṭhākura said; *khāṅnera kathā*—the plans of Rāmacandra Khān; *saba*—all; *āmi jāni*—I know; *ajña mūrkha sei*—he is an ignorant fool; *tāre*—by that; *duḥkha nāhi māni*—I do not feel unhappiness.

TRANSLATION

Haridāsa Ṭhākura replied, "I know everything about the conspiracy of Rāmacandra Khān. He is nothing but an ignorant fool. Therefore his activities do not make me feel unhappy.

TEXT 134

সেইদিন যাইতাম এস্থান ছাড়িয়া ।
তিন দিন রহিলাঙ তোমা নিস্তার লাগিয়া ॥ ১৩৪ ॥

sei-dina yāitāma e-sthāna chāḍiyā
tina dina rahilāṅa tomā nistāra lāgiyā

SYNONYMS

sei-dina—on that very day; *yāitāma*—I would have left; *e-sthāna*—this place; *chāḍiyā*—giving up; *tina dina*—for three days; *rahilāṅa*—I stayed; *tomā*—you; *nistāra lāgiyā*—for delivering.

TRANSLATION

"On the very day Rāmacandra Khān was planning his intrigue against me, I would have left this place immediately, but because you came to me I stayed here for three days to deliver you."

TEXT 135

বেশ্যা কহে,—"কৃপা করি' করহ উপদেশ ।
কি মোর কর্তব্য, যাতে যায় ভব-ক্লেশ ॥" ১৩৫ ॥

veśyā kahe,——"kṛpā kari' karaha upadeśa
ki mora kartavya, yāte yāya bhava-kleśa"

SYNONYMS

veśyā kahe—the prostitute said; *kṛpā kari'*—being merciful; *karaha upadeśa*—please give instructions; *ki*—what; *mora kartavya*—my duty; *yāte*—by which; *yāya*—go away; *bhava-kleśa*—all material tribulations.

TRANSLATION

The prostitute said, "Kindly act as my spiritual master. Instruct me in my duty by which to get relief from material existence."

TEXT 136

ঠাকুর কহে,—"ঘরের দ্রব্য ব্রাহ্মণে কর দান ।
এই ঘরে আসি' তুমি করহ বিশ্রাম ॥ ১৩৬ ॥

ṭhākura kahe,——"gharera dravya brāhmaṇe kara dāna
ei ghare āsi' tumi karaha viśrāma

SYNONYMS

ṭhākura kahe—Śrīla Haridāsa Ṭhākura said; *gharera*—at home; *dravya*—articles; *brāhmaṇe*—to the *brāhmaṇas*; *kara dāna*—give as charity; *ei ghare*—in this room; *āsi'*—returning; *tumi*—you; *karaha viśrāma*—stay.

TRANSLATION

Haridāsa Ṭhākura replied, "Immediately go home and distribute to the brāhmaṇas whatever property you have. Then come back to this room and stay here forever in Kṛṣṇa consciousness.

PURPORT

Haridāsa Ṭhākura's instruction that the prostitute should distribute to the *brāhmaṇas* all the property she had at home is very significant. Haridāsa Ṭhākura never advised the prostitute to give charity to the so-called *daridra-nārāyaṇa* ("poor Nārāyaṇa") or any other such persons. According to Vedic civilization, charity should be given only to the qualified *brāhmaṇas.* As stated in *Bhagavad-gītā* (18.42):

śamo damas tapaḥ śaucaṁ
kṣāntir ārjavam eva ca
jñānaṁ vijñānam āstikyaṁ
brahma-karma svabhāva-jam

The brahminical qualifications are truthfulness, control of the senses and mind, tolerance, simplicity, knowledge, practical application of transcendental knowledge in one's life, and full faith in the Supreme Personality of Godhead. Persons engaged in pursuing spiritual understanding have no time to earn their livelihood. They depend completely on the mercy of the Lord, who says in *Bhagavad-gītā* (9.22) that He personally carries to them all their necessities (*yoga-kṣemaṁ vahāmy aham*). The Vedic civilization recommends that one give charity to *brāhmaṇas* and *sannyāsīs*, not to the so-called *daridra-nārāyaṇa*. Nārāyaṇa cannot be *daridra*, nor can *daridra* be Nārāyaṇa, for these are contradictory terms. Atheistic men invent such concoctions and preach them to fools, but charity should actually be given to *brāhmaṇas* and *sannyāsīs* because whatever money they get they spend for Kṛṣṇa. Whatever charity one gives to a *brāhmaṇa* goes to Kṛṣṇa, who says in *Bhagavad-gītā* (9.27):

yat karoṣi yad aśnāsi
yaj juhoṣi dadāsi yat
yat tapasyasi kaunteya
tat kuruṣva mad-arpaṇam

"O son of Kuntī, all that you do, all that you eat, all that you offer and give away, as well as all austerities that you may perform, should be done as an offering unto Me." Everything actually belongs to Kṛṣṇa, but so-called civilized men unfortunately think that everything belongs to them. This is the mistake of materialistic civilization. The prostitute (*veśyā*) had earned money by questionable means, and therefore Haridāsa Ṭhākura advised her to distribute to the *brāhmaṇas* whatever she possessed. When Śrīla Rūpa Gosvāmī retired from family life, he distributed fifty percent of his income to the *brāhmaṇas* and Vaiṣṇavas. A *brāhmaṇa* knows what the Absolute Truth is, and a Vaiṣṇava, knowing the Absolute Truth, acts on behalf of the Absolute Truth, the Supreme Personality of Godhead. Generally one earns money by many questionable means. Therefore at some time one should retire and distribute whatever one has to the *brāhmaṇas* and Vaiṣṇavas who engage in devotional service by preaching the glories of the Supreme Personality of Godhead.

TEXT 137

নিরন্তর নাম লও, কর তুলসী সেবন ।
অচিরাৎ পাবে তবে কৃষ্ণের চরণ ॥" ১৩৭ ॥

nirantara nāma lao, kara tulasī sevana
acirāt pābe tabe kṛṣṇera caraṇa"

SYNONYMS

nirantara—twenty-four hours a day; *nāma lao*—chant the Hare Kṛṣṇa *mantra*; *kara*—perform; *tulasī sevana*—worship of the *tulasī* plant; *acirāt*—very soon; *pābe*—you will get; *tabe*—then; *kṛṣṇera caraṇa*—the lotus feet of Kṛṣṇa.

TRANSLATION

"Chant the Hare Kṛṣṇa mantra continuously and render service to the tulasī plant by watering her and offering prayers to her. In this way you will very soon get the opportunity to be sheltered at the lotus feet of Kṛṣṇa."

PURPORT

At least five thousand years ago, Lord Śrī Kṛṣṇa expressed His desire that everyone surrender to Him (*sarva-dharmān parityajya mām ekaṁ śaraṇaṁ vraja*). Why is it that people cannot do this? Kṛṣṇa assures, *ahaṁ tvāṁ sarva-pāpebhyo mokṣayiṣyāmi mā śucaḥ:* "I shall deliver you from all sinful reactions. Do not fear." Everyone is suffering from the results of sinful activities, but Kṛṣṇa says that if one surrenders unto Him, He will protect one from sinful reactions. Modern civilization, however, is interested neither in Kṛṣṇa nor in getting relief from sinful acts. Therefore men are suffering. Surrender is the ultimate instruction of *Bhagavad-gītā,* but for one who cannot surrender to the lotus feet of Kṛṣṇa, it is better to chant the Hare Kṛṣṇa *mantra* constantly, under the instruction of Haridāsa Ṭhākura.

In our Kṛṣṇa consciousness movement we are teaching our followers to chant the Hare Kṛṣṇa *mantra* continuously on beads. Even those who are not accustomed to this practice are advised to chant at least sixteen rounds on their beads so that they may be trained. Otherwise, Śrī Caitanya Mahāprabhu recommended:

tṛṇād api sunīcena
taror api sahiṣṇunā
amāninā mānadena
kīrtanīyaḥ sadā hariḥ

"One should chant the holy name of the Lord in a humble state of mind, thinking oneself lower than the straw in the street. One should be more tolerant than a tree, devoid of all sense of false prestige, and ready to offer all respect to others. In such a state of mind one can chant the holy name of the Lord constantly." *Sadā* means "always." Haridāsa Ṭhākura says, *nirantara nāma lao:* "Chant the Hare Kṛṣṇa *mantra* without stopping."

Although Kṛṣṇa wants everyone to surrender to His lotus feet, because of people's sinful activities they cannot do this. *Na māṁ duṣkṛtino mūḍhāḥ prapadyante narādhamāḥ:* rascals and fools, the lowest of men, who engage in sinful activities, cannot suddenly surrender to the lotus feet of Kṛṣṇa. Nevertheless, if they begin chanting the Hare Kṛṣṇa *mantra* and rendering service unto the *tulasī* plant, they will very soon be able to surrender. One's real duty is to surrender to the lotus feet of Kṛṣṇa but if one is unable to do so, he should adopt this process, as introduced by Śrī Caitanya Mahāprabhu and His most confidential servant,

Nāmācārya Śrīla Haridāsa Ṭhākura. This is the way to achieve success in Kṛṣṇa consciousness.

TEXT 138

এত বলি' তারে 'নাম' উপদেশ করি'।
উঠিয়া চলিলা ঠাকুর বলি' 'হরি' 'হরি' ॥ ১৩৮ ॥

eta bali' tāre 'nāma' upadeśa kari'
uṭhiyā calilā ṭhākura bali' 'hari' 'hari'

SYNONYMS

eta bali'—saying this; *tāre*—her; *nāma upadeśa kari'*—instructing about the process of chanting the Hare Kṛṣṇa *mahā-mantra*; *uṭhiyā*—standing up; *calilā*—left; *ṭhākura*—Haridāsa Ṭhākura; *bali'*—chanting; *hari hari*—the Hare Kṛṣṇa *mahā-mantra.*

TRANSLATION

After thus instructing the prostitute about the process of chanting the Hare Kṛṣṇa mantra, Haridāsa Ṭhākura stood up and left, continuously chanting "Hari, Hari."

TEXT 139

তবে সেই বেশ্যা গুরুর আজ্ঞা লইল।
গৃহবিত্ত যেবা ছিল, ব্রাহ্মণেরে দিল ॥ ১৩৯ ॥

tabe sei veśyā gurura ājñā la-ila
gṛha-vitta yebā chila, brāhmaṇere dila

SYNONYMS

tabe—thereafter; *sei*—that; *veśyā*—prostitute; *gurura*—of the spiritual master; *ājñā*—order; *la-ila*—took; *gṛha-vitta*—all household possessions; *yebā*—whatever; *chila*—there was; *brāhmaṇere*—to the *brāhmaṇas*; *dila*—gave.

TRANSLATION

Thereafter, the prostitute distributed to the brāhmaṇas whatever household possessions she had, following the order of her spiritual master.

PURPORT

Sometimes the word *gṛha-vṛtti* is substituted for the word *gṛha-vitta. Vṛtti* means "profession." The *gṛha-vṛtti* of the prostitute was to enchant foolish people and induce them to indulge in sex. Here, however, *gṛha-vṛtti* is not a suitable word. The proper word is *gṛha-vitta,* which means "all the possessions she had in her home." All the girl's possessions had been earned by professional prostitution and were therefore products of her sinful life. When such possessions are given to *brāhmaṇas* and Vaiṣṇavas who can engage them in the service of the Lord because of their advancement in spiritual life, this indirectly helps the person who gives the charity, for he is thus relieved of sinful reactions. As Kṛṣṇa promises, *ahaṁ tvāṁ sarva-pāpebhyo mokṣayiṣyāmi:* "I shall save you from all sinful reactions." When our Kṛṣṇa conscious devotees go out to beg charity or collect contributions in the form of membership fees, the money thus coming to the Kṛṣṇa consciousness movement is strictly employed to advance Kṛṣṇa consciousness all over the world. The Kṛṣṇa conscious devotees collect the money of others for the service of Kṛṣṇa, and they are satisfied with Kṛṣṇa's *prasāda* and whatever He gives them for their maintenance. They do not desire material comforts. However, they go to great pains to engage the possessions of prostitutes, or persons who are more or less like prostitutes, in the service of the Lord and thus free them from sinful reactions. A Vaiṣṇava *guru* accepts money or other contributions, but he does not employ such contributions for sense gratification. A pure Vaiṣṇava thinks himself unfit to help free even one person from the reactions of sinful life, but he engages one's hard-earned money in the service of the Lord and thus frees one from sinful reactions. A Vaiṣṇava *guru* is never dependent on the contributions of his disciples. Following the instructions of Haridāsa Ṭhākura, a pure Vaiṣṇava does not personally take even a single paisa from anyone, but he induces his followers to spend for the service of the Lord whatever possessions they have.

TEXT 140

মাথা মুড়ি' একবস্ত্রে রহিল সেই ঘরে ।
রাত্রি-দিনে তিন-লক্ষ নাম গ্রহণ করে ॥ ১৪০ ॥

māthā muḍi' eka-vastre rahila sei ghare
rātri-dine tina-lakṣa nāma grahaṇa kare

SYNONYMS

māthā muḍi'—shaving her head; *eka-vastre*—wearing one cloth; *rahila*—remained; *sei ghare*—in that room; *rātri-dine*—throughout the entire day and night; *tina-lakṣa*—300,000; *nāma*—holy names; *grahaṇa kare*—chants.

TRANSLATION

The prostitute shaved her head clean in accordance with Vaiṣṇava principles and stayed in that room wearing only one cloth. Following in the footsteps of her spiritual master, she began chanting the Hare Kṛṣṇa mahā-mantra 300,000 times a day. She chanted throughout the entire day and night.

TEXT 141

তুলসী সেবন করে, চর্বণ, উপবাস।
ইন্দ্রিয়-দমন হৈল, প্রেমের প্রকাশ ॥ ১৪১ ॥

tulasī sevana kare, carvaṇa, upavāsa
indriya-damana haila, premera prakāśa

SYNONYMS

tulasī—the *tulasī* plant; *sevana kare*—she worshiped; *carvaṇa*—chewing; *upavāsa*—fasting; *indriya-damana*—controlling the senses; *haila*—there was; *premera prakāśa*—manifestations symptomizing love of Godhead.

TRANSLATION

She worshiped the tulasī plant, following in the footsteps of her spiritual master. Instead of eating regularly, she chewed whatever food she received as alms, and if nothing was supplied she would fast. Thus by eating frugally and fasting she conquered her senses, and as soon as her senses were controlled, symptoms of love of Godhead appeared in her person.

TEXT 142

প্রসিদ্ধা বৈষ্ণবী হৈল পরম-মহান্তী।
বড় বড় বৈষ্ণব তাঁর দর্শনেতে যান্তি ॥ ১৪২ ॥

prasiddhā vaiṣṇavī haila parama-mahāntī
baḍa baḍa vaiṣṇava tāṅra darśanete yānti

SYNONYMS

prasiddhā—celebrated; *vaiṣṇavī*—devotee of the Lord; *haila*—became; *parama-mahāntī*—very advanced; *baḍa baḍa vaiṣṇava*—many recognized, highly situated devotees; *tāṅra*—her; *darśanete*—to see; *yānti*—used to go.

TRANSLATION

Thus the prostitute became a celebrated devotee. She became very advanced in spiritual life, and many stalwart Vaiṣṇavas would come to see her.

PURPORT

Stalwart, highly advanced Vaiṣṇava devotees are not interested in seeing prostitutes, but when a prostitute or any other fallen soul becomes a Vaiṣṇava, stalwart Vaiṣṇavas are interested in seeing them. Anyone can be turned into a

Vaiṣṇava if he or she follows the Vaiṣṇava principles. A devotee who follows these principles is no longer on the material platform. Therefore, it is one's strict adherence to the principles that should be considered, not the country of one's birth. Many devotees join our Kṛṣṇa consciousness movement from Europe and America, but one should not therefore consider them European Vaiṣṇavas or American Vaiṣṇavas. A Vaiṣṇava is a Vaiṣṇava and should therefore be given all the respect due a Vaiṣṇava.

TEXT 143

বেশ্যার চরিত্র দেখি' লোকে চমৎকার ।
হরিদাসের মহিমা কহে করি' নমস্কার ॥ ১৪৩ ॥

veśyāra caritra dekhi' loke camatkāra
haridāsera mahimā kahe kari' namaskāra

SYNONYMS

veśyāra—of the prostitute; *caritra*—character; *dekhi'*—seeing; *loke*—all people; *camatkāra*—astonished; *haridāsera*—of Ṭhākura Haridāsa; *mahimā*—glories; *kahe*—speak; *kari' namaskāra*—offering obeisances.

TRANSLATION

Seeing the sublime character of the prostitute, everyone was astonished. Everyone glorified the influence of Haridāsa Ṭhākura and offered him obeisances.

PURPORT

It is said, *phalena paricīyate:* one is recognized by the result of his actions. In Vaiṣṇava society there are many types of Vaiṣṇavas. Some of them are called *gosvāmīs,* some are called *svāmīs,* some are *prabhus,* and some are *prabhupāda.* One is not recognized, however, simply by such a name. A spiritual master is recognized as an actual *guru* when it is seen that he has changed the character of his disciples. Haridāsa Ṭhākura actually changed the character of the professional prostitute. People greatly appreciated this, and therefore they all offered obeisances to Haridāsa Ṭhākura and glorified him.

TEXT 144

রামচন্দ্র খাঁন অপরাধ-বীজ কৈল ।
সেই বীজ বৃক্ষ হঞা আগেতে ফলিল ॥ ১৪৪ ॥

rāmacandra khāṅna aparādha-bīja kaila
sei bīja vṛkṣa hañā āgete phalila

SYNONYMS

rāmacandra khāṅna—Rāmacandra Khān; *aparādha*—of the offense; *bīja*—seed; *kaila*—caused to germinate; *sei bīja*—that seed; *vṛkṣa hañā*—becoming a tree; *āgete*—later; *phalila*—fructified.

TRANSLATION

By inducing a prostitute to disturb Haridāsa Ṭhākura, Rāmacandra Khān caused a seed of offense at his lotus feet to germinate. This seed later became a tree, and when it fructified, Rāmacandra Khān ate its fruits.

TEXT 145

মহদপরাধের ফল অদ্ভুত কথন ।
প্রস্তাব পাঞা কহি, শুন, ভক্তগণ ॥ ১৪৫ ॥

mahad-aparādhera phala adbhuta kathana
prastāva pāñā kahi, śuna, bhakta-gaṇa

SYNONYMS

mahat-aparādhera—of a great offense at the feet of the exalted devotee; *phala*—the result; *adbhuta*—wonderful; *kathana*—narration; *prastāva*—opportunity; *pāñā*—taking advantage of; *kahi*—I say; *śuna*—hear; *bhakta-gaṇa*—O devotees.

TRANSLATION

This offense at the lotus feet of an exalted devotee has resulted in a wonderful narration. Taking advantage of the opportunity afforded by these incidents, I shall explain what happened. O devotees, please listen.

TEXT 146

সহজেই অবৈষ্ণব রামচন্দ্র-খাঁন ।
হরিদাসের অপরাধে হৈল অসুর-সমান ॥ ১৪৬ ॥

sahajei avaiṣṇava rāmacandra-khāṅna
haridāsera aparādhe haila asura-samāna

SYNONYMS

sahajei—naturally; *avaiṣṇava*—nondevotee; *rāmacandra-khāṅna*—Rāmacandra Khān; *haridāsera*—at the lotus feet of Haridāsa; *aparādhe*—by offenses; *haila*—was; *asura-samāna*—exactly like a demon.

TRANSLATION

Rāmacandra Khān was naturally a nondevotee. Now, having offended the lotus feet of Haridāsa Ṭhākura, he became just like a demoniac atheist.

TEXT 147

বৈষ্ণবধর্ম নিন্দা করে, বৈষ্ণব-অপমান।
বহুদিনের অপরাধে পাইল পরিণাম ॥ ১৪৭ ॥

vaiṣṇava-dharma nindā kare, vaiṣṇava-apamāna
bahu-dinera aparādhe pāila pariṇāma

SYNONYMS

vaiṣṇava-dharma—the cult of Vaiṣṇavism; *nindā kare*—blasphemes; *vaiṣṇava apamāna*—insults to the devotees; *bahu-dinera*—for a long time; *aparādhe*—by offensive activities; *pāila*—got; *pariṇāma*—the resultant action.

TRANSLATION

Because of blaspheming the cult of Vaiṣṇavism and insulting the devotees for a long time, he now received the results of his offensive activities.

PURPORT

Rāmacandra Khān was a great offender at the lotus feet of the Vaiṣṇavas and Viṣṇu. Just as Rāvaṇa, although born of a *brāhmaṇa* father, Viśvaśravā, was nevertheless called an *asura* or *rākṣasa* because of his offenses against Lord Rāmacandra (Viṣṇu) and Hanumān (a Vaiṣṇava), so Rāmacandra Khān also became such an *asura* because of his offenses against Haridāsa Ṭhākura and many others.

TEXT 148

নিত্যানন্দ-গোসাঞি গৌড়ে যবে আইলা।
প্রেম প্রচারিতে তবে ভ্রমিতে লাগিলা ॥ ১৪৮ ॥

nityānanda-gosāñi gauḍe yabe āilā
prema pracārite tabe bhramite lāgilā

SYNONYMS

nityānanda-gosāñi—Lord Nityānanda; *gauḍe*—in Bengal; *yabe*—when; *āilā*—came back; *prema pracārite*—to preach the cult of *bhakti,* love of Godhead; *tabe*—at that time; *bhramite lāgilā*—began to tour.

TRANSLATION

When Lord Nityānanda returned to Bengal to preach the cult of bhakti, love of Godhead, He began touring all over the country.

TEXT 149

প্রেম-প্রচারণ আর পাষণ্ডদলন ।
দুইকার্যে অবধূত করেন ভ্রমণ ॥ ১৪৯ ॥

prema-pracāraṇa āra pāṣaṇḍa-dalana
dui-kārye avadhūta karena bhramaṇa

SYNONYMS

prema-pracāraṇa—preaching the cult of *bhakti*; *āra*—and; *pāṣaṇḍa-dalana*—subduing atheistic men; *dui-kārye*—with two kinds of activities; *avadhūta*—the great devotee and mendicant; *karena*—does; *bhramaṇa*—touring.

TRANSLATION

For two purposes—to spread the cult of bhakti and to defeat and subdue the atheists—Lord Nityānanda, the most dedicated devotee of the Lord, moved throughout the country.

PURPORT

As stated in *Bhagavad-gītā* (4.8):

paritrāṇāya sādhūnāṁ
vināśāya ca duṣkṛtām
dharma-saṁsthāpanārthāya
saṁbhavāmi yuge yuge

Lord Kṛṣṇa appears in every millennium for two purposes, namely to deliver the devotees and kill the nondevotees. His devotees also have two similar purposes—to preach the *bhakti* cult of Kṛṣṇa consciousness and defeat all kinds of agnostics and atheistic demons. Nityānanda Prabhu carried out the order of Lord Śrī Caitanya Mahāprabhu in this way, and those who strictly follow Nityānanda

Prabhu perform the same activities. There are two classes of devotees. One is called *goṣṭhyānandī,* and the other is called *bhajanānandī.* A devotee who does not preach but always engages in devotional activities is called a *bhajanānandī,* whereas a devotee who not only is expert in devotional service but who also preaches the cult of *bhakti* and defeats all kinds of agnostics is called a *goṣṭhyā-nandī.*

TEXT 150

সর্বজ্ঞ নিত্যানন্দ আইলা তার ঘরে ।
আসিয়া বসিলা দুর্গামণ্ডপ-উপরে ॥ ১৫০ ॥

sarvajña nityānanda āilā tāra ghare
āsiyā vasilā durgā-maṇḍapa-upare

SYNONYMS

sarva-jña—omniscient; *nityānanda*—Lord Nityānanda; *āilā*—came; *tāra ghare*—at his house; *āsiyā*—coming; *vasilā*—sat down; *durgā-maṇḍapa-upare*—on the altar of the Durgā-maṇḍapa.

TRANSLATION

Lord Nityānanda, who is omniscient because He is the Supreme Personality of Godhead, came to the house of Rāmacandra Khān and sat down on the altar of the Durgā-maṇḍapa.

PURPORT

Well-to-do Hindu gentlemen constructed their houses with a place called the Durgā-maṇḍapa for the worship of the goddess Durgā. There they generally held worship of the goddess every year in the month of Āśvina (October). Rāmacandra Khān possessed such a Durgā-maṇḍapa at his residence.

TEXT 151

অনেক লোকজন সঙ্গে অঙ্গন ভরিল ।
ভিতর হৈতে রামচন্দ্র সেবক পাঠাইল ॥ ১৫১ ॥

aneka loka-jana saṅge aṅgana bharila
bhitara haite rāmacandra sevaka pāṭhāila

SYNONYMS

aneka—many; *loka-jana*—crowds of people; *saṅge*—accompanied by; *aṅgana*—the courtyard; *bharila*—became filled; *bhitara haite*—from inside; *rāma-candra*—Rāmacandra Khān; *sevaka*—servant; *pāṭhāila*—sent.

TRANSLATION

When the Durgā-maṇḍapa and courtyard were filled with crowds of men, Rāmacandra Khān, who was inside the house, sent his servant to Lord Nityānanda.

PURPORT

In those days, and also even now, the palatial buildings of respectable people, expecially in the villages of Bengal, were divided into two parts. The inside part was especially meant for the family, and the ladies would live there unexposed to men. That part was called the *bhitara-bāḍi,* or inside house. In the outside house, or *bahir-bāḍi,* the respectable gentleman received visitors and kept his business office. The Durgā-maṇḍapa would be part of the outside house. Thus when Lord Nityānanda entered the outside house, Rāmacandra Khān was in the inside house with the members of his family. When Nityānanda Prabhu arrived, Rāmacandra Khān did not receive Him personally but sent his servant to inform Him indirectly to go away.

TEXT 152

সেবক বলে—"গোসাঞি, মোরে পাঠাইল খাঁন ।
গৃহস্থের ঘরে তোমায় দিব বাসাস্থান ॥ ১৫২ ॥

sevaka bale——"gosāñi, more pāṭhāila khāṅna
gṛhasthera ghare tomāya diba vāsā-sthāna

SYNONYMS

sevaka bale—the servant said; *gosāñi*—my dear Lord; *more*—me; *pāṭhāila*—sent; *khāṅna*—Rāmacandra Khān; *gṛhasthera ghare*—at the house of some ordinary person; *tomāya*—unto You; *diba*—I shall give; *vāsā-sthāna*—residential place.

TRANSLATION

The servant informed Lord Nityānanda, "My dear sir, Rāmacandra Khān has sent me to accommodate You in some common man's house.

TEXT 153

গোয়ালার গোশালা হয় অত্যন্ত বিস্তার ।
ইহাঁ সঙ্কীর্ণ-স্থল, তোমার মনুষ্য—অপার"॥ ১৫৩ ॥

goyālāra gośālā haya atyanta vistāra
ihāṅ saṅkīrṇa-sthala, tomāra manuṣya——apāra"

SYNONYMS

goyālāra—of a milkman; *go-śālā*—cow shed; *haya*—is; *atyanta*—very; *vistāra*—spacious; *ihāṅ*—here; *saṅkīrṇa-sthala*—very narrow place; *tomāra*—Your; *manuṣya*—adherents; *apāra*—unlimited.

TRANSLATION

"You might go to the house of a milkman, for the cow shed is spacious, whereas the space here in the Durgā-maṇḍapa is insufficient because You have many followers with You."

TEXT 154

ভিতরে আছিলা, শুনি' ক্রোধে বাহিরিলা ।
অট্ট অট্ট হাসি' গোসাঞি কহিতে লাগিলা ॥ ১৫৪ ॥

bhitare āchilā, śuni' krodhe bāhirilā
aṭṭa aṭṭa hāsi' gosāñi kahite lāgilā

SYNONYMS

bhitare āchilā—was staying inside; *śuni'*—hearing; *krodhe*—in anger; *bāhirilā*—came out; *aṭṭa aṭṭa*—very loudly; *hāsi'*—laughing; *gosāñi*—Lord Nityānanda Prabhu; *kahite lāgilā*—began to say.

TRANSLATION

When Nityānanda Prabhu heard this order from the servant of Rāmacandra Khān, He became very angry and came out. Laughing very loudly, He spoke as follows.

TEXT 155

"সত্য কহে,—এই ঘর মোর যোগ্য নয় ।
ম্লেচ্ছ গো-বধ করে, তার যোগ্য হয় ॥" ১৫৫ ॥

"satya kahe,——ei ghara mora yogya naya
mleccha go-vadha kare, tāra yogya haya"

SYNONYMS

satya kahe—Rāmacandra Khān says rightly; *ei ghara*—this house; *mora*—for Me; *yogya naya*—is not fit; *mleccha*—the meateaters; *go-vadha kare*—who kill cows; *tāra*—for them; *yogya haya*—it is fit.

TRANSLATION

"Rāmacandra Khān has spoken rightly. This place is unfit for Me. It is fit for cow-killing meateaters."

TEXT 156

এত বলি' ক্রোধে গোসাঞি উঠিয়া চলিলা ।
তারে দণ্ড দিতে সে গ্রামে না রহিলা ॥ ১৫৬ ॥

eta bali' krodhe gosāñi uṭhiyā calilā
tāre daṇḍa dite se grāme nā rahilā

SYNONYMS

eta bali'—saying this; *krodhe*—in anger; *gosāñi*—Lord Nityānanda; *uṭhiyā calilā*—got up and left; *tāre*—him; *daṇḍa dite*—to chastise; *se*—that; *grāme*—in the village; *nā rahilā*—did not stay.

TRANSLATION

Having said this, Lord Nityānanda stood up and left in an angry mood. To chastise Rāmacandra Khān, He did not even stay in that village.

TEXT 157

ইহাঁ রামচন্দ্র খান সেবকে আজ্ঞা দিল ।
গোসাঞি যাহাঁ বসিলা, তার মাটী খোদাইল ॥১৫৭॥

ihāṅ rāmacandra khāna sevake ājñā dila
gosāñi yāhāṅ vasilā, tāra māṭī khodāila

SYNONYMS

ihāṅ—here; *rāmacandra khāna*—Rāmacandra Khān; *sevake*—to the servant; *ājñā dila*—ordered; *gosāñi*—Lord Nityānanda Prabhu; *yāhāṅ*—where; *vasilā*—sat down; *tāra*—of that place; *māṭī*—earth; *khodāila*—caused to dig.

TRANSLATION

Rāmacandra Khān ordered the servant to dig up the dirt in the place where Nityānanda Prabhu had sat.

TEXT 158

গোময়-জলে লেপিলা সব মন্দির-প্রাঙ্গণ ।
তবু রামচন্দ্রের মন না হৈল পরসন্ন ॥ ১৫৮ ॥

gomaya-jale lepilā saba mandira-prāṅgaṇa
tabu rāmacandrera mana nā haila parasanna

SYNONYMS

go-maya-jale—with water mixed with cow dung; *lepilā*—smeared; *saba*—all; *mandira*—the Durgā-maṇḍapa temple; *prāṅgaṇa*—the courtyard; *tabu*—still; *rāmacandrera mana*—the mind of Rāmacandra Khān; *nā haila parasanna*—was not happy.

TRANSLATION

To purify the Durgā-maṇḍapa temple and the courtyard, Rāmacandra Khān sprinkled and smeared it with water mixed with cow dung, but still his mind was unsatisfied.

TEXT 159

দস্যুবৃত্তি করে রামচন্দ্র রাজারে না দেয় কর ।
ক্রুদ্ধ হঞা ম্লেচ্ছ উজির আইল তার ঘর ॥ ১৫৯ ॥

dasyu-vṛtti kare rāmacandra rājāre nā deya kara
kruddha hañā mleccha ujira āila tāra ghara

SYNONYMS

dasyu-vṛtti—the business of a thief; *kare*—does; *rāmacandra*—Rāmacandra; *rājāre*—to the government; *nā*—does not; *deya*—pay; *kara*—tax; *kruddha hañā*—being angry; *mleccha*—the Mohammedan; *ujira*—minister; *āila*—came; *tāra ghara*—to his house.

TRANSLATION

Rāmacandra Khān's business was questionable, for he tried to avoid paying income tax to the government. Therefore the government's minister of finance was angry and came to his residence.

TEXT 160

আসি' সেই দুর্গামণ্ডপে বাসা কৈল ।
অবধ্য বধ করি' মাংস সে-ঘরে রান্ধাইল ॥ ১৬০ ॥

āsi' sei durgā-maṇḍape vāsā kaila
avadhya vadha kari' māṁsa se-ghare rāndhāila

SYNONYMS

āsi'—coming; *sei durgā-maṇḍape*—at that very place of the Durgā-maṇḍapa; *vāsā kaila*—made his residence; *avadhya*—a cow or calf, which is not to be killed; *vadha kari'*—killing; *māṁsa*—meat; *se-ghare*—in that place; *rāndhāila*—cooked.

TRANSLATION

The Mohammedan minister made his residence in the Durgā-maṇḍapa of Rāmacandra Khān. He killed a cow and cooked the meat at that very place.

TEXT 161

স্ত্রী-পুত্র-সহিত রামচন্দ্রেরে বান্ধিয়া ।
তার ঘর-গ্রাম লুটে তিনদিন রহিয়া ॥ ১৬১ ॥

strī-putra-sahita rāmacandrere bāndhiyā
tāra ghara-grāma luṭe tina-dina rahiyā

SYNONYMS

strī-putra—his wife and children; *sahita*—with; *rāmacandrere bāndhiyā*—arresting Rāmacandra Khān; *tāra*—his; *ghara-grāma*—house and village; *luṭe*—plundered; *tina-dina rahiyā*—staying three days.

TRANSLATION

He arrested Rāmacandra Khān, along with his wife and sons, and then he continuously plundered the house and village for three days.

TEXT 162

সেই ঘরে তিন দিন করে অমেধ্য রন্ধন ।
আর দিন সবা লঞা করিলা গমন ॥ ১৬২ ॥

sei ghare tina dina kare amedhya randhana
āra dina sabā lañā karilā gamana

SYNONYMS

sei ghare—in that room; *tina dina*—for three days; *kare*—does; *amedhya randhana*—cooking the flesh of a cow; *āra dina*—the next day; *sabā lañā*—accompanied by his followers; *karilā gamana*—left.

TRANSLATION

In that very room he cooked the flesh of a cow for three consecutive days. Then the next day he left, accompanied by his followers.

TEXT 163

জাতি-ধন-জন খানের সকল লইল ।
বহুদিন পর্যন্ত গ্রাম উজাড় রহিল ॥ ১৬৩ ॥

jāti-dhana-jana khānera sakala la-ila
bahu-dina paryanta grāma ujāḍa rahila

SYNONYMS

jāti—birthright; *dhana*—riches; *jana*—followers; *khānera*—of Rāmacandra Khān; *sakala*—everything; *la-ila*—he took away; *bahu-dina*—a long time; *paryanta*—for; *grāma*—the village; *ujāḍa rahila*—remained deserted.

TRANSLATION

The Mohammedan minister took away Rāmacandra Khān's position, wealth and followers. For many days the village remained deserted.

TEXT 164

মহান্তের অপমান যে দেশ-গ্রামে হয় ।
এক জনার দোষে সব দেশ উজাড়য় ॥ ১৬৪ ॥

mahāntera apamāna ye deśa-grāme haya
eka janāra doṣe saba deśa ujāḍaya

SYNONYMS

mahāntera—of persons who are highly advanced in spiritual life; *apamāna*—disrespect; *ye deśa-grāme*—in which country or village; *haya*—is; *eka janāra*—of one man; *doṣe*—for the fault; *saba deśa*—the whole country; *ujāḍaya*—becomes afflicted.

TRANSLATION

Wherever an advanced devotee is insulted, for one man's fault the entire town or place is afflicted.

TEXT 165

হরিদাস-ঠাকুর চলি' আইলা চান্দপুরে ।
আসিয়া রহিলা বলরাম-আচার্যের ঘরে ॥ ১৬৫ ॥

haridāsa-ṭhākura cali' āilā cāndapure
āsiyā rahilā balarāma-ācāryera ghare

SYNONYMS

haridāsa-ṭhākura—Haridāsa Ṭhākura; *cali'*—walking; *āilā*—came; *cāndapure*—in the village known as Cāndapura; *āsiyā*—coming; *rahilā*—remained; *balarāma-ācāryera ghare*—at the residence of Balarāma Ācārya.

TRANSLATION

Haridāsa Ṭhākura walked until he came to the village known as Cāndapura. There he stayed at the house of Balarāma Ācārya.

PURPORT

The village of Cāndapura is situated near the confluence of the rivers Ganges and Yamunā at Saptagrāma in the district of Huglī. Cāndapura is just east of the house of the two brothers Hiraṇya and Govardhana, the father and uncle of Raghunātha dāsa Gosvāmī. In Cāndapura lived Balarāma Ācārya and Yadunandana Ācārya, the priests of these two personalities, and when Haridāsa Ṭhākura went there he lived with them. Śrīla Bhaktisiddhānta Sarasvatī Ṭhākura says that the name of this village was later changed to Kṛṣṇapura.

TEXT 166

হিরণ্য, গোবর্ধন—দুই মুলুকের মজুমদার ।
তার পুরোহিত—'বলরাম' নাম তাঁর ॥ ১৬৬ ॥

hiraṇya, govardhana——dui mulukera majumadāra
tāra purohita——'balarāma' nāma tāṅra

SYNONYMS

hiraṇya—Hiraṇya; *govardhana*—Govardhana; *dui*—two; *mulukera*—of that country; *majumadāra*—treasurers of the government; *tāra*—their; *purohita*—priest; *balarāma*—Balarāma; *nāma*—name; *tāṅra*—his.

TRANSLATION

Hiraṇya and Govardhana were the two governmental treasurers in that division of the country. Their priest was named Balarāma Ācārya.

PURPORT

The word *majumadāra* refers to a treasurer who keeps accounts of revenue.

TEXT 167

হরিদাসের কৃপাপাত্র, তাতে ভক্তিমানে ।
যত্ন করি' ঠাকুরেরে রাখিলা সেই গ্রামে ॥ ১৬৭ ॥

haridāsera kṛpā-pātra, tāte bhakti-māne
yatna kari' ṭhākurere rākhilā sei grāme

SYNONYMS

haridāsera kṛpā-pātra—favored by Haridāsa Ṭhākura; *tāte*—therefore; *bhakti-māne*—a great devotee of Haridāsa Ṭhākura; *yatna kari'*—with great care and attention; *ṭhākurere*—Haridāsa Ṭhākura; *rākhilā*—kept; *sei grāme*—in the village.

TRANSLATION

Balarāma Ācārya, being favored by Haridāsa Ṭhākura, was very attached to him. Therefore he kept Haridāsa Ṭhākura in the village with great care and attention.

TEXT 168

নির্জন পর্ণশালায় করেন কীর্তন ।
বলরাম-আচার্য-গৃহে ভিক্ষা-নির্বাহণ ॥ ১৬৮ ॥

nirjana parṇa-śālāya karena kīrtana
balarāma-ācārya-gṛhe bhikṣā-nirvāhaṇa

SYNONYMS

nirjana—solitary; *parṇa-śālāya*—in a thatched cottage; *karena*—performs; *kīrtana*—chanting of the Hare Kṛṣṇa *mantra*; *balarāma-ācārya-gṛhe*—at the house of Balarāma Ācārya; *bhikṣā-nirvāhaṇa*—accepting alms.

TRANSLATION

In the village, Haridāsa Ṭhākura was given a solitary thatched cottage, where he performed the chanting of the Hare Kṛṣṇa mahā-mantra. He accepted prasāda at the house of Balarāma Ācārya.

TEXT 169

রঘুনাথ-দাস বালক করেন অধ্যয়ন ।
হরিদাস-ঠাকুরেরে যাই' করেন দর্শন ॥ ১৬৯ ॥

raghunātha-dāsa bālaka karena adhyayana
haridāsa-ṭhākurere yāi' karena darśana

SYNONYMS

raghunātha-dāsa—Raghunātha dāsa; *bālaka*—a boy; *karena adhyayana*—was engaged in study; *haridāsa-ṭhākurere*—to Haridāsa Ṭhākura; *yāi'*—going; *karena darśana*—used to see.

TRANSLATION

Raghunātha dāsa, who was the son of Hiraṇya Majumadāra and was later to become Raghunātha dāsa Gosvāmī, was at that time a boy engaged in study. He came to see Haridāsa Ṭhākura daily.

TEXT 170

হরিদাস কৃপা করে তাঁহার উপরে ।
সেই কৃপা 'কারণ' হৈল চৈতন্য পাইবারে ॥ ১৭০ ॥

haridāsa kṛpā kare tāṅhāra upare
sei kṛpā 'kāraṇa' haila caitanya pāibāre

SYNONYMS

haridāsa—Ṭhākura Haridāsa; *kṛpā kare*—shows mercy; *tāṅhāra upare*—upon him; *sei kṛpā*—that mercy; *kāraṇa*—the cause; *haila*—became; *caitanya*—Śrī Caitanya Mahāprabhu; *pāibāre*—to attain.

TRANSLATION

Naturally Haridāsa Ṭhākura was merciful toward him, and because of the merciful benediction of this Vaiṣṇava, he later attained the shelter of Śrī Caitanya Mahāprabhu's lotus feet.

TEXT 171

তাহাঁ যৈছে হৈল হরিদাসের মহিমা কথন ।
ব্যাখ্যান,—অদ্ভুত কথা শুন, ভক্তগণ ॥ ১৭১ ॥

tāhāṅ yaiche haila haridāsera mahimā kathana
vyākhyāna,——adbhuta kathā śuna, bhakta-gaṇa

SYNONYMS

tāhāṅ—at that place; *yaiche*—just as; *haila*—there was; *haridāsera*—of Haridāsa Ṭhākura; *mahimā*—glories; *kathana*—discussion; *vyākhyāna*—discourse; *adbhuta*—wonderful; *kathā*—incident; *śuna*—hear; *bhakta-gaṇa*—O devotees.

TRANSLATION

At the residence of Hiraṇya and Govardhana, discourses took place by which Haridāsa Ṭhākura was glorified. O devotees, please listen to that wonderful story.

TEXT 172

একদিন বলরাম মিনতি করিয়া ।
মজুমদারের সভায় আইলা ঠাকুরে লঞা ॥ ১৭২ ॥

eka-dina balarāma minati kariyā
majumadārera sabhāya āilā ṭhākure lañā

SYNONYMS

eka-dina—one day; *balarāma*—Balarāma Ācārya; *minati kariyā*—in great humility; *majumadārera*—of the Majumadāras, Hiraṇya and Govardhana; *sabhāya*—at the assembly; *āilā*—came; *ṭhākure*—Haridāsa Ṭhākura; *lañā*—taking with him.

TRANSLATION

One day Balarāma Ācārya requested Haridāsa Ṭhākura with great humility to come to the assembly of the Majumadāras, Hiraṇya and Govardhana. Thus Balarāma Ācārya went there with Haridāsa Ṭhākura.

TEXT 173

ঠাকুর দেখি' দুই ভাই কৈলা অভ্যুত্থান ।
পায় পড়ি' আসন দিলা করিয়া সম্মান ॥ ১৭৩ ॥

ṭhākura dekhi' dui bhāi kailā abhyutthāna
pāya paḍi' āsana dilā kariyā sammāna

SYNONYMS

ṭhākura dekhi'—seeing Haridāsa Ṭhākura; *dui bhāi*—the two brothers; *kailā abhyutthāna*—stood up; *pāya paḍi'*—falling at the lotus feet; *āsana dilā*—offered a sitting place; *kariyā sammāna*—with great respect.

TRANSLATION

Seeing Haridāsa Ṭhākura, the two brothers immediately stood up and fell at his lotus feet. Then with great respect they offered him a place to sit.

TEXT 174

অনেক পণ্ডিত সভায়, ব্রাহ্মণ, সজ্জন।
দুই ভাই মহাপণ্ডিত—হিরণ্য, গোবর্ধন ॥ ১৭৪ ॥

aneka paṇḍita sabhāya, brāhmaṇa, sajjana
dui bhāi mahā-paṇḍita——hiraṇya, govardhana

SYNONYMS

aneka paṇḍita—many learned scholars; *sabhāya*—in that assembly; *brāhmaṇa*—*brāhmaṇas*; *sat-jana*—respectable gentlemen; *dui bhāi*—the two brothers; *mahā-paṇḍita*—very learned scholars; *hiraṇya*—Hiraṇya; *govardhana*—Govardhana.

TRANSLATION

In that assembly were many learned scholars, brāhmaṇas and respectable gentlemen. The two brothers Hiraṇya and Govardhana were also greatly learned.

TEXT 175

হরিদাসের গুণ সবে কহে পঞ্চমুখে।
শুনিয়া ত' দুই ভাই পাইলা বড় সুখে ॥ ১৭৫ ॥

haridāsera guṇa sabe kahe pañca-mukhe
śuniyā ta' dui bhāi pāilā baḍa sukhe

SYNONYMS

haridāsera—of Haridāsa Ṭhākura; *guṇa*—the qualities; *sabe*—all of them; *kahe*—began to speak; *pañca-mukhe*—as if speaking with five mouths; *śuniyā*—hearing; *ta'*—certainly; *dui bhāi*—the two brothers; *pāilā*—got; *baḍa sukhe*—very great happiness.

TRANSLATION

Everyone there began to speak of Haridāsa Ṭhākura's great qualities as if they had five mouths. Hearing this, both brothers were extremely happy.

TEXT 176

তিন-লক্ষ নাম ঠাকুর করেন কীর্তন ।
নামের মহিমা উঠাইল পণ্ডিতগণ ॥ ১৭৬ ॥

tina-lakṣa nāma ṭhākura karena kīrtana
nāmera mahimā uṭhāila paṇḍita-gaṇa

SYNONYMS

tina-lakṣa—300,000; *nāma*—holy names of the Lord; *ṭhākura*—Haridāsa Ṭhākura; *karena kīrtana*—used to chant; *nāmera*—of the holy name; *mahimā*—glories; *uṭhāila*—raised; *paṇḍita-gaṇa*—all the learned scholars.

TRANSLATION

It was mentioned in the assembly that Haridāsa Ṭhākura chanted the holy names of Kṛṣṇa 300,000 times a day. Thus all the learned scholars began to discuss the glories of the holy name.

TEXT 177

কেহ বলে,—'নাম হৈতে হয় পাপক্ষয়' ।
কেহ বলে,—'নাম হৈতে জীবের মোক্ষ হয় ॥' ১৭৭ ॥

keha bale, —'nāma haite haya pāpa-kṣaya'
keha bale, —'nāma haite jīvera mokṣa haya'

SYNONYMS

keha bale—some of them said; *nāma haite*—by chanting the Hare Kṛṣṇa *mantra; haya*—there is; *pāpa-kṣaya*—disappearance of all reactions to sinful activities; *keha bale*—some of them said; *nāma haite*—by chanting the holy name; *jīvera*—of the living entities; *mokṣa haya*—there is liberation.

TRANSLATION

Some of them said, "By chanting the holy name of the Lord, one is freed from the reactions of all sinful life." Others said, "Simply by chanting the holy name of the Lord, a living being is liberated from material bondage."

TEXT 178

হরিদাস কহেন,—"নামের এই দুই ফল নয় ।
নামের ফলে কৃষ্ণপদে প্রেম উপজয় ॥ ১৭৮ ॥

haridāsa kahena, —"nāmera ei dui phala naya
nāmera phale kṛṣṇa-pade prema upajaya

SYNONYMS

haridāsa kahena—Haridāsa Ṭhākura replied; *nāmera*—of chanting the holy name of the Lord; *ei*—these; *dui*—two; *phala*—results; *naya*—are not; *nāmera phale*—by the result of chanting the holy name; *kṛṣṇa-pade*—at the lotus feet of Kṛṣṇa; *prema upajaya*—awakening of ecstatic love.

TRANSLATION

Haridāsa Ṭhākura protested, "These two benedictions are not the true result of chanting the holy name. By actually chanting the holy name without offenses, one awakens his ecstatic love for the lotus feet of Kṛṣṇa.

TEXT 179

এবংব্রতঃ স্বপ্রিয়নামকীর্ত্যা
জাতানুরাগো দ্রুতচিত্ত উচ্চৈঃ ।
হসত্যথো রোদিতি রৌতি গায়-
ত্যুন্মাদবন্নৃত্যতি লোকবাহ্যঃ ॥ ১৭৯ ॥

evaṁ-vrataḥ sva-priya-nāma-kīrtyā
jātānurāgo druta-citta uccaiḥ
hasaty atho roditi rauti gāyaty
unmādavan nṛtyati loka-bāhyaḥ

SYNONYMS

evaṃ-vrataḥ—when one thus engages in the vow to chant and dance; *sva*—own; *priya*—very dear; *nāma*—holy name; *kīrtyā*—by chanting; *jāta*—in this way develops; *anurāgaḥ*—attachment; *druta-cittaḥ*—very eagerly; *uccaiḥ*—loudly; *hasati*—laughs; *atho*—also; *roditi*—cries; *rauti*—becomes agitated; *gāyati*—chants; *unmāda-vat*—like a madman; *nṛtyati*—dances; *loka-bāhyaḥ*—not caring for outsiders.

TRANSLATION

" 'When a person is actually advanced and takes pleasure in chanting the holy name of the Lord, who is very dear to him, he is agitated and loudly chants the holy name. He also laughs, cries, becomes agitated and chants just like a madman, not caring for outsiders.'

PURPORT

For an explanation of this verse (*Bhāg.* 11.2.40) one may consult Chapter Seven, text 94, of the *Ādi-līlā.*

TEXT 180

আনুষঙ্গিক ফল নামের –'মুক্তি', 'পাপনাশ' ।
তাহার দৃষ্টান্ত যৈছে সূর্যের প্রকাশ ॥ ১৮০ ॥

ānuṣaṅgika phala nāmera——'mukti', 'pāpa-nāśa'
tāhāra dṛṣṭānta yaiche sūryera prakāśa

SYNONYMS

ānuṣaṅgika—concomitant; *phala*—result; *nāmera*—of the holy name; *mukti*—liberation; *pāpa-nāśa*—extinction of the resultant actions of sinful life; *tāhāra*—of that; *dṛṣṭānta*—example; *yaiche*—as; *sūryera prakāśa*—light of the sun.

TRANSLATION

"Liberation and extinction of the reactions of sinful life are two concomitant by-products of chanting the holy name of the Lord. An example is found in the gleams of morning sunlight.

TEXT 181

অংহঃ সংহরদখিলং সকৃদুদয়াদেব সকল-লোকস্য ।
তরণিরিব তিমিরজলধিং জয়তি জগন্মঙ্গলং হরের্নাম ॥১৮১॥

aṁhaḥ saṁharad akhilaṁ sakṛd
udayād eva sakala-lokasya
taraṇir iva timira-jaladhiṁ
jayati jagan-maṅgalaṁ harer nāma

SYNONYMS

aṁhaḥ—the resultant action of sinful life, which causes material bondage; *saṁharat*—completely eradicating; *akhilam*—all; *sakṛt*—once only; *udayāt*—by rising; *eva*—certainly; *sakala*—all; *lokasya*—of the people of the world; *taraṇiḥ*—the sun; *iva*—like; *timira*—of darkness; *jala-dhim*—the ocean; *jayati*—all glories to; *jagat-maṅgalam*—auspicious for the whole world; *hareḥ nāma*—the holy name of the Lord.

TRANSLATION

" 'As the rising sun immediately dissipates all the world's darkness, which is deep like an ocean, so the holy name of the Lord, if chanted once without offenses, can dissipate all the reactions of a living being's sinful life. All glories to that holy name of the Lord, which is auspicious for the entire world.' "

PURPORT

This verse is found in the *Padyāvalī* (16).

TEXT 182

এই শ্লোকের অর্থ কর পণ্ডিতের গণ ।"
সবে কহে,—'তুমি কহ অর্থ-বিবরণ' ॥ ১৮২ ॥

ei ślokera artha kara paṇḍitera gaṇa"
sabe kahe, ——'tumi kaha artha-vivaraṇa'

SYNONYMS

ei ślokera—of this verse; *artha*—meaning; *kara*—explain; *paṇḍitera gaṇa*—O groups of learned scholars; *sabe kahe*—everyone said; *tumi kaha*—you speak; *artha-vivaraṇa*—the meaning and explanation.

TRANSLATION

After reciting this verse, Haridāsa Ṭhākura said, "O learned scholars, please explain the meaning of this verse." But the audience requested Haridāsa Ṭhākura, "It is better for you to explain the meaning of this important verse."

TEXT 183

হরিদাস কহেন,—"যৈছে সূর্যের উদয় ।
উদয় না হৈতে আরম্ভে তমের হয় ক্ষয় ॥ ১৮৩ ॥

haridāsa kahena, ——"yaiche sūryera udaya
udaya nā haite ārambhe tamera haya kṣaya

SYNONYMS

haridāsa kahena—Haridāsa Ṭhākura began to explain; *yaiche*—like; *sūryera udaya*—sunrise; *udaya nā haite*—although not visible; *ārambhe*—from the beginning; *tamera*—of darkness; *haya kṣaya*—there is dissipation.

TRANSLATION

Haridāsa Ṭhākura said, "As the sun begins to rise, even before visible it dissipates the darkness of night.

TEXT 184

চৌর-প্রেত-রাক্ষসাদির ভয় হয় নাশ।
উদয় হৈলে ধর্ম-কর্ম-আদি পরকাশ ॥ ১৮৪ ॥

caura-preta-rākṣasādira bhaya haya nāśa
udaya haile dharma-karma-ādi parakāśa

SYNONYMS

caura—thieves; *preta*—ghosts; *rākṣasa*—demons; *ādira*—of them and others; *bhaya*—fear; *haya*—becomes; *nāśa*—destroyed; *udaya haile*—when the sunrise is actually visible; *dharma-karma*—all religious activities and regulative principles; *ādi*—everything; *parakāśa*—becomes manifest.

TRANSLATION

"With the first glimpse of sunlight, fear of thieves, ghosts and demons immediately disappears, and when the sun is actually visible, everything is manifest, and everyone begins performing his religious activities and regulative duties.

TEXT 185

ঐছে নামোদয়ারম্ভে পাপ-আদির ক্ষয়।
উদয় কৈলে কৃষ্ণপদে হয় প্রেমোদয় ॥ ১৮৫ ॥

aiche nāmodayārambhe pāpa-ādira kṣaya
udaya kaile kṛṣṇa-pade haya premodaya

SYNONYMS

aiche—similarly; *nāma-udaya*—of the appearance of the holy name; *ārambhe*—by the beginning; *pāpa*—reactions of sinful activities; *ādira*—of them and others; *kṣaya*—dissipation; *udaya kaile*—when there is actually awakening of offenseless chanting; *kṛṣṇa-pade*—at the lotus feet of Kṛṣṇa; *haya prema-udaya*—there is awakening of ecstatic love.

TRANSLATION

"Similarly, the first hint that offenseless chanting of the Lord's holy name has awakened dissipates the reactions of sinful life immediately. And when

one chants the holy name offenselessly, one awakens to service in ecstatic love at the lotus feet of Kṛṣṇa.

TEXT 186

'মুক্তি' তুচ্ছ-ফল হয় নামাভাস হৈতে ॥ ১৮৬ ॥

'mukti' tuccha-phala haya nāmābhāsa haite

SYNONYMS

mukti—liberation; *tuccha-phala*—insignificant result; *haya*—is; *nāma-ābhāsa haite*—from a glimpse of awakening of offenseless chanting of the holy name.

TRANSLATION

"Liberation is the insignificant result derived from a glimpse of awakening of offenseless chanting of the holy name.

TEXT 187

ম্রিয়মাণো হরের্নাম গৃণন্ পুত্রোপচারিতম্ ।
অজামিলোঽপ্যগাদ্ধাম কিমুত শ্রদ্ধয়া গৃণন্ ॥ ১৮৭ ॥

mriyamāṇo harer nāma
gṛṇan putropacāritam
ajāmilo 'py agād dhāma
kim uta śraddhayā gṛṇan

SYNONYMS

mriyamāṇaḥ—dying; *hareḥ nāma*—the holy name of the Supreme Lord; *gṛṇan*—chanting; *putra-upacāritam*—though spoken for his son; *ajāmilaḥ*—Ajāmila; *api*—also; *agāt*—attained; *dhāma*—the spiritual world; *kim uta*—what to speak of; *śraddhayā*—with faith and reverence; *gṛṇan*—chanting.

TRANSLATION

" 'While dying, Ajāmila chanted the holy name of the Lord, intending to call his son Nārāyaṇa. Nevertheless, he attained the spiritual world. What then to speak of those who chant the holy name with faith and reverence?'

PURPORT

This is a verse from *Śrīmad-Bhāgavatam* (6.2.49).

TEXT 188

যে মুক্তি ভক্ত না লয়, সে কৃষ্ণ চাহে দিতে ॥"১৮৮ ॥

ye mukti bhakta nā laya, se kṛṣṇa cāhe dite"

SYNONYMS

ye—which; *mukti*—liberation; *bhakta*—a devotee; *nā laya*—does not take; *se*—that; *kṛṣṇa*—Lord Kṛṣṇa; *cāhe dite*—wants to offer.

TRANSLATION

"Liberation, which is unacceptable for a pure devotee, is always offered by Kṛṣṇa without difficulty.

TEXT 189

সালোক্য-সার্ষ্টি-সারূপ্য-সামীপ্যৈকত্বমপ্যুত ।
দীয়মানং ন গৃহ্ণন্তি বিনা মৎসেবনং জনাঃ ॥ ১৮৯ ॥

sālokya-sārṣṭi-sārūpya-
sāmīpyaikatvam apy uta
dīyamānaṁ na gṛhṇanti
vinā mat-sevanaṁ janāḥ

SYNONYMS

sālokya—to live on the same planet; *sārṣṭi*—to acquire the same opulence; *sārūpya*—to achieve the same bodily features; *sāmīpya*—to live always near the Supreme Lord; *ekatvam*—to merge into the existence of the Lord; *api*—even; *uta*—certainly; *dīyamānam*—being offered; *na gṛhṇanti*—do not take; *vinā*—without; *mat-sevanam*—My service; *janāḥ*—the devotees.

TRANSLATION

" 'My devotees do not accept sālokya, sārṣṭi, sārūpya, sāmīpya, or oneness with Me—even if I offer these liberations—in preference to serving Me.' "

PURPORT

This verse is spoken by Lord Kapila, an *avatāra* of the Supreme Personality of Godhead, in *Śrīmad-Bhāgavatam* (3.29.13).

TEXT 190

'গোপাল চক্রবর্ত্তী' নাম একজন ।
মজুমদারের ঘরে সেই আরিন্দা প্রধান ॥ ১৯০ ॥

'gopāla cakravartī' nāma eka-jana
majumadārera ghare sei ārindā pradhāna

SYNONYMS

gopāla cakravartī—Gopāla Cakravartī; *nāma*—named; *eka-jana*—one person; *majumadārera ghare*—at the residence of Hiraṇya and Govardhana Majumadāra; *sei*—he; *ārindā pradhāna*—the chief tax collector.

TRANSLATION

At the house of Hiraṇya and Govardhana Majumadāra, a person named Gopāla Cakravartī was officially the chief tax collector.

TEXT 191

গৌড়ে রহি' পাৎসাহা-আগে আরিন্দাগিরি করে ।
বার-লক্ষ মুদ্রা সেই পাৎসার ঠাঞি ভরে ॥ ১৯১ ॥

gauḍe rahi' pātsāhā-āge ārindā-giri kare
bāra-lakṣa mudrā sei pātsāra ṭhāñi bhare

SYNONYMS

gauḍe rahi'—living in Bengal; *pātsāhā-āge*—on behalf of the emperor; *ārindā-giri kare*—acts as the chief tax collector; *bāra-lakṣa*—twelve hundred thousand; *mudrā*—coins; *sei*—he; *pātsāra ṭhāñi*—for the emperor; *bhare*—collects.

TRANSLATION

This Gopāla Cakravartī lived in Bengal. His duty as chief tax collector was to collect 1,200,000 coins to deposit in the treasury of the emperor.

TEXT 192

পরম-সুন্দর, পণ্ডিত, নূতন-যৌবন ।
নামাভাসে 'মুক্তি' শুনি' না হইল সহন ॥ ১৯২ ॥

parama-sundara, paṇḍita, nūtana-yauvana
nāmābhāse 'mukti' śuni' nā ha-ila sahana

SYNONYMS

parama-sundara—very beautiful; *paṇḍita*—learned; *nūtana*—new; *yauvana*—youth; *nāma-ābhāse*—by the glimpse of awakening of pure chanting of the holy name; *mukti*—liberation; *śuni'*—hearing; *nā ha-ila sahana*—could not tolerate.

TRANSLATION

He had handsome bodily features, and he was learned and youthful, but he could not tolerate the statement that simply by glimpsing the awakening of the Lord's holy name one can attain liberation.

PURPORT

Vaiṣṇavas strictly follow the directions of the *śāstras* regarding how one can be liberated simply by a slight awakening of pure chanting of the holy name. Māyāvādīs cannot tolerate the statements of the *śāstras* about how easily liberation can be achieved, for as stated in *Bhagavad-gītā* (12.5), *kleśo 'dhikaratas teṣām avyaktāsakta-cetasām:* impersonalists must work hard for many, many births, and only then will they perhaps be liberated. Vaiṣṇavas know that simply by chanting the holy name of the Lord offenselessly, one achieves liberation as a by-product. Thus there is no need to endeavor separately for liberation. Śrīla Bilvamaṅgala Ṭhākura has said, *muktiḥ svayaṁ mukulitāñjali sevate 'smān:* liberation stands at one's door, ready to render any kind of service, if one is a pure devotee with unflinching faith and reverence. This the Māyāvādīs cannot tolerate. Therefore the *ārindā pradhāna,* chief tax collector, although very learned, handsome and youthful, could not tolerate the statements of Haridāsa Ṭhākura.

TEXT 193

ক্রুদ্ধ হঞা বলে সেই সরোষ বচন ।
"ভাবুকের সিদ্ধান্ত শুন, পণ্ডিতের গণ ॥ ১৯৩ ॥

kruddha hañā bale sei saroṣa vacana
"bhāvukera siddhānta śuna, paṇḍitera gaṇa

SYNONYMS

kruddha hañā—becoming very angry; *bale*—said; *sei*—he; *sa-roṣa vacana*—angry words; *bhāvukera*—of an emotional person; *siddhānta*—conclusion; *śuna*—just hear; *paṇḍitera gaṇa*—O assembly of learned scholars.

TRANSLATION

This young man, Gopāla Cakravartī, became very angry upon hearing the statements of Haridāsa Ṭhākura. He immediately criticized him. "O assembly of learned scholars," he said, "just hear the conclusion of the emotional devotee.

TEXT 194

কোটি-জন্মে ব্রহ্মজ্ঞানে যেই 'মুক্তি' নয় ।
এই কহে,—নামাভাসে সেই 'মুক্তি' হয় ॥"১৯৪ ॥

koṭi-janme brahma-jñāne yei 'mukti' naya
ei kahe, ——nāmābhāse sei 'mukti' haya"

SYNONYMS

koṭi-janme—after millions upon millions of births; *brahma-jñāne*—by absolute knowledge; *yei*—which; *mukti naya*—liberation is not possible; *ei*—this person; *kahe*—says; *nāma-ābhāse*—simply by the awakening of a glimpse of the pure chanting of the holy name; *sei*—that; *mukti*—liberation; *haya*—becomes possible.

TRANSLATION

"After many millions upon millions of births, when one is complete in absolute knowledge, one still may not attain liberation, yet this man says that one may attain it simply by the awakening of a glimpse of the holy name."

TEXT 195

হরিদাস কহেন,— কেনে করহ সংশয় ?
শাস্ত্রে কহে,—নামাভাস-মাত্রে 'মুক্তি' হয় ॥ ১৯৫ ॥

haridāsa kahena, ——kene karaha saṁśaya?
śāstre kahe, ——nāmābhāsa-mātre 'mukti' haya

SYNONYMS

haridāsa kahena—Haridāsa Ṭhākura said; *kene*—why; *karaha saṁśaya*—are you doubtful; *śāstre kahe*—it is stated in the revealed scriptures; *nāma-ābhāsa-mātre*—simply by a glimpse of the chanting of the holy name; *mukti haya*—there is liberation.

TRANSLATION

Haridāsa Ṭhākura said, "Why are you doubtful? The revealed scriptures say that one can attain liberation simply by a glimpse of offenseless chanting of the holy name.

TEXT 196

ভক্তিসুখ-আগে 'মুক্তি' অতি-তুচ্ছ হয় ।
অতএব ভক্তগণ 'মুক্তি' নাহি লয় ॥ ১৯৬ ॥

bhakti-sukha-āge 'mukti' ati-tuccha haya
ataeva bhakta-gaṇa 'mukti' nāhi laya

SYNONYMS

bhakti-sukha—transcendental bliss derived from devotional service; *āge*—before; *mukti*—liberation; *ati-tuccha*—extremely insignificant; *haya*—is; *ataeva*—therefore; *bhakta-gaṇa*—pure devotees; *mukti*—liberation; *nāhi laya*—do not accept.

TRANSLATION

"For a devotee who enjoys the transcendental bliss of devotional service, liberation is most insignificant. Therefore pure devotees never desire to achieve liberation.

TEXT 197

ত্বৎসাক্ষাৎকরণাহ্লাদবিশুদ্ধাব্ধিস্থিতস্য মে।
সুখানি গোষ্পদায়ন্তে ব্রাহ্মাণ্যপি জগদ্গুরো ॥ ১৯৭ ॥

tvat-sākṣātkaraṇāhlāda-
viśuddhābdhi-sthitasya me
sukhāni goṣpadāyante
brāhmāṇy api jagad-guro

SYNONYMS

tvat—You; *sākṣāt-karaṇa*—by meeting; *āhlāda*—of pleasure; *viśuddha*—spiritually purified; *abdhi*—in an ocean; *sthitasya*—situated; *me*—of me; *sukhāni*—happiness; *goṣpadāyante*—is like a calf's hoofprint; *brāhmāṇi*—derived from understanding of impersonal Brahman; *api*—also; *jagat-guro*—O master of the universe.

TRANSLATION

" 'My dear Lord, O master of the universe, since I have directly seen You, my transcendental bliss has taken the shape of a great ocean. Being situated in that ocean, I now realize all other so-called happiness, including even brahmānanda, to be like the water contained in the hoofprint of a calf.' "

PURPORT

This verse is quoted from the *Hari-bhakti-sudhodaya* (14.36).

TEXT 198

বিপ্র কহে,—"নামাভাসে যদি 'মুক্তি' নয়।
তবে তোমার নাক কাটি' করহ নিশ্চয় ॥" ১৯৮ ॥

vipra kahe, —"nāmābhāse yadi 'mukti' naya
tabe tomāra nāka kāṭi' karaha niścaya"

SYNONYMS

vipra kahe—the *brāhmaṇa* said; *nāma-ābhāse*—simply by the awakening of offenseless chanting of the holy name; *yadi*—if; *mukti naya*—liberation is not attainable; *tabe*—then; *tomāra*—your; *nāka*—nose; *kāṭi'*—I shall cut off; *karaha niścaya*—take it as certain.

TRANSLATION

Gopāla Cakravartī said, "If one is not liberated by nāmābhāsa, then you may be certain that I shall cut off your nose."

TEXT 199

হরিদাস কহেন,—"যদি নামাভাসে 'মুক্তি' নয়।
তবে আমার নাক কাটিমু,—এই সুনিশ্চয়॥"১৯৯॥

haridāsa kahena, ——"yadi nāmābhāse 'mukti' naya
tabe āmāra nāka kāṭimu, ——ei suniścaya"

SYNONYMS

haridāsa kahena—Haridāsa Ṭhākura said; *yadi*—if; *nāma-ābhāse*—simply by the awakening of the holy name of the Lord; *mukti naya*—*mukti* is not available; *tabe*—then; *āmāra*—my; *nāka*—nose; *kāṭimu*—I shall cut off; *ei*—this; *suniścaya*—certain.

TRANSLATION

Then Haridāsa Ṭhākura accepted the challenge offered by Gopāla Cakravartī. "If by nāmābhāsa liberation is not available," he said, "certainly I shall cut off my nose."

TEXT 200

শুনি' সভাসদ্ উঠে করি' হাহাকার।
মজুমদার সেই বিপ্রে করিল ধিক্কার॥ ২০০ ॥

śuni' sabhā-sad uṭhe kari' hāhākāra
majumadāra sei vipre karila dhikkāra

SYNONYMS

śuni'—hearing; *sabhā-sat*—all the members of the assembly; *uṭhe*—got up; *kari' hāhā-kāra*—making a tumultuous sound; *majumadāra*—Hiraṇya and Govardhana Majumadāra; *sei vipre*—unto that *brāhmaṇa* who was their servant; *karila*—made; *dhik-kāra*—chastisement.

TRANSLATION

All the members of the assembly who had heard the challenge were greatly agitated, and they got up, making a tumultuous sound. Hiraṇya and Govardhana Majumadāra both immediately chastised the brāhmaṇa tax collector.

TEXT 201

বলাই-পুরোহিত তারে করিলা ভর্ৎসন ।
"ঘট-পটিয়া মূর্খ তুঞি ভক্তি কাঁহা জান ? ২০১ ॥

balāi-purohita tāre karilā bhartsana
"ghaṭa-paṭiyā mūrkha tuñi bhakti kāṅhā jāna?

SYNONYMS

balāi-purohita—the priest named Balarāma Ācārya; *tāre*—unto Gopāla Cakravartī; *karilā*—did; *bhartsana*—chastisement; *ghaṭa-paṭiyā*—interested in the pot and the earth; *mūrkha*—fool; *tuñi*—you; *bhakti*—devotional service; *kāṅhā*—what; *jāna*—do know.

TRANSLATION

The priest named Balarāma Ācārya chastised Gopāla Cakravartī. "You are a foolish logician," he said. "What do you know about the devotional service of the Lord?

PURPORT

The philosophy enunciated by the Māyāvādīs is called *ghaṭa-paṭiyā* philosophy. According to this philosophy, everything is one, everything is earth, and therefore anything made of earth, such as different pots, is also the same earth. Such philosophers see no distinction between a pot made of earth and the earth itself. Since Gopāla Cakravartī was a *ghaṭa-paṭiyā* logician, a gross materialist, what could he understand about the transcendental devotional service of the Lord?

TEXT 202

হরিদাস-ঠাকুরে তুঞি কৈলি অপমান !
সর্বনাশ হবে তোর, না হবে কল্যাণ ॥"২০২ ॥

haridāsa-ṭhākure tuñi kaili apamāna!
sarva-nāśa habe tora, nā habe kalyāṇa"

SYNONYMS

haridāsa-ṭhākure—unto Haridāsa Ṭhākura; *tuñi*—you; *kaili*—did; *apamāna*—insult; *sarva-nāśa*—destruction of everything; *habe*—there will be; *tora*—your; *nā*—not; *habe*—will be; *kalyāṇa*—auspicious result.

TRANSLATION

"You have insulted Haridāsa Ṭhākura. Thus there will be a dangerous position for you. You should not expect anything auspicious."

TEXT 203

শুনি' হরিদাস তবে উঠিয়া চলিলা ।
মজুমদার সেই বিপ্রে ত্যাগ করিলা ॥ ২০৩ ॥

śuni' haridāsa tabe uṭhiyā calilā
majumadāra sei vipre tyāga karilā

SYNONYMS

śuni'—hearing; *haridāsa*—Haridāsa Ṭhākura; *tabe*—then; *uṭhiyā calilā*—got up and began to go away; *majumadāra*—Hiraṇya and Govardhana Majumadāra; *sei vipre*—this *brāhmaṇa*; *tyāga karilā*—kicked out.

TRANSLATION

Then Haridāsa Ṭhākura got up to leave, and the Majumadāras, the masters of Gopāla Cakravartī, immediately dismissed Gopāla Cakravartī from their service.

TEXT 204

সভা-সহিতে হরিদাসের পড়িলা চরণে ।
হরিদাস হাসি' কহে মধুর-বচনে ॥ ২০৪ ॥

sabhā-sahite haridāsera paḍilā caraṇe
haridāsa hāsi' kahe madhura-vacane

SYNONYMS

sabhā-sahite—with all the members of the assembly; *haridāsera*—of Haridāsa Ṭhākura; *paḍilā caraṇe*—fell down at the lotus feet; *haridāsa*—Haridāsa Ṭhākura; *hāsi'*—smiling; *kahe*—said; *madhura-vacane*—in a sweet voice.

TRANSLATION

With all the members of the assembly, the two Majumadāras fell at the lotus feet of Haridāsa Ṭhākura. Haridāsa Ṭhākura was smiling, however, and he spoke in a sweet voice.

TEXT 205

"তোমা-সবার দোষ নাহি, এই অজ্ঞ ব্রাহ্মণ ।
তার দোষ নাহি, তার তর্কনিষ্ঠ মন ॥ ২০৫ ॥

"tomā-sabāra doṣa nāhi, ei ajña brāhmaṇa
tāra doṣa nāhi, tāra tarka-niṣṭha mana

SYNONYMS

tomā-sabāra—of all of you; *doṣa*—fault; *nāhi*—there is not; *ei*—this; *ajña*—ignorant; *brāhmaṇa*—so-called *brāhmaṇa*; *tāra doṣa nāhi*—he is also not at fault; *tāra*—his; *tarka-niṣṭha*—accustomed to speculation; *mana*—mind.

TRANSLATION

"None of you are at fault," he said. "Indeed, even this ignorant so-called brāhmaṇa is not at fault, for he is accustomed to dry speculation and logic.

TEXT 206

তর্কের গোচর নহে নামের মহত্ত্ব ।
কোথা হৈতে জানিবে সে এই সব তত্ত্ব ? ২০৬ ॥

tarkera gocara nahe nāmera mahattva
kothā haite jānibe se ei saba tattva?

SYNONYMS

tarkera—by argument and logic; *gocara*—appreciable; *nahe*—is not; *nāmera*—of the holy name; *mahattva*—the glory; *kothā haite*—from where; *jānibe*—will know; *se*—he; *ei*—this; *saba*—all; *tattva*—truth.

TRANSLATION

"One cannot understand the glories of the holy name simply by logic and argument. Therefore this man cannot possibly understand the glories of the holy name.

TEXT 207

যাহ ঘর, কৃষ্ণ করুন কুশল সবার।
আমার সম্বন্ধে দুঃখ না হউক কাহার॥" ২০৭ ॥

yāha ghara, kṛṣṇa karuna kuśala sabāra
āmāra sambandhe duḥkha nā ha-uka kāhāra"

SYNONYMS

yāha ghara—go to your homes; *kṛṣṇa karuna*—may Lord Kṛṣṇa bestow; *kuśala sabāra*—blessings to everyone; *āmāra sambandhe*—on my account; *duḥkha*—unhappiness; *nā ha-uka*—may there not be; *kāhāra*—of anyone.

TRANSLATION

"All of you may now go to your homes. May Lord Kṛṣṇa bestow his blessings upon you all. Do not be sorry because of my being insulted."

PURPORT

From this statement by Haridāsa Ṭhākura, it is understood that a pure Vaiṣṇava never takes anyone's insults seriously. This is the teaching of Śrī Caitanya Mahāprabhu:

tṛṇād api sunīcena
taror api sahiṣṇunā
amāninā mānadena
kīrtanīyaḥ sadā hariḥ

"One should chant the holy name of the Lord in a humble state of mind, thinking oneself lower than the straw in the street. One should be more tolerant than a tree, devoid of all sense of false prestige and ready to offer all respects to others. In such a state of mind one can chant the holy name of the Lord constantly." A Vaiṣṇava is always tolerant and submissive like trees and grass. He tolerates insults offered by others, for he is simply interested in chanting the holy name of the Lord without being disturbed.

TEXT 208

তবে সে হিরণ্যদাস নিজ ঘরে আইল।
সেই ব্রাহ্মণে নিজ দ্বার-মানা কৈল॥ ২০৮ ॥

tabe se hiraṇya-dāsa nija ghare āila
sei brāhmaṇe nija dvāra-mānā kaila

SYNONYMS

tabe—thereupon; *se*—that; *hiraṇya-dāsa*—Hiraṇya Majumadāra; *nija*—own; *ghare*—to home; *āila*—returned; *sei*—that; *brāhmaṇe*—to Gopāla Cakravartī; *nija*—own; *dvāra*—door; *mānā*—prohibition; *kaila*—issued.

TRANSLATION

Then Hiraṇya dāsa Majumadāra returned to his home and ordered that Gopāla Cakravartī not be admitted therein.

TEXT 209

তিন দিন ভিতরে সেই বিপ্রের 'কুষ্ঠ' হৈল ।
অতি উচ্চ নাসা তার গলিয়া পড়িল ॥ ২০৯ ॥

tina dina bhitare sei viprera 'kuṣṭha' haila
ati ucca nāsā tāra galiyā paḍila

SYNONYMS

tina dina—three days; *bhitare*—within; *sei*—that; *viprera*—of the *brāhmaṇa*; *kuṣṭha*—leprosy; *haila*—appeared; *ati*—very; *ucca*—raised; *nāsā*—nose; *tāra*—his; *galiyā*—melting; *paḍila*—fell.

TRANSLATION

Within three days that brāhmaṇa was attacked by leprosy, and as a result his highly raised nose melted away and fell off.

TEXT 210

চম্পক-কলি-সম হস্ত-পদাঙ্গুলি ।
কোঁকড় হইল সব, কুষ্ঠে গেল গলি' ॥ ২১০ ॥

campaka-kali-sama hasta-padāṅguli
koṅkaḍa ha-ila saba, kuṣṭhe gela gali'

SYNONYMS

campaka—of a golden-hued flower; *kali*—buds; *sama*—like; *hasta-pada-aṅguli*—fingers and toes; *koṅkaḍa ha-ila*—became crumpled; *saba*—all; *kuṣṭhe*—because of leprosy; *gela gali'*—melted away.

TRANSLATION

The brāhmaṇa's toes and fingers were beautiful like golden-colored campaka buds, but because of leprosy they all withered and gradually melted away.

TEXT 211

দেখিয়া সকল লোক হৈল চমৎকার ।
হরিদাসে প্রশংসি' তাঁরে করে নমস্কার ॥ ২১১ ॥

dekhiyā sakala loka haila camatkāra
haridāse praśaṁsi' tāṅre kare namaskāra

SYNONYMS

dekhiyā—seeing; *sakala loka*—all people; *haila*—became; *camatkāra*—astonished; *haridāse*—Haridāsa Ṭhākura; *praśaṁsi'*—praising; *tāṅre*—unto him; *kare*—offer; *namaskāra*—obeisances.

TRANSLATION

Seeing the condition of Gopāla Cakravartī, everyone was astonished. Everyone praised the influence of Haridāsa Ṭhākura and offered him obeisances.

TEXT 212

যদ্যপি হরিদাস বিপ্রের দোষ না লইলা ।
তথাপি ঈশ্বর তারে ফল ভুঞ্জাইলা ॥ ২১২ ॥

yadyapi haridāsa viprera doṣa nā la-ilā
tathāpi īśvara tāre phala bhuñjāilā

SYNONYMS

yadyapi—although; *haridāsa*—Haridāsa Ṭhākura; *viprera*—of the *brāhmaṇa*; *doṣa*—offense; *nā*—did not; *la-ilā*—take seriously; *tathāpi*—still; *īśvara*—the Supreme Personality of Godhead; *tāre*—unto him; *phala*—the result of insulting a Vaiṣṇava; *bhuñjāilā*—made to suffer.

TRANSLATION

Although Haridāsa Ṭhākura, as a Vaiṣṇava, did not take seriously the brāhmaṇa's offense, the Supreme Personality of Godhead could not tolerate it, and thus he made the brāhmaṇa suffer the consequences.

TEXT 213

ভক্ত-স্বভাব,—অজ্ঞ-দোষ ক্ষমা করে।
কৃষ্ণ-স্বভাব,— ভক্ত-নিন্দা সহিতে না পারে ॥ ২১৩ ॥

bhakta-svabhāva, —ajña-doṣa kṣamā kare
kṛṣṇa-svabhāva, —bhakta-nindā sahite nā pāre

SYNONYMS

bhakta-svabhāva—the characteristic of a pure devotee; *ajña-doṣa*—offense by an ignorant rascal; *kṣamā kare*—excuses; *kṛṣṇa-svabhāva*—the characteristic of Kṛṣṇa; *bhakta-nindā*—blaspheming the devotees; *sahite nā pāre*—cannot tolerate.

TRANSLATION

A characteristic of a pure devotee is that he excuses any offense by an ignorant rascal. The characteristic of Kṛṣṇa, however, is that He cannot tolerate blasphemy of His devotees.

PURPORT

Śrī Caitanya Mahāprabhu taught:

tṛṇād api sunīcena
taror api sahiṣṇunā
amāninā mānadena
kīrtanīyaḥ sadā hariḥ

A Vaiṣṇava strictly follows this principle of being humbler than the grass and more tolerant than a tree, expecting no honor from others but offering honor to everyone. In this way, a Vaiṣṇava is simply interested in chanting about the Supreme Personality of Godhead and glorifying Him. Haridāsa Ṭhākura epitomized this foremost order of Vaiṣṇavism. Kṛṣṇa cannot tolerate any insults or blasphemy against a Vaiṣṇava. For example, Prahlāda Mahārāja was chastised by his father, Hiraṇyakaśipu, in so many ways, but although Prahlāda tolerated this, Kṛṣṇa did not. The Lord therefore came in the form of Nṛsiṁhadeva to kill Hiraṇyakaśipu. Similarly, although Śrīla Haridāsa Ṭhākura tolerated the insult by Gopāla Cakravartī, Kṛṣṇa could not. The Lord immediately punished Gopāla Cakravartī by making him suffer from leprosy. While instructing Śrīla Rūpa Gosvāmī about the many restrictive rules and regulations for Vaiṣṇavas, Śrī Caitanya Mahāprabhu has very vividly described the effects of offenses at the lotus feet of a Vaiṣṇava. *Yadi vaiṣṇava-aparādha uṭhe hātī mātā* (*Madhya* 19.156). Offending or blaspheming a Vaiṣṇava has been described as the greatest offense, and it has been compared to a mad elephant. When a mad elephant enters a garden, it ruins all the creepers, flowers and trees. Similarly, if a devotee properly executing his devotional service becomes an offender at the lotus feet of his spiritual master or a Vaiṣṇava, his devotional service is spoiled.

TEXT 214

বিপ্রের কুষ্ঠ শুনি' হরিদাস মনে দুঃখী হৈলা।
বলাই-পুরোহিতে কহি' শান্তিপুর আইলা ॥২১৪ ॥

viprera kuṣṭha śuni' haridāsa mane duḥkhī hailā
balāi-purohite kahi' śāntipura āilā

SYNONYMS

viprera—of the *brāhmaṇa*; *kuṣṭha*—leprosy; *śuni'*—hearing; *haridāsa*—Haridāsa Ṭhākura; *mane*—within the mind; *duḥkhī hailā*—became unhappy; *balāi-purohite*—unto Balarāma Ācārya; *kahi'*—speaking; *śāntipura āilā*—came to Śāntipura.

TRANSLATION

Haridāsa Ṭhākura was unhappy when he heard that the brāhmaṇa Gopāla Cakravartī had been attacked by leprosy. Thus after informing Balarāma Ācārya, the priest of Hiraṇya Majumadāra, he went to Śāntipura, the home of Advaita Ācārya.

TEXT 215

আচার্যে মিলিয়া কৈলা দণ্ডবৎ প্রণাম।
অদ্বৈত আলিঙ্গন করি' করিলা সম্মান ॥ ২১৫ ॥

ācārye miliyā kailā daṇḍavat praṇāma
advaita āliṅgana kari' karilā sammāna

SYNONYMS

ācārye miliyā—meeting Advaita Ācārya; *kailā*—offered; *daṇḍavat praṇāma*—obeisances and respects; *advaita*—Advaita Ācārya; *āliṅgana kari'*—embracing; *karilā sammāna*—showed respect.

TRANSLATION

Upon meeting Advaita Ācārya, Haridāsa Ṭhākura offered Him respect and obeisances. Advaita Ācārya embraced him and showed respect to him in return.

TEXT 216

গঙ্গা তীরে গোঁফা করি' নির্জনে তাঁরে দিলা।
ভাগবত-গীতার ভক্তি-অর্থ শুনাইলা ॥২১৬॥

gaṅgā-tīre goṅphā kari' nirjane tāṅre dilā
bhāgavata-gītāra bhakti-artha śunāilā

SYNONYMS

gaṅgā-tīre—on the bank of the Ganges; *goṅphā kari'*—constructing a small cavelike residence; *nirjane*—in a solitary place; *tāṅre*—unto him; *dilā*—offered; *bhāgavata*—of *Śrīmad-Bhāgavatam; gītāra*—of *Bhagavad-gītā; bhakti-artha*—the real meaning of devotional service; *śunāilā*—spoke to him.

TRANSLATION

On the bank of the Ganges, in a solitary place, Advaita Ācārya made a cavelike home for Haridāsa Ṭhākura and spoke to him about the real meaning of Śrīmad-Bhāgavatam and Bhagavad-gītā in terms of devotional service.

TEXT 217

আচার্যের ঘরে নিত্য ভিক্ষা-নির্বাহণ।
তুই জনা মিলি' কৃষ্ণ-কথা-আস্বাদন ॥ ২১৭ ॥

ācāryera ghare nitya bhikṣā-nirvāhaṇa
dui janā mili' kṛṣṇa-kathā-āsvādana

SYNONYMS

ācāryera ghare—at the house of Advaita Ācārya; *nitya*—daily; *bhikṣā-nirvāhaṇa*—accepting food as alms; *dui janā*—the two of them; *mili'*—meeting together; *kṛṣṇa-kathā*—discourses on the subject matter of Kṛṣṇa; *āsvādana*—tasting.

TRANSLATION

Haridāsa Ṭhākura accepted food daily at the house of Advaita Ācārya. Meeting together, the two of them would taste the nectar of discourses on the subject matter of Kṛṣṇa.

TEXT 218

হরিদাস কহে,—"গোসাঞি, করি নিবেদনে।
মোরে প্রত্যহ অন্ন দেহ' কোন্ প্রয়োজনে? ২১৮ ॥

haridāsa kahe, —"gosāñi, kari nivedane
more pratyaha anna deha' kon prayojane?

SYNONYMS

haridāsa kahe—Haridāsa Ṭhākura said; *gosāñi*—my dear Advaita Ācārya; *kari nivedane*—let me submit one prayer; *more*—unto me; *prati-aha*—daily; *anna deha'*—You give food; *kon prayojane*—what is the necessity.

TRANSLATION

Haridāsa Ṭhākura said, "My dear Advaita Ācārya, let me submit something before Your Honor. Every day You give me alms of food to eat. What is the necessity of this?

TEXT 219

মহা-মহা-বিপ্র এথা কুলীন-সমাজ।
নীচে আদর কর, না বাসহ ভয় লাজ !! ২১৯ ॥

mahā-mahā-vipra ethā kulīna-samāja
nīce ādara kara, nā vāsaha bhaya lāja!!

SYNONYMS

mahā-mahā-vipra—great, great *brāhmaṇas*; *ethā*—here; *kulīna-samāja*—aristocratic society; *nīce*—to a low-class person; *ādara kara*—You show honor; *nā vāsaha*—You do not care for; *bhaya lāja*—fear or shame.

TRANSLATION

"Sir, You are living within a society of great, great brāhmaṇas and aristocrats, but without fear or shame You adore a lower-class man like me.

TEXT 220

অলৌকিক আচার তোমার কহিতে পাই ভয়।
সেই কৃপা করিবা,—যাতে মোর রক্ষা হয় ॥"২২০ ॥

alaukika ācāra tomāra kahite pāi bhaya
sei kṛpā karibā, —yāte mora rakṣā haya"

SYNONYMS

alaukika ācāra—uncommon behavior; *tomāra*—Your; *kahite*—to speak; *pāi bhaya*—I am afraid; *sei kṛpā*—that favor; *karibā*—kindly do; *yāte*—by which; *mora*—my; *rakṣā*—protection; *haya*—there is.

TRANSLATION

"My dear sir, Your behavior is uncommon. Indeed, sometimes I am afraid to speak to You. But please favor me by protecting me from the behavior of society."

PURPORT

While Haridāsa Ṭhākura was staying under the care of Advaita Ācārya, he was afraid of the behavior of society in Śāntipura, Navadvīpa, which was full of exceedingly aristocratic *brāhmaṇas, kṣatriyas* and *vaiśyas.* Haridāsa Ṭhākura was born in a Mohammedan family and was later recognized as a great Vaiṣṇava, but nevertheless the *brāhmaṇas* were very critical of him. Thus Haridāsa Ṭhākura was afraid that Advaita Ācārya would be put into some difficulty because of His familiarity with Haridāsa Ṭhākura. Śrī Advaita Ācārya treated Haridāsa Ṭhākura as a most elevated Vaiṣṇava, but others, like Rāmacandra Khān, were envious of Haridāsa Ṭhākura. Of course, we have to follow in the footsteps of Advaita Ācārya, not caring for people like Rāmacandra Khān. At present, many Vaiṣṇavas are coming to our Kṛṣṇa consciousness movement from among the Europeans and Americans, and although a man like Rāmacandra Khān is always envious of such Vaiṣṇavas, one should follow in the footsteps of Śrī Advaita Ācārya by treating all of them as Vaiṣṇavas. Although they are not as exalted as Haridāsa Ṭhākura, such Americans and Europeans, having accepted the principles of Vaiṣṇava philosophy and behavior, should never be excluded from Vaiṣṇava society.

TEXT 221

আচার্য কহেন,—"তুমি না করিহ ভয় ।
সেই আচরিব, যেই শাস্ত্রমত হয় ॥ ২২১ ॥

ācārya kahena, —"tumi nā kariha bhaya
sei ācariba, yei śāstra-mata haya

SYNONYMS

ācārya kahena—Advaita Ācārya said; *tumi*—you; *nā*—not; *kariha*—do; *bhaya*—fear; *sei ācariba*—I shall behave in that way; *yei*—whatever; *śāstra-mata*—sanctioned by the revealed scriptures; *haya*—is.

TRANSLATION

Advaita Ācārya replied, "My dear Haridāsa, do not be afraid. I shall behave strictly according to the principles of the revealed scriptures.

PURPORT

Śrīla Advaita Ācārya was not afraid of the strict brahminical culture and customs of society. As stated in the śāstric injunctions, which are the true medium of evidence or proof, anyone can go back to Godhead, even if born of a low family. Kṛṣṇa says in *Bhagavad-gītā:*

māṁ hi pārtha vyapāśritya
ye 'pi syuḥ pāpa-yonayaḥ
striyo vaiśyās tathā śūdrās
te 'pi yānti parāṁ gatim

"O son of Pṛthā, those who take shelter in Me, though they be of lower birth—women, *vaiśyas* [merchants], as well as *śūdras* [workers]—can approach the supreme destination." (Bg. 9.32) Though having taken a low birth in human society, one who accepts Kṛṣṇa as the Supreme Personality of Godhead is quite competent to go back home, back to Godhead; and one who is a bona fide candidate for going back to Godhead should not be considered lowborn, or *caṇḍāla.* That is also a śāstric injunction. As stated in *Śrīmad-Bhāgavatam* (2.4.18):

kirāta-hūṇāndhra-pulinda-pulkaśā
ābhīra-śumbhā yavanāḥ khasādayaḥ
ye 'nye ca pāpā yad-apāśrayāśrayāḥ
śudhyanti tasmai prabhaviṣṇave namaḥ

Not only the *yavanas* and *khasādayaḥ* but even those born in still lower families can be purified (*śudhyanti*) by the grace of a devotee of Lord Kṛṣṇa, for Kṛṣṇa empowers such devotees to perform this purification. Advaita Ācārya had confidence in the śāstric evidence and did not care about social customs. The Kṛṣṇa consciousness movement, therefore, is a cultural movement that does not care about local social conventions. Following in the footsteps of Śrī Caitanya Mahāprabhu and Advaita Ācārya, we can accept a devotee from any part of the world and recognize him as a *brāhmaṇa* as soon as he is qualified due to following the principles of Vaiṣṇava behavior.

TEXT 222

তুমি খাইলে হয় কোটিব্রাহ্মণ-ভোজন ।"
এত বলি, শ্রাদ্ধ-পাত্র করাইলা ভোজন ॥ ২২২ ॥

tumi khāile haya koṭi-brāhmaṇa-bhojana"
eta bali, śrāddha-pātra karāilā bhojana

SYNONYMS

tumi khāile—if you eat; *haya*—there is; *koṭi-brāhmaṇa-bhojana*—feeding ten million *brāhmaṇas;* *eta bali*—saying this; *śrāddha-pātra*—the dish offered to the forefathers; *karāilā bhojana*—made to eat.

TRANSLATION

"Feeding you is equal to feeding ten million brāhmaṇas," Advaita Ācārya said. "Therefore, accept this śrāddha-pātra." Thus Advaita Ācārya made him eat.

PURPORT

Śrāddha is *prasāda* offered to the forefathers at a certain date of the year or month. The *śrāddha-pātra,* or plate offered to the forefathers, is then offered to the best of the *brāhmaṇas* in society. Instead of offering the *śrāddha-pātra* to any other *brāhmaṇa,* Advaita Ācārya offered it to Haridāsa Ṭhākura, considering him greater than any of the foremost *brāhmaṇas.* This act by Śrī Advaita Ācārya proves that Haridāsa Ṭhākura was always situated in a transcendental position and was therefore always greater than even the most exalted *brāhmaṇa,* for he was situated above the mode of goodness of the material world. Referring to the *Bhakti-sandarbha,* verse 177, Śrīla Bhaktisiddhānta Sarasvatī Ṭhākura quotes the following statements from the *Garuḍa Purāṇa* in this connection:

brāhmaṇānāṁ sahasrebhyaḥ
satra-yājī viśiṣyate
satra-yāji-sahasrebhyaḥ
sarva-vedānta-pāragaḥ

sarva-vedānta-vit-koṭyā
viṣṇu-bhakto viśiṣyate
vaiṣṇavānāṁ sahasrebhya
ekānty eko viśiṣyate

"A *brāhmaṇa* qualified to offer sacrifices is better than an ordinary *brāhmaṇa,* and better than such a *brāhmaṇa* is one who has studied all the Vedic scriptures. Among many such *brāhmaṇas,* one who is a devotee of Lord Viṣṇu is the best; and among many such Vaiṣṇavas, one who fully engages in the service of the Lord is the best."

bhaktir aṣṭa-vidhā hy eṣā
yasmin mlecche 'pi vartate
sa viprendro muni-śreṣṭhaḥ
sa jñānī sa ca paṇḍitaḥ
tasmai deyaṁ tato grāhyaṁ
sa ca pūjyo yathā hariḥ

"There are many different kinds of devotees, but even a Vaiṣṇava coming from a family of *mlecchas* or *yavanas* is understood to be a learned scholar, complete in knowledge, if he knows the Vaiṣṇava philosophy. He should therefore be given charity, for such a Vaiṣṇava is as worshipable as the Supreme Personality of Godhead."

na me 'bhaktaś catur-vedī
mad-bhaktaḥ śva-pacaḥ priyaḥ
tasmai deyaṁ tato grāhyaṁ
sa ca pūjyo yathā hy aham

Lord Kṛṣṇa says, "Even if a nondevotee comes from a *brāhmaṇa* family and is expert in studying the *Vedas,* he is not very dear to Me, whereas even if a sincere devotee comes from a low family of meat-eaters, he is very dear to Me. Such a sincere pure devotee should be given charity, for he is as worshipable as I."

TEXT 223

জগৎ-নিস্তার লাগি' করেন চিন্তন ।
অবৈষ্ণব-জগৎ কেমনে হইবে মোচন ? ২২৩ ॥

jagat-nistāra lāgi' karena cintana
avaiṣṇava-jagat kemane ha-ibe mocana?

SYNONYMS

jagat-nistāra—the deliverance of the people of the whole world; *lāgi'*—for; *karena cintana*—was always thinking; *avaiṣṇava*—full of nondevotees; *jagat*—the whole world; *kemane*—how; *ha-ibe mocana*—will be delivered.

TRANSLATION

Advaita Ācārya was always absorbed in thoughts of how to deliver the fallen souls of the entire world. "The entire world is full of nondevotees," He thought. "How will they be delivered?"

PURPORT

Śrīla Advaita Ācārya sets the standard for *ācāryas* in the Vaiṣṇava *sampradāya.* An *ācārya* must always be eager to deliver the fallen souls. A person who establishes a temple or *maṭha* to take advantage of people's sentiments by using for his livelihood what people contribute for the worship of the Deity cannot be called a *gosvāmī* or *ācārya.* One who knows the conclusion of the *śāstras,* follows in the footsteps of his predecessors and endeavors to preach the *bhakti* cult all over the world is to be considered an *ācārya.* The role of an *ācārya* is not to earn his livelihood through the income of the temple. Śrīla Bhaktisiddhānta Sarasvatī

Ṭhākura used to say that if one earns his livelihood by displaying the Deity in the temple, he is not an *ācārya* or *gosvāmī*. It would be better for him to accept service even as a sweeper in the street, for that is a more honorable means of earning one's living.

TEXT 224

কৃষ্ণে অবতারিতে অদ্বৈত প্রতিজ্ঞা করিলা ।
জল-তুলসী দিয়া পূজা করিতে লাগিলা ॥ ২২৪ ॥

kṛṣṇe avatārite advaita pratijñā karilā
jala-tulasī diyā pūjā karite lāgilā

SYNONYMS

kṛṣṇe—Lord Kṛṣṇa; *avatārite*—to cause to descend; *advaita*—Advaita Ācārya; *pratijñā*—promise; *karilā*—made; *jala-tulasī*—Ganges water and *tulasī* leaves; *diyā*—offering; *pūjā*—worship; *karite*—to do; *lāgilā*—began.

TRANSLATION

Determined to deliver all the fallen souls, Advaita Ācārya decided to cause Kṛṣṇa to descend. With this vow, he began to offer Ganges water and tulasī leaves to worship the Lord.

TEXT 225

হরিদাস করে গোঁফায় নাম-সঙ্কীর্তন ।
কৃষ্ণ অবতীর্ণ হইবেন,— এই তাঁর মন ॥ ২২৫ ॥

haridāsa kare goṅphāya nāma-saṅkīrtana
kṛṣṇa avatīrṇa ha-ibena,——ei tāṅra mana

SYNONYMS

haridāsa—Haridāsa Ṭhākura; *kare*—performed; *goṅphāya*—in the cave; *nāma-saṅkīrtana*—chanting of the holy name of the Lord; *kṛṣṇa*—Lord Kṛṣṇa; *avatīrṇa ha-ibena*—will descend; *ei*—this; *tāṅra mana*—his mind.

TRANSLATION

Similarly, Haridāsa Ṭhākura chanted in his cave on the bank of the Ganges with the intention to cause Kṛṣṇa's descent.

TEXT 226

দুইজনের ভক্ত্যে চৈতন্য কৈলা অবতার।
নাম-প্রেম প্রচারি' কৈলা জগৎ উদ্ধার ॥ ২২৬ ॥

dui-janera bhaktye caitanya kailā avatāra
nāma-prema pracāri' kailā jagat uddhāra

SYNONYMS

dui-janera—of these two persons; *bhaktye*—because of the devotional service; *caitanya*—Lord Śrī Caitanya Mahāprabhu; *kailā*—made; *avatāra*—incarnation; *nāma-prema*—the holy name and love of Kṛṣṇa; *pracāri'*—preaching; *kailā*—did; *jagat uddhāra*—deliverance of the whole world.

TRANSLATION

Because of the devotional service of these two persons, Lord Śrī Caitanya Mahāprabhu descended as an incarnation. Thus He preached the holy name of the Lord and ecstatic love of Kṛṣṇa to deliver the entire world.

TEXT 227

আর অলৌকিক এক চরিত্র তাঁহার।
যাহার শ্রবণে লোকে হয় চমৎকার ॥ ২২৭ ॥

āra alaukika eka caritra tāṅhāra
yāhāra śravaṇe loke haya camatkāra

SYNONYMS

āra—another; *alaukika*—uncommon; *eka*—one; *caritra*—characteristic; *tāṅhāra*—of Haridāsa Ṭhākura; *yāhāra śravaṇe*—in hearing which; *loke*—in human society; *haya*—there is; *camatkāra*—astonishment.

TRANSLATION

There is another incident concerning Haridāsa Ṭhākura's uncommon behavior. One will be astonished to hear about it.

TEXT 228

তর্ক না করিহ, তর্কাগোচর তাঁর রীতি।
বিশ্বাস করিয়া শুন করিয়া প্রতীতি ॥ ২২৮ ॥

tarka nā kariha, tarkāgocara tāṅra rīti
viśvāsa kariyā śuna kariyā pratīti

SYNONYMS

tarka nā kariha—do not argue; *tarka-agocara*—beyond argument; *tāṅra*—his; *rīti*—behavior; *viśvāsa kariyā*—believing; *śuna*—listen; *kariyā pratīti*—having confidence.

TRANSLATION

Hear about such incidents without putting forth dry arguments, for these incidents are beyond our material reasoning. One must believe in them with faith.

TEXT 229

একদিন হরিদাস গোঁফাতে বসিয়া ।
নাম-সঙ্কীর্তন করেন উচ্চ করিয়া ॥ ২২৯ ॥

eka-dina haridāsa goṅphāte vasiyā
nāma-saṅkīrtana karena ucca kariyā

SYNONYMS

eka-dina—one day; *haridāsa*—Haridāsa Ṭhākura; *goṅphāte vasiyā*—sitting in his cave; *nāma-saṅkīrtana karena*—was chanting the holy name of the Lord; *ucca kariyā*—resounding very loudly.

TRANSLATION

One day Haridāsa Ṭhākura was sitting in his cave, reciting very loudly the holy name of the Lord.

TEXT 230

জ্যোৎস্নাবতী রাত্রি, দশ দিক্ সুনির্মল ।
গঙ্গার লহরী জ্যোৎস্নায় করে ঝল-মল ॥ ২৩০ ॥

jyotsnāvatī rātri, daśa dik sunirmala
gaṅgāra laharī jyotsnāya kare jhala-mala

SYNONYMS

jyotsnāvatī—full of moonlight; *rātri*—the night; *daśa dik*—ten directions; *su-nirmala*—very clear and bright; *gaṅgāra laharī*—the waves of the Ganges; *jyotsnāya*—in the moonlight; *kare jhala-mala*—appear dazzling.

TRANSLATION

The night was full of moonlight, which made the waves of the Ganges look dazzling. All directions were clear and bright.

TEXT 231

দ্বারে তুলসী লেপা-পিণ্ডির উপর ।
গোঁফার শোভা দেখি' লোকের জুড়ায় অন্তর ॥২৩১॥

dvāre tulasī lepā-piṇḍira upara
goṅphāra śobhā dekhi' lokera juḍāya antara

SYNONYMS

dvāre—at the door; *tulasī*—the *tulasī* plant; *lepā*—very clean; *piṇḍira upara*—on the altar; *goṅphāra śobhā*—the beauty of the cave; *dekhi'*—seeing; *lokera*—of everyone; *juḍāya*—was satisfied; *antara*—the heart.

TRANSLATION

Thus everyone who saw the beauty of the cave, with the tulasī plant on a clean altar, was astonished and satisfied at heart.

TEXT 232

হেনকালে এক নারী অঙ্গনে আইল ।
তাঁর অঙ্গকান্ত্যে স্থান পীতবর্ণ হইল ॥ ২৩২ ॥

hena-kāle eka nārī aṅgane āila
tāṅra aṅga-kāntye sthāna pīta-varṇa ha-ila

SYNONYMS

hena-kāle—at this time; *eka*—one; *nārī*—woman; *aṅgane āila*—came to the courtyard; *tāṅra*—her; *aṅga-kāntye*—by the beauty of the body; *sthāna*—that place; *pīta-varṇa ha-ila*—became yellowish.

TRANSLATION

At that time, in that beautiful scene, a woman appeared in the courtyard. The beauty of her body was so bright that it tinged the entire place with a hue of yellow.

TEXT 233

তাঁর অঙ্গ-গন্ধে দশ দিক্ আমোদিত ।
ভূষণ-ধ্বনিতে কর্ণ হয় চমকিত ॥ ২৩৩ ॥

tāṅra aṅga-gandhe daśa dik āmodita
bhūṣaṇa-dhvanite karṇa haya camakita

SYNONYMS

tāṅra—her; *aṅga-gandhe*—the scent of the body; *daśa dik*—ten directions; *āmodita*—perfumed; *bhūṣaṇa-dhvanite*—by the tinkling of her ornaments; *karṇa*—the ear; *haya*—becomes; *camakita*—startled.

TRANSLATION

The scent of her body perfumed all directions, and the tinkling of her ornaments startled the ear.

TEXT 234

আসিয়া তুলসীরে সেই কৈলা নমস্কার ।
তুলসী পরিক্রমা করি' গেলা গোঁফা-দ্বার ॥ ২৩৪ ॥

āsiyā tulasīre sei kailā namaskāra
tulasī parikramā kari' gelā goṅphā-dvāra

SYNONYMS

āsiyā—coming; *tulasīre*—unto the *tulasī* plant; *sei*—that woman; *kailā*—did; *namaskāra*—obeisances; *tulasī*—the *tulasī* plant; *parikramā*—circumambulating; *kari'*—doing; *gelā*—went; *goṅphā-dvāra*—to the door of the cave.

TRANSLATION

After coming there, the woman offered obeisances to the tulasī plant, and after circumambulating the tulasī plant she came to the door of the cave where Haridāsa Ṭhākura was sitting.

TEXT 235

যোড়-হাতে হরিদাসের বন্দিলা চরণ ।
দ্বারে বসি' কহে কিছু মধুর বচন ॥ ২৩৫ ॥

yoḍa-hāte haridāsera vandilā caraṇa
dvāre vasi' kahe kichu madhura vacana

SYNONYMS

yoḍa-hāte—with folded hands; *haridāsera*—of Haridāsa Ṭhākura; *vandilā caraṇa*—offered prayers at the lotus feet; *dvāre vasi'*—sitting at the door; *kahe*—says; *kichu*—some; *madhura vacana*—sweet words.

TRANSLATION

With folded hands she offered obeisances at the lotus feet of Haridāsa Ṭhākura. Sitting at the door, she then spoke in a very sweet voice.

TEXT 236

"জগতের বন্ধু তুমি রূপগুণবান্।
তব সঙ্গ লাগি' মোর এথাকে প্রয়াণ ॥ ২৩৬ ॥

"jagatera bandhu tumi rūpa-guṇavān
tava saṅga lāgi' mora ethāke prayāṇa

SYNONYMS

jagatera—of the whole world; *bandhu*—friend; *tumi*—you; *rūpa-guṇa-vān*—so beautiful and qualified; *tava saṅga*—your union; *lāgi'*—for; *mora*—my; *ethāke prayāṇa*—coming here.

TRANSLATION

"My dear friend," she said, "you are the friend of the entire world. You are so beautiful and qualified. I have come here only for union with you.

TEXT 237

মোরে অঙ্গীকার কর হঞা সদয়।
দীনে দয়া করে,—এই সাধু-স্বভাব হয় ॥" ২৩৭ ॥

more aṅgīkāra kara hañā sadaya
dīne dayā kare, ——ei sādhu-svabhāva haya"

SYNONYMS

more—me; *aṅgīkāra kara*—accept; *hañā sa-daya*—being very kind; *dīne*—to the fallen souls; *dayā kare*—show favor; *ei*—this; *sādhu-svabhāva*—the characteristic of saintly persons; *haya*—is.

TRANSLATION

"My dear sir, kindly accept me and be merciful toward me, for it is a characteristic of all saintly persons to be kind toward the poor and fallen."

TEXT 238

এত বলি' নানা-ভাব করয়ে প্রকাশ ।
যাহার দর্শনে মুনির হয় ধৈর্যনাশ ॥ ২৩৮ ॥

eta bali' nānā-bhāva karaye prakāśa
yāhāra darśane munira haya dhairya-nāśa

SYNONYMS

eta bali'—saying this; *nānā-bhāva*—various postures; *karaye prakāśa*—began to manifest; *yāhāra darśane*—seeing which; *munira*—of even the great philosophers; *haya*—there is; *dhairya-nāśa*—loss of patience.

TRANSLATION

After saying this, she began to manifest various postures, which even the greatest philosopher would lose his patience upon seeing.

TEXT 239

নির্বিকার হরিদাস গম্ভীর-আশয় ।
বলিতে লাগিলা তাঁরে হঞা সদয় ॥ ২৩৯ ॥

nirvikāra haridāsa gambhīra-āśaya
balite lāgilā tāṅre hañā sadaya

SYNONYMS

nirvikāra—unmoved; *haridāsa*—Haridāsa Ṭhākura; *gambhīra*—very deep; *āśaya*—determination; *balite lāgilā*—began to speak; *tāṅre*—unto her; *hañā sadaya*—being merciful.

TRANSLATION

Haridāsa Ṭhākura was immovable, for he was deeply determined. He began to speak to her, being very merciful toward her.

TEXT 240

"সংখ্যা-নাম-সঙ্কীর্তন— এই 'মহাযজ্ঞ' মন্যে ।
তাহাতে দীক্ষিত আমি হই প্রতিদিনে ॥ ২৪০ ॥

"saṅkhyā-nāma-saṅkīrtana——ei 'mahā-yajña' manye
tāhāte dīkṣita āmi ha-i prati-dine

SYNONYMS

saṅkhyā-nāma-saṅkīrtana—numerical chanting of the holy name; *ei*—this; *mahā-yajña*—great sacrifice; *manye*—I have vowed; *tāhāte dīkṣita*—initiated in that; *āmi*—I; *ha-i*—am; *prati-dine*—every day.

TRANSLATION

"I have been initiated into a vow to perform a great sacrifice by chanting the holy name a certain number of times every day.

TEXT 241

যাবৎ কীর্তন সমাপ্ত নহে, না করি অন্য কাম।
কীর্তন সমাপ্ত হৈলে, হয় দীক্ষার বিশ্রাম ॥ ২৪১ ॥

yāvat kīrtana samāpta nahe, nā kari anya kāma
kīrtana samāpta haile, haya dīkṣāra viśrāma

SYNONYMS

yāvat—as long as; *kīrtana*—chanting; *samāpta*—finished; *nahe*—is not; *nā*—not; *kari*—I do; *anya*—other; *kāma*—desire; *kīrtana*—chanting; *samāpta*—finished; *haile*—becoming; *haya*—there is; *dīkṣāra*—of initiation; *viśrāma*—rest.

TRANSLATION

"As long as the vow to chant is unfulfilled, I do not desire anything else. When I finish my chanting, then I have an opportunity to do anything.

TEXT 242

দ্বারে বসি' শুন তুমি নাম-সঙ্কীর্তন।
নাম সমাপ্ত হৈলে করিমু তব প্রীতি-আচরণ ॥ ২৪২ ॥

dvāre vasi' śuna tumi nāma-saṅkīrtana
nāma samāpta haile karimu tava prīti-ācaraṇa

SYNONYMS

dvāre vasi'—sitting at the door; *śuna*—hear; *tumi*—you; *nāma-saṅkīrtana*—chanting of the holy names; *nāma*—the holy name; *samāpta haile*—when finished; *karimu*—I shall do; *tava*—your; *prīti*—pleasure; *ācaraṇa*—activities.

TRANSLATION

"Sit down at the door and hear the chanting of the Hare Kṛṣṇa mahā-mantra. As soon as the chanting is finished, I shall satisfy you as you desire."

TEXT 243

এত বলি' করেন তেঁহো নাম-সঙ্কীর্তন ।
সেই নারী বসি' করে শ্রীনাম-শ্রবণ ॥ ২৪৩ ॥

eta bali' karena teṅho nāma-saṅkīrtana
sei nārī vasi' kare śrī-nāma-śravaṇa

SYNONYMS

eta bali'—saying this; *karena*—performs; *teṅho*—he; *nāma-saṅkīrtana*—chanting of the holy name; *sei nārī*—that woman; *vasi'*—sitting; *kare*—does; *śrī-nāma-śravaṇa*—hearing the holy name.

TRANSLATION

After saying this, Haridāsa Ṭhākura continued to chant the holy name of the Lord. Thus the woman sitting before him began to hear the chanting of the holy name.

TEXT 244

কীর্তন করিতে আসি' প্রাতঃকাল হৈল ।
প্রাতঃকাল দেখি' নারী উঠিয়া চলিল ॥ ২৪৪ ॥

kīrtana karite āsi' prātaḥ-kāla haila
prātaḥ-kāla dekhi' nārī uṭhiyā calila

SYNONYMS

kīrtana karite—chanting and chanting; *āsi'*—coming; *prātaḥ-kāla*—morning; *haila*—appeared; *prātaḥ-kāla dekhi'*—seeing the morning light; *nārī*—the woman; *uṭhiyā calila*—got up and left.

TRANSLATION

In this way, as he chanted and chanted, the morning approached, and when the woman saw that it was morning, she got up and left.

TEXT 245

এইমত তিনদিন করে আগমন।
নানা ভাব দেখায়, যাতে ব্রহ্মার হরে মন ॥ ২৪৫ ॥

ei-mata tina-dina kare āgamana
nānā bhāva dekhāya, yāte brahmāra hare mana

SYNONYMS

ei-mata—in this way; *tina-dina*—three days; *kare*—she does; *āgamana*—approaching; *nānā bhāva*—all kinds of feminine postures; *dekhāya*—exhibits; *yāte*—by which; *brahmāra*—even of Lord Brahmā; *hare*—attracts; *mana*—mind.

TRANSLATION

For three days she approached Haridāsa Ṭhākura in this way, exhibiting various feminine postures that would bewilder the mind of even Lord Brahmā.

TEXT 246

কৃষ্ণে নামাবিষ্ট-মনা সদা হরিদাস।
অরণ্যে রোদিত হৈল স্ত্রীভাব-প্রকাশ ॥ ২৪৬ ॥

kṛṣṇe nāmāviṣṭa-manā sadā haridāsa
araṇye rodita haila strī-bhāva-prakāśa

SYNONYMS

kṛṣṇe—unto Lord Kṛṣṇa; *nāma-āviṣṭa*—absorbed in chanting the holy name; *manā*—mind; *sadā*—always; *haridāsa*—Haridāsa Ṭhākura; *araṇye*—in the wilderness; *rodita*—crying; *haila*—became; *strī-bhāva-prakāśa*—exhibition of feminine postures.

TRANSLATION

Haridāsa Ṭhākura was always absorbed in thoughts of Kṛṣṇa and the holy name of Kṛṣṇa. Therefore the feminine poses the woman exhibited were just like crying in the forest.

TEXT 247

তৃতীয় দিবসের রাত্রি-শেষ যবে হৈল।
ঠাকুরের স্থানে নারী কহিতে লাগিল ॥ ২৪৭ ॥

tṛtīya divasera rātri-śeṣa yabe haila
ṭhākurera sthāne nārī kahite lāgila

SYNONYMS

tṛtīya divasera—of the third day; *rātri-śeṣa*—the end of the night; *yabe*—when; *haila*—there was; *ṭhākurera*—of Haridāsa Ṭhākura; *sthāne*—at the place; *nārī*—the woman; *kahite lāgila*—began to speak.

TRANSLATION

At the end of the night of the third day, the woman spoke to Haridāsa Ṭhākura as follows.

TEXT 248

"তিন দিন বঞ্চিলা আমা করি' আশ্বাসন।
রাত্রি-দিনে নহে তোমার নাম-সমাপন ॥" ২৪৮ ॥

"tina dina vañcilā āmā kari' āśvāsana
rātri-dine nahe tomāra nāma-samāpana"

SYNONYMS

tina dina—for three days; *vañcilā*—you have cheated; *āmā*—me; *kari' āśvāsana*—giving assurance; *rātri-dine*—throughout the entire day and night; *nahe*—is not; *tomāra*—your; *nāma-samāpana*—finishing of the chanting of the holy name.

TRANSLATION

"My dear sir, for three days you have cheated me by giving me false assurances, for I see that throughout the entire day and night your chanting of the holy name is never finished."

TEXT 249

হরিদাস ঠাকুর কহেন,—"আমি কি করিমু ?
নিয়ম করিয়াছি, তাহা কেমনে ছাড়িমু ?" ২৪৯ ॥

haridāsa ṭhākura kahena, —"āmi ki karimu?
niyama kariyāchi, tāhā kemane chāḍimu?"

SYNONYMS

haridāsa ṭhākura—Haridāsa Ṭhākura; *kahena*—said; *āmi ki karimu*—what shall I do; *niyama kariyāchi*—I have made a vow; *tāhā*—that; *kemane*—how; *chāḍimu*—shall I give up.

TRANSLATION

Haridāsa Ṭhākura said, "My dear friend, what can I do? I have made a vow. How, then, can I give it up?"

TEXT 250

তবে নারী কহে তাঁরে করি' নমস্কার।
'আমি—মায়া' করিতে আইলাঙ পরীক্ষা তোমার॥২৫০॥

tabe nārī kahe tāṅre kari' namaskāra
'āmi——māyā' karite āilāṅa parīkṣā tomāra

SYNONYMS

tabe—at that time; *nārī*—the woman; *kahe*—said; *tāṅre*—unto Haridāsa Ṭhākura; *kari' namaskāra*—offering obeisances; *āmi*—I; *māyā*—the illusory energy; *karite*—to do; *āilāṅa*—I came; *parīkṣā*—testing; *tomāra*—your.

TRANSLATION

After offering obeisances to Haridāsa Ṭhākura, the woman said: "I am the illusory energy of the Supreme Personality of Godhead. I came here to test you.

PURPORT

In *Bhagavad-gītā* (7.14) Lord Kṛṣṇa says:

daivī hy eṣā guṇamayī
mama māyā duratyayā
mām eva ye prapadyante
māyām etāṁ taranti te

"This divine energy of Mine, consisting of the three modes of material nature, is difficult to overcome. But those who have surrendered unto Me can easily cross beyond it." This was actually proved by the behavior of Haridāsa Ṭhākura. *Māyā* enchants the entire world. Indeed, people have forgotten the ultimate goal of life because of the dazzling attractions of the material world. But this dazzling attraction, especially the attractive beauty of a woman, is meant for persons who are not surrendered to the Supreme Personality of Godhead. The Lord says, *mām eva ye prapadyante māyām etāṁ taranti te*: "One who is surrendered unto Me cannot be conquered by the illusory energy." The illusory energy personally came to test Haridāsa Ṭhākura, but herein she admits her defeat, for she was unable to captivate him. How is this possible? It was because Haridāsa Ṭhākura, fully surrendered to the lotus feet of Kṛṣṇa, was always absorbed in thoughts of Kṛṣṇa by chanting the holy names of the Lord 300,000 times daily as a vow.

TEXT 251

ব্রহ্মাদি জীব, আমি সবারে মোহিলুঁ ।
একেলা তোমারে আমি মোহিতে নারিলুঁ ॥ ২৫১ ॥

brahmādi jīva, āmi sabāre mohiluṅ
ekelā tomāre āmi mohite nāriluṅ

SYNONYMS

brahma-ādi jīva—all living entities, beginning from Lord Brahmā; *āmi*—I; *sabāre mohiluṅ*—captivated everyone; *ekelā*—alone; *tomāre*—you; *āmi*—I; *mohite nāriluṅ*—could not attract.

TRANSLATION

"I have previously captivated the mind of even Brahmā, not to speak of others. Your mind alone have I failed to attract.

PURPORT

Beginning from Lord Brahmā down to the insignificant ant, everyone, without exception, is attracted by the illusory energy of the Supreme Personality of Godhead. The demigods, human beings, animals, birds, beasts, trees and plants are all attracted by sexual desire. That is the illusion of *māyā.* Everyone, whether man or woman, thinks that he is the enjoyer of the illusory energy. In this way, everyone is captivated and engaged in material activities. However, because Haridāsa Ṭhākura was always thinking of the Supreme Personality of Godhead and was always busy satisfying the senses of the Lord, this process alone saved him from the captivation of *māyā.* This is practical proof of the strength of devotional service. Because of his full engagement in the service of the Lord, he could not be induced to enjoy *māyā.* The verdict of the *śāstras* is that a pure Vaiṣṇava, or devotee of the Lord, never thinks of enjoying the material world, which culminates in sex life. He never thinks himself an enjoyer; instead, he always wants to be enjoyed by the Supreme Personality of Godhead. Therefore the conclusion is that the Supreme Personality of Godhead is eternal, transcendental, beyond the perception of sense gratification and beyond the material qualities. Only if a living entity gives up the false conception that the body is the self and always thinks himself an eternal servant of Kṛṣṇa and the Vaiṣṇavas can he surpass the influence of *māyā* (*mām eva ye prapadyante māyām etāṁ taranti te*). A pure living entity who thus attains the stage of *anartha-nivṛtti,* cessation of everything unwanted, has nothing to enjoy in the material world. One attains this stage only by properly performing the functions of devotional service. Śrīla Rūpa Gosvāmī has written:

adau śraddhā tataḥ sādhu-saṅgo 'tha bhajana-kriyā
tato 'nartha-nivṛttiḥ syāt tato niṣṭhā rucis tataḥ

"In the beginning one must have a preliminary desire for self-realization. This will bring one to the stage of trying to associate with persons who are spiritually elevated. In the next stage, one becomes initiated by an elevated spiritual master, and under his instruction the neophyte devotee begins the process of devotional service. By execution of devotional service under the guidance of the spiritual master, one becomes freed from all material attachments, attains steadiness in self-realization and acquires a taste for hearing about the Absolute Personality of Godhead, Śrī Kṛṣṇa." (B.r.s. 1.4.15) If one is actually executing devotional service, then *anarthas,* the unwanted things associated with material enjoyment, will automatically disappear.

TEXTS 252-253

মহাভাগবত তুমি,—তোমার দর্শনে ।
তোমার কৃষ্ণনাম-কীর্তন-শ্রবণে ॥ ২৫২ ॥
চিত্ত শুদ্ধ হৈল, চাহে কৃষ্ণনাম লৈতে ।
কৃষ্ণনাম উপদেশি' কৃপা কর মোতে ॥ ২৫৩ ॥

mahā-bhāgavata tumi,——tomāra darśane
tomāra kṛṣṇa-nāma-kīrtana-śravaṇe

citta śuddha haila, cāhe kṛṣṇa-nāma laite
kṛṣṇa-nāma upadeśi' kṛpā kara mote

SYNONYMS

mahā-bhāgavata—the foremost devotee; *tumi*—you; *tomāra darśane*—by seeing you; *tomāra*—your; *kṛṣṇa-nāma*—of the holy name of Kṛṣṇa; *kīrtana*—chanting; *śravaṇe*—by hearing; *citta*—consciousness; *śuddha haila*—became purified; *cāhe*—wants; *kṛṣṇa-nāma laite*—to chant the holy name of Lord Kṛṣṇa; *kṛṣṇa-nāma upadeśi'*—instructing about chanting the Hare Kṛṣṇa *mahā-mantra*; *kṛpā kara*—show mercy; *mote*—unto me.

TRANSLATION

"My dear sir, you are the foremost devotee. Simply seeing you and hearing you chant the holy name of Kṛṣṇa has purified my consciousness. Now I want to chant the holy name of the Lord. Please be kind to me by instructing me about the ecstasy of chanting the Hare Kṛṣṇa mahā-mantra.

TEXT 254

চৈতন্যাবতারে বহে প্রেমামৃত-বন্যা ।
সব জীব প্রেমে ভাসে, পৃথিবী হৈল ধন্যা ॥ ২৫৪ ॥

caitanyāvatāre vahe premāmṛta-vanyā
saba jīva preme bhāse, pṛthivī haila dhanyā

SYNONYMS

caitanya-avatāre—by the incarnation of Śrī Caitanya Mahāprabhu; *vahe*—flows; *prema-amṛta*—of the eternal nectar of love of Godhead; *vanyā*—the flood; *saba jīva*—all living entities; *preme*—in ecstatic love; *bhāse*—float; *pṛthivī*—the whole world; *haila*—became; *dhanyā*—thankful.

TRANSLATION

"There is now a flood of the eternal nectar of love of Godhead due to the incarnation of Lord Caitanya. All living entities are floating in that flood. The entire world is now thankful to the Lord.

TEXT 255

এ-বন্যায় যে না ভাসে, সেই জীব ছার ।
কোটিকল্পে কভু তার নাহিক নিস্তার ॥ ২৫৫ ॥

e-vanyāya ye nā bhāse, sei jīva chāra
koṭi-kalpe kabhu tāra nāhika nistāra

SYNONYMS

e-vanyāya—in this inundation; *ye*—anyone who; *nā bhāse*—does not float; *sei*—that; *jīva*—living entity; *chāra*—most condemned; *koṭi-kalpe*—in millions of *kalpas*; *kabhu*—at any time; *tāra*—his; *nāhika*—there is not; *nistāra*—deliverance.

TRANSLATION

"Anyone who does not float in this inundation is most condemned. Such a person cannot be delivered for millions of kalpas.

PURPORT

The *kalpa* is explained in *Bhagavad-gītā. Sahasra-yuga-paryantam ahar yad brahmaṇo viduḥ*. One day of Brahmā is called a *kalpa*. A *yuga,* or *mahā-yuga,* consists of 4,320,000 years, and one thousand such *mahā-yugas* constitute one *kalpa*.

The author of *Śrī Caitanya-caritāmṛta* says that if one does not take advantage of the Kṛṣṇa consciousness movement of Śrī Caitanya Mahāprabhu, he cannot be delivered for millions of such *kalpas.*

TEXT 256

পূর্বে আমি রাম-নাম পাঞাছি 'শিব' হৈতে।
তোমার সঙ্গে লোভ হৈল কৃষ্ণনাম লৈতে ॥ ২৫৬ ॥

pūrve āmi rāma-nāma pāñāchi 'śiva' haite
tomāra saṅge lobha haila kṛṣṇa-nāma laite

SYNONYMS

pūrve—formerly; *āmi*—I; *rāma-nāma*—the holy name of Lord Rāma; *pāñāchi*—got; *śiva haite*—from Lord Śiva; *tomāra saṅge*—by your association; *lobha haila*—I became greedy; *kṛṣṇa-nāma laite*—to chant the Hare Kṛṣṇa *mahā-mantra.*

TRANSLATION

"Formerly I received the holy name of Lord Rāma from Lord Śiva, but now, due to your association, I am greatly eager to chant the holy name of Lord Kṛṣṇa.

TEXT 257

মুক্তি-হেতুক তারক হয় 'রামনাম'।
'কৃষ্ণনাম' পারক হঞা করে প্রেমদান ॥ ২৫৭ ॥

mukti-hetuka tāraka haya 'rāma-nāma'
'kṛṣṇa-nāma' pāraka hañā kare prema-dāna

SYNONYMS

mukti-hetuka—the cause of liberation; *tāraka*—deliverer; *haya*—is; *rāma-nāma*—the holy name of Lord Rāma; *kṛṣṇa-nāma*—the holy name of Lord Kṛṣṇa; *pāraka*—that which gets one to the other side of the ocean of nescience; *hañā*—being; *kare*—gives; *prema-dāna*—the gift of love of Kṛṣṇa.

TRANSLATION

"The holy name of Lord Rāma certainly gives liberation, but the holy name of Kṛṣṇa transports one to the other side of the ocean of nescience and at last gives one ecstatic love of Kṛṣṇa.

PURPORT

In an indirect way, this verse explains the chanting of the Hare Kṛṣṇa *mahā-mantra.* The Hare Kṛṣṇa *mahā-mantra*—Hare Kṛṣṇa, Hare Kṛṣṇa, Kṛṣṇa Kṛṣṇa, Hare Hare/ Hare Rāma, Hare Rāma, Rāma Rāma, Hare Hare—includes both the holy name of Lord Kṛṣṇa and the name of Lord Rāma. Lord Rāma gives one the opportunity to be liberated, but simply by liberation one does not get actual spiritual benefit. Sometimes if one is liberated from the material world but has no shelter at the lotus feet of Kṛṣṇa, one falls down to the material world again. Liberation is like a state of convalescence, in which one is free from a fever but is still not healthy. Even in the stage of convalescence, if one is not very careful, one may have a relapse. Similarly, liberation does not offer as much security as the shelter of the lotus feet of Kṛṣṇa. It is stated in the *śāstra:*

ye 'nye 'ravindākṣa vimukta-māninas
tvayy asta-bhāvād aviśuddha-buddhayaḥ
āruhya kṛcchreṇa paraṁ padaṁ tataḥ
patanty adho 'nādṛta-yuṣmad-aṅghrayaḥ

"O Lord, the intelligence of those who think themselves liberated but who have no devotion is impure. Even though they rise to the highest point of liberation by dint of severe penances and austerities, they are sure to fall down again into material existence, for they do not take shelter at Your lotus feet." (*Śrīmad-Bhāgavatam* 10.2.32) *Yuṣmad-aṅghrayaḥ* refers to the lotus feet of Kṛṣṇa. If one does not take shelter of Kṛṣṇa's lotus feet, he falls down (*patanty adhaḥ*), even from liberation. The Hare Kṛṣṇa *mahā-mantra,* however, gives liberation and at the same time offers shelter at the lotus feet of Kṛṣṇa. If one takes shelter at the lotus feet of Kṛṣṇa after liberation, he develops his dormant ecstatic love for Kṛṣṇa. That is the highest perfection of life.

TEXT 258

কৃষ্ণনাম দেহ' তুমি মোরে কর ধন্যা ।
আমারে ভাসায় যৈছে এই প্রেমবন্যা ॥ ২৫৮ ॥

kṛṣṇa-nāma deha' tumi more kara dhanyā
āmāre bhāsāya yaiche ei prema-vanyā

SYNONYMS

kṛṣṇa nāma—the holy name of Lord Kṛṣṇa; *deha'*—please give; *tumi*—you; *more*—me; *kara dhanyā*—make fortunate; *āmāre*—me; *bhāsāya*—may cause to float; *yaiche*—so that; *ei*—this; *prema-vanyā*—inundation of ecstatic love of Lord Kṛṣṇa.

TRANSLATION

"Please give me the holy name of Kṛṣṇa and thus make me fortunate, so that I also may float in the flood of love of Godhead inaugurated by Śrī Caitanya Mahāprabhu."

TEXT 259

এত বলি' বন্দিলা হরিদাসের চরণ ।
হরিদাস কহে,—"কর কৃষ্ণ-সঙ্কীর্তন" ॥ ২৫৯ ॥

eta bali' vandilā haridāsera caraṇa
haridāsa kahe,——"kara kṛṣṇa-saṅkīrtana"

SYNONYMS

eta bali'—saying this; *vandilā*—worshiped; *haridāsera caraṇa*—the lotus feet of Haridāsa Ṭhākura; *haridāsa kahe*—Haridāsa said; *kara*—just perform; *kṛṣṇa-saṅkīrtana*—chanting of the holy name of Kṛṣṇa.

TRANSLATION

After speaking in this way, Māyā worshiped the lotus feet of Haridāsa Ṭhākura, who initiated her by saying, "Just perform chanting of the Hare Kṛṣṇa mahā-mantra."

PURPORT

Now even Māyā wanted to be favored by Haridāsa Ṭhākura. Therefore Haridāsa Ṭhākura formally initiated her by asking her to chant the Hare Kṛṣṇa *mahā-mantra.*

TEXT 260

উপদেশ পাঞা মায়া চলিলা হঞা প্রীত ।
এ-সব কথাতে কারো না জন্মে প্রতীত ॥ ২৬০ ॥

upadeśa pāñā māyā calilā hañā prīta
e-saba kathāte kāro nā janme pratīta

SYNONYMS

upadeśa pāñā—getting this instruction; *māyā*—Māyā; *calilā*—left; *hañā prīta*—being very pleased; *e-saba kathāte*—in all these narrations; *kāro*—of someone; *nā*—not; *janme*—there is; *pratīta*—faith.

TRANSLATION

After thus being instructed by Haridāsa Ṭhākura, Māyā left with great pleasure. Unfortunately, some people have no faith in these narrations.

TEXT 261

প্রতীত করিতে কহি কারণ ইহার।
যাহার শ্রবণে হয় বিশ্বাস সবার ॥ ২৬১ ॥

pratīta karite kahi kāraṇa ihāra
yāhāra śravaṇe haya viśvāsa sabāra

SYNONYMS

pratīta karite—just to make one faithful; *kahi*—I say; *kāraṇa ihāra*—the reason for this; *yāhāra śravaṇe*—hearing which; *haya*—there is; *viśvāsa*—faith; *sabāra*—of everyone.

TRANSLATION

Therefore I shall explain the reasons why people should have faith. Everyone who hears this will be faithful.

TEXT 262

চৈতন্যাবতারে কৃষ্ণপ্রেমে লুব্ধ হঞা।
ব্রহ্ম-শিব-সনকাদি পৃথিবীতে জন্মিয়া ॥ ২৬২ ॥

caitanyāvatāre kṛṣṇa-preme lubdha hañā
brahma-śiva-sanakādi pṛthivīte janmiyā

SYNONYMS

caitanya-avatāre—in the incarnation of Śrī Caitanya Mahāprabhu; *kṛṣṇa-preme*—for ecstatic love of Kṛṣṇa; *lubdha hañā*—being very greedy; *brahma*—Lord Brahmā; *śiva*—Lord Śiva; *sanaka-ādi*—the Kumāras and others; *pṛthivīte*—on this earth; *janmiyā*—taking birth.

TRANSLATION

During the incarnation of Lord Caitanya to inaugurate the Kṛṣṇa consciousness movement, even such personalities as Lord Brahmā, Lord Śiva and the four Kumāras took birth upon this earth, being allured by ecstatic love of Lord Kṛṣṇa.

TEXT 263

কৃষ্ণনাম লঞা নাচে, প্রেমবন্যায় ভাসে।
নারদ-প্রহ্লাদাদি আসে মনুষ্য-প্রকাশে ॥ ২৬৩ ॥

kṛṣṇa-nāma lañā nāce, prema-vanyāya bhāse
nārada-prahlādādi āse manuṣya-prakāśe

SYNONYMS

kṛṣṇa-nāma—the holy name of Lord Kṛṣṇa; *lañā*—chanting; *nāce*—dance; *prema-vanyāya*—in the inundation of the flood of love of Godhead; *bhāse*—float; *nārada*—the sage Nārada; *prahlāda-ādi*—and devotees like Prahlāda; *āse*—come; *manuṣya-prakāśe*—as if human beings.

TRANSLATION

All of them, including the great sage Nārada and devotees like Prahlāda, came here as if human beings, chanting the holy names of Lord Kṛṣṇa together and dancing and floating in the inundation of love of Godhead.

TEXT 264

লক্ষ্মী-আদি করি' কৃষ্ণপ্রেমে লুব্ধ হঞা ।
নাম-প্রেম আস্বাদিলা মনুষ্যে জন্মিয়া ॥ ২৬৪ ॥

lakṣmī-ādi kari' kṛṣṇa-preme lubdha hañā
nāma-prema āsvādilā manuṣye janmiyā

SYNONYMS

lakṣmī-ādi—the goddess of fortune and others; *kari'*—in this way; *kṛṣṇa-preme*—for love of Kṛṣṇa; *lubdha hañā*—being greedy; *nāma-prema*—the holy name of Kṛṣṇa in love; *āsvādilā*—tasted; *manuṣye janmiyā*—taking birth in human society.

TRANSLATION

The goddess of fortune and others, allured by love of Kṛṣṇa, also came down in the form of human beings and tasted the holy name of the Lord in love.

TEXT 265

অন্যের কা কথা, আপনে ব্রজেন্দ্রনন্দন ।
অবতরি' করেন প্রেম-রস আস্বাদন ॥ ২৬৫ ॥

anyera kā kathā, āpane vrajendra-nandana
avatari' karena prema-rasa āsvādana

SYNONYMS

anyera kā kathā—what to speak of others; *āpane*—personally; *vrajendra-nandana*—the son of Nanda Mahārāja, Kṛṣṇa; *avatari'*—descending; *karena*—performs; *prema-rasa āsvādana*—tasting of the nectar of love of Kṛṣṇa.

TRANSLATION

What to speak of others, even Kṛṣṇa, the son of Nanda Mahārāja, personally descends to taste the nectar of love of Godhead in the form of the chanting of Hare Kṛṣṇa.

TEXT 266

মায়া-দাসী 'প্রেম' মাগে,—ইথে কি বিস্ময় ?
'সাধুকৃপা'-'নাম' বিনা 'প্রেম' না জন্ময় ॥ ২৬৬ ॥

māyā-dāsī 'prema' māge,——ithe ki vismaya?
'sādhu-kṛpā-'nāma' vinā 'prema' nā janmaya

SYNONYMS

māyā-dāsī—the external energy is a maidservant; *prema māge*—she wants love of Godhead; *ithe*—in this; *ki vismaya*—what is the wonder; *sādhu-kṛpā*—the mercy of the devotee; *nāma*—chanting of the holy name; *vinā*—without; *prema*—love of Godhead; *nā janmaya*—is not possible.

TRANSLATION

What is the wonder if the maidservant of Kṛṣṇa, His external energy, begs for love of Godhead? Without the mercy of a devotee and without the chanting of the holy name of the Lord, love of Godhead cannot be possible.

TEXT 267

চৈতন্য-গোসাঞির লীলার এই ত' স্বভাব ।
ত্রিভুবন নাচে, গায়, পাঞা প্রেমভাব ॥ ২৬৭ ॥

caitanya-gosāñira līlāra ei ta' svabhāva
tribhuvana nāce, gāya, pāñā prema-bhāva

SYNONYMS

caitanya-gosāñira—of Lord Śrī Caitanya Mahāprabhu; *līlāra*—of the pastimes; *ei*—this; *ta'*—certainly; *sva-bhāva*—the characteristic; *tri-bhuvana nāce*—the three worlds dance; *gāya*—chant; *pāñā*—getting; *prema-bhāva*—love of Kṛṣṇa.

TRANSLATION

In the activities of Lord Śrī Caitanya Mahāprabhu, the three worlds dance and chant, having come in touch with love of Godhead. This is the characteristic of His pastimes.

TEXT 268

কৃষ্ণ-আদি, আর যত স্থাবর-জঙ্গমে।
কৃষ্ণপ্রেমে মত্ত করে কৃষ্ণ-সঙ্কীর্তনে ॥ ২৬৮ ॥

kṛṣṇa-ādi, āra yata sthāvara-jaṅgame
kṛṣṇa-preme matta kare kṛṣṇa-saṅkīrtane

SYNONYMS

kṛṣṇa-ādi—beginning from Kṛṣṇa; *āra*—and; *yata*—all; *sthāvara-jaṅgame*—moving and nonmoving creatures; *kṛṣṇa-preme*—in love of Kṛṣṇa; *matta*—maddened; *kare*—make; *kṛṣṇa-saṅkīrtane*—chanting the holy name of Kṛṣṇa.

TRANSLATION

The holy name of Kṛṣṇa is so attractive that anyone who chants it—including all living entities, moving and nonmoving, and even Lord Kṛṣṇa Himself—becomes imbued with love of Kṛṣṇa. This is the effect of chanting the Hare Kṛṣṇa mahā-mantra.

TEXT 269

স্বরূপ-গোসাঞি কড়চায় যে-লীলা লিখিল।
রঘুনাথদাস-মুখে যে সব শুনিল ॥ ২৬৯ ॥

svarūpa-gosāñi kaḍacāya ye-līlā likhila
raghunātha-dāsa-mukhe ye saba śunila

SYNONYMS

svarūpa-gosāñi—Svarūpa Dāmodara Gosvāmī; *kaḍacāya*—in his notes; *ye*—whatever; *līlā*—pastimes; *likhila*—has noted; *raghunātha-dāsa-mukhe*—from the mouth of Raghunātha dāsa Gosvāmī; *ye*—that; *saba*—all; *śunila*—I have heard.

TRANSLATION

I have heard from the mouth of Raghunātha dāsa Gosvāmī all that Svarūpa Dāmodara Gosvāmī recorded in his notes about the pastimes of Śrī Caitanya Mahāprabhu.

TEXT 270

সেই সব লীলা কহি সংক্ষেপ করিয়া ।
চৈতন্য-কৃপাতে লিখি ক্ষুদ্রজীব হঞা ॥ ২৭০ ॥

sei saba līlā kahi saṅkṣepa kariyā
caitanya-kṛpāte likhi kṣudra-jīva hañā

SYNONYMS

sei saba—all those; *līlā*—pastimes; *kahi*—I say; *saṅkṣepa kariyā*—in brief; *caitanya-kṛpāte*—by the mercy of Lord Śrī Caitanya Mahāprabhu; *likhi*—I write; *kṣudra-jīva hañā*—being a very insignificant living entity.

TRANSLATION

I have briefly described those pastimes. Whatever I have written is by the mercy of Śrī Caitanya Mahāprabhu, since I am an insignificant living being.

TEXT 271

হরিদাস ঠাকুরের কহিলুঁ মহিমার কণ ।
যাহার শ্রবণে ভক্তের জুড়ায় শ্রবণ ॥ ২৭১ ॥

haridāsa ṭhākurera kahiluṅ mahimāra kaṇa
yāhāra śravaṇe bhaktera juḍāya śravaṇa

SYNONYMS

haridāsa ṭhākurera—of Haridāsa Ṭhākura; *kahiluṅ*—I have described; *mahimāra*—of the glories; *kaṇa*—a fragment; *yāhāra*—of which; *śravaṇe*—the hearing; *bhaktera*—of the devotees; *juḍāya*—satisfies; *śravaṇa*—the aural reception.

TRANSLATION

I have described but a fragment of the glories of Haridāsa Ṭhākura. Hearing this satisfies the aural reception of every devotee.

TEXT 272

শ্রীরূপ-রঘুনাথ-পদে যার আশ ।
চৈতন্যচরিতামৃত কহে কৃষ্ণদাস ॥ ২৭২ ॥

śrī-rūpa-raghunātha-pade yāra āśa
caitanya-caritāmṛta kahe kṛṣṇadāsa

SYNONYMS

śrī-rūpa—Śrīla Rūpa Gosvāmī; *raghunātha*—Śrīla Raghunātha dāsa Gosvāmī; *pade*—at the lotus feet; *yāra*—whose; *āśa*—expectation; *caitanya-caritāmṛta*—the book named *Caitanya-caritāmṛta; kahe*—describes; *kṛṣṇa-dāsa*—Śrīla Kṛṣṇadāsa Kavirāja Gosvāmī.

TRANSLATION

Praying at the lotus feet of Śrī Rūpa and Śrī Raghunātha, always desiring their mercy, I, Kṛṣṇadāsa, narrate Śrī Caitanya-caritāmṛta, following in their footsteps.

Thus end the Bhaktivedanta purports to the Śrī Caitanya-caritāmṛta, Antya-līlā, *Third Chapter, describing the glories of Śrīla Haridāsa Ṭhākura.*

References

The statements of *Śrī Caitanya-caritāmṛta* are all confirmed by standard Vedic authorities. The following authentic scriptures are quoted in this book on the pages listed. Numerals in bold type refer the reader to *Śrī Caitanya-caritāmṛta's* translations. Numerals in regular type are references to its purports.

Amṛta-pravāha-bhāṣya (Bhaktivinoda Ṭhākura), 1,141

Bhagavad-gītā, 45, 106, 112, **119,** 248, 272, 276, 277, 278, 285, 306, 321, 335, 338

Bhakti-rasāmṛta-sindhu (Rūpa Gosvāmī), **54, 120, 240, 337**

Bhakti-sandarbha (Jīva Gosvāmī), 332

Bhāratī-vṛtti, 104

Brahma-saṁhitā, 222

Caitanya-maṅgala (Vṛndāvana dāsa Ṭhākura), **256**

Garuḍa Purāṇa, 322

Hari-bhakti-sudhodaya, 308

Laghu-Bhāgavatāmṛta (Rūpa Gosvāmī), 33

Lalita-mādhava (Rūpa Gosvāmī), 35, **64, 93-95, 98-99, 106-109**

Manu-saṁhitā, 181

Sāhitya-darpaṇa, 19, 68, 71, 104, **105**

Śaraṇāgati (Bhaktivinoda Ṭhākura), 13

Śikṣāṣṭaka (Caitanya Mahāprabhu), 278, 313

Śrī-bhāṣya (Rāmānujācārya), 169

Śrīmad-Bhāgavatam, 7, 46, **241, 250,** 270, **300, 303, 304,** 321, 340

Stotra-ratna (Yāmunācārya), **254**

Glossary

A

Āmānī—that food which is not offered to Lord Jagannātha.
Amukha—technical term for drama introduction, further classified into five kinds.
Anartha-nivṛtti—the cessation of everything unwanted.
Antya-līlā—last pastimes of Caitanya.
Aruṇa gems—rubies decorating Kṛṣṇa's flute.
Asaṁskṛtāḥ—unreformed.
Asura—a demon.
Ātapa-cāula—white rice.
Avatāra—one who descends from the spiritual sky.
Āveśa-avatāras—incarnations, or empowered living beings.

B

Bābājī—renounced order beyond *sannyāsa,* in which one chants and reads.
Bhajanānandī—a devotee who always engages in devotional activities but doesn't preach.
Brahmānanda—pleasure derived from impersonal liberation.

C

Caṇḍāla—lowborn.
Cāturmāsya—four months of the rainy season when *sannyāsis* do not travel.

D

Dharma-dhvajī—one who accepts *sannyāsa* but again becomes agitated by senses.
Dharma-kalaṅka—one who accepts *sannyāsa* but again becomes agitated by senses.

G

Gandharvas—celestial singers.
Gaura-gopāla *mantra*—mantra composed of four syllables: rā-dhā-kṛṣ-ṇa.
Gaura *mantra*—Gau-ra-aṅga.
Ghara-bhāta—rice prepared at home, not offered to Lord Jagannātha at temple.
Ghaṭa-paṭiyā—Māyāvāda philosophy which sees no distinctions, stating that everything is one.
Gosāñi—a teacher or *ācārya.*
Goṣṭhyānandī—a devotee who is expert in devotional activities and is also a preacher.
Guṇḍicā-mārjana—washing and cleansing the temple Guṇḍicā.

I

Indra-nīla—gems decorating Kṛṣṇa's flute.

J

Jīva—the living entity.

K

Kalpa—a day of Brahmā.
Kāma-lekha—exchanges of letters between a young boy and young girl concerning their awakening of attachment for one another.
Karmīs—fruitive workers.
Kevalādvaita-vādīs—Māyāvādī philosophers.
Khasādayaḥ—low born.
Kriyā-hīnāḥ—devoid of spiritual behavior.

M

Mad elephant offense—offense against the lotus feet of a Vaiṣṇava.
Mahā-bhāgāvata—highly elevated devotee.
Mānā—standard of measurement in Orissa for rice and grains.
Manu-saṁhitā—lawbook for mankind.
Markaṭa-vairāgya—renunciation of the monkeys.
Maṭha—temple.
Māyā—the external energy of the Lord.
Mlecchas—men who are unclean in their habits.
Mukta-puruṣa—a liberated soul.

N

Nāmābhāsa—awakening of the offenseless chanting of the holy name.
Nanda Mahārāja—father of Kṛṣṇa.
Nāndī-śloka—the introductory portion of a drama, which is written to invoke good fortune.
Niṣkiñcana—free from all material possessions.
Nirguṇa—having no material qualities.

P

Patita-pāvana—Lord Caitanya, the deliverer of all fallen souls.

Pātra—players in a drama.
Prarocanā—the method inducing the audience to become more and more eager to hear by praising the time and place, the hero and the audience.
Prasāda—mercy of Kṛṣṇa.
Prasādī—food offered to Lord Jagannātha.
Prasāda—remnants of foodstuff offered to Kṛṣṇa.
Pravartaka—introduction to a drama, when the players first enter the stage in response to the time.

R

Rādhikā—same as Rādhārāṇī.

S

Sādhu—saintly person.
Sādhu-saṅga—association with devotees.
Sālokya—liberation of living on a Vaikuṇṭha planet.
Sāmīpya—liberation of living as a personal associate of the Lord.
Sampradāya-ācāryas—Śrī Rāmānujācārya, Madhvācārya, Viṣṇusvāmī and Nimbarka.
Saṅkīrtana—congregational chanting of the holy name.
Saṁskṛta—purified.
Sapta-dvīpa—the seven islands.
Saralatā—simplicity.
Sārīraka-bhāṣya—Śaṅkarācārya's commentary on Vedānta.
Sārṣṭi—liberation of achieving opulences equal to those of the Lord.
Sārūpya—liberation of having a form the same as the Lord's.
Śāstras—Vedic scriptures.
Sāttvika—the material quality of goodness.
Siddha-cāula—brown rice.
Śikhariṇī—a blend of yogurt and sugar candy.
Śrī-bhāṣya—commentary on Vedānta by Rāmānujācārya.
Śukla-cāula—white rice.
Śrāddha—*prasāda* offered to the forefathers at a certain date of the year or month.
Śrāddha-pātra—plate offered to the forefathers and then to the best of the *brāhmaṇas*.
Strī-sambhāṣaṇa—talking with women.

T

Tulasī—a pure devotee in the form of a tree, most beloved by Kṛṣṇa.

U

Udghātyaka—a dancing appearance of a player in drama.

V

Vaiṣṇava-aparādha—offenses at the lotus feet of a Vaiṣṇava.
Vidagdha-mādhava—a seven-act play written by Śrīla Rūpa Gosvāmī describing the pastimes of Śrī Kṛṣṇa in Vṛndāvana.
Vidyā—knowledge.
Vairāgya—renunciation.
Vaikuṇṭha—the spiritual kingdom.
Viśiṣṭādvaita-vāda—philosophy established by the commentary *Śrī-bhāṣya* by Rāmānujācārya.
Vīthī—beginning of a drama consisting of only one scene.

Y

Yadukumāra—Kṛṣṇa who manifests pastimes in Mathurā and Dvārakā, known as.
Yajña—sacrifice.
Yavanas—men who are bereft of Vedic culture and unclean in their habits.

Bengali Pronunciation Guide

BENGALI DIACRITICAL EQUIVALENTS AND PRONUNCIATION

Vowels

অ a　আ ā　ই i　ঈ ī　উ u　ঊ ū　ঋ ṛ

ৠ ṝ　এ e　ঐ ai　ও o　ঔ au

ং ṁ *(anusvāra)*　ঁ ṅ *(candra-bindu)*　ঃ ḥ *(visarga)*

Consonants

Gutterals:	ক ka	খ kha	গ ga	ঘ gha	ঙ ṅa
Palatals:	চ ca	ছ cha	জ ja	ঝ jha	ঞ ña
Cerebrals:	ট ṭa	ঠ ṭha	ড ḍa	ঢ ḍha	ণ ṇa
Dentals:	ত ta	থ tha	দ da	ধ dha	ন na
Labials:	প pa	ফ pha	ব ba	ভ bha	ম ma
Semivowels:	য ya	র ra	ল la	ব va	
Sibilants:	শ śa	ষ ṣa	স sa	হ ha	

Vowel Symbols

The vowels are written as follows after a consonant:

া ā　ি i　ী ī　ু u　ূ ū　ৃ ṛ　ৄ ṝ　ে e　ৈ ai　ো o　ৌ au

For example:　কা kā　কি ki　কী kī　কু ku　কূ kū　কৃ kṛ

কৄ kṝ　কে ke　কৈ kai　কো ko　কৌ kau

The letter *a* is implied after a consonant with no vowel symbol.

The symbol *virāma* (্) indicates that there is no final vowel. ক্ k

The letters above should be pronounced as follows:

a —like the *o* in h*o*t; sometimes like the *o* in go; final *a* is usually silent.
ā —like the *a* in f*a*r.
i, ī —like the *ee* in m*ee*t.
u, ū —like the *u* in r*u*le.
ṛ —like the *ri* in *ri*m.
ṝ —like the *ree* in *ree*d.
e —like the *ai* in p*ai*n; rarely like *e* in b*e*t.
ai —like the *oi* in b*oi*l.
o —like the *o* in g*o*.
au —like the *ow* in *ow*l.
ṁ —*(anusvāra)* like the *ng* in so*ng*.
ḥ —*(visarga)* a final *h* sound like in Ah.
ṅ —*(candra-bindu)* a nasal *n* sound like in the French word *bon*.
k —like the *k* in *k*ite.
kh —like the *kh* in Ec*kh*art.
g —like the *g* in *g*ot.
gh —like the *gh* in bi*g-h*ouse.
ṅ —like the *n* in ba*n*k.
c —like the *ch* in *ch*alk.
ch —like the *chh* in mu*ch-h*aste.
j —like the *j* in *j*oy.
jh —like the *geh* in colle*ge-h*all.
ñ —like the *n* in bu*n*ch.
ṭ —like the *t* in *t*alk.
ṭh —like the *th* in ho*t-h*ouse.
ḍ —like the *d* in *d*awn.
ḍh —like the *dh* in goo*d-h*ouse.
ṇ —like the *n* in *gn*aw.
t—as in *t*alk but with the tongue against the the teeth.
th—as in ho*t-h*ouse but with the tongue against the teeth.
d—as in *d*awn but with the tongue against the teeth.
dh—as in goo*d-h*ouse but with the tongue against the teeth.
n—as in *n*or but with the tongue against the teeth.
p —like the *p* in *p*ine.
ph —like the *ph* in *ph*ilosopher.
b —like the *b* in *b*ird.
bh —like the *bh* in ru*b-h*ard.
m —like the *m* in *m*other.
y —like the *j* in *j*aw. য
y —like the *y* in *y*ear. য়
r —like the *r* in *r*un.
l —like the *l* in *l*aw.
v —like the *b* in *b*ird or like the *w* in d*w*arf.
ś, ṣ —like the *sh* in *sh*op.
s —like the *s* in *s*un.
h—like the *h* in *h*ome.

This is a general guide to Bengali pronunciation. The Bengali transliterations in this book accurately show the original Bengali spelling of the text. One should note, however, that in Bengali, as in English, spelling is not always a true indication of how a word is pronounced. Tape recordings of His Divine Grace A.C. Bhaktivedanta Swami Prabhupāda chanting the original Bengali verses are available from the International Society for Krishna Consciousness, 3959 Landmark St., Culver City, California 90230.

Index of Bengali and Sanskrit Verses

This index constitutes a complete alphabetical listing of the first and third line of each four-line erse and both lines of each two-line verse in *Śrī Caitanya-caritāmṛta*. In the first column the trans- eration is given, and in the second and third columns respectively the chapter-verse references d page number for each verse are to be found.

A

B

E

P

T

U

V

General Index

Numerals in bold type indicate references to *Śrī Caitanya-caritāmṛta's* verses. Numerals in regular type are references to its purports.

A

Ācārya
- preaches *bhakti* cult all over the world, 323
- role not to earn living through temple income, 323

Adau śraddhā tataḥ sādhu-saṅgo
- verses quoted, 337

Advaita Ācārya
- always meditating on deliverance of fallen souls, **323**
- associates with Haridāsa Ṭhākura, **318-322**
- decided to cause Kṛṣṇa to descend, **324**
- embraced Rūpa Gosvāmī, **117**
- meets with Haridāsa Ṭhākura, **317**
- not afraid of brahminical culture and customs, 321
- offered Ganges water and *tulasī* leaves, **324**
- set standard for Vaiṣṇava *sampradāya,* 323
- showed respect to Haridāsa Ṭhākura, **317**
- stayed back awaiting arrival of Caitanya, 147

Ahaṁ tvāṁ sarva-pāpebhyo
- quoted, 280

Aindraṁ kaśeru sakalaṁ kila
- verse quoted, 132

Ajāmila
- saved by holy name, **235, 241**

Ālālanātha
- Paramānanda Purī begged to go to, **187**

Amṛta-pravāha-bhāṣya
- cited on Gaura-gopāla *mantra,* 141
- summary of First Chapter given in, 1

Ananta
- affected by Kṛṣṇa's flute, **91**

Anger
- Caitanya manifests external, **100**
- not manifested against the envious, **54**

Animals
- dog liberated by Śivānanda Sena, **9-18**
- doglike persons do not appreciate Kṛṣṇa consciousness, 59
- lion kills elephants of desire, 67
- people less than in Kali-yuga, 231

Antya-līlā
- cited, 69

Anupama
- as brother of Rūpa, 20
- death of, **20-21, 26**

Arjuna
- advised to rise above modes of nature, 106

Asaṁskṛtāḥ kriyā-hīnā
- verse quoted, 46, 270

Aṣṭābhir daśabhir yuktā
- verses quoted, 19

Ataḥ śrī-kṛṣṇa-nāmādi
- quoted, 51

Atheists
- find fault with devotees, 261

Attachment
- as cause of loving affairs, **73**
- to dog by Śivānanda Sena, 13
- to Kṛṣṇa described by Rādhārāṇī, **75**

Avaiṣṇava-mukhodgīrṇam
- verse quoted, 51, 119

Āyodhyā
- Rāmacandra took residents of from world, **248**

B

Balabhadra Bhaṭṭācārya
- as servant of Caitanya, **245**

Balarāma
- describes Vṛndāvana, 87

Balarāma Ācārya
- as priest of Hiraṇya Majumadāra, **317**
- attached to Haridāsa, 293-**294**
- chastised Gopāla Cakravartī, **310**

D

E

F

G

I

J

K

L

Pious activities
attain maturity in devotional service, **72**
of Kṛṣṇa's flute, **90**
Pluto
his kingdom as destination of sinful, **84**
Pradyumna Brahmacārī
See : Nṛsiṁhānanda Brahmacārī
Prahlāda Mahārāja
came to earth at time of Caitanya, **343**
tolerated his father's chastisement, 316
Prasāda
brought to Rūpa and Haridāsa by Caitanya, **29,32**
by eating one can be promoted to Vaikuṇṭhaloka, 17
devotees satisfied with, 280
Kṛṣṇa conscious candidate must eat, 45
leaders must eat, 46
sent by Caitanya to Śacī, **226**
taken by Caitanya at houses of Vaiṣṇavas, 259
taken by Haridāsa at house of Balarāma Ācārya, **294**
Prastāvanāyās tu mukhe
verses quoted, 19
Prayāga
Caitanya met Rūpa Gosvāmī at, **112**
Junior Haridāsa died at, **194**
Premāñjana-cchurita-bhakti-
verses quoted, 222
Prostitutes
as devotees, 261
devotees engage possessions of, 280
Pṛthivīte āche yata nagarādi-grāma
verse quoted, 59
Pure devotees
as worshipable as Kṛṣṇa, 323
excuse any offense, **316**
liberation stands at door of, 306
liberation unacceptable by, **304**
never desire liberation, **308**
never take insults seriously, 313
qualities of 114-115
Pūrṇaprajña-bhāṣya
Mādhvacarya's commentary on *Vedānta,* 169
Puruṣottama
Supreme Personality of Godhead known as, **54**

R

Rādhārāṇī
affected by Kṛṣṇa's flute, **107**
as qualified with all transcendental attributes, **103**
as intelligent, **84**
beauty of described, **95**
compared to Ganges, **109**
compared to river, **85**
describes attachment to Kṛṣṇa, **75**
Her ecstatic symptoms described, **76-77**
Her face compared with lotus, **96**
Her face compared with moon, **96**
Kṛṣṇa's pastimes with increase in beauty, **70**
mistreated by Kṛṣṇa, 82
Paurṇamāsī as Her grandmother, 77
projects Her funeral, **78**
quoted on attraction of Kṛṣṇa, **108**
quoted on Kṛṣṇa's bodily features, 94
referred to by Rūpa, **39, 57**
violates vow of dedication to husband, **82**
Rāghava Paṇḍita
Caitanya appears in house of, 130, **143, 161**
Raghunātha dāsa Gosvāmī
as son of Hiraṇya, **295**
Kṛṣṇadāsa Kavirāja prays to, **125**
Rajo-guṇa
covers Kṛṣṇa's pastimes with *gopīs,* 106-107
Rāmacandra
name of chanted by *yavanas,* **233**
name of gives liberation, **339**-340
praised poetry of Rūpa Gosvāmī, **109**-111
took residents of Āyodhyā from world, **248**

S

W

Y